DATE DUE

DEMCO, INC. 38-2931

What are the key features of unionised labour markets? This important book analyses the nature of contracts between unions and management, and evaluates the results for wages, employment and productivity. It synthesises the two major strands of research on trade unions – the findings of empirical investigation and of theoretical inquiry. In this book, Alison Booth, a leading researcher in the field, explains the theoretical predictions and links these to widely observed outcomes. She argues that the theory of trade unions can also be applied to nonunion settings where workers have some market power, but that differences in institutions of the labour market will influence the outcomes. While the book focuses primarily on Britain and the USA, it also has a wider relevance to other industrialised economies.

The economics of the trade union is aimed at undergraduates and masters students studying labour economics and industrial relations. It presents some quite technical research in an accessible non-technical fashion, and in addition appendixes are provided that clearly set out the mathematical techniques used to obtain the main results.

The economics of the trade union

The economics
of the trade union

ALISON L. BOOTH

University of Essex

CAMBRIDGE
UNIVERSITY PRESS

Published by the Press Syndicate of the University of Cambridge
The Pitt Building, Trumpington Street, Cambridge CB2 1RP
40 West 20th Street, New York, NY 10011–4211, USA
10 Stamford Road, Oakleigh, Victoria 3166, Australia

First published 1995

Printed in Great Britain at the University Press, Cambridge

A catalogue record for this book is available from the British Library

Library of Congress cataloguing in publication data

Booth, Alison L.
    The economics of the trade union / Alison L. Booth.
        p.   cm.
    Includes bibliographical references (p.   ) and index.
    ISBN 0 521 46467 6 (hc) – ISBN 0 521 46839 6 (pbk)
    1. Trade unions – Economic aspects – Great Britain.   2. Trade unions – Economic
aspects – United States.   3. Labor market – Great Britain.   4. Labor market – United
States.   I. Title.
    HD6664.B598   1995
    331.88′0941–dc20   93-50224   CIP

ISBN 0 521 46467 6 hardback
ISBN 0 521 46839 6 paperback

To my parents

Contents

Figures

Tables

Preface

Over the past two decades, there has been an extraordinary expansion of the economic theory of the trade union. There has also emerged a huge literature that describes and quantifies the impact of the trade union on a host of labour market outcomes. The purpose of this book is to impose some structure on this literature, in order to make it easily accessible to the student of the economics of the trade union or the economics of industrial relations. The models in the book refer to collective agreements between a labour union and management. However, these models are also relevant to a much wider class of situations than those in which a trade union explicitly represents workers. Indeed, union collective bargaining agreements may be viewed simply as an explicit formulation of a wider variety of labour contracts that are found in labour markets wherever workers have some degree of bargaining power.

Work on this book was begun in late 1989, when it became clear that, following the expansion in the theoretical and applied literature on the economics of the trade union over the preceding decade, there was a gap in the labour economics literature that might usefully be filled. For teaching purposes in particular, there appeared to be a dearth of material suitable for third year undergraduates in the British system. Although there were a number of short survey articles, and an extensive and largely empirical survey of the US literature, there appeared to be scope for a textbook that would impose some structure on this huge body of literature, in a form suitable for economics students or more general readers with some economics background. It is my hope that this book may go some way in making the existing literature on the trade union more easily accessible to students at the third-year undergraduate level or the MSc level.[1]

Most of the research for the book, and a large part of the writing, was completed during the 1990–1 academic year, when I held a Nuffield Foundation Social Science Research Fellowship expressly for the purpose

[1] The excellent book by Pencavel (1991) provides a synthesis of empirical and theoretical work on trade unions at a more advanced level than this book.

of writing this book. One of the chapters of the book was written while I held a Visiting Research Fellowship at the Research School of Social Sciences at the Australian National University for ten weeks in 1990. I am very grateful to the Nuffield Foundation for the opportunity to spend uninterrupted time working on the book, and to the Research School of Social Sciences at the Australian National University for its hospitality. The views expressed in this book are not necessarily those of the Nuffield Foundation nor of the ANU.

A number of colleagues and friends read various chapters of the first draft of the book, and I am very grateful for their comments. In particular, I would like to thank Wendy Carlin, Monojit Chatterji, Jonathan Haskel, Tim Hatton, Deborah Mabbett, David Metcalf, Hassan Molana, Andrew Oswald and John Pencavel for their many helpful suggestions. I would also like to thank Patrick McCartan of Cambridge University Press for his enthusiasm and encouragement, Chris Doubleday for his stylistic suggestions, and Frank Cowell who first suggested that I write this book. Alexandra Small provided very capable assistance with the tables and figures. Most of the chapters of the book were tried out on students taking the labour economics option in the MSc programme at Birkbeck College Economics Department; I am grateful to students on this course for their comments and suggestions. Finally, I would like to thank Tim Hatton for his unfailing support and encouragement.

1 Introduction

Over the past two decades, there has been an extraordinary expansion of the economic theory of the trade union. There is also a huge empirical literature describing and quantifying the impact of the trade union on a host of labour market outcomes.[1] The purpose of this book is to impose some structure on this body of literature, in order to make it easily accessible to the student of the economics of the trade union or the economics of industrial relations. The book is not intended to be a comprehensive survey of the literature. Rather, it aims to provide a selective review of the crucial features of the analytical framework used by economists in modelling trade unions, a framework that is also potentially applicable to nonunionised labour markets where workers have some market power. Certain issues have been deliberately omitted in the interests of keeping the book to a manageable size for the readership for which it is intended. The book aims to be accessible in the main to third-year undergraduates and MSc students in economics, as well as to general readers with some basic training in economics and quantitative techniques. The main technical parts of the analytical framework have been confined to appendixes where appropriate, in order to avoid distracting the reader's attention from the main themes.

The book is written on the assumption that the reader is familiar with the perfectly competitive model of the labour market, in which labour is treated essentially as a commodity in a spot market. It is also assumed that the reader is aware of the weaknesses of this model, and in particular of the features of labour that distinguish it from other inputs, and which mean that labour cannot be treated in quite the same way as other factor inputs (Marshall, 1948). The two principal distinguishing characteristics of labour are, first, that workers retain ownership of their human capital (in the absence of slavery), and, secondly, that workers must be present at the workplace for the delivery of their skills. The fact that workers retain

---

[1] See, for example, references in the surveys by Oswald (1985), Pencavel (1985), Farber (1986), Hirsch and Addison (1986) and Ulph and Ulph (1990).

1

ownership of their human capital has the implication that any education or skills associated with employment are the property of the worker, who can therefore exercise some control over the use of these skills, and perhaps extract any surplus associated with them. The fact that workers must be present for the delivery of their skills means that workers must live near the workplace, which may constrain the opportunities of other family members, and make workers vulnerable to monopsonistic behaviour. It also means that the social aspects of the work environment are important for the worker.

There are a number of other important characteristics of labour; the differences between capital and labour with respect to these characteristics are sometimes of degree only, for capital may share some of these characteristics. An obvious feature of labour is that it is perishable; if a worker's skills become obsolete, the time and cost of training may mean that retraining is uneconomic. Moreover, the time and cost of training for workers, whose lifetime is finite, preclude labour from diversifying its portfolio of human capital. This specialisation of labour in one particular skill type, which may become obsolete, may leave the worker vulnerable to exploitation by the employer. The worker may, however, have some bargaining power through the fact that it takes time to provide additional supplies of specialised labour. Moreover, new employees may be imperfect substitutes for incumbent workers, for example where the incumbent worker has better information than management about work effort and production at the shop-floor level. In such a situation, the worker may refuse to reveal this information to management or to a new employee unless it is in his or her interest to do so, a fact that gives the incumbent some bargaining power. In general, in circumstances where it is costly for the firm to replace existing workers by outsiders for whatever reason, the incumbent workers have some market power.

Another important characteristic of labour is that the production process involves the bringing together of workers, giving greater opportunity for collective action. This also facilitates the development of personal relationships between workers, and sometimes between workers and management, which obviously does not happen with physical capital. Some of these characteristics of labour are conducive to collective action by workers, for the production process typically involves grouping workers together in a situation where there may be opportunities for exploitation by agents – either management or workers or both – of any surplus that might arise at the workplace. Where both workers and management have some bargaining power, bargaining may be either between individuals and management, or between an agent of the workers and management, where the agent could be a trade union. While bargaining may be more effective between a trade union and management, there may still be scope for individual bargaining with management in some production processes, owing to the presence of labour turnover costs, which give workers some monopoly power.

The models in this book refer to labour contracts between a trade union and management. However, these models are also relevant to a much wider class of situations than those in which a trade union explicitly represents workers, and have been extensively used in the insider–outsider literature (see Lindbeck and Snower, 1988) and the implicit contract literature. Individual incumbent workers in labour markets characterised by labour turnover or transactions costs possess a degree of monopoly power which, through individual or group bargaining even in the absence of trade unions, might be used to induce rent-sharing by management. Indeed, union contracts may be viewed simply as an explicit formulation of a wider variety of labour contracts that are found in labour markets. It is the explicit nature of union collective agreements that has allowed empirical research on union wage and employment determination, an avenue of research that is rather more difficult where bargaining agreements are not clearly specified in generally accessible written agreements.

The focus of the empirical work referred to in this book is primarily on Britain, but reference is also made to some major empirical findings from US studies. The institutional structure, and the stylised facts, associated with trade unionisation to which the book refers, relate both to Britain and the USA. However, there are considerable institutional differences between these two countries, which are highlighted in chapter 2 and also, where appropriate, in discussion of the theoretical models. Many of the innovations in the microeconometric modelling of union effects first emerged in the USA, where large cross-section and panel survey data at the individual level have been available since the late 1960s. For this reason, when discussing stylised facts or empirical regularities associated with trade unions, we sometimes refer to pioneering US work.

Much of the *theoretical* modelling referred to is appropriate to the unionised economies of Europe, Australia and New Zealand, and to the unionised sectors of the USA. None the less, it must be emphasised that there are important institutional differences across countries. In the introduction to chapter 2 we pay particular attention to the institutional differences in collective bargaining between Britain and the USA. It is important that students and researchers are aware of these differences, in order to avoid the pitfall of inappropriate applications of theoretical models characterising the behaviour of unions in one particular country to another country with a different institutional structure.

A reader might observe that there is some irony in the fact that,

Table 1.1 *An international comparison of union membership as a percentage of all employees 1970–85*

Country	1970	1975	1980	1985
Australia	51	54	52	51
Canada	36	34	30	31
France	23	23	19	na
Germany (FR)	37	39	39	37
Holland	38	39	37	29
Ireland	52	53	55	46
Italy	33	42	43	40
Japan	35	34	31	29
New Zealand	40	43	46	41
Norway	62	61	65	na
Sweden	74	79	88	88
United Kingdom	49	51	53	44
United States	27	25	23	16

Notes:
(i) 'na' denotes no data available.
(ii) Membership figures for the US are from the Bureau of Labor Statistics (see the notes to table 2.1 for discussion of US data sources for membership).
(iii) Break in the continuity of measurement in Canadian data in 1978 causes a fall of approximately 4 percentage points.
(iv) See Price (1989) for extensive discussion of data sources and data problems.
Sources: Price (1989) and Brown and Wadhwani (1990).

concurrent with the recent blossoming of research on trade unions, there has been a decline in trade union density in most major industrialised economies. Table 1.1 shows union density in eleven countries for the period 1970–85, where the definition of density is trade union membership as a percentage of the employed workforce. The table shows that density has declined over the period 1980 to 1985 for most countries, the exceptions being Canada and Sweden where density has remained constant. The USA had the lowest union density in 1985, with just 16% of all employees being trade union members.

Given that union density appears to be declining in most industrialised countries, and that in some countries only a minority of the workforce is unionised, do we really need to worry about providing appropriate models of trade union behaviour? For example, in the case of the US where union density is only 16%, might we be better advised to adhere to other theories of wage setting and worker behaviour? At the start of this chapter, the generality of union bargaining models was emphasised. While the models in this book refer to explicit labour contracts between a trade union and management, these mòdels are also relevant to a broader class of situations than those in which a trade union explicitly represents workers.

Moreover, trade union influence in a particular economy extends beyond the direct measure of union power suggested by the union density figures. Industrial relations and labour researchers in the USA, where union density has been declining since the mid-1950s, have for a long time suggested that union influence extends well beyond the unionised sector. For example, the threat of union organisation of a nonunion sector may provoke management to provide wages and working conditions that mimic those negotiated in union firms. The idea is that the nonunion workers, therefore, will be less prone to unionise, since there is little difference between their welfare in a union firm and in a nonunion firm providing matching benefits. In addition, the threat of union organisation may provoke management into directing resources into anti-union activities, and resource allocation in the non-union sector will therefore be indirectly affected by trade unionism. Furthermore, modelling the behaviour of the trade union in partially unionised economies is obviously of importance for sectoral analysis of the parts of the economy that *are* heavily unionised, or where a powerful sector is unionised and there are knock-on effects for the rest of the economy through particular institutional aspects of wage setting.

For European countries and Australia and New Zealand, the influence of trade unions at the macroeconomic level is perhaps better indicated by the extent of coverage of the workforce by union collective agreements, rather than by the measure of union density. According to Layard, Nickell and Jackman (1991: 52), all European countries with the exception of Switzerland have over three-quarters of employees covered by collective agreements, as does Australia. Using data for full-time employees in a permanent job from the 1991 British Household Panel Study (BHPS), I have calculated that 57% of British male workers are covered by collective agreements, while only 44% are trade union members. The comparable figures for women are 57% and 40% respectively. Part of the difference between Layard *et al.*'s (1991) figures for UK coverage and the 1991 BHPS figures arises from the fact that Layard *et al.* include Wages Council workers in their 'covered' category. Of the major industrial countries, only in the USA are less than one-quarter of workers covered by union collective agreements. In 1991, union membership density in the USA stood at 16%, while contract coverage stood at 18% of employed civilian wage and salary workers (Hirsch and Macpherson, 1993).[2] This suggests that an understanding of the economics of the trade union is vital for analysis of the

---

[2] These figures are calculated using data from the 1991 Current Population Survey.

workings of the macroeconomy for most industrialised countries, and that at the microeconomic level it is also important for the USA.

In order to understand unionised labour markets, it is desirable to construct analytical models of trade union behaviour and test these against the data, and also to measure the impact of unions on economic performance. The theoretical analysis of trade unions has, to a large extent, proceeded separately from empirical measurement, and there is a far larger literature devoted to the latter. Indeed, there is an enormous body of empirical research on trade unions; in particular, on the observed differences between union and nonunion wages, and, to a lesser extent, on union and nonunion sectors, jobs and outcomes. This is particularly the case for the USA, where many of the results have been surveyed in Freeman and Medoff (1984), Lewis (1986), Hirsch and Addison (1986) and Addison and Hirsch (1989).[3] Much of the literature measuring the impact of trade unions on various outcomes has been largely descriptive with no theoretical foundation. But our knowledge as to why there are differences between union and nonunion labour markets is incomplete. As Farber noted in 1986, a comment that is still relevant today,

there is quite a bit of controversy about what these differences mean. Are they accurate measures of the *effects* of unions, are they biased estimates of the effects, or are they statistical artifacts? How can these estimates be used to predict union response to changing economic conditions? Without a complete understanding of union behavior and how the outcomes of collective bargaining are determined it is difficult to answer these questions. (Farber, 1986: 1040.)

In essence, while descriptive empirical research is instructive in summarising data sets and suggesting stylised facts that require explanation, care should be taken in using it to make inferences about the impact of trade unions, as will be emphasised in the chapters in this book covering descriptive empirical research on union effects.

In chapter 2, we shall be examining the institutional structure of unionism and collective bargaining in both Britain and the USA. Examination of the trade union and its collective bargaining framework is the primary focus of the discipline of industrial relations, but it is also of crucial concern to economists wishing to model the behaviour of unionised labour markets. Trade unions in Britain and the USA are institutions that have evolved over several hundred years. To understand their structure, it is necessary for the student to have some knowledge of their historical development and the forces that led to their assuming a particular institutional form at the present time. Moreover, an understanding of their historical development can shed some light on the economic factors

[3] For a survey of Australian studies, see Miller and Mulvey (1993).

associated with union emergence, existence and stability, which will be helpful to the discussion of trade union theories in later chapters. Such an understanding can also illuminate current-day phenomena, such as British attitudes to European Community legislation on labour market issues. Owing to space limitations, the historical outline of chapter 2 is confined to a broadbrush approach, including only those factors that are believed to be relevant to explaining the present collective bargaining framework, as well as union emergence, existence and power.

The standard view of trade unions is that they are organisations whose purpose is to improve the material welfare of members, principally by raising wages above the competitive wage level. There is little dispute that unions are frequently able to push wages above the competitive level – what is called the 'monopoly' role of trade unions. There is an enormous body of literature documenting the impact of unionism on wage gains. Some of this will be examined in chapter 6. There is also a somewhat smaller body of literature examining the impact of unions on other variables, such as wage dispersion, productivity, profitability, investment and employment. Some of these studies will be examined in chapter 7. All of this literature is focusing on finding an answer to the important question: what do unions do? and thereby providing stylised facts or empirical regularities associated with trade unions. To the extent that these studies provide stylised facts associated with unionism, the reader familiar with the accepted economic methodology might expect an outline of these empirical regularities before the derivation of the theory.[4] However, since some of the more recent of these studies are based on the theory of trade unions developed in chapters 3–5, it seems more appropriate to place the empirical work aiming to measure trade union effects *after* the development of the theory. We therefore defer a review of empirical measurement of union effects until after a broad theoretical framework has been presented in those chapters.

Chapter 3 sketches what have become known as 'the two faces' of unionism – the monopoly role of unions, and the possible efficiency-enhancing role (Freeman and Medoff, 1979). The monopoly face of unions

---

[4] The accepted methodology of economics is that, following observation of an empirical regularity, economists can formulate a theory to attempt to explain the stylised fact. For simplicity and tractability, the theory necessarily abstracts from reality. In so doing, it makes simplifying assumptions. From the theory can be logically derived predictions for the economy or for particular economic variables. These predictions can then be tested against the available data. Thus the theory is inspired by empirical observation, and its predictions are also tested against the data. Since such testing is carried out with data sets with limited numbers of observations (rather than against the whole population), the theory can only ever be accepted or rejected probabilistically. It would be fair to say that few economic theories of the trade union have yet been adequately tested against the data. There are some notable exceptions to this, which will be discussed in association with the relevant theories in later chapters.

represents the orthodox textbook approach to unionisation, and is sum-marised in the first part of chapter 3. However, this chapter also provides a broad theoretical overview of the economic theory which attempts to answer some of these questions about how unions obtain the power to extract wage increases. Some of the theory is, as yet, undeveloped, and the chapter necessarily provides only a sketch of the major issues. Other parts of the theory have been well developed, in particular the analysis of union objectives and union–firm wage determination. Some of this latter work, now widely used in the literature, is expanded more formally in chapters 4 and 5. Because chapter 3 provides only an overview of the theoretical issues, the use of algebra is kept to a minimum, with broad discussion of the important issues and diagrammatic exposition where appropriate.

Chapters 4 and 5 show the formal derivation of the theoretical models that have achieved orthodoxy in the economics literature, and with which all labour economics students need to be familiar in order to read journal articles in the field. Chapter 4 considers ways of modelling the differing objectives of both the trade union and the firm, and examines the simplest method of reconciling the objectives of trade union and management: the monopoly union model. This method does not rely on any bargaining between the two parties. Instead, it supposes that the union is able to act as a monopolist in the supply of labour, and to impose a wage rate on the firm. The firm, however, retains its managerial prerogative to determine the number of workers to employ at the union wage rate. All workers are typically assumed to be identical in this type of model. We do, however, also examine the median voter model of trade union behaviour, where workers are assumed to be heterogeneous; the membership implications of a simple version of this model are considered.

Chapter 5 examines more sophisticated methods of reconciling the differing preferences of union and management, using a bargaining approach. Bargaining models of strike behaviour, and union–firm bargain-ing over standard hours, are also examined. The class of models developed in chapters 4 and 5 is widely used in theoretical work, and also in some empirical work aiming to estimate wage and employment equations based on a theoretical foundation. Emphasis is placed in these chapters on the simplifying assumptions underlying these models, the relaxation of which may well provide scope for future research.

With a broad theoretical framework in place, chapters 6 and 7 examine the impact of unions in Britain and the USA, and discuss which union effects appear to have the status of stylised facts. Chapter 6 focuses on the union–nonunion wage differential, which has often been used as a measure of union power. Macroeconomic models and models of the aggregate labour market commonly use the union wage markup for this purpose, since it is argued to be positively correlated with union power (Layard and Nickell, 1985, 1986). In chapter 3 it is argued that, at the microeconomic level, the existence of economic rents is a necessary condition for union wage markups, but that higher union wages will be found only where the trade union has the power to force the firm to give up some of its surplus. Therefore, the union wage markup will be positively correlated with union power, as suggested in macroeconomic work. But calculation of the union wage differential is sensitive to the method of estimation and the degree of aggregation of the data. Estimates from aggregate data are typically much larger than those from individual level survey data, which are in turn larger than estimates from panel studies. Which estimates can we believe? Is it a stylised fact that unions raise wages by 70% as one British researcher has claimed, or by just 7% as claimed by another? What are the problems involved in the calculation of these estimates? To understand the issues involved, it is important that we understand the methods used in estimation of union wage markups, and the econometric problems facing researchers in this field. To this end, chapter 6 examines just a few empirical studies which have attempted to quantify the impact of unions on wages, with discussion of the econometric issues throughout. These are presented non-technically in the main, so that the argument can be understood by a reader who has followed a standard econometric course.

A condition for a union to achieve wage gains is that the union has the necessary power to force the firm to share any surplus with the union; an alternative is that the firm may be willing to grant higher wages in return for increases in productivity that increase the surplus available to the firm. While the 'monopoly face' view of trade unions stresses the negative aspects of unionism, an alternative view is that in some circumstances they might be productivity-enhancing. Although unions may cause wages to increase in the union sector, neither employment nor firms' profitability need necessarily be greatly affected, since firms' higher labour costs may be offset by improved productivity. Since there are a variety of theories suggesting opposing union effects on productivity, it is ultimately an empirical issue as to whether unions are associated with increased or decreased productivity. Chapter 7 examines some empirical studies estimating union effects on productivity and productivity growth, investment, profitability, hours and employment.

Chapter 8 of the book turns to macroeconomic issues, in particular, the modelling of trade unions in the aggregate labour market. The chapter examines how the formal union models of chapters 4 and 5, which are microeconomic in flavour, might be applied to the macroeconomy. Over the past decade, macroeconomic modelling has been shifting increasingly from the Walrasian market-clearing approach to one in which account is taken of the fact that agents in the economy may be able to act strategically. The 'New Keynesian' approach to macroeconomics emerged in the 1980s as a response to the inability of the received macroeconomics to explain the phenomena of the period. By the 1980s, there were changes in the performance of the major advanced economies compared with the 1960s and 1970s. Growth almost halved, unemployment increased dramatically through both the 1970s and 1980s, and inflation accelerated in the 1970s, falling back in the 1980s to a level that was, none the less, higher than in the 1950s and 1960s. Moreover, while the OECD countries generally had a poorer economic performance in the 1970s and 1980s, there were considerable differences among countries with respect to growth, unemployment and inflation. These changes contributed to a re-evaluation of macroeconomic modelling, of which the 'New Keynesianism' emerging in the 1980s was one outcome; this approach is based on imperfect competition and combines Keynesian features with equilibrium unemployment. It attempts to obtain price and wage stickiness through modelling the imperfectly competitive behaviour of firms and workers, thereby providing microeconomic foundations for the behaviour of macroeconomic aggregates such as output, unemployment and inflation.

Chapter 8 examines the contribution of the recent microeconomic trade union literature to the New Keynesian approach to macroeconomics. The framework used in this chapter draws in particular on the approach of Carlin and Soskice (1990), Layard et al. (1991) and Blanchard and Fischer (1989). The chapter examines the implications of trade unions for wage and unemployment determination at the aggregate level, and draws principally on the monopoly union model of chapter 4. Of course, equilibrium unemployment may also be affected by the collective bargaining structure. Chapter 8 therefore examines the implications of the collective bargaining structure – in particular, the degree of centralisation of wage bargaining – for aggregate models of union behaviour and wages, prices, and unemployment. The implications of the macro-model for unemployment persistence, or hysteresis, are also considered, as is the validity of the model for economies which are only partially unionised.

The final chapter of the book draws some conclusions, and highlights areas where further research would appear to the author to be desirable. Students who are interested in further reading in any particular areas are referred to the references given throughout the book, and in the case of the extensive US empirical literature to the survey works of Freeman and Medoff (1984), Hirsch and Addison (1986) and Addison and Hirsch (1989).

While union membership and power have declined in many developed countries in the 1980s, it is unlikely that trade unions will vanish from European labour markets. Moreover, while the models in this book refer to explicit labour contracts between a trade union and management, these models are also relevant to a much wider class of situations than those in which a trade union explicitly represents workers. Individual incumbent workers in labour markets characterised by labour turnover or transaction costs possess a degree of monopoly power which, through individual or group bargaining even in the absence of trade unions, might be used to induce rent-sharing by management. The type of analysis used in modelling explicit labour contracts in unionised labour markets is also potentially applicable, with a few minor modifications, to these nonunion labour markets where incumbent workers have some market power.

The economic analysis of unionised labour markets has progressed enormously over the past two decades. However, there are omissions and oversimplifications in the literature, some of which are pointed out in the book. Therefore, much work remains to be done by the next generation of researchers in this interesting field.

2 The development of the union movements of Britain and the United States

2.1 Introduction

Why has a unique set of collective bargaining procedures and institutions emerged in Britain and the USA? How has the trade union movement managed to obtain the power that it still wields in Britain? Why is the US labour movement more fragmented? This chapter offers some answers to these questions by providing a brief outline of the development of the British and the US trade union movement up to the present. An examination of the broad historical influences associated with the development of the union movement is helpful in understanding the institutional peculiarities of the collective bargaining structure. History also informs the development of theoretical models, since historical analysis suggests necessary conditions for trade union emergence, stability and power. It must be emphasised that, in sketching a broad historical picture, many developments that are peripheral to the main theme are necessarily ignored. The interested reader wishing to pursue historical analysis is therefore referred to books that deal solely with trade union and economic history.[1]

Table 2.1 shows trade union density, the proportion of the civilian workforce unionised, for Britain and the USA over the period 1900 to 1990. Trade union density expanded fairly steadily for both countries from 1900. An important period of union growth for Britain was the period 1905–20, whereas for the USA the main period of growth was 1935–45. For both countries, these periods of rapid growth match the introduction of a statutory right to strike (Polachek and Siebert, 1993: 280).[2] From 1911, union density in Britain entered a period of very rapid expansion, reaching a peak of 45% in 1920. After this, British density declined during the years

[1] See, for example, Clegg, Fox and Thompson (1964), Phelps Brown (1986) and Pelling (1987) for Britain. For the US, see Taylor and Witney (1971), Reynolds (1978), Phelps Brown (1986) and references therein.
[2] This was given by the Trades Dispute Act of 1906 in Britain and by the Wagner Act of 1935 in the USA.

Table 2.1. *Trade union density for Britain and the United States (%)*

	Britain	USA
1900	13	3
1905	12	6
1910	15	6
1915	24	7
1920	45	12
1925	30	8
1930	25	8
1935	25	7
1940	33	13
1945	39	23
1950	44	23
1955	44	25
1960	44	22
1965	44	25
1970	49	25
1975	52	24
1980	53	20
1985	44	16
1990	39	16

Note:
Density is here defined as membership expressed as a percentage of the civilian workforce (excluding employers and the self-employed). The US membership figures are the Troy–NBER figures, largely derived from financial information from individual unions and associations, and available from 1897. See Price (1989) for a comparison of the two US membership data series – the Troy-NBER series and the more recent one provided by the Bureau of Labor Statistics (BLS).
Sources: Bain and Price (1980), Troy and Sheflin (1985), Hirsch and Addison (1986), Riley (1992) and Hirsch and Macpherson (1993).

of post-First World War depression, reaching a low of 23% in the years 1932–3. By 1934, British density began steadily increasing again, reaching a plateau in the mid-1940s. By 1948, it had regained the peak of 45% previously achieved in 1920. In 1969, British density again moved off the plateau on which it had been for almost a quarter of a century, and increased to an all-time maximum of 56% in 1979, after which time it declined again, and has continued declining up to the present. Union density in the USA also grew during the First World War, and declined in the post-war depression. US density growth was stimulated from the mid-1930s by the passage of the National Labor Relations Act (the Wagner Act) of 1935, and by the Second World War. Thus 1935–45 represents a period of major expansion of the US union movement. However, from 1955 union density began to fall, and it has declined continuously up to the present. In this chapter we will be looking at the historical development of the British and US union movements, reflected in table 2.1 through one indicator of union strength.

The remainder of this chapter is set out as follows. Section 2.2 provides a broad picture of the development of the union movement and collective bargaining institutions in Britain, right up to the present day. Section 2.3 outlines salient features of the development of the union movement in the USA that are important to an understanding of the US collective bargaining framework. Finally, section 2.4 compares and contrasts the collective bargaining frameworks of the USA and Britain. We believe that it is important for students to be aware of the points of similarity and of divergence in collective bargaining structures between the two countries. This is because trade union models developed for the institutional structure of the USA may not always be appropriate for Britain's, and vice versa.

2.2 The development of the British union movement

2.2.1 The early years

How did trade unions emerge in Britain? The first traces of organisation among crafts for much of the seventeenth century had been for social purposes, but by the end of that century workers also combined for mutual insurance against sickness, unemployment, death and sometimes old age (Pelling, 1987). These friendly societies were found throughout Britain during the eighteenth century. Combinations for mutual insurance purposes were given legal status, and their funds protection, by the 1793 Friendly Societies Act. This Act thereby made possible the use of a friendly society as a cover for the illegal activity of combining for the purpose of wage fixing. Trade societies had from their beginnings been open to legal repression. Under common law, they were illegal 'conspiracies' acting in restraint of trade. They were also illegal under statute law.[3]

---

[3] For example, under the Statute of Artificers of 1563, workers could be punished for leaving work unfinished if they went on strike. They could also be penalised under the 'master and servant' law of contract. Moreover, there had been many Acts against combinations in particular trades during the eighteenth century (Musson, 1972: 22).

By the start of the eighteenth century, a number of developments –
technological innovation, economies of scale and specialisation, improvements in communication and the rapid development of commerce – had led
to an increasing divergence between the interests of master craftsmen and
their employees, the journeymen. Economies of scale and specialisation
were associated with an increase in the size of workshops, and journeymen
could no longer expect to become self-employed masters. The guild system
therefore began to wither away (Pelling, 1987), with trade societies emerging among craft workers.[4] These craft societies formed the backbone of the
trade union movement until the late nineteenth century. Craft unionism
became established because of a combination of high demand for skilled
labour during industrial growth and the fact that craftsmen were able to
control the supply of trained labour. This was possible because craftsmen
were in charge of training the next cohort of skilled labour, and were able to
constrain numbers through the apprenticeship system that was already
established from the old guilds. Craft unions thereby obtained their power
by controlling entry into the particular skill category; they were able to
manipulate the supply of skilled labour to maintain their welfare. Moreover, in the event of a strike of craftsmen, employers are not immediately
able to replace organised workers, since it takes some time to develop these
skills in new workers.

What was the legal position of the emergent trade unions? The expansion
and effectiveness of trade unions or combinations in the late eighteenth
century, coupled with government fears of labour unrest following the
French Revolution and during the war with France, led to the passage of
the Combination Laws of 1799 and 1800. These Acts represented the first
general statutory outlawing of all combinations, and provided for summary
trial, albeit with mild penalties (Pelling, 1987). There was some use of the
legal system against combinations in the early nineteenth century,
especially in areas where there was rapid technological change and extensive outwork, and where combinations sometimes employed violence. But
in the older skilled craft industries, trade societies often negotiated openly
with employers over wages. Indeed, the Select Committee on Artisans and
Machinery of 1824 heard considerable evidence that some employers
preferred collective bargaining to the alternative of seeking legal redress.

---

[4] It is a popular view that the guilds of mediaeval Britain represented the first trade unions,
but this is not the case. A trade union represents an independent organisation of employees
which determines wages and conditions through negotiation with their employers. However, the guilds were combinations of both masters and journeymen sharing common
interests. The journeymen were skilled workers who had served an apprenticeship in the
trade, and who expected eventually to become self-employed masters. The guilds restricted
entry to a particular craft by the apprenticeship system, and regulated product price and the
journeyman piece rate.

In 1824, Parliament repealed all statutes against combination, including the Combination Laws. Thus trade unions or combinations were no longer illegal. But union demands for wage increases and work regulation, often accompanied by strikes and some violence, led to Parliament in 1825 increasing the provisions of the 1824 Act against violence and intimidation. Although trade unions remained lawful, members' activities could none the less be interpreted by law as criminally molesting or intimidating, and many prosecutions were made in subsequent years on this basis.

The ensuing period was characterised by an expansion of trade union objectives to include political and social ideas. But with the major depression of the early 1840s, the trade unions that managed to survive were of the skilled, sectional type. From the mid-nineteenth century, manufacturing industry became increasingly factory-based, with technical innovations increasing the scale of output. Developments in transportation (with the railways, and then steam shipping) and a growing population contributed to an expansion of the market for manufactured goods and an increased demand for labour. Improved communications facilitated labour mobility and the circulation of ideas through the radical press, which could be read by more workers as literacy spread. These factors all contributed to the development of national trade union organisations in the organised trades. In 1868, organised trades established the Trades Union Congress (TUC) to promote discussion of union issues.[5]

Two pieces of legislation favourable to trade unions were enacted in the 1850s: the Friendly Societies Act of 1855 giving legal protection to societies with benefit functions, and the Molestation of Workmen Act of 1859 legalising peaceful picketing in trade disputes over wages and hours. Union officials were becoming increasingly politically involved in campaigns to enfranchise working men and for reform of the old master-and-servant law of contract. Following intimidation of nonunionists in the 'Sheffield outrages'[6] of 1866, a Royal Commission was established to investigate trade unionism, and reported on trade unions favourably. The net result of the spate of legislation following in the 1870s was the removal of the law of conspiracy from trade disputes (unless actions under the dispute were criminal *per se*) and the establishment of the legal right for unionists to picket peacefully. The master-and-servant legislation was replaced by the Employers and Workmen Act, limiting the penalty for breach of contract to payment of civil damages, and thus at last allowing for the equal treatment of employers and workers under the law.[7]

---

[5] It is interesting that the establishment of this Congress was stimulated by the National Social Science Association Congresses (Pelling, 1987).

[6] So called, because they involved acts of violence against nonunionists in the Sheffield cutlery trade.

[7] See Clegg, Fox and Thompson (1964), Musson (1972) and Pelling (1987) for interesting accounts.

The emergence of general or industrial unions of unskilled or semi-skilled workers followed a very different pattern to the development of craft unions. Why was this the case? In the course of industrialisation, there was a huge surplus of unskilled displaced agricultural labour (due to agrarian reforms); thus manipulation of labour supply by workers was not possible. Displaced agricultural workers flocked to the factories, making it easy for employers to substitute labour in the face of any threat of labour withdrawal by incumbent workers, and therefore hard for emergent unions to gain any monopoly power. Trade unions in such an environment were vulnerable to economic fluctuations: a depression coupled with a ready pool of available substitute workers could decimate a trade union. In such conditions, it was important for the union to gain political support and/or high levels of membership.

Unions of semi-skilled workers had begun to organise in the boom of the early 1870s, but were largely wiped out by the Great Depression in the late 1870s. It was not until the late 1880s that there emerged permanent unions of unskilled and semi-skilled workers – the 'new unionism' – against a background of a working class which was more cohesive owing to increasing literacy (following state-provided education from 1870), improvements in communications and the growth of cities. Moreover, the enfranchisement of working men by the Second and Third Reform Acts of 1867 and 1884 encouraged some politicians to take a more favourable attitude to unionism, and made workers more aware of their political clout (Pelling, 1987: 86).[8] Union membership increased from approximately 750,000 in 1888 to 1,576,000 in 1892, and union density grew from 6.2% to 13.0% over the period (Clegg, Fox and Thompson, 1964: 467, 1489). Although the term 'new unionism' refers to the first permanent unions of low-skilled workers, skilled membership increased over the period by an even larger absolute amount.[9]

For most of the nineteenth century, the technological lead of British industry had enabled Britain's manufacturers to shelter from international competition. However, by the last decade of that century foreign competition was increasing, in particular from the USA and Germany. At the same time, union membership was also increasing, and the labour movement appeared to be changing its attitudes, both through the 'new unionism' of unskilled and semi-skilled workers and the increasing militancy of some craft unions, particularly in engineering. The introduction of

[8] British trade unions from early on used both industrial and political means to pursue their goals. The cotton unions lobbied for factory legislation limiting hours and regulating safety from early in the nineteenth century, while the miners lobbied for safety regulation from 1844, and the railway workers for hours and safety in the late nineteenth century. See Clegg (1985: 11–14).

[9] See Boyer, Hatton and Bailey (1994) for a study of the union–nonunion wage differential for the period.

new technology in engineering displaced craft skills, while the introduction of management science techniques displaced custom and practice. The structure of industry was also evolving: organisation size was increasing, while the private owner was being replaced by professional managers. How did labour and capital respond to these changes? Labour responded by organised resistance, and shop stewards and committees began to emerge to protect craftsmen's interests. These forces also contributed to the development of employers' associations. In 1896, an industry-wide employers' association was founded in engineering – the Employers' Federation of Engineering Associations. This association began a pro-longed wrangle with the engineering workers over the issue of new machinery and payment mechanisms, culminating in a major lockout in 1897. This represents a landmark in British trade union history, for it resulted in an extension of collective bargaining in an important industry – engineering – from the district to the national level. Moreover, it was the first major dispute over workshop control, and marks 'a first provision for industrial relations within the firm' (Phelps Brown, 1986: 139).

In response to the growth in union membership, employers' federations emerged and strengthened in other industries, and by 1898 employers had established a new general employers' organisation, the Employers' Parliamentary Council, to counterbalance the Trades Union Congress. By this time, the legal position of trade unions (as set out by the 1871 Trade Union Act, the 1875 Conspiracy and Protection Act and the 1875 Employers and Workmen Act) was being undermined by interpretation by the judiciary. As a response, union leaders in 1900 formed the Labour Representation Committee, in order to strengthen politically the union movement. The famous Taff Vale case of 1901 determined that union funds were liable for damages inflicted by union officials. As a result, union leaders not only provided greater support than originally envisaged for the Labour Representation Committee, but they also took an important additional step to facilitate representation in politics. They decided in 1903 to raise funds to pay Labour members of parliament (MPs) via a compulsory political levy on unions, and to insist that Labour parliamentary candidates were not to affiliate with either Liberal or Conservative parties. In the 1906 election, the Labour Representation Committee gained 54 Lib-Lab or Labour MPs,[10] and changed its name. Thus was born the Labour Party, the child of the union movement.

By this time there were three broad types of union: the craft unions, the operatives' unions, and the general unions encompassing the 'new unions' of the late 1880s (Phelps Brown, 1959). The craft unions, though by now

---

[10] Lib-Lab refers to Liberal-Labour candidates, who were typically trade union men adopted by the local Liberal Party caucuses. Of the 54 Lib-Lab or Labour MPs, 29 were Labour. See Phelps Brown (1986: 62).

national, were still concerned with entry restrictions and the maintenance of scarcity through the apprenticeship system, which in itself had provided a motive for combining nationally to control entry. The operatives' unions were, like the crafts, segregated by occupation, viz. the miners and the cotton operatives. But they were not characterised by an apprenticeship system, and were semi-skilled. Negotiation over wages and hours occurred at the district level, and the unions also lobbied Parliament. The general unions covered workers in *different* occupations and industries, and were characterised by low dues, few friendly society benefits, and a belief in the necessity of alliance with a general labour or socialist movement. These unions were most vulnerable to the business cycle, and wanted to reinforce their industrial gains through legislation (Pelling, 1987: 100). This appeared to be an achievable ambition, with the birth of the Labour Party, and the passage in 1906 of the Trades Disputes Act, protecting union members' right to strike and to engage in picketing.[11]

Legislative reform by the Liberal Party, under Asquith, encouraged union membership, in particular through an innovative programme of social reform, establishing labour exchanges and a state system of health and unemployment insurance, for which trade unions and friendly societies became the approved agents.[12] Trade union membership increased from 3.139 million in 1911 when the National Insurance Act was passed (a density of 17.7%), to 4.135 million in 1913 (23.0%). This growth in union membership was to continue throughout the First World War.

2.2.2 Two world wars and the Great Depression

At the start of the First World War, most collective bargaining in each organised industry took place at the district level, between the local employers' association and each union, or group of unions, that had agreed on joint negotiation (Phelps Brown, 1959: 359). With the outbreak of war, the state began to play a major role in the collective bargaining system, introducing in 1915 compulsory arbitration, and state control of industries that were important to the war effort, and in which pay was determined at the industrial level. This encouraged the development of industry-wide organisation of both employers and unions in other industries. Union

[11] This legislated to prevent union officials being liable for damages through any strike action breaking the employment contract. It thereby aimed to avoid the situation where a union might, after a dispute, be sued for such large damages that it could never entertain the thought of a strike again. As Phelps Brown suggests, this is rather a draconian way of protecting the right to strike.

[12] The Liberal Party also introduced state payments of MPs, thereby preventing financial embarrassment for Labour MPs following the Osborne judgement of 1909. This judgement restrained unions from raising a political levy and contributing to Labour Party funds (Pelling, 1987: 129–30). Predictably, the judgement raised the wrath of the trade union movement, and was overturned by the 1913 Trade Union Act.

leaders and the government agreed on the temporary removal of certain restrictive practices, for example to allow unskilled workers, in particular women, to take over jobs that were traditionally the preserve of skilled men. War profits were also limited (Pelling, 1987: 153). During the war years, wages were increased following price inflation, but in a haphazard fashion, 'outraging wage earners' sense of equity' (Phelps Brown, 1959: 359). Membership of trade unions increased from 4.145 million in 1914 to 6.533 million in 1918 (Bain, Bacon and Pimlott, 1972). Excess demand and cost-plus contracts disguised competitive forces, while the government used industry-wide bargaining to attempt to reduce the continual threat of strikes.[13] The war years also saw an important new development – the appearance of shop stewards and *workplace* industrial relations in the munitions industries, where full employment gave skilled men 'confidence in taking action without support or control by their trade union officials' (Phelps Brown, 1986: 141).

The predominant occupational structure of British trade unions had fostered industry-wide bargaining. Indeed, the occupational structure of unionism precluded bargaining at the enterprise level, since workplaces with different types of skills were characterised by multi-unionism, and there was no single workplace federating organisation. Industry-wide bargaining appeared to suit management, for employers were thereby guaranteed that all firms in close competition in the product market would be paying the same wage rate. Furthermore, they did not have to argue with union employees in their own workplace and retained the right to manage. Inherent disadvantages of the system were that wage determination could not be related to productivity at the enterprise level, and that there remained a 'gap' in the workplace. This gap occurred since 'usually there was no recognized organ or agent of the unionists there to look after them in their daily dealings with management, and provide management with a means of securing the agreement of the men in measures affecting them' (Phelps Brown, 1959: 363), in spite of the workshop committees that had emerged before the First World War, and the extension of the shop steward system.

War-time conditions meant that unions were in a position to exert pressure on government, both through Labour Party involvement in the coalition governments and the threat of industrial disputes. The latter

---

[13] The Whitley Committee, set up to investigate the industrial unrest, recommended in its reports in 1917 the establishment of industry-wide collective bargaining in each industry. The establishment of trade boards in unorganised industries was also advocated. The Trade Boards Act of 1918 provided for industry-wide wage regulation throughout an industry, where workers and employers were insufficiently organised to maintain or introduce industry-wide bargaining. The Whitley Committee also recommended the establishment of works committees to fill in the perceived void in workplace industrial relations institutions (Clegg, 1985). Although many works committees were established, few survived for long.

could be so potentially damaging that the government would exert pressure on employers to reach a settlement. Industrial unrest increased over the period 1917 to 1920, exacerbated by the immediate post-war boom and conditions of full employment which characterised this period. By 1921 the boom had collapsed, and employers attempted to reduce labour costs by cutting money wages, provoking much industrial unrest.[14] Unemployment increased from 2% in 1920 to 12.9% in 1921, and was to remain above 1 million until the Second World War. Union density was 45.2% in 1920, but fell to 35.8% in 1921.

Although by 1924 the worst of the slump was over, Britain returned to the Gold Standard on pre-war parity, with the result that sterling was overvalued. Employers in export industries, such as coal and textiles, faced with even greater foreign competition, announced wage cuts. In 1925, to avert a threatened national strike, the government agreed to subsidise the coal industry for nine months to remove wage pressure. This respite enabled government and the mine owners to prepare for a renewal of the conflict. The General Strike began on 2 May 1926 with a remarkable display of labour solidarity throughout the country, orchestrated by the General Council of the TUC to whom the miners had appealed for help. But the government had made careful plans to maintain supplies of essential goods and services. In the face of the government's determination to hold out, and fearful of a drift back to work, the TUC called off the strike on 12 May, following a tentative government offer to renew the coal subsidy for an unspecified period. The TUC obtained no guarantees that striking workers would be reinstated on their former terms of employment. Moreover, the end of the General Strike did not mark the end of the miners' lockout. Widespread employer victimisation of striking workers followed, particularly by the railway companies (Clegg, 1985: 410–11). The miners eventually reached settlements with the owners on a district by district basis, with the reduction in labour costs being achieved predominantly by an increase in hours. The miners were not to recover their bargaining power until the Second World War.

The failure of the General Strike had a profound impact on the union movement. After it, the government passed in 1927 the Trade Disputes and Trade Unions Bill. This outlawed general and sympathetic strikes, curtailed some industrial action as intimidation, and introduced contracting-in (instead of contracting-out) for the political levy for the Labour Party.[15]

---

[14] During 1921, 85.9 million working days were lost owing to industrial unrest.
[15] The General Strike also raised the issue that widespread industrial action represented a challenge to the authority of a democratically elected government. Because the TUC backed off from this challenge and accepted an early end to the strike, it 'was in effect decisively setting its face against the revolutionary elements in the movement' (Lovell and Roberts, 1968: 94).

Meanwhile, unemployment was continuing to increase. It had been high in the 1920s, but the world-wide depression of 1929–32 saw it soar, reaching 22% of the insured working population by 1932, and remaining above 2 million until 1936 (Lovell and Roberts, 1968: 128). By 1933, union membership stood at 4.392 million workers (representing a density of 22.6%), the lowest level since 1914 (Bain *et al.*, 1972). Since the peak in 1920, nearly 4 million members had been lost. Nevertheless the TUC still was able to strengthen its position during the inter-war years. This was remarkable, because these years were largely a period of union weakness in the face of major depression, huge membership losses and the failure of the General Strike. The success of the TUC was in part due to the new moderation of its leadership, and its willingness to become more knowledgeable about economic policy. The TUC adopted a Keynesian line, and lobbied the government to adopt an expenditure policy maintaining consumer spending during the economic crisis of 1931.[16] The rise of Nazism in Germany and Fascism in Italy was associated with the destruction of the union movement in those countries. Worries about the possible spread of these tendencies prompted the TUC to push for rearmament in 1937, even with a Conservative government in power. But in spite of the weakness of the unions and the strengthening of the position of the TUC, the latter was unsuccessful in reforming trade union structure, which had for some years been regarded as in need of change. There remained problems of competition between unions, with no consensus as to how reorganisation might be achieved.

In the early months of the Second World War, the Chamberlain government took little action with respect to manpower planning, but with the formation of the Churchill coalition government in 1940, trade union leaders began to take an active part in the war effort and in government. Strikes and lockouts were made illegal for the duration of the war, and binding arbitration was introduced. Yet normal collective bargaining continued, with the voluntary cooperation of trade unions and employer associations. National and regional production boards were established,

[16] In 1928 the TUC decided to participate in the Mond–Turner talks, a series of discussions on industrial issues which had been initiated by a group of influential employers. The willingness of the TUC to participate was a manifestation of the new moderate view of the leadership that discussion with industrial leaders was not incompatible with its political objectives. The talks also encouraged the TUC to become more knowledgeable about economic policy. The TUC adopted a Keynesian line on economic policy, arguing for the maintenance of consumer spending during the economic crisis of 1931, and against any cuts in unemployment benefits. In 1932, Roosevelt became President of the United States, and immediately initiated the New Deal, a programme of national recovery that was similar to the TUC policies in its emphasis on public expenditure, and its maintenance of purchasing power (Lovell and Roberts, 1968: 130). This encouraged the TUC to lobby the government for a similar public expenditure programme.

and at the plant level consultative machinery was set up to find ways of
increasing efficiency (Pelling, 1987: ch.11). Trade union membership
increased from 6.298 million in 1939 to 7.875 million by 1945, and density
from 31.6% to 38.6%. The reputation of trade unions also grew over the
period. The growth of trade union power plus government commitment to
post-war full employment raised the question as to whether the trade union
movement could exercise its power responsibly in the national interest after
the war. The answer to this question clearly depended on the structure of
the movement and its ability to co-ordinate its activities. While the TUC
was aware of the need for rationalisation on the basis of industry, any
moves in this direction were blocked by the powerful general and occupational unions (Lovell and Roberts, 1968: 152–4).

2.2.3 The aftermath of the Second World War

A Labour government was elected in 1945, and it at once repealed the 1927
Trade Disputes and Trade Unions Act. The government also embarked on
a nationalisation programme, and appointed many of the more able trade
union leaders to the boards of the nationalised industries. The trade union
movement continued to behave co-operatively during this period, no doubt
in part because the nationalisation programme and the expansion of the
welfare state were in accordance with TUC policy. By 1951 when a
Conservative government was elected, union membership stood at 9.530
million, and density at 45.0%. The new government 'felt obliged to move
forward only in agreement with the union leaders: to attempt to do
otherwise would be to violate the accepted conventions of industrial
relations' (Pelling, 1987: 240). The government removed economic
controls, and allowed private consumption and wages to increase.

Through much of the twentieth century, and especially after the Second
World War, trade unions were regarded as constructive forces, embodying
the conflict of interest between employer and worker, but also providing a
means of resolution of this conflict (Lewis, 1991). This view justified the
traditional British non-interventionist approach to industrial relations over
this period. However, problems were in evidence by the mid-1950s. By
1955, Britain was encountering difficulties with the balance of payments.
From this time, industrial relations worsened, with problems of demarcation and unofficial disputes. By the time the Labour Party returned to
power in 1964, the collective bargaining system was seen to be flawed in
several respects. Since 1947, unemployment had been consistently less than
3%, in sharp contrast to the high levels that characterised the inter-war
years. But Britain was performing badly relative to her competitors, with
slow growth, recurrent balance-of-payments problems, and growing

inflation. Industry was hampered by restrictive practices, opposition to technical change, uncoordinated and inflationary wage settlements, and unions which were apparently unable to control shop stewards (Roberts and Rothwell, 1973). Moreover, industrial conflict was increasing. In the face of these problems, the Labour government in 1964 appointed a Royal Commission on Trade Unions and Employers' Associations, to indicate 'with particular reference to the Law' what changes might be necessary to the flawed system of industrial relations.

2.2.4 Attempts to reform collective bargaining

The report of the Royal Commission – the Donovan Report – was published in 1968. It argued that the traditional system of industry-wide collective bargaining had been replaced by two tiers of collective bargaining, a formal system comprising official institutions at national level, and an informal system at the enterprise level. Since there were often no established procedures at the enterprise level, and no effective links between the two systems, industrial relations were characterised by unofficial disputes, lack of order, and uncoordinated wage increases that were unrelated to productivity. The Commission did not favour any legislative reform of industrial relations, since it viewed legislative intervention as foreign to the British tradition of voluntarism in industrial relations. It recommended instead that firms and employees should move *voluntarily* to organisation- or plant-level collective bargaining, to allow wage increases to be related to productivity. It advocated the establishment of a Commission for Industrial Relations with advisory functions, and state imposition of industrial arbitration where there was no collective bargaining.[17]

It is interesting to consider how this dual system of industrial relations had emerged. The Second World War had seen the creation in 1941–2 of Joint Production Committees, most of which terminated after the war, leaving a legacy of shop stewards in many industries (Phelps Brown, 1986: 148). Strong labour demand since the Second World War had allowed shop stewards to increase their bargaining power and extend their activities. Owing to labour shortages, employers were more willing to increase local wages above the nationally agreed industry level in response to shop stewards' demands. Because the structure of trade union organisation was largely occupational or general, many enterprises were characterised by multi-unionism. Each union was represented by its own shop steward. Hence shop stewards' committees on site comprised members of different unions, were not governed by particular union rules, and possessed considerable autonomy. Since there was no effective link between this

---

[17] The Report has been criticised for focusing on manufacturing, in particular engineering; it tended to understate diversity (Bamber and Snape, 1987: 42).

informal system and the industry-level system, shop stewards had come to rely on unofficial strikes to solve many of their problems. Moreover, many firms now had specialised industrial relations personnel, and preferred tailor-made agreements to industry-wide ones (Roberts and Rothwell, 1973: 356–7).

Dissatisfaction with industrial relations continued into the 1970s. In 1971, the Conservative government passed its Industrial Relations Act. At the time, it was clear that the previously uncodified but well-established practice of industrial relations was collapsing; unofficial strikes and the number of working days lost were increasing, and union leaders were apparently unable to control their members. Yet there was widespread opposition to the Act, which was passed with little consultation with either the union movement or employers. The Act, influenced by the US Taft–Hartley Act of 1947, established legally enforceable collective bargaining, compulsory ballots before strikes, and a conciliation pause before any strike that might endanger the national interest.[18] The Act was long, complex, and the 'understanding and use of the new Act evidently called for the work of many lawyers' (Phelps Brown, 1986: 193). Neither the trade unions nor the CBI were keen to entrust industrial relations to the legal profession, and British managers were unused to dealing with issues of labour law. Few employers enlisted the help of the Act in issues of unfair industrial practices,[19] and unions were vehemently opposed to it.

Following the election of the Labour Party in 1974, the Wilson government immediately repealed the Act. In return for union agreement for a voluntary incomes policy – the 'Social Contract' – the government passed legislation extending union and individual rights at the workplace. The 1974 Trade Union and Labour Relations Act restored union immunities to the 1971 position. Individual employment rights were extended with the 1975 Employment Protection Act (re-enacted in 1978), which also enabled unions to obtain statutory recognition through the Advisory, Conciliation and Arbitration Service (ACAS).[20] Union membership stood at 11.764

---

[18] The Act set up a National Industrial Relations Court to settle most industrial disputes, and explicitly defined unfair industrial practices on the part of both workers and employers. The Court was empowered to require a strike ballot and a conciliation pause in strikes affecting the national interest. The pre-entry closed shop was made illegal, and replaced by the 'agency shop', where a union could acquire sole bargaining rights if a secret ballot indicated that a majority of workers was in favour, or if the employer was in agreement.

[19] For example, the attempts by the Act to curtail the closed shop were not successful. Weekes, Mellish, Dickens and Lloyd (1975: 63) found that 'employers defended [the closed shop] almost as tenaciously as did workers ... by using persuasion, the recruitment interview, induction, and a variety of techniques, managers set out to frustrate the intention of the law'.

[20] The government rejected the proposals of the 1977 Bullock Report, which advocated trade union directors for companies to increase industrial democracy. This rejection is viewed by some commentators as reflecting the essentially reformist, rather than radical, aims of the Labour Party with respect to industrial relations (Lewis, 1991: 64).

million in 1974 (a density of 50.4%). Encouraged by statutory and government recognition and a vigorous union recruitment drive, it was to grow to an all-time peak of 13.289 million (55.4%) by 1979.

Over this period, the number of shop stewards also increased, often with employer support and payment of stewards' costs and salaries. Shop stewards became more important as the trend to plant- or company-level collective bargaining continued. Closed-shop agreements became more widespread, also with some employer support.[21] Management was increasingly willing to help unions maintain membership by deducting union dues from employees' pay, a procedure guaranteeing a regular flow of dues income to the union, and transferring collection costs to the employer (Roberts 1985: 107). The numbers of single-employer bargains increased, as did the number of personnel specialists in firms (Metcalf, 1989). Union bargaining power increased over the decade, owing to the fact that statutory protection had increased, that incomes policies effectively deferred any bargaining about restrictive working practices, and state subsidies were granted to companies experiencing difficulties (Metcalf, 1989).

Although formal procedures at the workplace had been strengthened, there was no evidence of the improvement in industrial relations that had been predicted by the Donovan Commission. Inflation had become a major problem, and productivity was low.[22] Unions were unwilling to allow the introduction of new technology or the removal of restrictive practices. Unemployment was also growing. The 'Social Contract', whereby unions were to seek pay rises only to keep up with the cost-of-living, lasted for three years. The 'winter of discontent' of 1978–9 – a series of strikes in essential services against the recommended pay norm – culminated in the defeat of the Labour government in the election in 1979. A Gallup poll in March 1979 indicated that 81% of respondents disapproved of the way the Labour government had handled industrial relations (Pelling, 1987: 299). Margaret Thatcher led the Conservative Party to victory in 1979 on an election platform in which trade union reform was a major issue.

---

[21] McCarthy (1964) estimated that in 1962 3.75 million workers were covered by closed-shop arrangements. Gennard, Dunn and Wright (1980) found that by 1978 at least 5.2 million workers were covered. Brown (1981: 57–9), reporting the results of a survey in 1977–8, found that management 'openly' supported three-quarters of closed-shop arrangements. Reasons given for management support were that the closed shop ensured that unions represented all workers, and that 'the closed shop is a procedural device that increases the representativeness and stability of collective bargaining'.

[22] UK productivity growth (GDP per person employed) was 3.0% for 1968–73, and fell to only 1.3% for the period 1973–9 (Haskel and Kay, 1991, table 2). Note that US productivity growth was also extremely low, being 1% in 1968–73, and 0% in 1973–9.

2.2.5 The Thatcher years

Conservative Party policy involved a shift to free-market rhetoric and monetarism, with restrictive monetary and fiscal policy, and a privatisation programme for the nationalised industries. Trade union power was to be reduced through legislative reform, in order to restrain inflationary wage increases and increase productivity. The Conservative Party appeared to have learnt, from its experiences with the 1971 Industrial Relations Act, that union reform would have to be gradual. The first of a series of acts affecting trade unions was passed in 1980, at a time when unemployment had reached 2 million as the economy entered a recession. The 1980 Employment Act limited secondary picketing, expanded exemptions from the closed shop and provided public funds for secret ballots prior to strikes, and for the periodic election of union officials. The statutory union recognition procedure set up in the early 1970s was repealed.[23] While the growth of recognition agreements has fallen since 1980 (Towers, 1989; Millward, 1990), derecognition has not been widespread (Claydon, 1989; Millward, Stevens, Smart and Hawes, 1992).[24]

Although trade unions opposed the narrowing of immunities implied by the 1980 Act, they were in no position to challenge it. Over the period 1980–2, the British economy was in a major recession.[25] Unemployment was high and rising, and the public mood was out of sympathy with the union movement following union militancy in the late 1970s. The government then moved to restrict union organisational immunities. Under the 1982 Employment Act, the definition of a trade dispute was narrowed to cover only disputes between workers and their own employer. Individuals or firms affected by unlawful industrial action could now sue for damages against the union. The pre-entry closed shop was outlawed; post-entry closed shops could exist only if 85% of a secret ballot of membership supported them. In 1982 the Fair Wages Resolution was rescinded. In spite of unemployment reaching 3 million, the Conservative government was re-elected in 1983, with an election manifesto of further trade union legisla-

[23] The voluntary procedure for union recognition was retained, where ACAS will conciliate in a recognition dispute if the union or employer so requests. However, the employer cannot be compelled to recognise the union (Towers, 1989: 168).

[24] The proportion of establishments with a recognised union has declined from 66% in 1984 to 53% in 1990 (Millward et al., 1992). Relatively small numbers of plants have either recognised or derecognised unions over the period; hence most of the fall in recognition appears to have arisen through the demise of plants with union recognition. See Disney, Gosling and Machin (1993) for an econometric analysis of recognition using Workplace Industrial Relations Survey (WIRS) data.

[25] The depth of the recession in Britain was due to the tight fiscal and monetary policy of the government, the world recession, and the appreciation in the sterling exchange rate (Haskel and Kay, 1991: 200).

tion. Increasing share ownership, through the privatisation programme, was recommended to increase worker democracy. Only 39% of union members voted for the Labour Party in the General Election of 1983, the lowest proportion since 1935 (Pelling, 1987: 305). In 1984 the Trade Union Act was passed; this required secret ballots every five years for the election of union executives, a secret ballot prior to any industrial action, and secret ballots every ten years for the political levy.

The more militant unions now began to test the new legislation. The coal-miners' strike of 1984–5 occurred in response to the National Coal Board's threatened pit closures as part of the streamlining of the industry. Although a national strike required, under the new legislation, a national membership ballot, this was not held. Instead, the strategy of the National Union of Miners was to encourage militant local-area unions to call a strike, and let this filter through to other locals, who were pressured as necessary by picketing. Although the government maintained a distance from the dispute, it clearly influenced the National Coal Board and authorised national use of the police force to control picketing. 'The strike illustrates many of the features of British industrial relations in the mid-1980s: a tougher management style; legal interventions; the weakness of the labour movement; and in the number of working miners and the increasing unpopularity of the strike, a public mood out of sympathy with militant union action.' (Bamber and Snape, 1987: 49.)

In 1986 the Wages Act restricted Wages Councils to setting single hourly and overtime wage rates, and removed all employees under the age of twenty-one from their coverage. Following another Conservative win in the 1987 election, the government proceeded with more reforms. Under the 1988 Employment Act, union members were enabled to obtain an injunction where the union had acted without a secret ballot, a Commissioner for the Rights of Trade Union Members was appointed to help workers taking action against their union, and union disciplinary powers were restricted. Members were also given the right to inspect union accounts, and remaining statutory support for the closed shop was removed; industrial action to enforce a closed shop was outlawed, and employees could not be dismissed for refusing to join a union even if 85% voted for the closed shop in a secret ballot. By the 1989 Employment Act, restrictions on working time for women and youths were lifted, and separate majority ballots were required for industrial action in multi-plant organisations. The 1990 Employment Act allowed for firms to dismiss selectively workers engaged in unofficial industrial disputes, and all remaining secondary action was outlawed. Unions were also made liable for unofficial strike action by shop stewards, unless this action had been formally repudiated by the union. Moreover, job applicants refused a job on the basis of *either* membership *or* non-membership of a union were now entitled to legal compensation[26].

From 1979, union membership began to fall for the first time since the interwar years, and it has continued falling right up to 1991 (latest figures available at the time of writing). In 1979, union membership in Britain stood at 13.289 million, but had fallen to 9.585 million by 1987 (Bird, Beatson and Butcher, 1993). This loss of 3.7 million members represents the longest period of sustained decline since records began in 1892, although the absolute number is not as great as for the period 1920–33, when almost 4 million were lost. (Membership fell from 8.348 million in 1920 to just 4.392 million by 1933.)[27] Reasons advanced for the fall in membership since 1979 include compositional changes, business cycle factors, anti-union legislation, the changing attitudes of both employers and union leaders to union organisation, and government willingness to stand out against industrial action (Booth, 1991; Metcalf, 1991; Millward *et al.*, 1992).

How have these factors affected membership? First, it has frequently been argued that structural change in the British economy has contributed to declining membership.[28] Concomitant with the decline of the heavily unionised older manufacturing industries (with a concentration of male workers) and the contraction of the public sector, there has been an expansion of the services sector, and growth of smaller enterprises and part-time and female employment, which have traditionally been harder to unionise. Secondly, there are business cycle factors. In particular, employment has declined since 1980, and unemployed members may have dropped out of their unions, especially if long-term unemployed.[29] The impact of unemployment on membership over time has been much discussed in business cycle theories of trade union membership.[30] What is at issue in current discussion of declining membership is whether the decline is due to a cyclical response around long-run trend patterns, or to a 'new industrial relations' inducing an alteration in trend growth.

A third reason often put forward for the decline in density is the legislative changes since the Thatcher government took office in 1979. Trade union legislation may affect the cost of union organisation and the extent of management opposition to unions (Freeman and Pelletier, 1990:

[26] See Metcalf (1990a) and Lewis (1991) for more detailed accounts of the legislation.
[27] Union density in 1920 was 45.2% and fell to a low of 22.6% by 1933.
[28] See for example MacInnes (1987), Carruth and Disney (1988), Richardson and Wood (1989), Metcalf (1989) and Booth (1989).
[29] According to the 1987 British Social Attitudes Survey, 11% of the unemployed are union members, compared with 41% of the employed (see Freeman and Pelletier, 1990: 160).
[30] See Bain and Elsheikh (1976), Richardson (1976), Booth (1983), Carruth and Disney (1988) and Freeman and Pelletier (1990), for example.

146). The legislation affects organisation through the constraints it estab-
lishes on employers' rights to oppose recognition, workers' rights to abstain
from membership, and union rights to withdraw labour and to pressure
management to recognise a union (through secondary picketing). If
workers perceive legislative changes as weakening trade unions, they may
abstain from membership, because the perceived future benefits are less.[31]
In addition, there is no doubt that the new legislation has put considerable
pressure on union leadership, since it has effectively changed the rules under
which unions operate, and thereby increased uncertainty. Inevitably these
changes have necessitated increased expenditure of union resources at a
time when membership has been declining.[32]

A fourth reason advanced for declining membership is the possibility of a
a change in industrial relations institutions over the period that might
parallel the switch in the USA from a collective bargaining system to a
'human resource management system', as described in Kochan, Katz and
McKersie (1986). But there is little evidence of this from the three
Workplace Industrial Relations Surveys (conducted in 1980, 1984 and
1990), apart from the decline in the extent of union representation, to which
we will return in the following subsection.

While there has been a tremendous amount of speculation about the
impact on membership density of compositional changes, the business cycle
and legislative changes, there has been relatively little empirical research
attempting to measure the impact of these factors. Carruth and Disney
(1988) estimate a business cycle model of the determinants of membership
growth over the period 1892–1984, where business cycle factors are proxied
by unemployment and nominal wage and price inflation. Their model
predicts the downturn in union density in 1979, and also finds that
unemployment, and both nominal and real wages growth, are negatively
related to membership. The latter finding is in sharp contrast to earlier
business cycle studies, where membership density has been found to
increase with wage growth.[33] In one of their specifications, Carruth and
Disney use a dummy variable taking the value '1' when Labour, Liberals or

[31] It is interesting that against this background of anti-union legislation, evidence has been
produced from Gallup polls since the 1950s that a growing proportion of the British
population believes unions are a 'good thing'. However, this finding may follow from the
decline in inflation and strikes, and may reflect union weakness rather than union strength
(see Edwards and Bain, 1988).
[32] In 1979, 84% of all union income came from members' subscriptions, as compared with
81% in 1986. The proportion of average weekly earnings represented by average subscriptions was 0.33% in 1979 as compared with 0.38% in 1985; this is below most other countries
(Towers, 1989: 178). Willman (1990), examining British unions over the period 1950–88,
found that the real financial worth of unions improved over the 1980s, and had worsened
over the period of membership expansion of the 1970s.
[33] See, for example, Bain and Elsheikh (1976) and Booth (1983).

a coalition was governing; they find this is significantly positive, and plays some part in determining steady-state union density.[34]

Freeman and Pelletier (1990), in a business cycle model estimated over the period 1945–86, explicitly take into account the impact of industrial relations legislation on union density. They do this by carefully constructing an index based on an ordinal ranking of the industrial relations legislation, which they then compress into a 1–5 scaling of the laws. Their approach leaves them open to criticisms of subjectivity, and there are also possible simultaneity problems with their specification, since the legislation may have been determined in part by union weakness reflected in lower density. None the less, the Freeman–Pelletier approach represents an interesting attempt to quantify the impact of legislation, which is held by many industrial relations experts to affect steady-state membership. Their estimates show density increasing significantly with the legal index, the manufacturing share of employment, inflation and unemployment. The unemployment effect differs in sign from earlier business cycle models, 'suggesting that its effect is particularly fragile and sensitive' (Freeman and Pelletier, 1990: 152). Their results lead them to conclude that '*the vast bulk of the observed 1980s decline in union density in the UK is due to the changed legal environment for industrial relations*' (Freeman and Pelletier, 1990: 156, emphasis in source), a result that contrasts with the findings of Carruth and Disney (1988) and Disney (1990) that business cycle factors are the principal cause.[35]

Disney *et al.*, (1993) use the Workplace Industrial Relations Survey data to examine union recognition over the period 1980 to 1990. Their results provide indirect evidence that business cycle factors have not been the sole reason for decline in union membership. In particular, they find that new establishments (emerging over the period 1980–90) were less likely to recognise a union and that 'it is this, rather than derecognition of unions in existing establishments, which has been driving the downturn in unionization' (Disney *et al.*, 1993: 12).

History suggests that the trade union movement has always been vulnerable to business cycle factors, and quantitative analyses generally support this view. Legislation, and the attitudes of the incumbent political party, have also been found to be important. It is interesting to place the recent decline in union density within an historical context.

[34] However, in the second half of the 1980s, outside their estimating period, unemployment fell dramatically, and yet union density continued its steady decline. Disney (1990), presenting the predictions for the Carruth–Disney model up to 1987, argues that this model is able to explain over 90% of the decline in union density in the 1980s.

[35] Unfortunately, in Britain we do not yet have the micro data-sets that would allow compositional impacts to be examined in the way that Farber (1987a, 1987b), for example, was able to do for the USA.

Table 1.1 showed density in a number of industrialised market economies. It is interesting to note that, for the period 1980 to 1985, *all* countries
except for Canada and Sweden have been characterised by declining
density.[36] Yet these countries have not experienced the anti-union legislation characterising Britain in the 1980s. Table 2.2 presents an international
comparison of strike activity over the period 1978–87, where the measure of
strike activity is working days lost per thousand employees in all employment. A comparison of the period 1978–82 with the period 1983–7 reveals
that only five of the twenty countries listed experienced an increase in strike
activity. As Brown and Wadhwani (1990: 60) argue, Britain was the seventh
most strike-prone country in each five-year period. Her decline in strike
activity over the 1980s reflected international trends, for fifteen out of
twenty countries also experienced declines over this period. Moreover,
most other countries experiencing a decline experienced a proportionately
greater decline than did Britain.

It is often argued that employer resistance has been a major factor
associated with declining union density in the USA, but this has not had the
same importance in Britain. There appears to have been no widening of the
union wage markup in Britain over the past decade (see chapter 6 and
Stewart (1990, 1993a)) nor any increase in the union share of profits
(Blanchflower and Oswald, 1988b), which in the USA increased the
incentive for employers to engage in anti-union activities. There has also
been little derecognition of British trade unions in established workplaces
since the new legislation has been in place (Claydon, 1989; Millward *et al.*,
1992). However, there is evidence that union recognition at 'greenfield' sites
is now often only granted by management where the union is willing to
accept a single-union deal (Metcalf, 1991), in an effort to overcome the
problems of multi-unionism on site.[37]

British trade unions in the late 1980s have responded to the perceived
crisis of declining membership levels and the hostile legislative environment
in a number of different ways. Merger activity has been increasing (Towers,

---

[36] This international comparison casts some doubts on the popular view in Britain that the
Thatcher industrial relations legislation was largely responsible for declining union density.
A basic question at issue is whether we observed in the 1980s a change in long-run trend
movements in unionisation, or simply a large deviation around an established trend. For
discussion of this question, see Neumann and Rissman (1984), Farber (1987a, 1987b) and
Dickens and Leonard (1985) for the USA; Carruth and Disney (1988), Booth (1989),
Metcalf (1989), Brown and Wadhwani (1990), Disney (1990) and Freeman and Pelletier
(1990) for the UK; and for an international comparison see Freeman (1988).

[37] The TUC, finding that its unions objected to TUC suggestions of membership swaps on
existing sites to reduce the extent of multi-unionism, has recommended single-table
bargaining (Metcalf, 1991). Here, all unions on site are brought together around a single
negotiating table.

Table 2.2 *An international comparison of strikes 1978–87 (working days lost per 1000 employees in all employment)*[a]

Country	1978–82	1983–87	1978–87
Australia	600	250	420
Austria	—	—	—
Canada	820	440	620
Denmark	120	250	190
Finland	300	520	420
France[b]	120	50	80
Germany (FR)	40	50	50
Greece	950	590	760
Ireland	800	400	600
Italy	1160	510	840
Japan	20	10	10
Netherlands	30	10	20
New Zealand[b]	350	550	450
Norway	60	140	100
Portugal	210	120	160
Spain	1110	560	850
Sweden	250	60	150
Switzerland	—	—	—
United Kingdom	540	400	470
United States[c]	200	100	150

Notes:

[a]   All figures shown in the table are rounded to the nearest 10 working days. The average working days lost are calculated using unrounded figures, and the ten-year average is reported using the appropriate ten-year figures (and not as an average of the two five-year figures).

[b]   Public sector strikes excluded.

[c]   Excludes strikes involving fewer than 1000 workers.

— less than five days lost per 1000 employees

Source: 'International Comparisons of Industrial Stoppages for 1987', *Employment Gazette*, June 1989, 309–13.

1989; Willman, 1989; Metcalf, 1991).[38] Some unions have been improving services offered to members as an incentive to unionise (Booth, 1991). Recruitment of members from the fast-growing, previously poorly organised sectors has also been attempted (Towers, 1989). There has also been revision of union goals, with issues like multi-unionism, single-union deals, no-strike deals and so on under discussion by both the TUC and individual unions. The need to work for a Labour government is also regarded as vital, but it is apparent that the Labour Party has lost the support of many traditionally Labour-voting unionists; the Labour Party has also announced it would leave in place much of the union legislation of the Thatcher years.

This is not the place for a detailed analysis of whether or not the Thatcher government's trade union legislation has had an impact on industrial relations outcomes. Many investigators have been exploring this impact with regard, for example, to productivity and investment, and some of these studies will be examined in chapter 5. The incidence of strikes in Britain declined in the 1980s, but since most other industrialised market economies experienced a similar fall, the reduction appears to be associated with the recession rather than the legislation (Brown and Wadhwani, 1990). As Haskel and Kay note when commenting on Thatcher policy and legislative changes: 'the consequences of these changes are hard to detect in aggregate economic statistics ... Between 1979 and 1989 GDP has grown at an average rate of 2.3 per cent per annum ... very much in line with the long term historical performance of the British economy.' However, productivity in British manufacturing industry has grown at the extraordinary average rate of 5.4% per annum, and commentators are generally in agreement that this is due to a large extent to 'macroeconomic restriction and a competitive, deregulated environment ... If the overall effect on economic performance is modest, it is partly because much of the economy was not much affected by either recession or competition' (Haskel and Kay, 1991: 197–8).

2.2.6 Collective bargaining in Britain today

What is the state of industrial relations in Britain today? The debate on the British industrial relations system has been enormously informed by the results of the Workplace Industrial Relations Surveys (WIRS) of 1980,

---

[38] Merger activity increases what Willman calls the 'market share' of a union. But it will only increase aggregate membership if there are economies of scale permitting the union to devote more resources to organisation drives, or if the merger involves some cross-subsidisation from a rich to a poor union allowing the latter to spend more resources on organisation.

1984 and 1990. This section draws on the sourcebooks from these three surveys, in particular on Millward *et al.* (1992). At the time of WIRS 1980, a central feature of the British system was voluntary collective bargaining between employers and employers' associations, and trade unions. Although the style of negotiation was adversarial, the system worked through largely voluntary procedures, and it applied to most of private manufacturing, to the whole of the public sector, and to large employers in private services (Millward *et al.*, 1992: 351). While there was little change to the British system between 1980 and 1984, as indicated by WIRS1 and WIRS2, considerable changes were apparent by the time of WIRS3 in 1990.

A striking feature of British collective bargaining by 1990 as revealed by the WIRS3 data was that the extent of multi-employer bargaining with trade unions had contracted. Moreover, the proportion of work places affiliated to employers' associations had been halved between 1980 and 1990. Since multi-employer bargaining occurred predominantly at the industry level, this represented an interesting shift away from the industry level of bargaining which has had its critics for many years. The proportion of plants bargaining at the establishment level remained unchanged, with an increase in the proportion bargaining at the organisation or company level.

A second striking feature of British collective bargaining is a *fall in the extent of trade union representation*, particularly over the period 1984–90. This decline is found in all aggregate indicators – union density, union recognition, coverage of employees by collective agreements, multi-union-ism, and the closed shop – but changes have tended to be concentrated in particular sectors (see Millward *et al.*, 1992 for details). In both 1980 and 1984, 73% of all workplaces had union members, but this had declined to 64% by 1990. In 1984, management recognised one or more unions (for collective bargaining over pay for some employees) in 66% of all work-places; but by 1990 this had dropped to just 53%. The corollary of the decline in recognition was that the proportion of employees covered by collective bargaining fell from 71% in 1984 to 54% in 1990. The extent of multi-unionism in the manual unionised sector remained unaltered, but declined for non-manuals. Perhaps the most dramatic change over the period was in the extent of the closed shop. For manual workers, 20% of establishments had a closed shop arrangement in 1984, while for non-manual workers 9% of establishments had a closed shop. By 1990, these figures had fallen to just 4% and 1% respectively. None the less, the WIRS data show that firms abandoning the closed shop over the period experienced only small falls in union density (Millward *et al.*, 1992: 359).

However, where trade union representation has persisted, industrial relations and collective bargaining structures remain largely unchanged.

Pay and conditions remain within the scope of collective bargaining; other issues such as physical working conditions, staffing levels, and redeployment within the establishment are often negotiated between management and recognised unions. Health and safety representation is still found to the same extent in the union sector, but it has declined in the nonunion sector. Interestingly, the proportion of union establishments with formal grievance procedures, and disciplinary and dismissal procedures, has grown (Millward *et al.*, 1992: 355). Finally, WIRS3 shows that the decline in union representation over the second half of the 1980s has not been accompanied by a reduction or 'downgrading' of personnel management, which some commentators had suggested was happening.

The salient features of British collective bargaining can be summarised as follows. British collective agreements are legally unenforceable, and the rules of the bargaining process are largely voluntarist, left to the unions and employers to determine. But individual and trade union rights have been extensively proscribed by trade union legislation over the past decade (Lewis, 1991). Unions must conduct postal ballots every five years to elect general secretaries and executive committees, and ballots every ten years to determine whether or not the political levy should continue. Unions must also secure 85% of a secret ballot to establish a closed shop, but individuals who do not wish to join a union retain the right to abstain. The corollary also holds; individuals who wish to join must not be penalised for doing so. Industrial action must also be preceded by a secret ballot, and immunities for strike action pertain only to official action *excluding* secondary action or picketing. As was also the case prior to 1979, individuals who strike are not entitled to statutory unemployment benefits (though they are entitled to means-tested state benefits), and if dismissed while on strike, they are not entitled to any statutory redundancy pay or compensation for unfair dismissal. There is no statutory right for employers to recognise a trade union, even if a majority of workers wants union representation. Individual members have the right to inspect trade union accounts, and members wishing to take legal action against their unions can seek assistance from the Commissioner for the Rights of Trade Union Members.

How do the US trade union movement and US collective bargaining institutions compare with those of Britain? The following section considers the principal features of the development of the US union movement and collective bargaining system.

2.3 The development of the US union movement

2.3.1 The early years

Trade unions began in the USA in much the same way as in Britain, with skilled craftsmen combining in local unions in the 1790s, in defensive moves to resist the reduction in pay caused by expanding and increasingly competitive markets. The success of the shoemakers' unions in Philadelphia stimulated the development of a shoemaker employers' association, which took the unions to court in 1806 alleging that unions were conspiracies, being the combination of two or more persons banded together to prejudice the rights of others. These rights were the property rights of employers to free access to labour and product markets, and the rights of workers to a job regardless of union status. The fact that unions had been declared unlawful in Britain was used as a precedent. Thus began the long history of litigation that has characterised the US labour movement (Taylor and Witney, 1971: 14). But workers continued to unionise in spite of the conspiracy cases. By the late 1830s there were hundreds of local trade unions and some city-wide federations in the major eastern cities, and some national labour organisations (Taylor and Witney, 1971; Reynolds, 1978). None of these survived the depression of 1837. But by an important court case in 1842 trade unions became lawful organisations.[39]

In the process of industrialisation in the nineteenth century, as in Britain, a new class of semi-skilled employees began to emerge in the USA, threatening the traditional craftsmen. As manufacturing processes became more sophisticated, production became factory-based. The growing population and the development of an extensive transportation system contributed to the expansion of the market for domestic manufactured goods. Improved transportation made labour more mobile. Labour mobility and the opening up of new markets allowed for greater competition, and the emergence of merchants who could facilitate the workings of the market mechanism. The new factory system initially employed unskilled women and children, and, later, immigrants from Europe. As in Britain, unionisation of industrial workers was slow, for factory workers could be easily replaced by a ready pool of available unskilled workers. The threat of labour withdrawal was therefore not a credible threat in industrial union attempts to gain any monopoly power.

Until the late nineteenth century, the unions that developed in the USA tended to be ephemeral organisations that were eliminated by depressions. The immediate post-Civil War depression of 1873–8 was the first that unions managed to survive, albeit with severely reduced membership. The period immediately following the Civil War was important for the growth of national unions. The development of national markets, with firms competing nationally, stimulated the formation of national unions, better able to survive depressions than local unions. These national unions took over, from the locals, control of benefits, apprenticeships, membership and strike regulation. They also became involved in contract negotiation and

[39] This was the *Commonwealth of Massachusetts* v. *Hunt* case; see Taylor and Witney (1971: 20) for details.

the organisation of new locals. It is still the case that full-time union officials, benefits and strikes are centrally financed and regulated. The development of national unions ensured that, in the event of a depression, a nucleus of the union could survive to begin organisation again afterwards. Union survival was also assisted by the appointment of full-time officials with a vested interest in the survival and expansion of their unions (Marshall, King and Briggs, 1980).

2.3.2 The beginnings of business unionism in the USA

In 1869, the Knights of Labor organisation was formed, with the aim of establishing a single union comprising workers of all types. However, its heterogeneity made consensus difficult. The fact that it comprised large numbers of unskilled workers contributed to its weakness, since unskilled workers could easily be replaced by employers. The Knights had an ideological outlook, looking 'to make industrial and moral worth, not wealth, the true standard of individual and national greatness'.[40] At that time in Britain, union leaders were also concerned with the moral uplift of their membership (Phelps Brown, 1986: 200).

Skilled workers, dissatisfied with the Knights of Labor, formed in 1886 the American Federation of Labor (AFL), which increasingly dominated the Knights. The AFL was a voluntary association of national craft unions, whose organisation was strongly influenced by its first president, Samuel Gompers. The establishment of the AFL marks the beginning of 'business unionism' in the USA. Gompers and his colleagues believed that workers should not become involved in politics and middle-class reform movements, since this might divide the labour movement and fragment its aims. The weakness of the Knights was perceived to arise in part from the tremendous heterogeneity of its membership. A perennial dilemma for the labour movement is whether to organise by occupation or craft, or instead by industry. The AFL organised by crafts; each of its constituent craft-based national unions was autonomous within the Federation. The AFL also resolved to pursue labour objectives through the process of collective bargaining with employers (Reynolds, 1978; Marshall et al., 1980). While the AFL strategy resulted in slow but irregular growth in craft unions, there remained with a few notable exceptions little organisation of semi-skilled and unskilled workers until the 1930s. The AFL remained dominated by craft unions, and it was not until 1938 that a breakaway group formed the Congress of Industrial Organisations (CIO) to organise industrial unions in manufacturing industry.

[40] This quotation is from the Knights' 1878 convention platform; see Marshall et al., 1980: 59.

The 1870s saw the introduction of the use of injunctions in labour disputes. An injunction is a court order directing an individual to follow, or to refrain from following, a particular action. It has traditionally been used to protect property rights. In the context of labour disputes, the relevant property right was the right to carry out a business in a profitable manner. The union could therefore be enjoined for any action that damaged the employer's right to do business. Injunctions are issued by a special type of court – the equity court – in which a judge alone determines the outcome. Thus from the late nineteenth century 'the judiciary literally enacted legislation', bypassing any public debate on the issue (Taylor and Witney, 1971: 31). The full force of the injunction was felt when in 1895 the Supreme Court allowed that the injunction could be used to enforce the 'yellow-dog' contract, an agreement between a worker and the employer in which the worker agreed not to join a union. As a result, employers could enjoin unions for inciting workers to break these contracts. This was to curtail unionisation and collective bargaining until the passage of the Norris–La Guardia Anti-injunction Act in 1932. None the less, the US trade union movement expanded in the late nineteenth century, increasing from 0.447 million members in 1897 to 2.687 million by 1914 (Wolman, 1924: 16). This paralleled the expansion of union membership in other countries such as Britain, Germany, France and Sweden (Phelps Brown, 1986).

While there are strong similarities in the development of the trade union movement in Britain and the USA up to the end of the nineteenth century, there are also some major points of divergence. In particular, the US union movement has always been weak relative to Britain. A number of reasons have been put forward for this. First, it is often argued that US industrial workers did not have the same impetus to unionise to achieve higher wages in the nineteenth century as did European workers. The wages of US factory workers were comparable to those of US farm workers, and higher than those in the European countries the immigrants had left behind (Lebergott, 1984; Wheeler, 1987; Boyer, Hatton and Bailey, 1994). More-over, the heterogeneity of the US labour force, which included immigrants and, after the Civil War, emancipated blacks, inhibited the organisation of the unskilled. In contrast, the British unskilled labour force was relatively homogeneous. The vast size of the USA also made it harder to organise nationally (Phelps Brown, 1986).

Secondly, US employers were quick to stamp on emerging unions, whereas British employers accepted unions, and sometimes even welcomed their presence. British employers in much of the nineteenth century were sheltered from competition through their technical lead from the Industrial Revolution. By the late nineteenth century, when the trade union movement was beginning to strengthen in the USA, British family firms were often well established and 'could enter into agreements with trade unions, and individually respect their men's working practices, without fear of losing their markets overnight to innovating or invading competitors' (Phelps Brown, 1986: 210). In contrast, US employers faced greater competitive pressures, and lacked the British technological lead. They therefore had a greater incentive to quash trade unions.

Thirdly, expectations of upward mobility in the new country hindered the development of worker solidarity. The British union movement was based on working-class solidarity, albeit with support from many intellectuals, and was characterised by 'corporate consciousness' (Kahn-Freund, 1977) and a commitment to trade union ideals. In contrast, US workers regarded themselves as equal citizens, and adult males were enfranchised decades before British workers, and therefore were not excluded from politics as they were in Britain until the late nineteenth century.[41] Furthermore, after the American revolution, individual rights were established constitutionally in the USA, in contrast to Britain which relies on custom and practice in many areas and where it was not until 1875 that master-and-servant legislation was replaced by the Employers and Workmen Act.

2.3.3 *The early years of the twentieth century*

The early years of the twentieth century in the USA were characterised by increasing industrial concentration and the reduction of competition. Anti-trust laws that were introduced in response also affected trade unions; in particular, the secondary boycott became illegal. Although unions were legal, and workers were legally entitled to join a union and to strike, the use of the injunction by hostile employers and the impact of the anti-trust laws put a strong brake on union development in the USA. While the First World War increased union power, this collapsed as in Britain just a few years after war ended. By 1930, union membership as a percentage of the civilian labour force (excluding employers and the self-employed) was only one-third of that of the United Kingdom (Bain and Elsheikh, 1976).

Until the 1930s, there had been a hostile attitude to the union movement on the part of both employers and the government. But the Great Depression saw a change in attitudes to the labour movement, and a move from judicial to legislative control of labour relations. The beginnings of this change were evinced in the passage of the Norris–La Guardia Act of 1932. This Act restricted the power of federal courts to issue injunctions

---

[41] Pennsylvania gave the vote to adult men in 1790, followed by Massachusetts in 1820 and New York in 1822 (Phelps Brown, 1986: 212). In Britain, adult men were not enfranchised until the Second and Third Reform Acts of 1867 and 1884.

against unions involved in peaceful activities, and made 'yellow-dog' contracts unenforceable in federal courts. The federal government's attitudes over the period 1933–55 were encouraging to the union movement, and as a result membership increased over the period. President Roosevelt's New Deal was based on the Keynesian view that restricted purchasing power and deficient aggregate demand had exacerbated the effects of the Depression. To make labour more equal in its relationship with big business, the policy reforms under the New Deal aimed to encourage union organisation.

2.3.4 The Wagner Act and the Second World War

In 1935, the National Labour Relations Act (the Wagner Act) was passed. This Act aimed to protect workers in their rights to organise and to bargain collectively. Proponents of the Act believed that institutionalised collective bargaining would stabilise and make more efficient employment relations, engendering cost savings that would cover any increased labour costs (Kochan *et al.*, 1986: 26). The Wagner Act has had a profound impact on the character of present-day US industrial relations. Under the provisions of the Wagner Act, employers were required to bargain collectively with trade unions chosen by a majority of workers, and were not allowed to pursue anti-union activities. The National Labor Relations Board (NLRB) was established to enforce the provisions of the Act; in particular, to investigate unfair labour practices, to issue orders enforceable in federal courts for employers to cease such practices, and to conduct union representation elections in appropriate bargaining units. The Wagner Act left the determination of substantive issues to collective bargaining by management and the union, but circumscribed the process by which the parties could reach a contract. Under this system of industrial relations, management retained control of strategic decision-making, which 'was also consistent with the American labor movement's business unionism philosophy' (Kochan *et al.*, 1986: 27).

Under the protection of the Wagner Act, the Congress of Industrial Organisations (CIO), established in 1938, organised the mass-production car and steel industries on an industry-wide basis. Union membership increased from 3.162 million in 1930 to 8.410 million at the start of US involvement in the Second World War in 1941 (Bain and Elsheikh, 1976: 138; National Bureau of Economic Research figures). During the period 1941–45, the War Labor Board facilitated trade union expansion (Taylor and Witney, 1971) and collective bargaining became institutionalised. However the growth in membership in the war years derived not from previously unorganised industries becoming unionised, but from the employment growth in the already organised industries, such as steel, cars, aircraft, shipbuilding, mining, electrical manufacture and transportation (Marshall *et al.*, 1980: 90). By the end of the war in 1945, union membership had increased to 12.088 million (Bain and Elsheikh, 1976: 138).

But towards the end of the war years, public opinion began to turn against the union movement, following a series of unofficial strikes in the coal industry. In response to this, the War Disputes Act (Smith–Connally Act) of 1943 required that, before any strike, there must be a thirty-day cooling-off period and an NLRB-conducted strike ballot. Seeking political support for the union movement, the CIO then established the Political Action Committee (PAC) in 1943, and the AFL in 1947 established Labor's League for Political Education (LLPE). While neither developed into an independent labour party along the lines of the British experience, the formation of these organisations or pressure groups marked a new development in the US labour movement – a recognition of the importance of formalising political lobbying.

2.3.5 The aftermath of the Second World War

The success of the Wagner Act in encouraging the growth and expansion of the union movement led to increasing efforts by employers and business interests to repeal the legislation. The end of the war also marked the end of war-time no-strike pledges, the abandonment of price and wage controls, and the surfacing of unresolved labour grievances that had accumulated during the war years.[42] Although the strikes were in part due to the ending of war-time controls that had pent up grievances over the war years, public opinion attributed the unrest to the Wagner Act. Moreover, abuses that had always characterised the union movement (such as discrimination, featherbedding, and corruption) became more apparent to the general public with the growing power of unions (Taylor and Witney, 1971: 202). Thus, in 1947, Congress amended (but did not displace) the Wagner Act by the Labor–Management Relations Act (the Taft–Hartley Act). While the Wagner Act had been concerned to restrict employer conduct, the Taft–Hartley Act aimed to restrict union conduct. It proscribed union unfair labour practices, outlined procedures for de-certification of a union as the exclusive bargaining agent, and required unions to bargain in good faith. The closed shop was prohibited, and the use of the union shop narrowed.[43]

---

[42] In 1946, 4,985 strikes occurred and 116 million working days (an estimated 1.43% of working time) were lost.

[43] In the US context, the closed shop requires that workers be union members before being employed, while the union shop allows the employer to hire non-union workers, who must

Unions were forbidden to engage in secondary boycotts, jurisdictional disputes were made illegal, and procedures were established to deal with labour disputes which might threaten national health or safety. The states were also allowed to establish 'right-to-work' laws, limiting the application of union shop provisions in union contracts (Freeman, 1972; Taylor and Witney, 1971).

The 1940s marked the gradual formalisation of collective bargaining procedures. In many of the industries into which unions had expanded, management and unions negotiated multi-year contracts covering wage increases, grievance and arbitration procedures, and a variety of fringe benefits (such as pensions, health and insurance). The strong industrial unions in the car, steel and coal industries were characterised by increasing centralisation of power, and provided contractual agreement models for the more decentralised national unions. Management specialists and personnel departments also emerged to deal with collective bargaining procedures (Kochan *et al.*, 1986).

Overall, the 1950s were characterised by a stability in collective bargaining, a continuation of the negotiation of multi-year contracts, and the expansion of the range of benefits covered in contracts. In 1955 the AFL and the CIO merged, and further stabilised industrial relations by eliminating competition between unions for the same group of members. In spite of the 1958–9 recession and the concomitant hard line adopted by management in bargaining, 'collective bargaining looked like a system that by 1960 had developed a set of permanently institutionalised practices in the nation's core industries' (Kochan *et al.*, 1986: 45).

2.3.6 The decline in union membership in the USA

However, while the 1950s saw an expansion in the range of benefits negotiated by unions, union membership density did not increase, and indeed began to decline from 1955 (see table 2.1). Between 1957 and 1959, Senator McClellan's Anti-racketeering Committee held sensational hearings on internal union corruption. As Freeman and Medoff (1984: 213) comment, '[h]onesty is dull; corruption is exciting', and in fact only a minority of unions were guilty of corruption. Following the McClellan hearings, union activities were further regulated with the passage in 1959 of the Labor–Management Reporting and Disclosure Act (the Landrum-Griffin Act), directed primarily at internal union practices. This Act

then join the union after starting work. Thus the 'closed' shop in US parlance is what is termed in Britain the 'pre-entry' closed shop, while the US 'union' shop is the British 'post-entry' closed shop. See Hanson, Jackson and Miller (1982) for a comparison of the closed shop in the USA, Britain and West Germany.

provided for regular election of union officials and disclosure of union finances, in order to ensure internal democracy and financial responsibility in unions, and the establishment of a 'bill of rights' for trade union members.[44]

Over the next two decades, there emerged an alternative nonunion system of industrial relations in enough industries and firms to pose a major challenge to unionised employment relations in the 1980s (Kochan *et al.*, 1986). Many nonunion firms mimicked the personnel and compensation practices of union firms, in order to pre-empt union organisation of their workplaces. The discipline of 'human resources management' also developed further, and provided a rationale for the development of work practices in which labour was regarded as a valuable asset. These work practices thereby also pre-empted the need for union organisation.

The USA has faced increased product market competition since the mid-1970s, with high quality imports and technological change threatening traditionally unionised industries such as car manufactures, textiles and steel. While in 1958 imports accounted for only 2.5% of US manufacturing sales, by 1977 they had increased to 7.2%, and by 1984 stood at 11.0%. Furthermore, the union–nonunion wage differential widened in the late 1970s (Johnson, 1984; Lewis, 1986), increasing the labour costs of unionised firms. The combination of increasing competition and a widening union wage markup reduced profits in unionised firms, and increased the incentive for employers to engage in anti-union activities. More recently, the deregulation of unionised industries such as transport and communications, and the consequent increased competition, have provided an added impetus to employer anti-union activities (Farber, 1987, 1990).

What are these anti-union activities pursued by US management? Employer resistance to unions has manifested itself in innovative personnel practices, involvement in anti-union litigation, a willingness to engage in unfair labour practices, the hiring of labour-management consultants specialising in anti-union tactics at certification elections, and the location of new plants in traditionally anti-union areas such as the South.[45] Since the 1960s, employers have increasingly engaged in illegal activities to prevent union success in representation elections (Dickens, 1983; Weiler, 1983; Freeman and Medoff, 1984; Flanagan, 1989). But penalties for illegal actions are small.[46]

---

[44] The Landrum–Griffin Act has been referred to as the 'Lawyers' Full Employment Act', owing to the vagueness of many of its provisions (Taylor and Witney, 1971: 499).

[45] See Freeman and Medoff (1984) and the references therein, Kochan *et al.* (1986), Farber (1990) and Rogers (1989).

[46] For an interesting account, see Rogers (1989), who points out that legal remedial orders are a limited deterrent, since they merely return the parties to the position before the activity, without any additional penalty. See also chapter 15 in Freeman and Medoff (1984).

The union movement, in response to employer abuses of labour law protecting workers' rights to organise, attempted in the late 1970s to reform the existing legislation. The Labor Law Reform Bill was introduced in 1977, with the aims of expediting the union representation procedure, providing more severe penalties against employers engaging in illegal labour practices, and providing unions with equal time to present the union case before a representation election (Freeman and Medoff, 1984; Wheeler, 1987). Although the proposed reforms were minor, the bill was unsuccessful, largely because of business opposition. Once again, the union movement failed to obtain legislation favourable to its interests.

Union membership as a percentage of the total labour force (union 'density') has declined inexorably since the 1950s. However, *public* sector union density has increased over the period, from 13% in 1956 to 36.9% in 1991.[47] Thus the aggregate figure disguises the magnitude of the drop in private sector union organisation. In 1962, federal public sector workers obtained the right to organise and bargain collectively, but cannot bargain generally over wages. From the 1960s, public sector union organisation for state and municipal employees was facilitated when many states legalised collective bargaining over wages and working conditions. In states with no such provision, public sector employees, none the less, are legally entitled to join a union (Hirsch and Addison, 1986). But US public sector workers in general have no right to strike, in contrast with the situation for British public sector workers.

Reasons advanced for the decline in *private* sector union membership since the mid-1950s include increased employer resistance in response to changes in compliance and enforcement incentives as described above, changes in labour force structure, and increased job satisfaction of non-union workers (Farber, 1987, 1990). The structure of the US labour force has changed considerably since the 1950s. Female participation increased from 29.4% in 1950 to 43.7% in 1984. The regional composition of employment has shifted from the traditionally more unionised Northeast and North Central regions towards the less unionised South. There has also been a shift from heavily unionised blue-collar occupations and manufacturing industries towards traditionally less unionised white-collar occupations and service industries. Yet investigators have found that these compositional changes account for only a small share of the decline in

---

[47] The figure for 1991 is from Hirsch and Macpherson (1993) using CPS data. Freeman and Medoff (1984: 243) attribute the growth in public sector unionisation to labour laws requiring union recognition for bargaining purposes. However, it also seems likely that public sector administration does not face the same competitive pressures as do private sector firms, and therefore has not had the same impetus to resist unionisation.

For further discussion of public sector unionisation in the USA, see Hamermesh (1975), Aaron, Grodin and Stern (1979) and Ehrenberg and Schwarz (1983).

union density.[48] Moreover, other countries experiencing similar structural changes have experienced an *increase* in union density since the 1950s (see Australia, Canada, and Britain until 1979). The consensus amongst investigators in this area is that while compositional changes play some part, the predominant factor associated with declining union density in the USA is employer resistance.

2.3.7 Collective bargaining in the USA today

Industrial relations in the USA are characterised by a number of features that distinguish the country from other advanced industrial countries, including Britain. The form of industrial relations has been shaped by the Wagner Act of 1935, amended in 1947 and again in 1959. This legislation has encouraged the formation of small, separate bargaining units, and hence the decentralisation or fragmentation of US collective bargaining. The legislation is *procedural* rather than substantive; that is, it regulates the procedures which unions must follow for recognition and bargaining.

Under the provisions of the Wagner Act, employers are compelled to bargain with any union with majority support in an 'appropriate unit' of employees, where the National Labor Relations Board (NLRB) has discretion to determine what constitutes an appropriate unit. The NLRB, in determining the bargaining scope, follows the principle that only workers with a 'substantial mutuality of interests' in wages, hours and working conditions should be included in a single bargaining unit (Rogers, 1989).

While union recognition can be achieved by voluntary employer recognition of a union with majority status, the more common procedure is that the union initially organises a minimum of 30% of what it considers to be a bargaining unit, and then petitions the NLRB to order a secret ballot election of employees in that unit. Once majority support has been obtained, the employer is compelled, via NLRB certification of the union as the bargaining representative, to recognise and bargain with the union 'in good faith'. The union has exclusive jurisdiction over that particular bargaining unit (typically a single location of a particular firm). Hence agreements are usually single-company contracts. Note that the decentralisation inherent in this procedure is unlikely to be conducive to worker solidarity across locations. Although the national unions control strike funds and strikes, union benefits and organising drives, the plant-based local unions control all aspects of collective bargaining.

Workers are legally allowed to strike over recognition issues, provided that before the strike reaches thirty days duration they have filed a petition for an NLRB election. Although striking workers cannot be fired, the

[48] See Neumann and Rissman (1984) and Farber (1987, 1990) for example.

employer is allowed to hire strike-breakers or 'scabs' permanently, and need not replace workers who were on strike until a new permanent position becomes available. As in Britain, workers whose unemployment follows from strike activity have reduced access to unemployment benefits; this varies across states. Once the union has achieved recognition, workers can strike in support of contract demands provided the strike is confined to 'mandatory' bargaining subjects, where the protection is the same as for recognition strikes. 'Mandatory' issues include wages, hours and working conditions. Strikes over 'permissive' matters (such as benefits affecting more than one bargaining unit) are unlawful. It is easy for employers to contravene the intention of the Act. Although once recognition has been achieved employers have a duty to bargain in 'good faith', they are under no obligation to reach an agreement or sign a contract, and can effectively contrive to continue nonunion (Freeman and Medoff, 1984).

Once a collective agreement has been reached, the contract can be enforced by non-judiciary means, namely arbitration (Rogers, 1989). There are no provisions for compulsory settlement of contract disputes (Reynolds, 1978). Workers are not allowed to strike during the period of the contract, which ranges between one and three years. Collective bargaining contracts are normally lengthy and very detailed documents, covering wages, hours, holidays, pensions, seniority rights, health and life insurance, union recognition, management rights, the management and arbitration of grievances, and sometimes cost-of-living adjustments (COLA), and safety provisions.[49] As Wheeler (1987: 72) comments, 'for unionised workers, the relative lack of government welfare programs in the USA is somewhat compensated for by the extensive protections included in these agreements'. In the 1980s, there have been two novel additions to the contracts. The first of these is *concession* bargaining, whereby unions have agreed to reductions in pay and benefits. The second is *two-tier wage structures*. US agreements have sometimes allowed employers to pay new workers less than incumbents for two to three years before paying them the full union rate, but in the 1980s some contracts allowed for this two-tier system to be permanent (Flanagan, 1990b).

2.4 A brief comparison of the British and the US collective bargaining systems

The previous sections have indicated that there are important differences between the USA and Britain in terms of the development of trade union

---

[49] The Bureau of National Affairs maintains a broadly representative sample of 400 major contracts. See Bureau of National Affairs (1986) and Wheeler (1987) for details of the percentage of these contracts that cover each of the benefits listed in the text.

institutions and in the extent of regulation over collective bargaining. Some of the salient differences are summarised in this section.

In the USA, there are three different classes of contract. These are single-employer–single-plant contracts; single-employer–multi-plant contracts; and multi-employer contracts. While most contracts are single-employer, most union workers are covered by multi-employer contracts.[50] There are in the USA, in the nonunion sector, employers' groups whose purpose is to avoid the unionisation of their members (Wheeler, 1987). Indeed, in the USA there is far more employer opposition to unions than in Britain. In the latter, bargaining occurs at a *variety of levels*, with company-level bargaining becoming increasingly prevalent. Multi-unionism – the presence of a number of different unions at a single workplace – further complicates the bargaining process in Britain. Although both Britain and the USA can be characterised as possessing a relatively decentralised collective bargaining structure, with the USA more decentralised than Britain, this categorisation conceals the fact that trade unions in the USA and Britain possess very different characteristics.

The USA is characterised by a very fragmented collective bargaining process; while most union contracts are single-employer, most union workers are covered by multi-employer contracts. Moreover, in the USA a recognised union has *exclusive* jurisdiction, whereas in Britain many different rival unions can represent workers at the one workplace. In the USA, contracts arising out of the bargaining process are typically very detailed, and may cover wages, hours, holidays, pensions, life and health insurance, management rights, seniority, union recognition and grievance procedures (Wheeler, 1987). Although the US collective bargaining process is decentralised and the determination of substantive issues is left to the local union–firm pair, the procedure for bargaining and recognition is carefully circumscribed by federal government regulation, and the agreements reached are legally enforceable. The more regulated industrial relations system in the USA affects the pattern of US strikes, which typically occur at the end of the life of a contract. In Britain, strikes tend to be more frequent and shorter than in the USA, since they can occur at any time (Polachek and Siebert, 1993).

Britain is characterised by bargaining at a number of levels, ranging from industry-wide bargaining between union and employer federations, through bargaining at the organisation level, to bargaining at the establishment or plant level. The rules of the bargaining process are left to the discretion of unions and management. Only recently has legislation regulated union procedures. British collective agreements reached cover a narrower range of issues than in the USA. In Britain, legislation regulates

[50] Information obtained from communication from John Pencavel.

many of the issues such as health insurance, pensions, redundancy or severance pay, and unfair dismissal, which are dealt with by union–firm agreements in the union sector in the USA. Moreover, collective agreements in Britain are not legally enforceable.

The US labour movement is characterised by a type of 'business unionism', by which is meant that the principal concern of American unions is to provide economic benefits to its existing membership, with only a secondary concern with broader issues of social reform. In contrast, trade unions in Britain have traditionally been associated both with social reform and with improving the economic welfare of their members. Moreover, the British trade union movement has strong affiliations with one of the two major parties in British politics, the Labour Party, while US trade unionism is essentially apolitical.

Not only do British and US trade unions possess different characteristics, but the extent of unionism and collective bargaining is very different in each country. The union movement in the USA never achieved the high levels of membership density and collective bargaining coverage reached in Britain. Although British membership density has been declining steadily since 1979, some 33% of the workforce was in a trade union in 1991.[51] In the USA, density has been declining since 1955, and in 1991 only 16% of the workforce was in a union. Moreover, coverage in Britain is much higher than in the USA.[52] The decline of union density does not spell the end of the union movement. In the USA, for example, public sector union density has been growing steadily. Moreover, in Britain the decline in union membership in the 1920s was worse in absolute numbers. While the loss since 1979 of 3.7 million members represents the longest period of sustained membership decline since records began in 1892, the absolute number is not as great as for the period 1920–33, when 3.96 million members were lost.

In chapter 8, we look at the connection between the institutional structure of wage bargaining and macroeconomic performance. It has been suggested that the degree of centralisation of wage bargaining may be particularly important in its impact on macroeconomic performance. The USA (and Canada, Japan and Switzerland) are the most decentralised of the OECD countries, while at the other end of the spectrum, where bargaining may be centralised to the economy level and where confede-

---

[51] This figure comes from the 1991 Labour Force Survey (LFS). See Beatson and Butcher (1993) for a discussion of these data, and a comparison of the LFS data and membership figures from the Certification Officer (used in table 2.1 since these data have a long time series).

[52] Hirsch and Macpherson (1993) show the extent of free-riders over the period 1983 to 1991 in the USA, using CPS data. The difference between contract coverage and union density ranges from a maximum of 3.19% in 1983 to a minimum of 2.11% in 1991. The proportion of free-riders is greater in the public sector, however.

rations of unions and employers negotiate wages, are Austria, Denmark, Finland and Sweden. Britain lies in between these two extremes. There appears to be some (as yet tentative) evidence that countries with very high or low degrees of centralisation suffer lower unemployment perturbations after major supply shocks (Calmfors and Driffill, 1988). The linkage between different countries' collective bargaining structure and economic performance remains an interesting area for research.

3　The orthodox theoretical framework: an overview

3.1 Introduction

The standard view of trade unions is that they are organisations whose purpose is to improve the material welfare of members, principally by raising wages above the competitive wage level. There is little dispute that unions are frequently able to push wages above the competitive level – what is called the 'monopoly' role of trade unions. There is an enormous body of literature documenting the impact of unionism on wage gains, some of which we will be examining in chapter 6. There is also a somewhat smaller body of literature examining the impact of unionism on other variables, such as wage dispersion, productivity, profitability, investment and employment, some of which we will consider in chapter 7. All of this literature is focused on finding an answer to the important question: what do unions do? However, there are many other interesting questions about trade unions that remain unanswered in most of the literature; for example, how do unions gain the power to obtain these wage increases? Under what conditions is the union able to raise wages above the nonunionised wage rate? What factors determine the magnitude of the union wage effect? Why do unions exist? In what circumstances might management acquiesce in the formation of a union or agree to recognise a union?

The first part of this chapter provides an overview of the trade union within the framework of competitive labour and product markets. It also examines the conditions under which a union can achieve a wage rate greater than the competitive level. In particular, there must be some surplus that can be shared, and the union or group of workers must have some bargaining power to induce the firm to share the surplus. Of course, in a competitive framework, the trade union does introduce into the economy a variety of distortions and inefficiencies, and we therefore examine issues of allocative and technical inefficiency associated with the emergence of a trade union in a competitive economy. The orthodox textbook analysis of unions and resource misallocation assumes that the union has emerged in an economy with perfectly competitive product and labour markets. Yet, if modern industrialised economies are characterised by imperfect competition in labour and product markets, it is not clear that replacement of individual bargaining by collective bargaining will result in the same efficiency losses.

Moreover, even within a framework of competitive labour and product markets, there are some arguments suggesting that, in the presence of imperfect information and uncertainty, trade unions may be efficiency enhancing. Unions may in some circumstances increase the available surplus to be shared between the firm and workers, to the extent that unions may provide services reducing labour turnover and negotiating costs, and may thereby be instrumental in shifting out the production possibility frontier. The second part of this chapter outlines the theory examining the conditions under which unions may increase efficiency. Emphasis is also placed on the interdependence of the monopoly and 'efficiency' roles of trade unions. Unions may not be able to increase efficiency without the union having some bargaining or monopoly power. The chapter then moves on to examine how a trade union might obtain this power.

These approaches to modelling the behaviour of the trade union go only some way towards answering the questions raised above, as we note at the end of the chapter. Some of the theory mentioned in the chapter is, as yet, undeveloped, and in discussing this work we can provide only a sketch of the issues, which suggest avenues for further research. Other parts of the theory have been well-developed, in particular the treatment of the distortions in a competitive economy caused by a union. Throughout this chapter, we treat trade union objectives and union-firm wage determination as exogenously given. The analysis of union objectives and wage determination will be expanded more rigorously in later chapters, where the empirical testing of the theory will also be discussed. Because this chapter is providing only an overview of the broad issues, we will not be using much algebra, but will instead rely on diagrammatic exposition where appropriate.

3.2 Trade unions in a perfectly competitive product market

This section looks at the development of the basic model of trade unions in a perfectly competitive product market. In subsection 3.2.1, we examine the conditions under which a union can achieve a wage rate greater than the competitive level. In particular, there must be some surplus that can be shared, and the union or group of workers must have some bargaining power to induce the firm to share the surplus. The concept of union wage gaps and wage gains is illustrated using a simple two-sector general equilibrium diagram. Subsection 3.2.2 looks at social welfare and allocative costs brought about through distortion of factor prices in a perfectly competitive product market, while subsection 3.2.3 examines trade unions and technical inefficiency.

3.2.1 Conditions under which a trade union can achieve a wage rate higher than the nonunion wage

What conditions are necessary for a union to achieve a wage rate higher than the nonunion level? The ability of a trade union to do this depends on the existence of economic rents or surplus in the product market, *and* on the power of the union to act as a monopolist in the supply of labour. Union power is of little use if there is no surplus which can be shared by the union and the firm. Thus for trade unions to exist as viable organisations, they must either create a surplus, or be able to capture a share of the surplus previously appropriated only by the firm. Existence of a (potential) surplus is a necessary condition for union success in its goal of improving union workers' welfare. The surplus may arise from a variety of sources, the most obvious being market imperfections or regulation of the particular industry. In *non-competitive* firms or industries where firms are making surpluses, unions with sufficient power can insist that management increases wages without threatening the demise of the firm. Thus one would expect a higher probability of union organisation in non-competitive industries than in competitive product markets.

In a *perfectly competitive* product market, the firm must be making positive profits when employing workers n at the perfectly competitive wage w_c, in order for the union to be able to appropriate any surplus. Thus the competitive firm's production function must be characterised by decreasing returns to labour in the neighbourhood of the equilibrium (see Ulph and Ulph, 1990a: 89). The union is therefore able to appropriate some of the firm's profits by negotiating a wage above w_c, without driving the firm out of business. This is illustrated in figure 3.1, where the firm's total revenue product function is denoted by $pq(n)$, where p is product price and $q(n)$ is the production function. For a given capital stock, the production function is assumed to be characterised by, first, increasing returns to labour at low levels of employment, and then by diminishing returns at higher levels, as illustrated in figure 3.1.[1] The firm's total factor outlay curve is given by $w_c n$ (capital is assumed fixed in the short run). The firm's profits Π are given by

---

[1] Thus $q'(n) > 0$ (where $q'(.)$ is the usual notation for the first derivative), and $q''(n) > 0$ for $n < \tilde{n}$ and $q''(n) < 0$ for $n > \tilde{n}$ (where $q''(.)$ denotes the second derivative of the production function). Note that an equivalent way of writing the derivative is $q'(n) = dq/dn$.

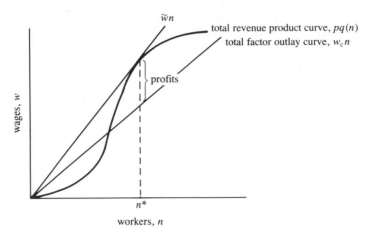

Figure 3.1. Profits in a competitive industry.

$$\Pi = pq(n) - w_c n \tag{1}$$

Clearly profits are greatest where the vertical distance between the total revenue product curve and the total factor outlay curve is at its greatest. If the union can set wages at some $w > w_c$, it can appropriate some of this surplus. The highest wage it can set without driving the firm out of business is $\tilde{w}$, as illustrated in figure 3.1.

In perfectly competitive situations where firms in the industry have different cost structures but there is a fixed number of firms, unions could organise only the firms with the lowest costs, thereby gaining a share of the supernormal profits of the inframarginal firms. However, if there is freedom of entry and exit of firms from the industry, unions may not be able to extract any surplus in the long run. This is because in the long run with freedom of entry and exit we would expect only the firms with the lowest costs to survive, and supernormal profits would be eroded.

Figure 3.2 illustrates the labour demand curve associated with the total revenue curve in figure 3.1. In a perfectly competitive market, the firm faces an exogenously given wage rate w_c. For this given wage, the firm recruits labour until the marginal benefit of hiring an additional worker is equal to the marginal cost; that is, where the value of output produced by the last worker employed is equal to the wage rate that must be paid to this worker. This can be seen by noting that, if the firm chooses labour n to maximise its profits, the first-order condition from maximisation of equation (1) is given by

$$\frac{d\Pi}{dn} = pq'(n) - w_c = 0 \tag{2}$$

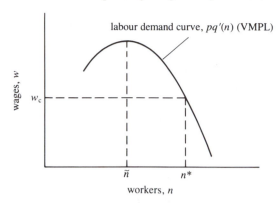

Figure 3.2. Labour demand curve.

and thus

$$pq'(n) = w_c \tag{3}$$

Equation (3) shows that in a perfectly competitive market, the firm recruits labour until the value of the marginal product of labour, given by $pq'(n)$ or VMPL, is equal to the marginal cost, given by w_c. This is illustrated in figure 3.2, where the *slope* of the VMPL curve or labour demand curve is given by the sign of the second derivative of the production function. Since it is assumed that the short-run production function is initially characterised by increasing returns ($q''(n) > 0$ for $n < \tilde{n}$), the VMPL curve is positive for $n < \tilde{n}$. But for higher levels of employment, the short-run production function is assumed characterised by diminishing returns ($q''(n) < 0$ for $n > \tilde{n}$); hence the VMPL curve is decreasing for $n > \tilde{n}$. Optimal employment is given by n^*, where $pq'(n) = w_c$. The area given by $w_c n^*$ represents the firm's wage bill. In figure 3.2, the competitive wage rate is exogenously given to the firm (since it is determined by the interaction of the industry labour demand and labour supply schedules). In chapters 4 and 5 we will be examining precisely how determination of the union wage rate might be modelled. The derivation of the labour demand curve for a monopolistic firm is given in appendix 3A, which also examines wage determination under monopsony and bilateral monopoly. (The monopsonist is of particular interest, because the emergence of a union where wages are set monopsonistically may result in an increase in employment, as is well known in the case of minimum wages.)

We have already noted that surplus existence is a necessary condition for union existence, in that it is unlikely that unions would emerge as viable organisations unless there was some chance that they could negotiate higher wages or better working conditions than those already offered by the firm. But surplus existence alone does not guarantee union success. Clearly, union success depends on one or both of the following conditions. Either the union must have sufficient power to force the firm to concede a share of the surplus to workers or, alternatively, the firm must be willing to share some of the surplus with the union in return for behaviour that guarantees a larger surplus (and thus the firm is not made worse off). But even in the latter situation, the union may need its monopoly power to ensure the firm does not cheat on any agreements once the surplus has been created by co-operative union behaviour. The view that unions may agree to co-operate to increase the available surplus has implications for empirical research attempting to estimate the magnitude of the union wage differential and the union productivity effect, as we shall see in chapters 6 and 7.

The notion that workers may have to battle to acquire sufficient power to induce the firm to concede any surplus accords with the Marxian analysis of the capitalist means of production. According to this approach (see, for example, Bowles (1985)), the production process has been specifically chosen by capitalists to maintain their control over labour, and to ensure that labour as class has no bargaining power. Given the inherent conflict of interest between employers and workers over work effort, and the fact that monitoring of workers is costly to the employer, it is in employers' interests to use unemployment as a means of promoting worker effort. If employees are paid a wage rate exceeding their next best alternative, there is some positive cost associated with being fired. Equilibrium wages in such a labour market are above the market-clearing wage, intuitively because the market-clearing wage is associated with zero unemployment (with the implication that the cost of a job loss is zero). Involuntary unemployment is associated with excess supply of labour, so that labour as a class is not in a position of bargaining strength to claim a share of any surplus.[2]

How is a trade union able to gain monopoly power? A union or group of workers is able to achieve power primarily through the threat of a strike; the union's threat of labour withdrawal will be credible only if there is no alternative pool of substitute workers available. Hence it is important for the union to be able to prevent the firm from employing alternative workers in the event of labour withdrawal. How can the union achieve such monopoly power? The union may be able to organise all workers, or the majority of workers, in the industry, thereby acting as a monopolist in the supply of labour. We saw in chapter 2 that the early successful unions in both Britain and the USA were craft unions, which were able to control the

[2] While having strong similarities to efficiency wage and other malfeasance/shirking models, this Marxian approach differs from shirking models in that the production process is argued to be chosen to ensure workers do not have the opportunity of gaining any bargaining power.

supply of skilled labour to the sector. The industrial or general unions emerged much later, and were unsuccessful at achieving any power until they had reached high levels of union density.[3] If a whole sector is organised, then a closed shop is said to operate in that sector (and this is what is assumed in most formal models of the trade union). Clearly, for the union to be able to act as a monopolist in the supply of labour, membership, denoted by m, must be large relative to the total pool of available workers, t. If not, firms could simply hire nonunion labour and produce at lower cost than unionised competitors, thereby driving the latter out of business and the union out of existence. For very large m relative to t, union organisation in the sector acts as a form of entry barrier, since entry by new firms is discouraged by the union threat to organise entrants. (Indeed, it is possible that existing firms may consider union organisation as a means of ultimately shifting to a more oligopolistic industrial structure.) However, such a scenario is not viable in industries open to international competition where foreign firms are able to hire nonunion labour. In chapter 2, we saw the importance for the historical development of the labour movement of union control of labour supply through these mechanisms.

In craft unions, workers may gain their bargaining power through the fact that it takes time to provide additional supplies of specialist labour. Moreover, in some circumstances unions can control the supply of labour (for example, the medical profession can control the supply of specialists, and printers can control skilled labour supply through apprenticeships), which gives them market power. But non-craft workers may also have a degree of market power if, for example, labour turnover costs make it expensive for management to replace incumbent workers by workers from outside the firm (see Lindbeck and Snower, 1988). Or new employees may be imperfect substitutes for incumbent workers, for example where the incumbent worker has better information than management about work effort and production at the shop floor. In such a situation, the worker or group of workers may refuse to reveal this information to management or to a new employee unless it is in their interests to do so, a situation which gives the incumbent workers some bargaining power and which may encourage them to form a union.

Even if a union does control all the labour supplied to a particular sector, it will not necessarily be able to negotiate a large wage increase relative to the competitive level. The magnitude of the union wage effect depends crucially on the wage elasticity of labour demand in the particular sector. Consider a sector in which a craft-style of union emerges and begins to control labour supply through entry restrictions. For a given level of labour

---

[3] In some cases, they were successful only where employers actively encouraged them, particularly in Britain. See, for example, Phelps Brown (1986) and Pelling (1987).

supply through entry restrictions, the wage gain will be larger the less elastic is the demand for labour. Now suppose that in another sector a general union emerges, which cannot exercise entry restrictions, but whose membership encompasses the whole sector. As this general union begins to raise wages above the competitive level, there will be employment losses as firms shift up their labour demand curves. The less elastic is the labour demand curve, the more the union can raise wages without suffering large employment losses. If the union cares about both wage increases and union employment (we will model this formally in chapters 4 and 5), we would expect to observe large wage gains where labour demand is inelastic, since employment losses are low. Conversely, where labour demand is *elastic*, union wage gains are likely to be smaller.

Factors affecting the elasticity of labour demand are given by Marshall's rules of derived demand. These rules state that, in the long run, where capital is variable, influences on labour demand can be considered under four headings. First and most obviously, labour demand will be affected by changes in demand for the final product. If there is an exogenous increase in product demand, then clearly labour demand will shift in the same direction. Secondly, labour demand will be affected by production substitution possibilities between labour and other inputs (which are determined by the particular production technology used). If the price of labour increases, firms may be able to substitute labour by other factor inputs. Thirdly, labour demand elasticity is affected by the share of labour in total costs. If this share is low, then a 10% increase in wages will have a smaller impact on total costs than if the share of labour is large. Finally, labour demand will also be affected by the elasticity of supply of other factors of production. For while factor substitution may be feasible with a particular technology, if the other factor is scarce there will be no point in substituting the scarce factor for labour when wages increase.

The majority of formal trade union models in the literature assume a perfectly competitive product market, presumably to allow the models to focus on union wage and employment determination in the simplest industrial environment. (Exceptions are Fellner (1947), Hieser (1970), Layard and Nickell (1985), Dixon (1988, 1991), Dowrick (1989) and Layard, Nickell and Jackman (1991).) Of course, the simplifying assumptions of a closed shop and a competitive product market in most formal models of the trade union allow concentration on the important issues of wage and employment determination in models that are not too complex. Furthermore, it is unlikely that the principal results of the models outlined in chapters 4 and 5 (which assume a closed shop and perfect competition) would be substantially altered by assuming imperfect competition. None the less, it is an empirical regularity that imperfections in the product and the labour markets are correlated. Stewart (1990) finds that for semi-skilled British workers, union–nonunion wage differentials in establishments facing competitive market conditions are zero, while in establishments that have some degree of product market power as a result of facing limited competition, the mean union pay differential is between 8 and 10%.[4] Moreover, allocative losses associated with the emergence of unions are likely to differ between competitive and non-competitive product and labour markets. It would therefore be interesting to see a more extensive modelling of the structure of the product market in future union theory.

We have seen that a union's power to achieve wage gains above the competitive level depends crucially on its ability to control labour supply and to prevent firms hiring nonunion labour in the event of labour withdrawal. We have also seen that wages can be raised only if there exist economic rents or surplus which can be shared by the union and the firm, with the union's share taking the form of wage gains. We also saw that the extent of these wage gains is related to the wage elasticity of labour demand.

When considering the impact of trade unions on relative wages, we need to distinguish carefully between two concepts of wage differentials. First, we might compare the union wage with wages that would pertain in the economy *with no trade unions at all*, which would be the competitive wage rate. This is termed by Lewis (1986) the wage *gain*. Secondly, we might compare the union wage with the nonunion wage *ceteris paribus*. This is termed the wage *gap*. These concepts are shown in figure 3.3, which illustrates a simple general equilibrium competitive model (Oswald, 1979). Suppose there are only two sectors in the economy, and that initially there is no trade union. The horizontal axis shows that there is a fixed supply of workers in the economy, given by $\bar{n} = n_1 + n_2$, where n_1 is the number in sector 1 and n_2 is the number in sector 2. The vertical axes show wages and the value of marginal product for each sector. Labour demand in sector 1 is given by the demand curve $VMPL_1$ and in sector 2 by $VMPL_2$. In the absence of any trade union, equilibrium wages are given by w_c, at point A. Here wages are equal in both sectors, so there is no incentive for workers to relocate. Moreover, from profit maximisation under perfect competition, wages in each sector are equal to workers' marginal products, which are the same across sectors.

Now suppose a trade union forms in sector 1 (which has a less elastic labour demand curve). Suppose this union is able to set wages in sector 1 at w_1, at point B on $VMPL_1$. (In chapters 4 and 5 we will examine models which formally analyse the determination of union wages and employ-

---

[4] Stewart argues that earlier econometric work, using the industry concentration ratio for the industry in which the firm operates, is not correct. This is because the measure represents the structure of the industry and not the firm.

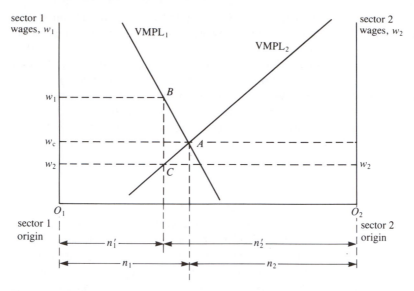

Figure 3.3. Union wage gaps and wage gains in a two-sector economy.

ment). If workers are mobile between sectors, those workers displaced from sector 1 will flood into the nonunion sector 2, driving down wages there to w_2 (where supply of workers to sector 2 given by n_2' is equal to demand $VMPL_2$, at point C in the diagram). Equilibrium employment will now be n_1' in sector 1 and n_2' in sector 2. The wage *gap* is given by $w_1 - w_2$, while the wage gain is given by $w_1 - w_c$. In this diagram, nonunion workers are made worse off by the presence of a trade union in sector 1 of the economy, since their wages have fallen relative to the competitive benchmark.

3.2.2 Trade unions, allocative costs and social welfare

The orthodox monopoly view of trade unions is that the union imposes allocative costs through the distortion of factor prices. Without unions, allocative efficiency is associated with the allocation of identical factor inputs such that their marginal products are equalised across sectors. This was given by w_c in figure 3.3. With unions and fixed capital stock in the short run, wage increases alter relative factor prices. With higher wages in the union sector, union firms employ fewer workers (since the higher wage must in equilibrium be set equal to marginal product, that is, union firms are shifting up the negatively sloped union labour demand curve). Displaced union workers crowd into the nonunion sector, lowering nonunion wages along the nonunion labour demand curve. As a result, too few workers are employed in the union sector where output falls, while too many workers are employed, and too many goods produced, in the nonunion sector.

How does unionisation affect social welfare according to this simple model? First, consider the efficiency loss. If the unionised labour market would otherwise have been competitive, there is an efficiency loss because the value of marginal products of labour in the two sectors are not equal. The deadweight loss to society owing to the unionisation of sector 1 is represented by the shaded triangles in figure 3.4. Triangle ABC measures the total deadweight loss.[5] This has two components: ABD is the deadweight loss in the union sector, while ADC is the deadweight loss in the nonunion sector.[6]

Secondly, consider equity issues. What is the impact of unionisation on income distribution? *Aggregate* labour income may increase or decrease, depending on whether the total economy-wide wage bill after unionisation is greater than or less than the total wage bill prior to unionisation. In other words, in figure 3.4, aggregate labour income will increase only if $(O_1w_1BF + FCw_2O_2) > (O_1w_cAE + EAw_cO_2)$. Capitalists will have gained (or lost), depending on whether the *post-unionisation* return to capital (given by the total area of the triangles $GBw_1 + HCw_2$) is greater than (or smaller than) the *pre-unionisation* return to capital (triangles $GAw_c + HAw_c$). If labour as a class has gained from unionisation, then capital will have lost, given that there is a fixed surplus available for distribution.

We now examine the impact of unionisation on employment and capital in the longer run, where capital is variable. It is useful to consider the simple *partial equilibrium* diagram in figure 3.5 in order to examine how the presence of a union might induce capital substitution in a competitive sector that has just become unionised. With variable capital, higher wages in the union sector cause the competitive firm to substitute capital for labour (the substitution effect). Figure 3.5 shows the isoquant (constant output) and the isocost (constant cost) curves, which are derived from the firm's profit function where both capital and output are variable and the product market is competitive. The profit function is

$$\Pi = pq(n,k) - wn - rk \qquad (4)$$

---

[5] This deadweight loss is equal to the loss in producers' surplus following unionisation, less the gain in workers' surplus.

[6] Conventional estimates of this deadweight loss are very small. Rees (1963) estimates an output loss for the US economy in 1957 of 0.14% of GNP. This calculation is based on the approach of Harberger (1954), and assumes a two-sector general equilibrium model, a 15% relative wage effect and equal labour demand elasticities in each sector. More recently, de Fina (1983) estimates an output loss for the US economy of 0.2% for a union wage gap of 25%, falling to only 0.02% for a union wage gap of 7.5%. De Fina's estimates are based on the explicit solution to a twelve-sector numerically specified computable general equilibrium model. Comparable calculations of deadweight loss have not been made for Britain.

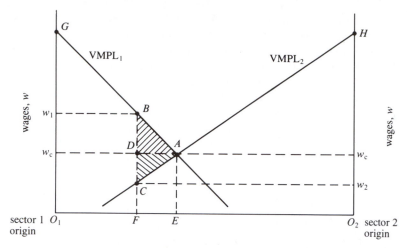

Figure 3.4. Allocative inefficiency in a two-sector economy with a unionised sector.

where r is the return to capital k, and $q(n,k)$ represents the production function, in which output is an increasing function of both capital and labour. The slope of the isoquant is the marginal rate of technical substitution, and is given by minus the ratio of the marginal products of labour and capital. The slope of the isocost curve is minus the ratio of factor input prices, w/r.[7] With the advent of unionisation, suppose that the union forces up the wage from w_0 to w_1, and thus the relative price ratio becomes steeper, as shown in figure 3.5. The intercept on the vertical axis remains unaltered. The total impact of the wage increase on the demand for labour and capital can be divided up into two constituent effects: the *substitution* effect, considering movements along the initial isoquant, and the *scale* or *output* effect, considering the impact on output produced of the higher price

---

[7] To find the slope of the isoquant, totally differentiate the firm's revenue function $q = q(n,k)$ with respect to k and n. Since output is held constant by definition along an isoquant, this yields

$$dq = 0 = p\frac{\partial q}{\partial n}.dn + p\frac{\partial q}{\partial k}.dk$$

Rearrangement produces

$$\frac{dk}{dn} = -\frac{\partial q}{\partial n}\bigg/\frac{\partial q}{\partial k}$$

which shows that the slope of the isoquant in (n,k) space is given by minus the ratio of the marginal products of labour and capital.

To find the slope in (n,k) space of the total factor cost curve, $TC = wn + rk$, rearrange the equation to obtain $k = \frac{TC}{r} - \frac{wn}{r}$. Differentiation with respect to n yields $dk/dn = -w/r$.

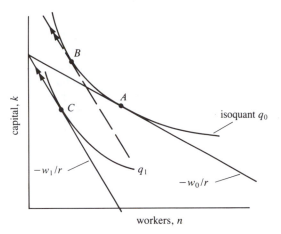

capital, k

B

A

C

isoquant q_0

$-w_1/r$

q_1

$-w_0/r$

workers, n

Figure 3.5. Substitution of capital for labour after unionisation.

of labour. First, consider the substitution effect. The higher wage induces the firm to substitute capital for labour as it moves along the initial isoquant q_0 from point A to point B. The number of workers employed will fall, and the number of machines will increase. Now consider the scale effect of the rise in wages. Because the isocost curve has shifted inwards, less output is produced following the wage increase – we are on the lower isoquant, denoted by q_1 in figure 3.5, at point C. The substitution effect of a wage increase on the demand for labour will always be negative, as shown; however, the scale effect may be either positive or negative. As illustrated in figure 3.5, the net impact of unionisation is a fall in the number of workers, while the number of machines has also declined. However, in principle, capital demand may increase or decrease as a result of a wage increase, depending on the relative strengths of the substitution and scale effects, and the production technology.

The analysis in this subsection of allocative inefficiency has assumed that a union has emerged in an economy characterised by competitive product and labour markets. But are nonunionised labour markets always perfectly competitive? Is it valid to assume that a nonunion economy has perfectly competitive product markets? There is considerable evidence that, in modern industrialised countries, many product markets are imperfectly competitive. Moreover, labour markets may be characterised by an incumbent workforce that has a degree of bargaining power. It is therefore interesting to consider what happens when a union emerges in *imperfectly competitive* labour and product markets. In such a situation, even prior to unionisation both workers and the firm will have bargaining power. Indeed, even in the absence of unionisation, the parties may be in a situation of bilateral monopoly, where employment and a range of possible wage rates may be determined as shown in appendix 3A. There is considerable evidence of such bargaining in nonunionised labour markets, and a significant literature modelling wage determination in situations where there are no trade unions, but where labour may have some bargaining power through, for example, specific training, mobility costs, or hiring and firing expenditures.[8] An important question then arises as to whether or not the replacement of individual bargaining by collective bargaining generates additional inefficiencies and misallocation of resources in situations where markets were previously not functioning in accordance with the textbook model of perfect competition. There is little analysis or discussion of this important question in the union literature.[9]

3.2.3 Unions and technical inefficiency

The existence of trade unions may be associated with technical inefficiency, since not only do unions affect wages, but they also often introduce restrictive practices, such as manning agreements or rules about work-pace (see Clegg, 1980). Manning agreements may be conceptualised as a fixed capital-to-labour ratio, while work-pace rules may be conceptualised as a fixed level of effort. With a fixed capital-to-labour ratio, no substitution is possible out of labour into capital when labour becomes relatively more expensive (the isoquants are L-shaped). With only the scale effect (reduced output), the demand for both labour and capital will fall when higher wages are introduced in the unionised sector.

There may also be a further loss of output associated with trade unions. Threats of strikes are essential to union power to achieve higher wages and restrictive practices. If this threat is ever used, there may be output losses if no intertemporal substitution of production is possible, or if such substitution is expensive, or if storage is expensive.

In the longer run (where capital is variable), with the advent of unionisation the firm may substitute its existing workforce by capital and higher quality labour. Where unions are able to push up wages for union jobs, there will be an excess supply of workers for the relatively better paid

---

[8] See the literature on specific training (Becker, 1962; Oi, 1962; Hashimoto, 1981); internal labour markets (Doeringer and Piore, 1971; Williamson, Wachter and Harris, 1975); efficiency wages (Akerlof and Yellen, 1986; Weiss, 1991); and insiders and outsiders (Lindbeck and Snower, 1988).

[9] Notable exceptions are Fellner (1947) and Pencavel (1991). Pencavel (1991: 103) notes some conditions under which union and management, bargaining over wages and employment, replicate the resource allocation of a profit-maximising monopolist facing a competitive labour price. (The model is an 'efficient bargaining' union model, which we will be examining in chapter 5.) Of course the division of the surplus differs, which is likely to affect capital in the long run.

union-covered jobs. If workers queueing for union-covered jobs are heterogeneous, union firms will be able to select the 'better quality' workers from the queue. This suggests that, in the longer run, union–nonunion wage differentials based on labour *efficiency* units will be small. The induced effect on capital demand may also be small.

The orthodox view about the impact of unions on capital demand and investment is challenged by the following argument that union presence may deter investment. Suppose that the firm is aware that, if it engages in any investment, it is driving a wedge between short-run average variable costs and average total costs. The standard perfectly competitive model shows that the firm will continue production provided that the exogenously given price is greater than or equal to its average variable costs. If product price is *greater* than average variable costs, there is a quasi-rent (the return on fixed capital) which might potentially be appropriated by the union. Note that this argument does not hinge critically on there being a trade union. The argument could also apply to investment by the firm in hiring and training (see Lindbeck and Snower, 1987).

Baldwin (1983), Grout (1984) and van der Ploeg (1987) provide formal models of the underinvestment result in a unionised setting. Grout shows that, in the absence of legally binding contracts, once the firm has invested in a particular level of capital, the union (or group of workers with bargaining power) will have an incentive to demand a higher wage in order to appropriate a share of quasi-rents. Firms, knowing this *ex ante*, have a reduced incentive to invest, and the demand for capital declines. This underinvestment problem would not arise if there were legally binding contracts such that workers could not demand a higher wage once the investment was in place. Baldwin (1983) outlines further mechanisms that would reduce the underinvestment problem.

Devereux and Lockwood (1991) produce a counter-example to the underinvestment result of Grout (1984). In a formal general equilibrium model with overlapping generations, they show that the redistribution of income from the owners of capital to workers implied by unionism increases the supply of capital at a given interest rate. This is because workers are savers (in the first period of their life-cycle), while the owners of capital are dissavers (being in the last period of their life-cycle). In such a framework, the net effect of unionism on the capital stock in a steady state is uncertain: it depends on whether or not the reduction in the demand for capital at a given interest rate (the 'Grout effect') is outweighed by the increased supply of capital.

An interesting extension to this debate is provided in a series of papers by Ulph and Ulph (1988, 1990b, 1994), in which they focus on a particular investment decision – innovation. They argue that the Grout style of model is inappropriate for research and development, or innovation. This is because of the fact that innovation investment can be viewed as a race between two or more competing firms, with only a single prize: the winner captures a larger market share after the introduction of the new technology. Under certain conditions, a stronger union can encourage a firm to bid more to win a patent race, thereby gaining market share and making both the union and the firm better off. However, this result depends crucially on the structure and timing of the bargaining between firm and union.

The preceding discussion emphasised the importance of surplus existence and union power to ensure union success in its goal of improving union workers' welfare. Such an improvement occurs at the expense of profits (as the firm's surplus or part thereof is now appropriated by the union), and of nonunion labour,[10] and could result in either under- or overinvestment in capital in the union sector. However, an alternative view of the presence of a trade union is that it may, under certain conditions, result in a larger surplus to be shared between the union and the firm. These alternative views of the union are referred to by Freeman and Medoff (1979), in a famous phrase, as the 'two faces' of unionism. The first face is the monopoly face, while the second is the collective or institutional response face. The first views the trade union as inefficient, while the second sees the trade union as an organisation that may increase economic efficiency.

The 'monopoly face' view of unions assumes that union presence results only in an increase in firms' costs (since the wage rate is above the competitive level) through the exercise of union monopoly power. But if union presence results in both wages increasing *and* efficiency (or productivity) increasing, then the net effect may be to leave firms' profits unaffected or even increased. In such circumstances, firms may gain from union recognition, even though it confers on the union some monopoly power. (And a necessary condition for union existence may no longer be the pre-existence of a surplus, but rather the creation of a surplus.) We now turn to a discussion of unions as a means of creating a surplus or promoting economic efficiency: the second face of unions.

3.3 Trade unions and improvements in economic efficiency

In a world of imperfect information and thus uncertainty, the union may be viewed as an organisation acting as the 'agent' of the workers, who are the 'principal'. There are many types of benefits provided by the union as agent,

---

[10] Note that nonunion labour may be unaffected if the advent of unionisation simply replaces individual bargaining by collective bargaining in the newly unionised sector. See the discussion at the end of subsection 3.2.2 on 'Trade unions, allocative costs and social welfare'.

and many of these benefits are relevant to the firm's performance (Faith and Reid, 1987). First, the union may provide information and contractual services to its membership. Secondly, it may monitor and evaluate the firm's contract performance ('governance' services). Thirdly, the union is able to communicate, to management, workers' preferences for wages, personnel practices and other collective benefits.

It is easier and cheaper for a single organisation, such as a labour union, to negotiate contracts and monitor and evaluate the firm's performance than it is for individuals. This is due to economies of scale in the production of these agency services. Rather than each individual hiring an economist, an accountant and a lawyer, the union can engage these specialists; the marginal cost of providing these services for an extra individual is close to zero.

But even if there were no economies of scale in the provision of agency services, there are compelling arguments against the individual worker providing these benefits himself. First, many aspects of labour contracts and workplace characteristics are collective in nature, for example, grievance and promotions procedures, safety, lighting and heating. The usual problems associated with preference revelation for public goods are therefore likely to arise (Freeman and Medoff, 1984: 9). Without the union, workers are unlikely individually to attempt to change conditions, since there are considerable individual costs to so doing, and all workers would reap the benefits (the free-rider problem). Secondly, individual workers are unlikely to reveal their true preferences to management through fear of management retaliation by, for example, dismissing complaining workers. Hence workers prefer what Hirschman (1970) calls 'voice', in other words, the use of the political mechanism of appointing a representative of workers to communicate their preferences. Unions provide just such a means of communication. They have the power, through the threat of total labour withdrawal, to prevent management retaliation. While the individual worker is not in a position to devise a credible punishment should the firm cheat – be it through reneging on a contract or through repression of individual expression of preferences – the union is able to do so through its threat of labour withdrawal. Thirdly, workers acting collectively are frequently protected by labour legislation.

Some of the agency benefits described above may also be desirable to management. If so, it follows that the union may be an efficient organisation from the viewpoint of both the worker and the firm, in that both parties are made better off *with* its existence than without. From the managerial perspective, information about workers' preferences may be gleaned from either labour turnover ('exit'), or from communication through the workers' agent, the trade union ('voice'). Since individual voice is unlikely to be heard (through individual fears of retaliation plus the free-rider problem), the management may prefer union voice to the alternative of losing dissatisfied workers at the margin. This argument holds most weight where the union executive is democratically elected, and *is* therefore representative of the membership. Here the *median* member's preferences are heard. Reliance on the 'exit' method of inferring workers' preferences is likely to reveal only the views of an unrepresentative group of workers – the younger more mobile and less specifically trained workers, who are more likely to quit at the *margin*. Furthermore, if there are substantial transaction costs associated with labour turnover – hiring, training and firing costs – exit behaviour may impose losses on the firm.

The firm's acceptance of unions as efficiency-augmenting organisations is likely to depend on the extent to which continuity is desirable in the employment relationship. In employment contracts in which continuity is desirable, but where there is uncertainty and where management necessarily has greater latitude over adjustment, both workers and management may prefer procedural safeguards for the resolution of disputes. Management may prefer to deal with the union as the workers' agent since it reduces the costs of negotiation and processing of grievances, with the union 'more aware of broad market considerations and more able to understand cost accounts than the average employee, especially if the agent has credibility with the employee' (Faith and Reid, 1987: 47).

Williamson (1985: 256) argues that union organisation is more likely in areas where workers are trained in firm-specific skills. Here both the worker and the firm share in the costs of specific human capital acquisition (Becker, 1962; Oi, 1962; Hashimoto, 1981) and both are interested in a long-term relationship to maximise the period over which the training investment can be amortised. The costs of monitoring and enforcing employment contracts are likely to be higher in such situations than in firms where employment continuity is unimportant. Thus specialised procedural arrangements are likely to be favoured where employment continuity is desired by both workers and management. Since unions facilitate the establishment of procedural arrangements, union organisation is likely to be favoured by firms when there is a high degree of specific human capital. Workers also have incentives to organise because, where skills are firm-specific, management is not easily or costlessly able to replace these workers.

For similar reasons, unions will also be more likely where there are high labour turnover costs, and *ex ante* uncertainty so that the firm has latitude over adjustment *ex post*. In such situations, there will be considerable scope for costly *ex post* disputes over the division of any economic rents (Lindbeck and Snower, 1987). Formalised procedural arrangements, such as those negotiated by a trade union and management, may therefore be efficiency-enhancing in the presence of high labour turnover costs. Conversely, where labour turnover costs are low and/or human capital specificity is low, there may be no efficiency gains from formalised procedural arrangements between employees and management.

These arguments for management recognition of unions are somewhat tenuous, however, because such productivity-enhancing procedures may be obtainable *without* the union. There is indeed a considerable theoretical literature on contractual or procedural arrangements between employees and management in which there is no trade union involvement, but where management finds it optimal to impose certain procedures on its workforce. The context for such models is generally a world of uncertainty, in which employment continuity is desired because of transaction costs or specific human capital. Here the firm may find it optimal to create incentive procedures since state-contingent contracts (where an outcome is specified for every state of the world) are unenforceable.[11] Moreover, in the presence of labour turnover costs which give the existing workforce some monopoly power, incumbent workers and the firm may agree, even in the absence of unions, on procedural arrangements which reduce the possibility of costly *ex post* disputes over the division of any economic rents.

Of course, the existence of a union may make it easier for the firm to negotiate and administer these practices, as noted earlier in this section. Survey evidence for the United Kingdom provides some support for this view. Brown (1981) found that management, as long as it has to deal with a trade union, strongly supports the closed shop. Some three-quarters of the closed shops in the survey had formal and open management support, with two reasons being given for this support. First, the closed shop ensures that all workers are recognised by unions, and are covered by negotiated procedures. Secondly, the closed shop stabilises the relationship between firm and workers, and facilitates collective bargaining. The disadvantages were viewed as being increased union strength, restricted recruiting of new workers, and inflexibility in dealing with individuals.

A rare formal model of the trade union as efficiency-enhancing is provided by Malcomson (1983), who shows the conditions under which the union can ensure more efficient risk-sharing between firm and workers, where both are assumed risk-averse. Malcomson emphasises the importance of the timing of decisions about production in an uncertain environment, when the 'state of the world' (demand conditions) may not be

[11] See, for example, the deferred compensation scheme of Lazear (1979), who explains mandatory retirement and severance payment schemes; Booth and Chatterji (1989), who explain redundancy payment schemes as a means of ensuring a supply of workers willing to share the costs of specific training when future product demand is uncertain; and Carmichael (1983) explaining seniority schemes.

revealed until after production decisions have been made. (An example might be where decisions about specific training are made in the first period, with both workers and firm sharing the costs, but where product demand is so bad in the second period that workers are sacked and production never occurs.) *Legally enforceable* state-contingent contracts are rarely observed. This may be due to both bounded rationality and problems in actual observation of the correct state.[12] Instead, in an uncertain world, the firm is often given considerable latitude about its *ex post* adjustment. If production decisions are not made before demand conditions are known, there is not a problem. But if they are made *ex ante*, the firm may *ex post* have an incentive to renege on legally non-enforceable *ex ante* agreements, and workers may not be paid. If the firm is concerned with its reputation in the labour market as a reliable employer, it is unlikely to cheat *ex post* since the short-term gains are less than any benefits from being able to use state-contingent arrangements in the future. Alternatively, workers may use a union to enforce any state-contingent contract that is preferred by the firm to a protracted strike. The union must clearly have the monopoly power over labour supply to do this. It is also in a position to investigate more thoroughly than individuals the firm's case. In other words, it can provide agency benefits of monitoring and evaluating the firm's performance. In so doing, the union ensures improved risk-sharing between firm and employees.

This example illustrates the interdependence of the monopoly and efficiency roles of the trade union. The union makes credible the firm's *ex ante* promise not to cheat on contracts in which the firm has considerable flexibility after the state of nature is revealed. Such a promise may be believed by workers, since they know the union has a credible punishment strategy should the firm try to cheat. The punishment strategy relies crucially on the union having some bargaining power – its monopoly face. Individual workers (in the absence of labour turnover costs) have no bargaining power *ex post*. Szymanski (1988) provides a formal model in a similar genre, in which the trade union is viewed as a means of enforcing contracts between workers and management.

Ultimately it is an empirical question as to whether or not the net effect of the trade union is efficiency-enhancing, and there is currently a lively debate on this issue in the empirical literature, as we shall see in chapter 7.

We began this section by noting that the union's ability to extract a surplus depends crucially on its monopoly power. We noted that the union may find the gaining of such power very much simpler where management

---

[12] Bounded rationality refers to the inability of the human mind to perceive and evaluate every possible future contingency. A state-contingent contract is one where the contract specifies, say, wage and employment levels for every conceivable contingency.

finds it advantageous to recognise unions. We now return to consideration of how the union may obtain its power in the *absence* of management approval.

3.4 How does a union obtain monopoly power?

In most formal models of the union, as we shall see in chapters 4, 5 and 8, it is assumed that the whole sector is unionised and that the firm is therefore forced to negotiate with the union. Should it not do so, it cannot hire any labour. Yet this assumption begs the question: how did the union arrive at this position of power? Under what conditions might the firm agree to union recognition prior to the existence of any closed shop institutions? If the union is able to control the supply of only a small proportion of the pool of available workers, then the firm can choose not to bargain over the surplus. It can simply hire nonunion labour. How then do unions achieve monopoly power over the supply of labour?

It is useful in discussing union monopoly power to recall the historical background to trade union emergence. The first trade unions were craft unions. Craft skills were regarded by the possessors as their property, and workers clubbed together to try to protect the value of their human capital by implementing entry restrictions. Craft unionism became established because of a combination of high demand for skilled labour during industrial growth and the control of trained labour by skilled workers. Such control was possible because craftsmen were in charge of training the next cohort of skilled labour and were able to constrain numbers through the apprenticeship system. Craft unions were therefore able to manipulate the supply of skilled labour to maintain their welfare.

The emergence of general or industrial unions followed a different process. In the course of industrialisation, there was a huge surplus of unskilled displaced agricultural labour and thus manipulation of labour supply was impossible. Trade unions in such an environment were vulnerable to economic fluctuations: a depression coupled with a ready pool of available substitute workers could decimate a trade union. In such conditions it was important for the trade union to gain political support and/or high levels of membership. To have high membership levels, a union needs to persuade workers to join the union. This may be difficult in its early stages at a time when there are no immediately obvious wage benefits; these are to come when the union has attained a position of monopoly power. Thus the Webbs wrote in 1897 that 'the prospect of securing support in sickness and unemployment is a greater inducement [for young men] to join the union ... than the less obvious advantages to be gained by the trade combination' (B. and S. Webb, 1897: 158).

In summary, union power derives from the ability of the union to inflict damage on the firm through labour withdrawal. The union therefore needs to control labour supply either by entry restrictions or, for a fixed labour supply, by having high levels of membership relative to the size of the sector. However, under certain conditions, a union or group of workers may be able to inflict damage on a firm through labour withdrawal even if it does not directly control the supply of labour. For example, if it is costly for the firm to hire an alternative workforce because there are high labour turnover costs, then the union can credibly threaten to inflict damage on the firm through labour withdrawal, and thereby gain bargaining power.

As noted by Mulvey (1978), it is more useful to replace the historical distinction between pure craft and industrial unions by Turner's (1962) distinction between 'open' and 'closed' unions. Closed unions are not necessarily craft unions in the traditional sense, but are characterised by entry restrictions. They have a small and stable membership, and no ambition to increase membership (since this dilutes labour supply and reduces wages). Examples are professional associations such as the British Medical Association, and a trade union such as the National Graphical Association. An open union, in contrast, derives its power from extensive organisation; most industrial, some craft, and all general unions are open. Such open unions have a strong impetus for union growth, to limit the potential for either labour or product market substitution against members.

This discussion emphasises the fact that union membership density may play a part in determining the power of the union to extract a share of any surplus from the firm. Consider a firm in a particular sector of the economy where labour possesses general skills, and where, therefore, its supply is fixed in the short run. Clearly in such a situation the level of membership affects the outside options available to the firm: as membership density increases, there is a contraction of the pool of skilled workers available to the firm should it choose not to employ unionised labour. Thus one would expect to find a minimum critical level of membership for any sector, below which firms would refuse to recognise and bargain with the trade union (see Osborne (1984) and Booth and Ulph (1990) for formal models).

It is important to note that, in such a context where the level of membership density is crucial to the union's monopoly power, the union must consider carefully how it can attract workers at the margin. Thus the next issue to consider is this: why do individual workers join the trade union? The answer to this question also provides an explanation of how unions can achieve a position of monopoly power. It also provides a partial answer as to why in some circumstances firms may agree to union recognition.

The basic problem for economists in explaining why workers join a trade union relates to free-riders. This arises because of the collective nature of many of the goods provided by the union. We briefly consider two situations. The first situation is where the union is not yet in existence, while the second is where the union is a viable organisation recognised by firms for collective bargaining over wages and working conditions.

Suppose that there are unorganised workers who could benefit from organisation to extract better working conditions and wages from employers. It seems reasonable to suppose that, if a few of these workers were to organise themselves into a union, it would not be possible to extract any immediate benefits from employers, because of the lack of bargaining strength of the newly emerged and presumably weak trade union. Benefits must be perceived by organisers as being anticipated future benefits – perhaps anticipated at quite some time in the future, when the union is in a stronger position with more members and with a consequent greater bargaining strength. In such a situation, the argument of Stigler (1974) for the emergence of small groups does not hold. This argument states that individuals may combine if the expected benefits to them individually from combination (regardless of the collective nature of such benefits) exceed their setting-up costs. In the case of union formation, the present discounted value of expected benefits to any individual would be very small, and would be far outweighed by the costs of union organisation. So far, the economics of the trade union has little to say about the formation and growth of unions.

The second situation is where the union is already in existence and negotiating with the firm. Here the level of wages and working conditions, in the absence of closed-shop agreements, represent a form of public good, since they are available to all workers covered by the collective agreement regardless of their union status. The literature on public-good provision by groups has traditionally emphasised the free-rider problem. If the group provides, or lobbies for the provision of, a good that is collective to potential members, then individuals can free-ride and enjoy the benefits of group action without incurring the costs. The free-rider problem is generally not considered insurmountable in small groups, as the benefits will not be achieved at all without co-operation, and it is easy with small numbers to subject potential beneficiaries to surveillance and control to ensure that they do not cheat. The larger the number of potential beneficiaries, the more difficult it is to overcome the free-rider problem, because of exclusion and surveillance difficulties, and the less likely is the collective good to be provided.[13]

---

[13] As noted in chapter 1, the extent of free-riding on trade union membership is greater in Britain than the USA.

Olson (1965) provides an explanation of why *large* groups manage to exist despite the free-rider problem. He argues that if a large group exists, it must have formed either because membership is compulsory, or because the group provides private goods and services accessible only to its members, with ancillary provision of the collective good as a 'by-product'.[14]

There is considerable evidence that friendly society benefits have been important historically in attracting workers to trade unions (see, for example, Boyer (1988)). Furthermore, this view of the importance of private benefit provision in maintaining membership levels is consistent with the agency theory of unionism explained in the previous section. According to the agency view, the trade union provides both collective and private agency benefits, with examples of the former being contractual services and of the latter being grievance procedures. Thus when considering why workers unionise in the absence of coercion, it is the private agency benefits that may provide the motivation, since the worker can free-ride on the collective benefits. These distinctions are important for economic models in which membership is endogenous.[15]

The preceding discussion has argued that control of labour supply or high membership density are important for union power. But these are not the only explanations. Clearly union power is also influenced by other factors, such as the elasticity of labour demand, managerial resistance, and the structure of collective bargaining. Suppose that labour demand is very elastic owing to a high elasticity of substitution of capital for labour (see Marshall, 1948), and that all workers in a particular sector are unionised. If the union threatens withdrawal of the entire workforce to induce the firm to share its surplus, the firm can simply substitute capital for labour. Thus what is important to union monopoly power is not just the degree of substitutability of nonunion labour, but also the degree of substitutability of any other factor of production.

The exercise of union power will also be affected by whether or not unionised labour is complementary in production with nonunion labour. Suppose there is a craft union operating in a largely nonunion industry, and that this union represents an important group of workers such as maintenance engineers who are complements in production with all other workers. As these workers represent only a small fraction of the sector, the union does not control the labour force of the sector. But it can nevertheless paralyse the industry if its membership goes on strike.

Trade union power and the degree of management resistance may, in

---

[14] See Cornes and Sandler (1984) for a general analysis of marketed goods that jointly provide public and private characteristics.

[15] For models of union membership considering these issues, see Booth (1985), Naylor (1989, 1990), Booth and Chatterji (1993a, 1993b) and Naylor and Raaum (1993).

some conditions, be simultaneously determined. Historically, US employers were quick to quash emerging unions, whereas British employers accepted unions and sometimes even welcomed their presence, as was noted in chapter 2. This difference between the attitudes of US and British employers to developing unionism was due to the fact that US employers faced greater competitive pressures and lacked Britain's technological lead; they therefore had a greater incentive to try to prevent unionisation. More recently, US nonunion employers have mimicked the personnel and compensation practices of unionised firms, in order to pre-empt union organisation of the workplace. Well-compensated nonunion workers are less likely to vote for union representation in NLRB elections, since there are not necessarily apparent gains from unionisation. This type of managerial resistance to unionisation is a reflection of union power in similar workplaces. So far, there has been relatively little theoretical work modelling employer resistance.[16]

The bargaining structure is also likely to be important for union power. (Here we use the industrial relations definition of the bargaining structure as the scope of a particular bargaining unit.) Unionised industrial economies exhibit a variety of bargaining structures, ranging from decentralised structures for pay bargaining (as in the USA, Canada, Japan and Switzerland) to centralised bargaining between employers' and unions' federations (as in Australia, Austria, Denmark, Finland, Norway and Sweden) (see Calmfors and Driffill, 1988). Britain lies somewhere in between, with a mixture of industry-wide bargaining, organisation-level bargaining and establishment-level bargaining, between single and multiple unions (see Millward *et al.*, 1992). As Ulph and Ulph (1990a: 119) point out, '[w]e need to ask not only how these different bargaining structures affect the resulting wage or employment levels but more importantly why particular institutional structures have emerged'. While historical accident no doubt plays some part, there is also likely to be an economic rationale for the choice of bargaining structure, which may affect the power of the relevant parties to increase any surplus or share thereof. The industrial relations literature outlines some conditions under which unions and firms might choose particular levels (see, for example, Deaton and Beaumont (1980), Purcell and Sisson (1983), Sisson and Brown (1983) and Booth (1989)).[17] Fine

---

[16] Examples of US management's anti-union activities are given by Dickens (1983), Weiler (1983), Freeman and Medoff (1984), Kochan *et al.* (1986), Farber (1987a), Flanagan (1989) and Rogers (1989). For theoretical models of employer resistance, see Abowd and Farber (1990), Naylor and Raaum (1993), and Disney, Gosling and Machin (1993).

[17] For example, multi-employer bargaining, where unions negotiate with firms through the medium of employers' associations, can lead to standardisation of conditions and pay, which may be desired by firms wishing to ensure that all firms have the same competitive advantage. It may also encourage both parties to consider macroeconomic factors in their

(1990) points out that management may be able to choose its bargaining structure so as to minimise costs. Thus in the British coal industry, management has specifically chosen its bargaining structure to avoid the implementation of equal pay. But so far the economics literature has little to say. With a handful of exceptions, for example Horn and Wolinsky (1988) and Dowrick (1992), theoretical models of union behaviour assume only one union and one firm, and thereby side-step the choice of bargaining structure, which may affect union power.

3.5 Conclusion

The standard view of trade unions is that they are organisations whose purpose is to improve the material welfare of members, principally by improving working conditions and raising wages above the competitive wage level. There is little dispute that, if unions emerge in competitive markets, higher union wages will introduce allocative inefficiencies into the economy. The ability of unions to achieve wage gains is called the 'monopoly' role of trade unions. The first part of this chapter provided an overview of the trade union within the framework of competitive labour and product markets. It also examined the conditions under which a union can achieve a wage rate greater than the competitive level. In particular, there must be some surplus that can be shared, and the union or group of workers must have some bargaining power to induce the firm to share the surplus. Of course, in a competitive framework, the trade union introduces into the economy a variety of distortions and inefficiencies, and we therefore briefly examined issues of allocative inefficiency associated with the trade union in a competitive economy.

However, even within a competitive framework there are arguments suggesting that, in the presence of imperfect information and uncertainty, trade unions may be efficiency-enhancing. Unions may in some circumstances increase the available surplus to be shared between the firm and workers, to the extent that unions may provide services reducing labour turnover and negotiating costs, and may thereby be instrumental in shifting out the production possibility frontier. The second part of this chapter

bargaining behaviour. There may also be economies of scale for firms in dealing collectively with unions. However, to the extent that industry-wide bargaining is dominated by the interests of the weaker firms, a firm may consider it can further its own interests by dealing with the union directly, either at the organisation or establishment level. A firm may prefer organisation bargaining to establishment bargaining because the former allows for conditions and pay to be standardised across plants, and because it separates union negotiations from the workplace and restricts the role of the shop stewards. However, payment mechanisms can be most easily related to performance and productivity as bargaining becomes more decentralised. See Booth (1989: 226–8).

outlined the theory examining the conditions under which unions may increase efficiency. Emphasis was also placed on the interdependence of the monopoly and 'efficiency' roles of trade unions. Unions may not be able to increase efficiency without the union having some bargaining or monopoly power.

It is important to remember that the analysis in this chapter of allocative inefficiency has assumed that a union has emerged in an economy characterised by competitive product and labour markets. There is considerable evidence that, in modern industrialised countries, many product markets are imperfectly competitive. Moreover, labour markets may be characterised by an incumbent workforce that has a degree of bargaining power through, for example, specific training, mobility costs, or hiring and firing expenditures. An important question then arises as to whether or not the replacement of individual bargaining by collective bargaining, through unionisation of imperfectly competitive markets, generates additional inefficiencies and misallocation of resources. There is little analysis of this important question in the union literature.

Throughout this chapter, we treated trade union objectives and union–firm wage determination as exogenously given. The analysis of union objectives and wage and employment determination will be expanded more rigorously in the following two chapters, where the empirical testing of the theory will also be discussed. After the theoretical framework has been established, we will examine, in chapters 6 and 7, empirical measurement of the impact of unions on a number of economic variables.

Appendix 3A

3A.1 Derivation of labour demand curve in a monopolistic industry

In this section, we develop the labour demand curve for a monopolistic industry, and compare it with the corresponding curve for a perfectly competitive firm. The monopolist's labour demand curve is more steeply sloping than that of the perfectly competitive firm, because the monopolist faces a downward-sloping product demand curve, and knows that additional output reduces the price and thus the revenue earned on previous units of output. To see this formally, suppose that the firm faces a demand curve for its product, given by $p = p(q)$, where p is product price and q is output. If $dp/dq = 0$, the demand curve is horizontal, and the firm sells in a competitive product market. If $dp/dq < 0$, the demand curve is negative, and the firm is a monopolist. A firm's revenue can be written generally as

$$R(q) = p(q).q \tag{A1}$$

where the firm's short-run production function is given by $q = q(n)$, assuming a fixed level of capital in the short run. The firm chooses n to maximise profits, given by

$$\max_{n} \Pi = p[q(n)].q(n) - wn \tag{A2}$$

The first-order condition is

$$\frac{d\Pi}{dn} = \frac{dp.dq}{dq\,dn}.q + p(.).\frac{dq}{dn} - w = 0 \tag{A3}$$

where dp/dq is marginal revenue and dq/dn is the marginal product of labour. Equation (A3) can be simplified by multiplying the first term on the left-hand side by p/p, which leaves its value unchanged but allows us to consider the term as containing an elasticity. Thus (A3) can be written as:

$$p\left(\frac{dp.q.dq}{dq\,p\,dn} + \frac{dq}{dn}\right) = w \tag{A4}$$

Noting that $\eta = -(dq/q)/(dp/p)$ (the elasticity of product demand) and $dq/dn = \text{MPL}$, we can rewrite (A4) as

$$p(1 - 1/\eta) = w/\text{MPL} \tag{A5}$$

The real wage is then given from this price-setting equation as

$$w/p = (1 - 1/\eta)\text{MPL} \tag{A6}$$

As $\eta \to \infty$, the real wage given by (A6) approaches the perfectly competitive real wage. The nominal wage is given by $w = (1 - 1/\eta)p.\text{MPL}$, where $p.\text{MPL}$ represents the value of the marginal product of labour, given by VMPL in figure 3A.1. The monopolist's labour demand curve $w = (1 - 1/\eta)p.\text{MPL}$ is termed the marginal revenue product of labour, denoted by MRPL in figure 3A.1.

Note also that, using the fact that marginal cost (MC) is given by w/MPL, we can rewrite (A5) as

$$(p - \text{MC})/p = 1/\eta \tag{A7}$$

which shows that the markup of price over marginal cost is inversely related to the elasticity of product demand η. To see this, rewrite (A6) as $\text{MC} = p[(\eta - 1)/\eta]$. Rearrangement yields (A7).

Equation (A6) provides a comparison of the real wage implied by price-setting behaviour in the perfectly competitive and monopolistic models, which is illustrated in figure 3A.1. Notice that the slopes of both curves are negative, and that for η that is constant across levels of output and employment, the monopolist's curve deviates from that of the perfectly competitive firm by a constant fraction. (See chapter 8 for discussion of the possibility that η may vary with output.)

3A.2 Employment and wages in a monopsonistic firm

Suppose that there is a firm that is a single buyer in the market for its input, and hence it faces an upward-sloping labour supply curve. Because of this, for each additional worker it employs at the margin, a higher wage must be paid to all the intramarginal workers already in employment (since all workers must be paid the same wage, in the absence of price discrimination). Hence the marginal cost to the

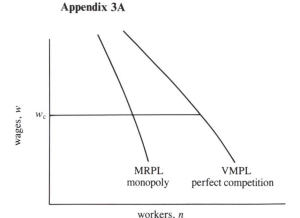

Figure 3A.1. Comparison of labour demand curves of perfectly competitive and monopolistic forms.

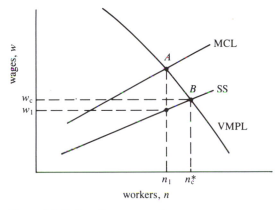

Figure 3A.2. Employment under monopsony.

monopsonistic firm of hiring an extra worker is not simply that worker's wage but the increase in the wage bill for all the workers already in employment. Thus the marginal cost of labour (MCL) is greater than the supply schedule (SS), as illustrated in figure 3A.2. The firm will be maximising profits where the marginal revenue from hiring an extra worker equals marginal cost, given by point A in the figure. While employment at this point is less than employment under perfect competition (at point B), hiring an extra worker beyond point A adds more to total labour cost than it contributes to total revenue. The wage rate paid to workers by the monopsonist is given by w_1, which is less than their marginal product. The competitive wage rate is given by w_c. Both wage and employment in the monopsonistic firm are below that of perfect competition. Clearly, if the advent of unionisation results in the union setting a wage rate w, where $w_1 < w \leq w_c$, then employment will increase under unionisation.

3A.3 Bilateral monopoly and the indeterminate nature of wages

In this section, we consider the bilateral monopoly model, in which a single seller of a good or input faces a single buyer. This situation may appear where there is imperfect competition in both the goods and the labour markets, such that both workers and management have some degree of monopoly power. This situation is illustrated in figure 3A.3, for the case of a single seller of labour (a monopolistic supplier) facing a single purchaser (a monopsonist buyer).

First, consider the single seller or monopolist, who supplies labour services to the market along a marginal cost curve given by SS in figure 3A.3. Under competitive conditions, SS represents the supply curve. Because the supplier is a monopolist, she determines n^S by equating marginal cost to the marginal revenue arising from the sale of her labour services, given by the intersection of the SS and MM curves in the figure (where MM is the monopolist's marginal revenue curve). The monopolist then reads off the wage rate, w^S, from the MRPL curve.

Now consider the single buyer or monopsonist, who equates the MRPL to the marginal cost of acquiring labour, given by the curve MCL in figure 3A.3, in order to determine n^B. The wage associated with n^B units of labour is given by w^B, as shown.

What is the outcome when the buyer and seller meet? It can be shown that the employment outcome is equivalent to that which would be reached were each party able to price discriminate, that is, the number of units of labour maximising the sum of the profits to be shared out between the two parties. This is given by n^* in figure 3A.3, and is shown more rigorously below (see Gravelle and Rees, 1983: 392).

Suppose that profits of the buyer of labour services can be represented by

$$\pi^B = R[q(n)] - wn \tag{A7}$$

where $R[q(n)]$ is revenue, given by $p[q(n)].q(n)$. The seller's profits are given by

$$\pi^S = wn - C(n) \tag{A8}$$

where $C(n)$ represents the seller's costs of supplying the amount n of labour services. The two parties choose n to maximise combined profits given by

$$\max_n \pi^B + \pi^S = R[q(n)] - C(n) \tag{A9}$$

and thus

$$\frac{d(\pi^B + \pi^S)}{dn} = \frac{dR}{dq}\cdot\frac{dq}{dn} - \frac{dC}{dn} = 0 \tag{A10}$$

Thus with employment chosen optimally to maximise the sum of profits, MRPL = MCL, as shown in figure 3A.3. We now examine what wage might be chosen by both parties. From (A9), the wage does not affect the sum of profits. However, it does affect the share of the surplus that each party will receive. The model yields only a range of wage rates, as shown. Differentiate (A7) and (A8) with respect to w, to obtain $\frac{\partial \pi^B}{\partial w} = -n$ and $\frac{\partial \pi^S}{\partial w} = n$. Thus the profits of the buyer are decreasing in w, while

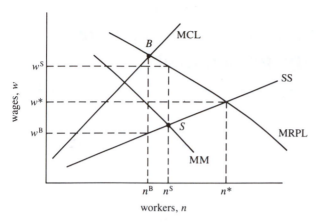

Figure 3A.3. Bilateral monopoly.

the profits of the seller are increasing in w. Therefore the former wants to set a low wage, while the latter prefers a high wage. We can determine the upper and lower limits of a range of wage rates by using the fact that each party will only agree to a bargain if it is at least as well off as a result than if no deal was reached. This condition can be written as

$$\pi^B = R[q(n)] - wn = pq - wn \geq 0 \tag{A11}$$

and

$$\pi^S = wn - C(n) \geq 0 \tag{A12}$$

From (A11) it can be seen that $w \leq pq/n$ and from (A12) it can be seen that $w \geq C(n)/n$. Thus we can combine these findings to give

$$pq/n \geq w \geq C(n)/n \tag{A13}$$

Notice that the LHS of the inequality of (A13) is the product of price and average product, and the RHS is average cost. These curves are not shown on figure 3A.3 for clarity; see Gravelle and Rees (1983: 393). The average cost curve $C(n)/n$ lies below the SS curve, while the curve pq/n for the monopolist seller lies above the MRPL curve in (w,n) space.

4   Trade union objectives and the monopoly union model

4.1 Introduction

'What is industrial relations? ... The answer ... is that it is the study of the rules governing employment, together with the ways in which the rules are made and changed, interpreted and administered ... The rules governing employment, and the ways in which they are made and interpreted, cannot be understood apart from the organizations that take part in the process. Industrial relations therefore includes the study of trade unions, management, employers' associations and the public bodies concerned with the regulation of employment. Each of these organizations has its own sources of authority, and wherever there are separate sources of authority there is the risk of conflict ...

The rules themselves are of two main types. There are the rules that settle such issues as pay, the length of the working day, over-time, holidays, and the way in which a job should be done and the time it should take. These are called *substantive* rules. Then there are the rules that settle the ways in which the substantive rules are made, and the ways in which they can be challenged, changed, interpreted and applied. These are *procedural* rules.' (Clegg, 1980: 1–2)

This quotation highlights several of the problems facing economists in constructing an analytical model of a unionised labour market, wherein it is necessary to abstract from the diversity of institutions, procedures and outcomes that characterise industrial relations in a unionised economy. The first problem is that there are many sets of actors, each with its own power base and organisational structure, and with possibly competing aims. As each set of agents pursues its own objectives, there is scope for conflict. The economist needs to model the objectives of the relevant actors, as well as the means by which these potentially conflicting objectives are resolved. Secondly, the various agents are concerned with both procedures *and* end results. Unions and firms have been concerned historically not simply with outcomes such as wage and employment levels, hours and manning arrangements, but also with procedures such as the level at which bargaining occurs, the extent of consultation and the role of custom and practice. Can the economist model both outcomes and processes? If only outcomes are examined, how sensitive are the results to alterations in procedural arrangements?

The economic model-maker faces a trade-off between tractability and realism. The accepted methodology of economics is that, following observation of an empirical regularity or 'stylised fact', the economist formulates a theory attempting to explain the empirical regularity. For tractability, the theory necessarily abstracts from reality; in so doing, simplifying assumptions must be made. From the theory can be logically derived predictions for the economy or particular economic variables. These predictions can then be tested against available data. The theory is inspired by empirical observation, and its predictions also tested empirically. Since such testing is carried out with data-sets comprising limited numbers of observations (rather than against the whole population), the theory can only be accepted or rejected probabilistically.[1]

What appropriate simplifying assumptions might be made for a tractable model of the unionised labour market? To begin with, it is necessary to consider the purpose of the model. Suppose the focus of economic interest is an examination of the determinants of wages and employment, or perhaps productivity or membership. While procedural arrangements may well impinge on these economic variables, and may also provide an additional rationale for union existence and viability, it seems reasonable to restrict our attention to *outcomes*, since these are vital to understanding the workings of the economy. (The processes can be treated as constraints within which the various agents operate.)[2] In this sense, the economists' approach is more delimited than that of the industrial relations literature, which is able to focus on individual trade unions' processes and outcomes. But at the same time the economists' analytical approach is also broader, since in trying to understand the way the economy works, it is searching for generalisations rather than analysing particular cases.

In the construction of a model of the unionised labour market, it is necessary to consider the objectives of the two principal actors – the trade union and management. The latter may be working through an employers' association or independently. It seems reasonable to suppose that the government's behaviour is exogenous. (It would be possible to model this explicitly, as in recent macroeconomic models of the political business cycle, but, this would be at the cost of considerably complicating the

---

[1] See Blaug (1990) for an interesting discussion of economics as a method of scientific inquiry.
[2] These processes and procedures differ across countries. In the USA, the rules of the bargaining process and some internal procedures of unions are established by legislation. US collective agreements are typically comprehensively specified, both in terms of procedures and outcomes. By contrast, in Britain the rules of the bargaining process are left to the unions; only recently has legislation regulated internal union procedures (see chapter 2).

analysis.)[3] Since the objectives of the trade union and management may be conflicting, it is also necessary to consider how conflicts might be resolved, within the constraints provided by the political, legal and product market environment. Discussion in chapter 2 indicated how important these constraints might be in determining the scope of union operation; it also emphasised how these constraints differed between the USA and Britain, and within each of these countries, through time.

It is also useful to consider the distinction between the *scope* and the *outcome* of collective bargaining. The scope covers the range of permissible issues that are within the purlieu of both the union and the firm. The outcome refers to the results of reconciliation of the perhaps conflicting preferences over these issues of the various agents interacting in a unionised labour market. What are the issues that are covered by collective bargaining? As noted in chapter 2, the range of issues covered by collective bargaining is narrower in Britain than in the USA. The fact that US collective agreements cover a broader set of issues than in Britain almost certainly reflects the relative lack of US social welfare legislation. In Britain, legislation regulates many of the issues, such as health insurance, pensions, redundancy pay and unfair dismissal, which are frequently dealt with by union–firm agreements in the USA.

In Britain, the issues over which there is negotiation between unions and management include pay, physical working conditions, redeployment, manning levels, redundancy procedure and redundancy payments, major changes in production methods, recruitment, holiday entitlement and length of the working week. Table 4.1 shows the percentage of British establishments with a recognised trade union or staff association that bargain over some of these issues, broken down by manual and non-manual status.[4] While the figures for manual workers suggest a slight decline in the percentage of plants reporting negotiation over non-pay issues over the period 1984–90, the non-manual figures suggest a small increase.

Oswald and Turnbull (1985) have compared British and US collective agreements; they note that the British agreements are more heterogeneous than in the USA (where there is frequently a common format apart from in the craft industries), and are typically far shorter. Procedures are also far less circumscribed in the British agreements, which are not legally enforceable, in contrast to the American situation.

In the USA, the issues covered by joint negotiation between unions and management include health and life insurance, pensions, severance pay, unfair dismissal, pay, hours, holidays, management rights and seniority

---

[3] For a survey of political business cycle models, see Alesina (1989).
[4] See Millward *et al.* (1992) for further breakdowns by sector and industry.

Table 4.1. *The extent of negotiation by management and the largest union over non-pay issues, 1984 and 1990*

Issue	All manual plants		All non-manual plants	
	1984	1990	1984	1990
Negotiated at some level				
Physical working conditions	78	76	76	78
Redeployment	62	57	61	62
Staffing levels	55	50	55	56
Size of redundancy pay	46	42	49	51
Recruitment	38	32	39	40
Reorganisation of working hours	—	78	—	46
Negotiated at establishment level				
Physical working conditions	39	42	30	34
Redeployment	33	32	26	30
Staffing levels	25	23	17	20
Size of redundancy pay	10	12	5	6
Recruitment	16	13	12	13
Reorganisation of working hours	—	40	—	31
Numbers of plants	1405	1134	1397	1072

Base: all establishments with one or more bargaining units.

Source: Millward *et al.* (1992: tables 7.16 and 7.17), based on the 1984 and 1990 Workplace Industrial Relations Surveys' Management Responses.

(see, for example, the Bureau of National Affairs (1983) and Wheeler (1987)).

Note that the level of *employment* is rarely determined by union–firm bargaining in either Britain or the USA (see Oswald, 1993). Many US collective agreements explicitly stipulate that management retains the right to determine the level of employment. While such a stipulation is not found in British contracts, trade unions typically do not bargain over this issue.[5] However, the evidence from the British Workplace Industrial Relations Surveys given in table 4.1 suggests that unions may affect employment *indirectly*, to the extent that they negotiate with management over redeployment, staffing levels, redundancy pay (which affects firms' layoff procedures) and recruitment. We will return to this issue in the following chapter, where we examine *bargaining* models of wage determination.

While there is considerable information on the outcomes of the collective bargaining process – such as wage increases – and the issues that are

[5] However, Oswald (1987) found that the printers and the miners in Britain do bargain over employment.

covered, it is difficult to make any inferences about union preferences from this information. This is because all that has been observed is the result of the *interaction* of union *and* management preferences through the collective bargaining process. It must be borne in mind when examining these outcomes that they may reflect managerial preferences and union weakness, or union preferences and management weakness, or some combination of the preferences of each party after reconciliation within the bargaining process. It is problematic to infer union objectives from these results, since the means of reconciliation of the conflicting objectives of the union and the firm is not known for certain and can only be hypothesised, as will be further discussed in chapter 5.

In this chapter, we consider ways of modelling the differing objectives of the trade union and the firm in sections 4.2 and 4.3 respectively. We then consider, in section 4.4, the simplest method of reconciling the objectives of the trade union and management: the monopoly union model. This method does not rely on any bargaining between the two parties. Instead, it supposes that the union is able to act as a monopolist in the supply of labour, and to impose a wage rate on the firm; the firm, however, retains its managerial prerogative to determine the number of workers employed at the union wage. Section 4.5 examines empirical work on trade union objectives within this simple framework. Section 4.6 outlines a simple extension to the monopoly union model – the median voter model, in which union membership is made endogenous, and where it is assumed that the union comprises an elected executive and a set of rank-and-file members. In the following chapter, we will consider more sophisticated methods of reconciling the differing preferences of union and management, using a bargaining approach. We will also show how the monopoly union model is nested, as a special case, within a simple bargaining model.

Formal analysis in this and the following chapter will be confined to what we term the 'orthodox approach' to modelling trade union behaviour, by which we mean the generally accepted class of models of wage and employment determination in a unionised sector of the economy. This class of models is widely used in theoretical work (see references in Oswald (1985), Pencavel (1985), Farber (1986), Ulph and Ulph (1990a) and Pencavel (1991)), and also in empirical work aiming to estimate wage and employment equations based on a theoretical foundation (see, for example, Layard *et al.*, (1991)). We will be highlighting the simplifying assumptions underlying these models, the relaxation of which may provide scope for future research.[6]

---

[6] In most of the theoretical models examined in this book, we ignore for simplicity the issue of hours determination, and instead focus on wages and employment. However, in chapter 5 we present a brief outline of a bargaining model of hours determination. See also Pencavel (1991).

4.2 The union objective function

'The implications of any model [of a unionised labour market] ... will rest heavily ... on what is assumed about the union's objectives. Unfortunately, our knowledge of these objectives is meagre. It rests on two types of information: first, on discursive accounts from the industrial relations literature where formal models are eschewed and, therefore, where analytical results are difficult, if not impossible, to discern; and second, on some quantitative studies by economists on a few, perhaps unrepresentative, trade unions. In view of this scanty knowledge, economists have good reason to adopt a very modest position ... in that at least one crucial component of our modelling of such markets is not at all well understood.' Pencavel (1991: 54)

What does the trade union maximise? Trade unions are concerned with a wide range of issues, from the basic aim of increasing wages to broader political issues concerned with the labour movement as a whole.[7] Of course, union objectives may sometimes be conflicting. For example, an increase in the wages of unionised workers may reduce available jobs in the union sector, resulting in unemployed union workers crowding into the nonunion sector, and driving down nonunion wages, as shown in figure 3.3. If a union is concerned with labour as a whole, this result might be expected to affect its behaviour. The industrial relations and labour history literature contains many examples of trade unions that are concerned with issues of equity. However, as the quotation at the start of this section points out, we have little systematic evidence as to what trade union objectives are. While we have considerable information about outcomes, and the issues that are bargained over, it is problematic to infer union preferences from this information, since the outcome reflects the preferences and constraints of *both* parties.

The orthodox union models assume that trade unions are concerned *only* with the economic welfare of the *unionised sector*. Suppose that this assumption holds. Even with trade union objectives bounded in this fashion, there are, none the less, still difficulties in determining union objectives. This is because there are different sets of actors *within the union organisation*, and each set may have conflicting objectives. Not only will the trade union typically contain a heterogeneous group of individuals with varying preferences as to the union's strategy, but also the organisational structure of the trade union is likely to be such that different groups of individuals have *conflicting* preferences about the union's objectives. In

---

[7] Examples of the latter are union embargoes of South African goods, and the 'green bans' by construction workers in Australia during the 1970s. These bans are particularly interesting, since the Builders' Labourers Federation (BLF) banned demolition of historic housing in inner city suburbs, even though this action meant the blocking of building projects that would have increased BLF employment.

particular, there are likely to be principal–agent problems associated with the fact that union leaders (agents) have objectives conflicting with the membership (the principal). These problems may arise because the leadership may be better informed than its membership, or because it is interested in self-aggrandisement.

The industrial relations literature charts a variety of union structures and constitutions, ranging from democratic, through bureaucratic, to totalitarian in organisation.[8] Trade unions in both Britain and the USA are generally large. Such large groups have complex organisational structures, concerned with representation of members' interests and with administration. The actual union structure and constitution differ across unions, but overall the union is clearly a heterogeneous body whose maximising strategy may be determined by the structure of its government and administration. Because the internal organisation of a trade union is typically hierarchical in structure, the question arises as to how well members' preferences are transmitted through the various levels, each of which may have conflicting aims. There is a small literature that does allow for union objectives to be affected by heterogeneity of membership or by a conflict of interests between leadership and membership. These models will be referred to in section 4.6. But the widely accepted models of trade union behaviour side-step these problems by assuming that all workers in the unionised sector are identical. There is thus no distinction between leadership and membership, nor is there any distinction between members and non-members. All workers are identical, and all are union members.

So far, two assumptions have been made about union objectives: first, that the union cares only about the economic welfare of the union sector, and, secondly, that all members are identical including the leadership and rank-and-file members.[9] What is meant in this context by economic welfare? Economic welfare covers a range of aspects associated with employee remuneration (such as working conditions and fringe benefits, as well as wages). For simplicity, we can suppose that employer-provided benefits are encapsulated in the wages variable, since these benefits typically involve a redistribution of the firm's surplus to each member. Because the union is also hypothesised to care about the employment of union workers as well as their wages, union objectives can now be specified as an increasing function of wages and employment. The *union objective function* can therefore be written as

8   See Clegg (1980: 200) and Freeman and Medoff (1984: 18).
9   Some writers do not explicitly assume that members are identical, but instead state that the union is concerned with the utility of the median member. If union members *are* identical, then maximisation of the utility of the median member is equivalent to maximisation of the utility of *any* member. If union members are *not* identical, they must be differentiated by some characteristic. Once the membership is regarded as heterogeneous, then union wage and employment outcomes may affect different members differently. See section 4.6.

$$U = U(w,n) \tag{1}$$

where U denotes union utility, w and n denote wages and employment respectively, and $\partial U/\partial w > 0$ and $\partial U/\partial n > 0$. It has often been argued that rules found in collective agreements, such as those covering 'manning' and work pace, can be interpreted as being the concern of the union because of their impact on employment. Therefore it is legitimate as a first approximation to subsume these rules within employment to avoid complicating the analysis. An alternative hypothesis is that these rules are the concern of unions because the rules affect worker *effort*, which is quite distinct from employment. According to this view, the union objective function should therefore include as arguments wages, employment and effort (see, for example, Nickell, Wadhwani and Wall (1992) and Rosen (1989)). We assume for the moment that the union considers only wages and employment.

In practice, in most of the recent literature, the union is assumed to maximise either a *utilitarian* objective function or an *expected utility* objective function. Before we examine these two approaches, it is worth briefly considering how earlier writers treated the union objective function. Dunlop (1944: 44) considered a number of possible union objectives.[10] He argued that the most convincing union objective function was maximisation of the *total wage bill* of the membership. He suggested that unions could be treated analogously to firms who maximise revenues less costs. In the case of a trade union, revenue can be thought of as the wage income of members; if subscription costs are negligible, then the trade union's 'expected profits' are simply revenues, given by the following function:

$$U = wn \tag{2}$$

where the right-hand side is the wage income of employed members – the wage bill. However, his view that trade unions could be treated as maximising something, using standard economic techniques, was challenged by Ross. The latter maintained that 'the wage policy of unions ... is not to be found in the mechanical application of any maximisation principle' (Ross, 1948: 8), and that economists' use of such a maximising approach ignored the vital political dimension of the trade union. By 'political dimension', he meant not the broader political aims that are associated with some British trade unions, but rather the fact that unions are political institutions in their own right. He argued that the union could not be treated as maximising revenue analogously to a firm, because a union

---

[10] These were maximisation of total union employment, maximisation of average wages, maximisation of the wage bill of the employed plus unemployment benefit payments of the unemployed and, lastly, the objective he favoured, maximisation of the total wage bill of members.

is a political institution concerned largely with collective action. While the union is clearly interested in providing benefits to its membership, '[t]he policies adopted by particular unions do not represent different degrees of enlightenment but different ranges of choice and cannot be understood until we recognize the primary importance of organizational survival as the central aim of the leadership' (Ross, 1948: 16). Although most economists would not take exception to these views, there is a dearth of analysis allowing for differences in preferences between leadership and membership.[11]

An alternative trade union objective that has some similarity to maximisation of the wage bill advocated by Dunlop is *rent maximisation* (see Rosen (1969), de Menil (1971) and Calvo (1978)). For example, de Menil assumes that the union cares about the 'real wage surplus', that is, the difference between the real wage bill in the union sector and that in the perfectly competitive sector. This rent maximisation objective function can be represented by

$$U = (w - w^c)n \tag{3}$$

where w denotes the union wage and w^c the competitive wage. Note that, in equations (2) and (3), the union utility function is assumed linear in wages (that is, workers are risk-neutral).

We now return to consideration of the two union objective functions used in most of the recent theoretical literature, viz. the utilitarian and the expected utility functions. First, consider the *utilitarian* objective function. Here it is supposed that the union maximises the sum of individual utilities u_i. Thus

$$U = \sum_{i=1}^{n} u_i(w) \qquad u'(w) > 0; \ u''(w) \leq 0 \tag{4}$$

where w denotes wages, n is the number of union workers, and $u(w)$ is the (indirect) utility of income. If individual utility is linear in wages (individuals are risk-neutral), (4) is equivalent to wage-bill maximisation. In practice in the literature, all union workers are assumed to be identical, and (4) is written as

$$U = nu(w) \tag{5}$$

The union comprises *identical* members who are all treated *identically* by the union, and therefore no distributional or normative judgements are being made by the utilitarian or Benthamite objective of (4). However, it is

---

[11] Notable exceptions are provided by Berkovitz (1954), Atherton (1973), Faith and Reid (1987) and Pemberton (1988). Atherton (1973: ch. 1) also provides a thoughtful review of the literature of union bargaining goals.

important to remember that, if workers were assumed to be heterogeneous, the use of (4) as the trade union objective would introduce normative judgements.[12] If individuals were *not* identical, it would be necessary to consider carefully why the utilitarian or Benthamite social welfare function should be adopted, rather than some alternative such as the Rawlsian maximin criterion, or perhaps even a more egalitarian approach.[13]

If the union's wage-setting behaviour results in some union members being unemployed, the utilitarian objective function of equation (4) can be written as

$$U = nu(w) + (t-n)u(b) \qquad w > b; \, 0 < n \leq t \qquad (6)$$

where n denotes employment in the union sector, t is the total number of union workers in the sector, and b is the alternative sector wage or the unemployment benefit. Since all workers in the sector are assumed union members, t also denotes membership. The first term on the right-hand side of (6) is the number of workers employed times the utility of an employed worker, while the second term is the number of unemployed workers, $t-n$, times the utility of an unemployed worker.

Now consider the second union objective function that has been popular in recent theoretical work, the *expected utility* approach. If membership (here denoted by t) is fixed, then equation (4) can be written equivalently in terms of expected utility. Since the union raises wages above the competitive level, each member will face some probability of being unemployed. If unemployed, a worker receives the alternative sector wage or the unemployment benefit, denoted by b. By assumption all union workers are identical, and n employees are selected at random from the total number of union members, t.[14] Therefore union workers each have an equal probability of being employed, given by n/t. The probability of being unemployed is given by $(1 - n/t)$, because there are only two possible states and probabilities must sum to one. The union maximises the expected utility of a representative union member, given by:

$$EU = \frac{n}{t}u(w) + \left(1 - \frac{n}{t}\right)u(b) \qquad u'(w) > 0; \, u''(w) \leq 0 \qquad (7)$$

---

[12] Pencavel (1991) discusses various alternative forms of social welfare function that might be adopted as the union objective function. An example is the Bernoulli–Nash form of union objective function where union utility is the *product* of individual utilities, and which is associated with an equal distribution of outcomes.

[13] Once the assumption of identical individuals is removed, it is necessary to consider whether this sort of social welfare function approach is suitable at all. Instead, it might be more appropriate for the model-maker to use positive theories of majority decision-making and social choice.

[14] Because all workers are identical, the firm is unable to distinguish between them and therefore follows a random hiring or firing rule.

where $u'(w) = du/dw$. Note that in both (6) and (7), union utility is non-decreasing in alternative wages. But in (6), union utility is increasing in membership, while in (7) it is decreasing in membership.[15]

However, provided that membership is held fixed, (6) and (7) are equivalent characterisations of union preferences. Thus the principal difference between the utilitarian and expected utility specifications lies in the role of membership t. This can be easily seen by rewriting (6) as

$$U = t\left[\frac{n}{t}u(w) + \left(1 - \frac{n}{t}\right)u(b)\right] = t.\text{EU} \tag{6a}$$

Equation (6) can also be rewritten as:

$$U = n[u(w) - u(b)] + tu(b) \tag{8}$$

This formulation nests the wage-bill and rent-maximisation objectives as special cases.[16]

From either (6) or (7) can be derived a union indifference curve in (w,n) space; the indifference curve indicates various pairs of w and n yielding constant utility. The slope of this indifference curve is obtained by total differentiation of either (6) or (7), keeping (expected) utility fixed.[17] Thus from (7)

$$d(\text{EU}) = 0 = dn[u(w) - u(b)] + nu'(w)\,dw \tag{9}$$

Thus

$$dw/dn = -[u(w) - u(b)]/nu'(w) \tag{10}$$

For fixed membership t, equation (10) also represents the slope of the indifference curve for (6). Equation (10) shows the marginal rate of substitution of wages for employment in the union objective function; it

[15] Thus from (6), it can be seen that $\partial U/\partial t = u(b) > 0$, and $\partial U/\partial b = (t-n)u'(b) \geq 0$. However, from (7), $\partial(\text{EU})/\partial t = -n[u(w) - u(b)]/t^2 < 0$. But $\partial(\text{EU})/\partial b = (1 - n/t)u'(b) \geq 0$.
[16] The last term on the right-hand side of (8) is treated by the union as a constant, since it is assumed in these models that the union does not control the alternative wage (plausible) nor membership (implausible). The effective maximand is therefore $n[u(w) - u(b)]$. If individuals have utility functions that are linear in wages, this maximand can be regarded as rent maximisation, $n(w - b)$. Now suppose that the alternative wage is zero and individual utility is linear in wages. The maximand is now wage-bill maximisation, nw.

The expected utility objective function of (7) can also nest the wage-bill and rent-maximisation objectives as special cases. Rewrite (7) as

$$\text{EU} = [u(w) - u(b)]n/t + u(b) \tag{7a}$$

The last term is a constant to the union. If $u(w)$ is linear in wages, the relevant maximand for the union is $n(w - b)/t$; here the union is concerned with per capita rent maximisation. If $u(w)$ is linear in wages but $b = 0$, the union's maximand is effectively nw/t, which is per capita wage-bill maximisation.
[17] Since the union indifference curve shows various pairs of w and n yielding constant utility, the change in utility $d(\text{EU})$ as one moves along a particular indifference curve is zero.

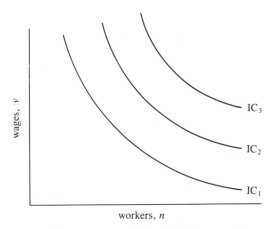

Figure 4.1. A family of union indifference curves.

indicates the union indifference curve is negatively sloped, because $[u(w) - u(b)] > 0$ for $w > b$, and $u'(w) > 0$. The indifference curve is asymptotic to b, since as $w \rightarrow b$, $dw/dn \rightarrow 0$. The indifference curve is convex, because $d^2w/dn^2 = [u(w) - u(b)]/n[u'(w)]^2 > 0$. A family of union indifference curves is illustrated in figure 4.1.[18]

Both the utilitarian and the expected utility objective functions have the implication that identical workers receive different outcomes *ex post*. Employed members receive the union wage, while unemployed workers receive b. If unemployed members effectively leave the union, the leadership will be concerned about the future union viability, since there will be a larger pool of nonunion labour who might undercut the union wage, and because union income through dues will be affected.[19] This is likely to affect union outcomes, and is an argument for inclusion of the level of membership in the union objective function as an endogenous variable. Pencavel (1991: 62) suggests that b may not be exogenous, for example if the union can affect remuneration for unemployed members through redistribution from the employed to the unemployed.[20] To ensure union survival, the union might want to treat identical members identically, and therefore redistribution schemes should be observed, adjusted for the disutility of work for those in employment.

[18] If the union cared only about wages and not about employment, the indifference curves would be horizontal at each wage rate in the utilitarian case (see, for example, Oswald (1985)).

[19] This point has been raised by, for example, Atherton (1973: 19), discussing the wage-bill hypothesis of Dunlop (1944), and Pencavel (1991: 62).

[20] See Kiander (1993) and Booth (1993) for union models where intra-union redistribution occurs through unemployment benefits and redundancy payments respectively.

What evidence is there for this hypothesis? Historically, many US and British unions paid unemployment benefits to out-of-work members, and some commentators, such as the Webbs (1897) and Boyer (1988), argue that this was important for union growth and survival. However, whilst unemployment benefits are still provided by many unions, the amounts are typically small and appear to be an historical legacy.[21] Other forms of redistribution might be severance payments or minimum income guarantees. In Britain in 1990, 42% of establishments bargained with a recognised manual union about the size of redundancy payments and 51% with a recognised non-manual union (see table 4.1), while in the USA, 39% of major collective agreements covered severance pay. However, it may be in a firm's interests to pay these. Worksharing arrangements are also a form of redistribution, but although in US contracts these are sometimes found, they are not often used (Pencavel, 1991: 65). Thus there is some evidence for redistribution schemes; with the exception of severance payments, these schemes are not widespread nor are the amounts involved typically large. Moreover, schemes such as unemployment compensation, severance payments and worksharing may exist for reasons apart from union concern to treat identical workers identically.[22]

4.3 The behaviour of the firm

We now consider the behaviour of the other important agent in the unionised labour market – the firm. In the modern theory of the firm, it is often suggested that management may have objectives other than profit maximisation. Given the separation of ownership and control in large firms, there may be a divergence of interest between managers who run the company and shareholders who own the company. Thus managers might be interested in maximising their own salaries or perquisites subject to achieving a certain level of profits, or in maximising company size proxied by sales revenues, rather than maximising only profits which accrue to shareholders. Shareholders typically hold a portfolio of shares in different companies, and are therefore not able to monitor effectively the behaviour of their agents (management) in different companies. However, in the private sector there is always the threat of potential takeover of an inefficient company (and a subsequent change of management) which, it is

[21] For the US, some 26% of members covered by major collective agreements are able to receive unemployment benefits (see Pencavel, 1991). A postal survey of the twenty-eight largest British unions affiliated with the TUC found that 39% of the responding unions paid unemployment benefits. The average unemployment benefit (calculated for unions paying this benefit) was £8.38 per week, in 1988 figures (see Booth, 1991).

[22] For example, firms and workers may want worksharing to avoid losing specifically trained workers.

argued, ensures that management broadly follows the profit maximisation objective. It therefore seems reasonable to suppose that, for private sector firms, management is concerned with maximising expected profits.[23]

What sort of product-market structure characterises unionised labour markets? It appears to be an empirical regularity that imperfections in the labour market are correlated with imperfections in the product market (see, for example, Mishel (1986), Stewart (1990) and Machin, Stewart and van Reenen (1993)). While some researchers modelling the unionised economy have assumed that product markets are *imperfectly* competitive (see, for example, Layard and Nickell (1986), Dixon (1988), Dowrick (1989) and Layard *et al.* (1991)), the vast majority of the trade union literature assumes a *perfectly* competitive product market but without free entry.[24] This is because such a simplifying assumption allows concentration on the important issues of wage and employment determination in models that are not too complex. Furthermore, these models show how unionisation can give rise to wage increases and unemployment quite independently of product market imperfections. However, the assumption of perfect competition means that there are certain issues that cannot be addressed. For example, it is not possible to examine what Dowrick (1989: 1124) terms: 'the macroeconomic questions of whether real wages and the functional distribution of income are determined in the labour market, characterised by bargaining between large firms and unions, or in the product market, characterised by oligopolistic price-setting'.

For a union to be able to negotiate wage increases above the competitive level, there must be available in the industry some rents or surplus which can be captured by the union. Chapter 3 discussed necessary conditions for a union to be able to appropriate any surplus, in a perfectly competitive product market, without driving the firm out of existence.[25] These conditions were very high levels of unionisation in the perfectly competitive industry, no nonunion foreign competition, entry barriers (which may be provided by the threat of immediate union organisation of new entrants), and inelastic product demand. Without the first three conditions, domestic firms, or foreign firms, or new firms entering the industry, could simply hire

---

[23] However, in *public sector* companies, management may pursue objectives that are different to profit maximisation, and they are free to do so because public sector companies or bureaucracies are not subject to the threat of takeover that, it is argued, keeps private sector management adhering to profit maximisation. For example, bureaucrats may wish to maximise their budgets, since that enhances their power and prestige. For this reason, it would be desirable to modify the management's maximisation strategy in models of public sector unionisation.

[24] With free entry, profits would have to be zero. Since there would be no available surplus to share, the union would not be able to demand any wage above the competitive level.

[25] As noted in chapter 3, unions may be able to increase the surplus available to both union and firm through co-operative behaviour.

nonunion labour and produce at a lower cost than unionised competitors, thereby driving them out of business. These conditions should be borne in mind when working with trade union models that assume a perfectly competitive product market.

The usual characterisation of the preferences of a firm is that management will maximise profits. If firms have no power in the labour market, they take wages as given. Thus their only choice variable is n. The optimisation problem facing the firm can therefore be written as:

$$\max_{n} \pi = pq(n) - wn \tag{11}$$

where π denotes profits, and the production function $q(n)$ is characterised by diminishing returns to labour, $q'(n) > 0, q''(n) < 0, q(0) = 0$. Product price is denoted by p. The first-order condition from (11) is

$$d\pi/dn = pq'(n) - w = 0 \tag{12}$$

and the second-order condition is

$$d^2\pi/dn^2 = pq''(n) < 0 \tag{13}$$

Note that (12) is the standard textbook result for the firm, in a perfectly competitive product market and labour market, employing workers up to the point where the value of their marginal product $pq'(n)$ equals the exogenously given wage. (The competitive labour demand curve is given by $pq'(n)$; see appendix 3A for the monopolist's labour demand curve.)

We can also use (11) to show the firm's *isoprofit* (constant profit) curve in (w,n) space, by totally differentiating (11) with respect to w and n, holding profits π fixed. Thus

$$d\pi = 0 = pq'(n)\,dn - w\,dn - n\,dw \tag{14}$$

Rearrangement of (14) yields the slope of the isoprofit curve:

$$dw/dn = [pq'(n) - w]/n \tag{15}$$

Equation (15) shows that the slope of the isoprofit curve is determined by the sign of $[pq'(n) - w]$. The labour demand curve is $pq'(n)$; all points to the left of the labour demand curve are where $w < pq'(n)$, while all points to the right of the demand curve are associated with $pq'(n) < w$. Thus, from (15), the slope of an isoprofit curve is positive to the left of the labour demand curve, and negative to the right; each isoprofit curve is concave. For each isoprofit curve, there is a unique wage rate associated with the turning-point of that curve (where $pq'(n) = w$). The locus of the turning-point of each isoprofit curve traces out the labour demand curve, as illustrated in figure 4.2a. Clearly, for any given level of employment n, profits will be

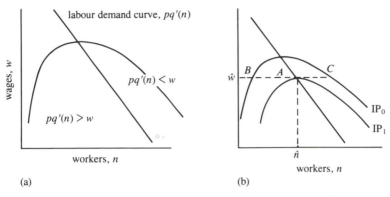

Figure 4.2. (a) The isoprofit curve; (b) optimal position for the firm at A.

greater the lower is the wage level. Hence *lower* isoprofit curves in (w,n) space are associated with *higher* levels of profits.

From the first-order condition of (12), the profit-maximising firm always chooses employment such that $w = pq'(n)$. Any other choice of employment is sub-optimal. To see this diagrammatically, suppose wages are exogenously given as $\hat{w}$, as shown in figure 4.2b. The firm is free to choose employment. If it chooses $n = \hat{n}$, it will be on isoprofit curve IP_1, at point A on the labour demand curve. But if it chooses $n < \hat{n}$, it will be at point B on an isoprofit curve yielding lower profits, IP_0. Analogously, if it chooses $n > \hat{n}$, it will be at point C, also yielding lower profits. Hence it will choose $n = \hat{n}$.

Having characterised the firm's behaviour in this section, and the union's preferences in the previous section, we are now in a position to bring these together and consider the simplest method of reconciling the objectives of each party – the *monopoly union model*.

4.4 The monopoly union model

In the *monopoly union model*, the union is assumed to set the wage level unilaterally, subject to the firm's labour demand curve. Once the wage is set by the union, the firm then simply reads off from the labour demand curve the number of workers to hire at that wage. In unilaterally choosing the wage, the union understands how the firm will behave in response to the wage. The monopoly union model has been objected to by some writers as being 'excessively simple'. For example, Layard *et al.* (1991: 96) write: 'The union never gets everything it wants. It bargains. Thus we reject an excessively simple model in common usage – the model of the "monopoly union". Under this model the union chooses wages on its own, with no

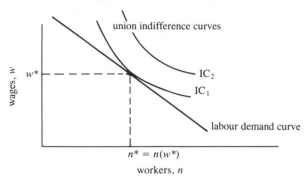

Figure 4.3. Monopoly union outcome.

bargaining.' While sympathising with this view, we consider the monopoly union model in some detail here, first, because it has been widely used in the literature and, secondly, because it turns out to be a special case of the bargaining model that will be developed in the following chapter. An understanding of the monopoly union model will therefore greatly assist the reader in understanding the models of the following chapter.

The monopoly union model can be illustrated diagrammatically with the union seeking its highest level of utility, subject to the constraint of the firm's labour demand curve. At the optimum, the union is thus equating its marginal rate of substitution of employment for wages with the slope of the labour demand curve, as shown in figure 4.3, where w^* and n^* are the optimal wage and employment levels.

Suppose that the union maximises the expected utility of a representative worker:

$$\max_{w} EU = (n/t)\, u(w) + (1 - n/t)\, u(b) \tag{16}$$

subject to

$$pq'(n) = w \tag{17}$$

The first-order condition of the maximisation problem of (16) and (17) can be found directly by equating the slope of the union indifference curve with the slope of the labour demand curve. We have already found the slope of the former in (10), and the slope of the labour demand curve is given by $q''(n)$. However, an equivalent but simpler way of dealing with the maximisation problem of (16) and (17) is to note the following. Once the union sets its optimal wage w^*, equilibrium employment is given by equating w^* with the firm's labour demand curve $pq'(n)$. From figure 4.3, equilibrium employment is thus $n^* = n(w^*/p)$. Thus an alternative way of writing the union's constraint (17) is:

$$n = n(w/p) \tag{18}$$

Substitution of (18) into (16) and maximisation with respect to w yields the following result where we set $p = 1$ for simplicity:

Proposition 4.1.
Wages will be set by the union such that the percentage increase in a member's utility due to a percentage increase in wages is exactly equal to the elasticity of labour demand (that is, the percentage reduction in employment due to the percentage wage increase). This is given by

$$\epsilon = w u'(w)/[u(w) - u(b)] \tag{19}$$

where $\epsilon = -n'(w)w/n$.

Proof. See appendix 4A.

Intuitively, this result arises because an increase in wages reduces employment in the union sector, and each worker therefore faces a greater chance of being unemployed. On the other hand, any member lucky enough to be employed will receive a higher wage. In equilibrium therefore, the percentage marginal benefit is equal to the percentage marginal cost, as given by (19). Note that (19) simply *characterises* the equilibrium solution for the monopoly union. In order to obtain a *specific* value for w, it is necessary to choose explicit functional forms for the utility function and the labour demand function. These can then be inserted into the generalised characterisation of (19) and solved for w.

Now consider how the wage set by the monopoly union will alter due to a change in each of the explanatory variables. This is of particular interest if we wish to see how the business cycle might affect the unionised sector of the economy (see, for example, McDonald and Solow (1981) and Oswald (1982, 1985)). The business cycle is likely to affect both labour demand and alternative opportunities (represented by b).

An increase in product demand will increase the demand for labour at each wage rate. Thus the labour demand curve in figure 4.3 will shift rightwards. However, if the *elasticity* of labour demand is unaffected, the union wage will remain constant. This can be seen from (19) in proposition 1: with fixed ϵ, the right-hand side of (19) must remain unaltered, and wages will not change. (An example of an isoelastic labour demand function is $n = \theta n(w)$, where θ is a demand shift parameter.) Thus wages are rigid during fluctuations in product price, and all adjustment occurs through employment.

Now consider the impact of an improvement in alternative opportunities, represented by an increase in b. Such an increase affects only union preferences; it does not affect labour demand. From (19), it is clear that the union wage will increase. The left-hand-side of (19) remains unaltered by an increase in b. For the right-hand-side also to remain unaltered, w must increase with an increase in b. This result suggests that union wages will move with the level of unemployment in the rest of the economy. For as alternative opportunities worsen (b declines), the union moderates its wage claims, and this wage moderation increases employment in the unionised sector.

How do changes in union membership affect the monopoly union model? Recall that the union is assumed to be a closed shop, so that membership is equal to the sector size, t: union density is 100 per cent. Since t does not enter into (19), then changing membership has no impact on the union wage, a curious result.

These results are summarised in the following proposition:

Proposition 4.2.

For a monopoly union:

(i)   An isoelastic increase in labour demand has no effect on union wages, but employment is increased.

(ii)   An improvement in alternative opportunities increases the union wage. Employment is reduced as we move up the labour demand curve.

(iii) An increase in membership or the size of the union wage has no effect on wages or the numbers employed.

Proof. See appendix 4A.

Since the business cycle is likely to affect b and labour demand simultaneously, it is useful to consider their combined impact on union wage behaviour. If the economy moves into a recession, product demand and alternative opportunities are likely to decline. A decline in product demand does not affect the union wage but does reduce employment, while a decline in b reduces the union wage and *increases* employment. Thus the monopoly union model predicts that the net effect of a recession is for union wages to decline, while the impact on employment is ambiguous. However, where there is little labour mobility between sectors in the short run, the impact of changes in alternative opportunities will be small. The negative employment effect of a decline in product prices might be expected to dominate and wages will be sticky. In a boom, if the product-market effect dominates the alternative opportunities effect, employment will increase and union wages will be sticky. Thus it can be seen that the model offers a microeconomic alternative to the implicit contract models of sticky wages and unemployment.

Finally, what are the empirically testable predictions of the monopoly union model? First, the alternative wage and unemployment benefit should affect wages directly. However, employment should be determined by the wage rate, and should not be affected by variables measuring alternative opportunities. Secondly, membership changes should have no impact on the union wage.

4.5 Empirical evaluation of union objectives

What can be inferred about trade union objectives from empirical work? There is a small body of applied work which attempts to establish the nature of union objectives over wage and employment determination. The principal problem in attempting to infer union objectives from outcomes has already been noted. Outcomes are reached by a process of negotiation between two parties – the union and management – who have conflicting objectives over the sharing of any surplus, and who are typically in a position of bilateral monopoly. The outcome of the negotiation process will be affected by the relative strengths of the two parties. In the extreme case of the monopoly union model, the union is assumed to have the strength to extract all the surplus, while the firm passively determines employment in response to what is, in effect, an *imposed* wage. If any industry could be found that approximated this situation, then the observed outcome could be held to reflect trade union preferences. (However, we would still be unable to distinguish the utilitarian objective function from the expected utility objective function: they are observationally equivalent.) Work by Farber (1978b, 1978c) represents the first application of these ideas in a pioneering and important application of the monopoly union model to the US bituminous coal industry, using annual data for the period 1948 to 1973. He argues that, over this period, the market structure of the coal industry was relatively fragmented and competitive, while the United Mineworkers' Union (UMW) was a united and 'dominant force'. The UMW could therefore impose its preferred wage on employers in the industry, who were then free to adjust employment.

Farber's model is considerably more sophisticated than the monopoly union model outlined in the previous section, because it embeds the monopoly union model within a structural model of the whole coal industry, and also because it draws on the median voter model, which we will not be examining until later in this chapter (where the assumption of a homogeneous membership will be relaxed). We briefly consider Farber's union objective function below, before turning to detailed discussion of

Carruth and Oswald (1985), who infer trade union objectives in a simpler model.

Farber assumes that union workers are differentiated by age. At each age, they prefer differing combinations of wages and fringe benefits (including pensions) in their remuneration package; thus his analysis extends the orthodox model by distinguishing between pay and benefits. Farber writes the union objective function as:

$$EU = \frac{n}{t}u(\omega_i) + \left(1 - \frac{n}{t}\right)u(\omega^a) \qquad (20)$$

where ω_i is total compensation per person-hour of the ith employed union worker, and ω^a is compensation per person-hour in the alternative sector. Note that ω_i is a weighted average of wages and fringe benefits, with the weights depending on the age of the worker. The union, in order to be re-elected, is assumed to choose a wage and fringe-benefit package to maximise the expected utility of the *median-aged* member (and thus the ith individual in (20) is replaced by the *median-aged* member), subject to the labour demand curve of the industry.[26] Specific functional forms were chosen for the underlying functions, and Farber then estimated a nine-equation simultaneous system based on the structural form of the model, using Full Information Maximum Likelihood.[27] We will return to his findings shortly.

To gain an understanding of the issues involved in actually *estimating* a monopoly union model of the form of equations (16) and (17), we now consider in some detail a simpler approach than that followed by Farber – the model of Carruth and Oswald (1985). Carruth and Oswald estimate wages and employment in the British coal industry over the period 1950 to 1980, and assume that the wage-setting policy of the National Union of Mineworkers (NUM) can be represented by the monopoly union model.[28] The British coal industry is nationalised; to circumvent the problem of modelling the objectives of a state-run industry, they postulate a reduced-form labour demand function which they reasonably argue 'can be derived for both a profit-maximising monopoly firm and a socially planned

---

[26] There are problems in using the median voter model when there is more than one choice variable (see, for example, Atkinson and Stiglitz (1980: 302–7)). In Farber's union objective function there are two choice variables – wages and benefits. Blair and Crawford (1984) point out that the equilibria in the Farber model will not generally exist.

[27] The full nine-equation model appears in Farber (1978c), while a subset of the results, focusing on the union objective function, appears in Farber (1978b).

[28] While Farber uses an hourly wage rate, Carruth and Oswald were constrained by data availability to using real weekly earnings of all workers in the coal industry (which included 'allowances in kind'). Such a measure may not be directly comparable with the microeconomic theory which considers wage rates and which is based on the assumption that hours are exogenously fixed. See Pencavel (1991: 92) for further discussion of this issue.

industry' (Carruth and Oswald, 1985: 1004).[29] They assume that the union follows the utilitarian strategy:

$$\max_{w} U = nu(w) + (t - n)u(b) \tag{21}$$

subject to

$$n = n(w, \theta) \tag{22}$$

where w is now the real wage, and θ represents demand shift parameters, including the price of coal substitutes, technological progress and other input prices. This is a restatement of the monopoly union model of equations (16) and (18). The wage and employment outcome of this maximisation process is illustrated diagrammatically in figure 4.3 as w^* and n^* respectively. We have already noted that, in order to solve explicitly for w^* and n^*, it is necessary to impose more structure on the model, and to assume explicit functional forms for the utility function $u(.)$ and the labour demand function $n(.)$. Consider the union objective function. Carruth and Oswald assume, like Farber, that individual worker utility is given by the constant relative risk aversion function:

$$u(w) = \frac{1}{1 - \gamma} w^{1 - \gamma} \qquad u'(w) = w^{-\gamma}; \, u''(w) = -\gamma w^{-(1 + \gamma)} \tag{23}$$

and

$$u(b) = \frac{1}{1 - \gamma} b^{1 - \gamma} \qquad u'(b) = b^{-\gamma}; \, u''(b) = -\gamma b^{-(1 + \gamma)} \tag{24}$$

This particular utility function has the property that relative risk aversion, defined as $-[u''(w)w]/u'(w)$, is given by γ. Since this is constant, it is possible in econometric work to *estimate* relative risk aversion. Clearly if the estimate of γ is insignificantly different from zero, then the utility function is linear in wages (risk-neutral in this context).

Substitution of equations (23) and (24) into the union objective function (21) yields:

$$\max_{w} U = n \left[\frac{1}{1 - \gamma} w^{1 - \gamma} - \frac{1}{1 - \gamma} b^{1 - \gamma} \right] + t \left[\frac{1}{1 - \gamma} b^{1 - \gamma} \right] \tag{25}$$

Observe that (25) nests the rent maximisation objective function as a special

---

[29] Of course, it might be argued that the British coal industry, where a single employer, the Coal Board, faced a single trade union, the National Union of Mineworkers, was a classic situation of bilateral monopoly, and might have been better characterised by a bargaining model of the type discussed in the following chapter. However, the Carruth and Oswald model is a remarkably clear exposition of the transformation of a theoretical model into one that can be estimated, which is why we examine it in detail here.

case if $\gamma = 0$. Carruth and Oswald assume that labour demand follows the linear approximation:

$$n_t = \beta_0 + \beta_1 \, w + \beta_2 \, \tau + \sum_{i=0}^{3} a_i p_{t-i}^0 + \sum_{i=0}^{3} \delta_i r_{t-i} + \epsilon_{2t} \tag{26}$$

where w is the real wage, r is the rental return to capital, p^0 is the price of oil, τ is a linear time trend to capture technical progress, and β_j ($j = 0,1,2$), a_i and δ_i are coefficients to be estimated. The subscript t denotes time, and the error term ϵ_{2t} reflects the stochastic nature of the data. Note that

$$n'(w) = \beta_1 \tag{27}$$

The first-order condition from maximisation of (25) subject to (26) yields:

$$n_t w^{-\gamma} + \beta_1 \left[\frac{1}{1-\gamma} (w_t^{1-\gamma} + b_t^{1-\gamma}) \right] = \epsilon_{2t} \tag{28}$$

We now have two equations, (26) and (28), in two unknowns; the endogenous variables of the system are, of course, wages and employment. A method of estimation of the structural coefficients of a simultaneous equation system is Full Information Maximum Likelihood (FIML) which involves, in this case, application of maximum likelihood to the two stochastic equations, (26) and (28), simultaneously. FIML produces estimates of the structural coefficients *directly*, and also takes into account correlation of error terms across equations and cross-equation restrictions (see Kmenta, 1971: 578).

Of particular interest are the FIML estimates of the coefficient of relative risk aversion, γ. Carruth and Oswald find γ to be 0.8 with a t-statistic of 23.2. For the US coal industry, Farber (1978b) estimates γ as 3.7, with a t-statistic of 11. Since γ is significantly different from zero in both countries, the rent maximisation hypothesis is rejected. These results suggest that in both the US and British coal industries workers are relatively risk-averse, and especially so in the USA. Indeed, the difference between the estimated relative risk aversion of US and British miners is quite startling. The UMW in the USA appears to place greater emphasis on the employment consequences of its wage policies than the NUM in Britain. Both Farber and Carruth and Oswald conclude that these estimates suggest the UMW and the NUM *do* care about employment when setting wages.[30] However,

---

[30] The question arises as to why there are such big differences in estimated γ between the US and British coal industries. Farber (1986: 1063) suggests that the difference in alternative income measures used in the two studies may affect the results. Another explanation may be that the means of reconciliation of the union and managerial preferences differs between the two countries. Farber argues fairly convincingly that at the time of his study the US coal industry was fragmented and weak, and that the UMW therefore had all the power. It is

neither paper tests whether employment matters to the union or not; in
other words, both papers take employment mattering to the union as a
maintained hypothesis. A way of *testing* whether employment matters or
not would be to rewrite (25) as

$$\max_{w} U = n^{\varphi}\left[\frac{w^{1-\gamma} - b^{1-\gamma}}{1-\gamma}\right] + t\left[\frac{b^{1-\gamma}}{1-\gamma}\right] \tag{25a}$$

Both φ and γ should be estimated, and then tested to see if each is
significantly different from zero. If $\varphi = 0$, then the union does not care
about employment. Note that (25) is a special case of (25a) with $\varphi = 1$, so
that in (25) the union has been *assumed* to care about employment without
testing to see if this is indeed the case.

In a model that overcomes this problem, Dertouzos and Pencavel (1981)
estimated wage and employment equations for US workers covered by each
of eight locals of the International Typographical Union (ITU), over the
period 1946 to 1965 (before the technological revolution in newspaper
composition). They carefully relate the structure of the ITU and the
newspaper printing industry to the model. They argue that over the
estimating period the newspaper printing industry is of fragmented market
structure, that contracts are negotiated at the local level between ITU
chapters and particular firms, that the ITU operates a closed shop so that it
is valid to suppose membership covers the whole sector, and that the
membership is homogeneous. Moreover, since the structure and constitution of the ITU is democratic, it is reasonable to suppose that leaders and
rank-and-file members do not have conflicting objectives. The union is also
argued to be 'in a dominant position vis-à-vis the firm. This provides some
support for interpreting the pattern of typographers' wages and employment over time as tracing out the union's preferences.' (Dertouzos and
Pencavel, 1981: 1166.) The authors assume that the union has the following
Stone–Geary objective function:[31]

$$U = (w - b)^{\kappa} (n - \bar{n})^{1 - \kappa} \tag{29}$$

where w is the hourly real wage rate, b is some comparison wage rate, n is
local union employment and $\bar{n}$ represents some minimum level of employment. Since the ITU is a pre-entry closed shop union, n can be thought of as

harder to argue this for the British coal industry. Furthermore, there is some evidence that
the British coal industry is one of those rare industries in which collective agreements
actually state that employment is bargained over in addition to wages (Layard *et al.* 1991:
91). This would suggest that there may be some rationale for also estimating the efficient
bargaining model of the next chapter for the British coal industry.
[31] The Stone–Geary utility function is commonly used in consumer theory in order to derive a
linear expenditure system of demand equations (see, for example, Layard and Walters
(1978: 163)).

membership, and indeed the estimation typically used local membership data instead of employment (except for the Cincinnati local). An advantage of the formulation of (29) is that it nests the wage-bill and rent maximisation hypotheses as special cases. Thus if $\kappa = 1/2$ and $b = \bar{n} = 0$, equation (29) represents wage-bill maximisation. Alternatively if $\kappa = 1/2$ and $\bar{n} = 0$, equation (29) represents rent maximisation. Finally, if $\kappa = 1$, the union cares only about wages. A test of whether or not κ is equal to one is a proper test for whether employment matters to the union.

The two-equation system estimated by Dertouzos and Pencavel is derived in a similar fashion to that of Carruth and Oswald (1985) described in detail above. Once again, there are two unknowns – wages and employment – and a two-equation simultaneous equation system represented by the first-order condition of the maximisation of (29) with respect to wages, plus the labour demand curve. Dertouzos and Pencavel used FIML to estimate the parameters of the stochastic form of this two-equation simultaneous equation system. What do their estimates reveal about the union objective function? First, the special cases of wage-bill and rent maximisation within the Stone–Geary formulation were rejected by the data. Secondly, the local unions appeared to be concerned with the excess of both wages and employment (or membership) above some reference levels – 'supernumerary' wages and employment.[32] Thirdly, there appeared to be considerable variation across the ITU locals in the relative weights estimated for supernumerary wages and supernumerary employment.

Pencavel (1984) used similar data to that of Dertouzos and Pencavel for ten locals of the ITU for the period 1946 to 1965, but he assumed the union objective function was addilog. An advantage of this particular functional form is that it nests the Stone–Geary, the wage-bill and the rent maximisation objective functions as special cases. Following the monopoly union model, the ITU chose wages to maximise its addilog objective function subject to a labour demand constraint whose slope was assumed to follow a particular functional form. Instead of estimating the model for each of the locals separately (as did Dertouzos and Pencavel (1981)), Pencavel chose to pool the data to estimate the model, and then to split the pooled data into two subsets – the five larger union locals, and the five smaller. The results suggest that, although there are considerable variations in preferences across different size locals, the wage-bill objective function was rejected in all specifications. The elasticity of substitution between wages and employment in the union's maximand was found to fall between zero and one, indicating limited substitution between wages and employment. Indeed, for

---

[32] 'Supernumerary' refers to the difference between the union outcome and the basic level, which, for wages is represented by $(w - b)$, and for employment or membership by $(n - \bar{n})$.

the larger locals, the results provided some support for the rent maximisation hypothesis. However, the smaller locals were relatively more concerned with employment than the larger locals.

While the union objective function of Pencavel (1984) is considerably more general than that of Dertouzos and Pencavel (1981), the labour demand function used in the later paper has a more specific functional form than the earlier model.

What conclusions about trade union preferences can be drawn from this empirical work? The principal conclusion is that employment as well as wages matter to trade unions in the two industries covered – the coal and newspaper printing industries. However, even within these two industries there is substantial variation in preferences. Mining trade unions in the USA and Britain appear to be characterised by differing degrees of relative risk aversion, with the UMW in the USA placing greater emphasis on the employment consequences of its wage policies than the NUM in Britain.[33] To a student of comparative industrial relations, this result is hardly surprising, since the institutional arrangements in the two countries are very different, and the results are perhaps a salutary reminder that generalisations of findings for one country to another may sometimes be misplaced. But even within an industry in one particular country – newspaper printing in the USA – there is evidence of considerable diversity in union preferences over the wage and employment trade-off among different local branches of the ITU.

Differences in measurement of wages and employment in the various studies, due to data availability, do not facilitate comparison. For example, the trade-off between wages and employment found by Dertouzos and Pencavel (1981) and Pencavel (1984), is actually a trade-off between wages and union membership.[34] The fact that the ITU is actually a pre-entry closed shop union, in which unemployed members are unlikely to leave the union, suggests that membership may not be an exact proxy for employment. None the less, the findings that the ITU cares about both wages and membership are interesting in their own right.

Measurement of the wage rate also differs across the studies. While Farber (1978b, 1978c), Dertouzos and Pencavel (1981), and Pencavel (1984) all use hourly wage rates, Carruth and Oswald (1985) are constrained by the available data to use of weekly earnings including allowances in kind. Hence the trade-off for the NUM in the British coal industry

---

[33] In other words, the NUM appears to have steeper indifference curves in (w,n) space than does the UMW.

[34] This is because membership figures were used in place of unobtainable employment figures for all the ITU locals (except for the *Cincinnati Post*, where employment figures were available).

is between this measure of earnings and employment.[35] In summary, however, while the extent to which unions care about the employment consequences of wage determination varies across unions, there is evidence for there being some sort of a trade-off in the industries so far studied.

It is important to bear in mind the assumption on which these studies were based, namely that the union is in a position to impose the wage level on a passive firm, which then determines the level of employment. This assumption conveniently simplifies the analysis by ignoring the means of reconciliation of the conflicting preferences of the union and management – the bargaining problem. For some applications, this assumption may well be appropriate, but none the less it remains a maintained hypothesis that has not been subject to testing. As Farber (1986: 1068) suggests, a problem with the use of this assumption is that the researcher may wrongly attribute moderation in wages to union concern for both wages *and* employment, whereas it may actually be the case that wage moderation has arisen from employer resistance to union demands. However, on a practical level 'it may not be possible to identify the form of the solution to the bargaining problem without assuming something about the structure of the union objective function', as we shall see in the following chapter.

4.6 The median voter model and models of endogenous membership

The monopoly union model developed in this chapter is based on the assumption of identical individuals and a fixed membership level. But should membership be included in the trade union objective function as a *variable* in addition to wages and employment? In this section we briefly consider reasons for allowing membership to be endogenous, and various ways in which membership can then be modelled.

The monopoly union model developed so far in this chapter predicts wage stickiness and employment fluctuations in response to demand fluctuations, provided that labour demand is less than the total number of union workers in the sector, given by t. However if, after a demand shock, labour demand increases so that the firm wants to hire $n > t$, then wages will increase, since the available pool of workers cannot be expanded beyond t. Since membership is important in this context, an interesting question is therefore: what are the determinants of membership size? There are other reasons for considering theories of the determinants of membership. As we shall see in chapter 6, some of the recent empirical literature on union wage gaps argues that union membership should be treated as endogenous in wage equations. However, in simultaneous equation empirical models of

---

[35] The microeconomic theory on which all the empirical specifications are based assumes that hours are exogenously fixed.

union wages and membership, the membership equation is typically specified in an *ad hoc* fashion. Any theories of the determinants of union membership will therefore shed some light on this issue. Union membership is also regarded in the 'insider–outsider' literature as being a potentially important influence on wages and employment, although as is made clear in Lindbeck and Snower (1988), the insider–outsider distinction can be made in the absence of trade unions.[36]

In most formal models of the trade union, it is assumed that the whole sector is unionised, and that the firm is therefore forced to negotiate with the union. Should it not do so, it cannot hire any labour. Yet this assumption begs the question (also raised in chapter 3): how did the union arrive at this position of power? If the union is able to control the supply of only a small proportion of the pool of available workers, then the firm can choose not to bargain over the surplus. It can simply hire nonunion labour. How then do unions achieve monopoly power over the supply of labour? Union membership density clearly plays a part in determining the power of the union to extract a share of any surplus from the firm. Consider a sector of the economy where the supply of labour is fixed, at least in the short run, perhaps because it takes time for labour to acquire the necessary skills. Here the level of membership affects the outside options available to the firm should it choose not to employ union labour. Thus one would expect to find a minimum critical level of membership for any sector, below which firms could refuse to recognise and bargain with the union. For formal models of trade union behaviour that explicitly take into account the size of the pool of nonunion workers, see Osborne (1984), Booth and Ulph (1990) and Naylor and Raaum (1993). Because the level of membership is crucial to the union's monopoly power, it is important for the union to consider how to maintain membership and attract workers at the margin. Thus some interesting questions are: why do individual workers join the union? How does membership enter into the objective function of unions? The answers to these questions may also provide an explanation of how unions can achieve a position of monopoly power.

One response in the literature to the observation that union membership is likely to evolve over time involves the dynamic formulation of the union monopoly model developed in this chapter. Typically, these dynamic models assume that membership in the current period is exactly equal to the level of employment in the previous period. Jones (1987) and Kidd and Oswald (1987) employ this assumption in a dynamic formulation of the monopoly union model with utilitarian preferences. They find that steady

---

[36] Insiders in this context are defined as experienced incumbent workers with protected employment, while outsiders are either unemployed or working in the informal or secondary sector of the labour market.

state employment is greater in the dynamic monopoly union model than in the usual static case. The intuition behind this result is straightforward: the *utilitarian* union is concerned about the sum of utilities of current and future members. Because union membership is conditional upon employment, the union prefers higher employment, and therefore membership, in steady state. It is also interesting that the model predicts that employment and membership will be perfectly positively correlated in steady state, a result that follows from the mechanistic assumption of the determinants of membership.

An interesting issue in the context of these dynamic models is whether or not the $\dot{n}$ locus is horizontal in (n,m) space, where $\dot{n}$ is the derivative of employment with respect to time. If it is horizontal, then membership and employment dynamics are independent, and membership can be neglected in analyses of employment dynamics, as suggested by Carruth and Oswald (1985). However Jones (1987) shows that this result is sensitive to the assumed form of the union objective function. If the instantaneous utility function of the union is both separable and linear in membership, as in the utilitarian union objective function, then the $\dot{n}$ locus is horizontal in (n,m) space. However, other plausible maximands do not produce this result. It is therefore clear that only with a very particular form of union maximand can membership dynamics be ignored when considering employment dynamics.

The assumption that this period's employment exactly determines next period's membership is a deterministic approach to membership, and one that is only likely to be valid, as Kidd and Oswald (1987) recognise, for a post-entry closed-shop union.[37] This approach to explaining the determinants of union membership does not rely on any microeconomic foundation as to why individuals might join a trade union in the absence of closed-shop agreements. This approach to membership is unsatisfactory for several reasons: first, because the closed shop is not a universal phenomenon in unionised labour markets, and is now illegal in Britain and in many US states with 'right-to-work' rulings. Secondly, historically where closed shops were legal, they were found only where the union had achieved sufficient power to force them on firms, and this power was itself related to membership density. Thus the union framework clearly requires extension to take into account other membership arrangements apart from the closed shop. For example, what happens to union membership when workers in the union sector can gain the benefits of union wages, which apply to all

---

[37] This is because the assumption does not allow $m_{t+1} > n_t$, where the subscripts denote time periods. But it might be the case that $m_{t+1} > n_t$ if union workers laid off this period retain union membership in the hope of getting a union job next period, as occurs with many pre-entry closed-shop unions.

covered workers irrespective of membership, without having to join the union? What are the membership implications of trade unions as hierarchical organisations, where the union executive and the rank-and-file workers may have conflicting goals? What happens to union models when employment is related to membership in a more complex fashion, for example when unions are characterised by seniority queues or 'last-in, first-out'?

Many writers have emphasised the potential conflict of interests between union leaders and membership (for example, Dunlop (1944), Ross (1948), Berkowitz (1954), Pencavel (1985), Farber (1986) and Faith and Reid (1987) *inter alia*). However, the only formal models of a trade union in this vein are Ashenfelter and Johnson (1969)[38] and Pemberton (1988). The essence of the Pemberton (1988) model is that the welfare of the union leadership is increasing in membership, while members' welfare is decreasing in membership. Various reasons have been advanced to explain why leaders might favour higher membership levels. Dunlop (1944:43) notes, for example, that 'The formal rationale of the union is to augment the economic welfare of its members; but a more vital institutional objective – survival and growth of the organisation – will take precedence whenever it comes into conflict with the formal purpose.' Pencavel (1985: 208) suggests that a larger membership is important in 'increasing the leader's constituency and ... furthering his larger aspirations in the trade union movement'. Pemberton (1988: 757), in addition, appeals to the literature modelling the firm as a bureaucracy in which bureaucrats are concerned with maximisation of firm size.

Another approach in the literature is to argue that unions should be modelled as political organisations, rather than as bureaucratic-style ones. One approach to modelling union membership in a democratic framework is to use a model in which the union's objectives are the outcome of the political process of majority voting.[39] This allows the use of the *median voter model* from social choice theory, which is based on the assumption that the leadership or executive is democratically elected by the voting population. Are trade unions democratically elected? Clegg (1980: 200–25) argues that British unions are quasi-democratic, for three principal reasons. First, there are often informal parties and factions competing for office, in spite of traditional union prejudices against organised opposition that might endanger union solidarity. Secondly, unions are partially democratic because of the growth over the past decades of workplace organisation in

---

[38] The Ashenfelter and Johnson (1969) model was developed for the analysis of strikes.

[39] We noted in section 4.2 that the union objective function can be viewed as some form of social welfare function, where the social planner is the trade union. When modelling union membership, some researchers have relied on heterogeneity of workers to explain why some workers unionise while others do not.

Britain, and the development of decentralised regional organisation, taking policy decisions closer to membership. Thirdly, the democratic argument is supported by the existence of workplace balloting, which has increased during the 1980s in Britain. Trade unions in the USA may also be regarded as quasi-democratic, because they require the approval of a majority of workers. Moreover, both union constitutions and legislation, in particular the 1959 Landrum–Griffin Act, impose democracy on trade unions (Freeman and Medoff, 1984: 18 and 212). For both the USA and Britain, democracy appears to work better at the local rather than the national level. In summary, it would appear likely that some unions fit an oligarchic model, while some can be characterised as democratic, and that both forms exist in the economy.

How can the *median voter model* be applied to shed some light on union wage, employment and membership determination? Suppose that the union consists of two sets of individuals, one set comprising union representatives who are responsible to another set – the rank-and-file membership. The union representatives are concerned with maximising the probability of re-election, as well as with the level of wages and employment. The membership is concerned only with wages and employment, and they are assumed to be differentiated from one another by one particular characteristic that does not affect their productivity. It is an insight of the median voter model of social choice theory that the union executive will maximise the utility of the *median voter* in order to be re-elected, under certain sufficient, but not necessary, assumptions.[40] Thus if the union executive were to choose an outcome lower than the median voter's preferred position, then a majority of voters will vote against this position. Conversely, if the executive chooses a higher outcome than the median's preferred position, then another majority of the electorate will vote against this higher outcome. Only the outcome preferred by the median voter will defeat all other potential outcomes in any sequence of pairwise elections. Note that in a representative democracy with two factions or parties, if the incumbent party were to choose an outcome different from the median voter's preferred position, it would be voted out and replaced by the competing faction at the next election. In order to maximise the probability of election, both parties will aim policy at the median voter.[41]

Since the median voter model introduces worker heterogeneity, what characterises differences in worker preferences? In the union literature using the median voter model, differences in union workers' preferences

---

[40] These are that there is a system of majority voting, that members vote sincerely, that there is a single decision, that individuals differ in only one characteristic at a time, and that preferences are single-peaked (Atkinson and Stiglitz, 1980: 302–7).

[41] See Atkinson and Stiglitz (1980) for further discussion.

have been assumed to arise from a variety of sources, including differences in age (Farber, 1978b), differing amounts of seniority which, it is argued, affect workers' job security (Grossman, 1983), differences in labour market opportunities (Booth, 1984), differing degrees of commitment to the union movement in a social custom style model (Booth and Chatterji, 1993a) and different preferences for a union-provided private good such as a grievance procedure (Booth and Chatterji, 1993b). We shall consider below in some detail a median voter model in which workers are differentiated by differences in their outside opportunities. We ignore the model with differences in seniority here, because of unresolved conceptual problems that remain with this model. In particular, the median voter model with seniority assumes that layoffs and hires are done on the basis of seniority, yet wages are unrelated to seniority. Given the prevalence of seniority wage scales in the union sector, this is an implausible assumption that might usefully be relaxed in future research.[42]

The monopoly union model can be readily extended to incorporate the median voter framework. The trade union continues to set the wage, but does so now by maximising the expected utility of the *median* member rather than that of the representative member. What is new in the model is the introduction of an equation explaining the individual decision to join a union. The model supposes that the individual worker decides to join the union if her expected utility from so doing exceeds that from abstaining. Workers are differentiated by some characteristic, and it is assumed that there is some exogenously given probability distribution of this characteristic across the workforce. The marginal worker is characterised by the condition that her expected utility from joining is equal to that from abstaining, for a given level of union-determined wages. Given that this *marginal* member determines the identity of the *median* member, the trade union then takes the median member as given, and sets wages to maximise the median's expected utility. The model generates a simultaneous equation system: membership at the margin is a function of the union set wage and other parameters, and union wages are a function of median membership. Once wages and membership have been determined in this simultaneous equation system, the firm sets employment unilaterally from the labour demand curve, as in the usual monopoly union model.

A very simple application of the median voter model to union wage and membership determination is given by Booth (1984). Suppose that workers are differentiated by alternative opportunities, given by b_j, $j=1,...,P$, where P is the total pool of available workers in the sector. Thus the b_j

---

[42] Interesting models of union seniority wage scales that are not in the median voter framework are given in Frank (1985) and Frank and Malcomson (1994). These models allow for both employment and wages to be related to seniority.

represent an index picking up differences between individuals due to different unemployment benefit entitlement, varying attitudes to work and leisure, alternative job opportunities and the income of other household members. The b_j are assumed to be uniformly distributed over the closed interval $[b_0, b_0 + h]$ according to the density function $f(b_j)$, where h is some positive constant. To generate an explicit solution, the model assumes specific functional forms for the utility function of workers, and for the labour demand curve. A union member in employment is assumed to have a constant elasticity utility function given by

$$V(w,a) = \frac{v}{\sigma}[w(1-a)]^\sigma \qquad \sigma < 1; \sigma \neq 0 \tag{30}$$

where w is the union wage, a is the subscription or other cost associated with union membership, v is some constant, and the parameter σ is a measure of risk aversion, since $-\frac{V''w}{V'} = 1 - \sigma$. An employed individual who is *not* a union member has utility $V(w) = \frac{v}{\sigma} w^\sigma$, which is equation (30) with $a = 0$. Any worker who is unemployed has a utility level given by

$$V(b) = \frac{v}{\sigma} b^\sigma \tag{31}$$

and it is assumed that unemployed unionists do not pay union dues. Labour demand is also assumed to be constant elasticity, and is given by

$$n = aw^{-\epsilon} \tag{32}$$

where a is some constant, and ϵ is our usual symbol for the elasticity of labour demand.[43] It is also assumed that firms employ union members before non-members when $n < P$. However, if employed union members are to be laid off, they are randomly selected from this group.

We now consider the individual membership decision. An individual worker takes the union-set wage as given and will join the union if the expected utility from so doing exceeds the utility from abstaining; this can be written generally as

$$\frac{n}{M} V(w,a) + \left(1 - \frac{n}{M}\right) > V(b_j) \tag{33}$$

where M here denotes the number of union members. Using our specific functional forms, we can simplify (33) to

$$w(1-a) > b_j \tag{34}$$

---

[43] We also assume that $\epsilon > 1$, in order to ensure a plausible solution to the union wage-setting function described below.

All individuals for whom inequality (34) holds will join the union. But we are particularly interested in the identity of the marginal member. The marginal member is defined as being an individual who is just indifferent to joining; that is, for the marginal member

$$w(1-a)=b_j \tag{35}$$

Equation (35) allows us to draw a line of indifference in (w,b) space, which represents the *membership curve*, given by

$$w=b_j/(1-a) \tag{36}$$

Because workers differ in b_j, which is increasing from $j=1$ to $j=P$, then the membership curve is increasing in (w,b) space as illustrated in figure 4.4. As b increases, the wage required to induce the jth individual to join is also increasing.

Membership of the union is given by $F(b_j)$, where F represents the cumulative distribution function. We can therefore write membership M of the union as

$$M=F(b_j)=\int_{b_0^j}^{b_j} f(b)db \tag{37}$$

where M is an increasing function of b_j.

How does the union executive set wages, given that the executive is facing a particular *median* member? The democratically elected union executive sets wages in order to maximise the probability of re-election, and it does this by maximising the expected utility of the median member. The relationship between median and marginal membership is given by $m=(M+1)/2$, where m denotes the median member and M is the marginal member, assuming an odd number of members. The union sets wages to maximise the expected utility of the median member given by

$$\max_w \mathrm{EU}_m=\frac{n}{M}V(w,a)+\left(1-\frac{n}{M}\right)V(b_m) \tag{38}$$

Insertion of the specific functional forms for utility and labour demand in (38), and maximisation, yields the union *wage-setting curve*:[44]

---

[44] The wage-setting curve (39) is obtained from the first-order condition from maximisation of (38) w.r.t. w, using our specific functional forms. Thus (38) can be rewritten, inserting these functional forms, as

$$\max_w (\mathrm{EU}_m)\cdot\frac{\sigma}{v}=\frac{a}{M}[w^{\sigma-\epsilon}(1-a)^\sigma-b^\sigma w^{-\epsilon}]+b^\sigma \tag{38a}$$

where we have omitted the subscript m from the b parameter for clarity. The first-order condition from maximisation of (38a) then yields

$$(\sigma-\epsilon)w^{\sigma-\epsilon-1}(1-a)^\sigma+\epsilon b^\sigma w^{-\epsilon-1}=0$$

which upon rearrangement yields (39) in the text. See Booth (1984) for the full derivation where constraints are also taken into account, and for the stability condition of the model.

$$w = \left(\frac{\epsilon}{\epsilon - \sigma_m}\right)^{1/\sigma_m} \cdot \frac{b_m}{(1-a)} \tag{39}$$

The union wage-setting curve is also illustrated in figure 4.4, and is positively sloped in (w,b) space. Equilibrium union wages and membership are given from the intersection of the membership curve and the wage-setting curve at w^*, b^*. The precise level of membership is obtained from substituting b^* into (37). The level of employment is then determined by the firm from the labour demand curve, for the equilibrium wage w^*. Comparative static predictions of this model can then be generated by examining how changes in the exogenous parameters of the model shift either or both of the membership and wage-setting curves.

The median voter model has provided a microeconomic foundation for the simultaneous determination of wages, membership and employment. But the union in the model above is effectively a closed shop, since union workers are hired before nonunion workers. Some recent research has focused on wage and membership determination using the median voter model in an open-shop framework.[45]

While all the median voter models of union wages, employment and membership assume a heterogeneous workforce, it must be emphasised that heterogeneity of membership is not a necessary condition for endogenising membership. Nor do all models with heterogeneous membership use the median voter model. (See, for example, Booth (1985) and Naylor (1989, 1990), who model membership in a social custom framework without explicitly modelling wage determination, and Naylor and Raaum (1993) who model wages and membership determination in a model that does not appeal to any social choice framework like the median voter model.)

4.7 Conclusion

A major purpose of this chapter was to outline a popular model in the trade union literature – the monopoly union model. Another goal, however, was to make the reader aware of some of the problems facing economists in constructing an analytical model of a unionised labour market, wherein it is necessary to abstract from the diversity of institutions, procedures and outcomes that characterise industrial relations in a unionised economy. In any labour market, there are many sets of actors, each with its own power base and organisational structure, and with possibly competing aims. As each set of agents pursues its own objectives, there is scope for conflict. The economist needs to model not only the objectives of the relevant actors, but also the means by which these potentially conflicting objectives are

[45] See Booth and Chatterji (1993a) and references therein.

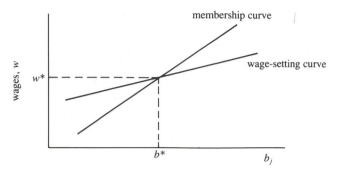

Figure 4.4. Wages and union membership in the median voter model.

resolved. The various agents are concerned both with procedures *and* with end results. Unions and firms have been historically concerned not simply with outcomes such as wage and employment levels, hours and manning arrangements, but also with procedures such as the level at which bargaining occurs, the extent of consultation, and the role of custom and practice. Economists focus principally on outcomes, which are the predictions arising from the economists' models; in constructing economic models, the model-maker faces a trade-off between tractability and realism. While procedural arrangements may well impinge on these economic variables, and may also provide an additional rationale for union existence and viability, it seems reasonable to restrict our attention as economists to *outcomes*, since these are vital to understanding the workings of the economy. (The processes can be treated as constraints within which the various agents operate.) In this sense, the economists' approach is more delimited than that of the industrial relations specialists, who are able to focus on individual trade unions' processes and outcomes. But at the same time the economists' analytical approach is also broader, since in trying to understand the way the economy works, it is searching for generalisations rather than analysing particular cases.

In the construction of a model of the unionised labour market, this chapter has considered the objectives of two principal actors – the union and management. Since the objectives of the trade union and management may be conflicting, it was also necessary to consider how conflicts might be resolved, within the constraints provided by the political, legal and product-market environment. In sections 4.2 and 4.3, we considered ways of modelling the differing objectives of the trade union and the firm. We then considered, in section 4.4, the simplest method of reconciling the objectives of the trade union and management: the monopoly union model. This method did not rely on any bargaining between the two parties. Instead, it supposed that the union is able to act as a monopolist in the supply of labour, and to impose a wage rate on the firm; the firm, however, retains its managerial prerogative to determine the number of workers employed at the union wage. In section 4.5, we examined empirical work on trade union objectives within this simple framework, while in section 4.6 we presented a simple median voter model that allowed for union membership to be endogenous in the framework of the monopoly union model.

In the following chapter, we will consider more sophisticated methods of reconciling the differing preferences of union and management, using a bargaining approach. We will also show how the monopoly union model is nested, as a special case, within a simple bargaining model.

Appendix 4A

Proof of proposition 4.1

The union chooses the wage rate w to maximise the expected utility of a representative worker, given by:

$$\max_{w} \text{EU} = \phi(w,b,\theta) = \theta \frac{n(w)}{t} [u(w) - u(b)] + u(b) \tag{A1}$$

Notice that labour demand is now written as $\theta n(w)$, where θ is a shift parameter and w is the real wage. (The shift parameter θ is introduced here to provide a proof for proposition 4.2 as well as proposition 4.1.) If the number of workers demanded at each wage rate increases, owing to, for example, a product demand increase, then we can think of θ increasing and shifting the labour demand curve to the right. The first-order condition for a maximum is

$$\phi_w(w,b,\theta) = \theta n'(w)[u(w) - u(b)] + \theta n(w)u'(w) = 0 \tag{A2}$$

where $\phi_w = \partial\phi/\partial w$. Multiplication of both sides of (A2) by w and rearrangement yields

$$\frac{-wn'(w)}{n(w)} = \frac{wu'(w)}{[u(w) - u(b)]} \tag{A3}$$

where

$$\epsilon = \frac{-wn'(w)}{n(w)}$$

For the second-order condition for a maximum to be satisfied, the following must hold. Rewrite (A1) more generally as

$$\max_{w} U = U[w,n(w)] \tag{A4}$$

and the first-order condition can be written as

$$U_1[w,n(w)] + U_2[w,n(w)]n'(w) = 0 \tag{A5}$$

where $U_1 = \partial U/\partial w$ and $U_2 = \partial U/\partial n$. Differentiation of (A5) with respect to w yields the second-order condition

$$U_{11} + 2U_{12}n'(w) + U_{22}n'(w)^2 + U_2 n''(w) < 0 \tag{A6}$$

where the first three terms are the quadratic form which must be negative for a maximum (see Chiang (1984), for example).

Proof of Proposition 4.2

The first part of this proposition is clear from (A2) above, where θ cancels out of the first-order condition for a maximum. The proof for the second part of proposition 4.2 is as follows. Equation (A2) represents the monopoly union optimal wage equation. We can therefore totally differentiate (A2) with respect to w and b to find the impact of a small increase in alternative opportunities b on the optimal wage. Thus

$$\phi_{ww}dw + \phi_{wb}db = 0$$

and

$$dw/db = -\phi_{wb}/\phi_{ww} \tag{A7}$$

For a maximum, $\phi_{ww} < 0$. Hence the sign of dw/db is given by the sign of ϕ_{wb}.

$$\phi_{wb} = -n'(w)u'(b) > 0 \tag{A8}$$

Thus the optimal union wage increases as alternative opportunities improve.

The third part of proposition 4.2 follows simply from the fact that t does not appear in (A2) and thus $\phi_{wt} = 0$. Changing the sector's size has no effect on union wages at the optimum.

Finally, note that if the impact of θ is modelled as $n = n(w,\theta)$ instead of the isoelastic specification in (A2), then the optimal union wage may rise, fall, or remain unaltered as θ increases. (The reader can verify this by substituting $n(w,\theta)$ into (A2) and proceeding to find the sign of $\phi_{w\theta}$.)

5 Bargaining models of the trade union

5.1 Introduction

The previous chapter examined the modelling of trade union preferences and managerial preferences, and a method of reconciliation of these preferences – the monopoly union model. In the monopoly union model, the labour union is assumed to have the power to impose its preferred wage policy on the firm, which then determines employment from its labour demand curve. While some researchers have argued that this model is a reasonable approximation for particular industries at particular times (for example, the US bituminous coal industry over the period 1948 to 1973 (Farber, 1978b, 1978c)), observation suggests that wages are more frequently *bargained over* by trade unions and management. Once it is assumed that wages are determined by bargaining between labour and management, we need to add to the model of the previous chapter a means of determining a solution to the bargaining process. When the firm and the union are bargaining over wages, they are in a bilateral monopoly situation, in which a single seller of labour confronts a single buyer. There is a single seller of labour in that the union controls the supply of labour to the firm, and nonunion workers cannot be easily or costlessly substituted by the firm for union workers. There is effectively also a single buyer of labour; if the firm locks out, or dismisses workers, they face costs in moving to another job, lost specific training investments, and perhaps the prospect of being unemployed. In such a bilateral monopoly situation, it is well known that the outcome is indeterminate, unless a further solution concept is introduced (see appendix 3A).

An important element in this bargaining process is the ability of each party to impose costs on the other party if it refuses to bargain and engages in a strike or lockout. We saw in chapter 2 that the right to strike differs in the USA and Britain. The situation in Britain, following the Thatcher government's trade union legislation over the 1980s, is that strikes are legal only if they result from disputes between workers and their own employer, and only after a secret majority ballot of membership. All secondary industrial action is illegal. However, in the USA, workers' legal right to strike is more curtailed. It is legal to strike over recognition issues provided that, before the strike is thirty days old, workers have filed a petition for National Labor Relations Board (NLRB) election. Once the union is recognised, workers can strike in support of contract demands provided the strike is confined to 'mandatory' bargaining issues. Once a collective bargain has been agreed, the contract can only be enforced by arbitration; it is illegal to strike during the period of the contract, which is typically three years. In contrast, British workers can be called on strike at any time by their union, provided the action is not secondary, and that the balloting requirements have been met. The fact that strikes are actually relatively infrequent does not mean that the strike or lockout weapon is not important: it is the *threat of withdrawal* that counts, as we shall see in a formal model below. What induces the two parties to bargain is the threat of facing costs imposed by the other party.[1]

What do the two parties bargain over? In chapter 4, we saw that bargaining typically takes place over a number of issues. For tractability in modelling union behaviour, researchers usually concatenate wages and other forms of employee compensation, such as fringe benefits, under the single heading of wages. We also noted in the previous chapter that union preferences appear to include employment as well as wages. But is employment also a bargaining *issue*? For the majority of unions, the answer appears to be no. It is rare to find instances of union–firm bargaining over both wages and employment. Oswald (1993) produces evidence from a survey of the largest British and US trade unions that employment is almost always set unilaterally by the firm, and that in US contracts this is explicitly set out in a 'management rights' clause. Oswald and Turnbull (1985) analyse data from the first Workplace Industrial Relations Survey (WIRS) and a sample of British collective bargaining units. They conclude that 'Unions do not bargain routinely about the level of total employment in the firm or sector ... Except in special cases it is the employer who has the unilateral right to fix the total number of jobs' (Oswald and Turnbull, 1985: 82).

Some researchers have argued that, although unions and management do not bargain over employment directly, they do so indirectly through bargaining over rules such as 'manning' levels (by which is meant capital-to-labour or labour-to-output ratios), which affect the level of employment

---

[1] Moene (1988), in a game-theoretic framework, examines how the outcome of bargaining will vary with the type of industrial action, viz. work-to-rule, 'go-slow', wild-cat strikes and official strikes or lockouts.

(McDonald and Solow, 1981; Johnson, 1990; Clark, 1990).[2] However, it is not clear that bargaining over the capital-to-labour ratio can be interpreted as bargaining over employment. This is because even where the capital-to-labour ratio is specified, the firm is free to vary capital (not bargained over) and the number of shifts per machine (Layard *et al.*, 1991: 96). An alternative interpretation of bargaining over the capital-to-labour ratio is that it represents bargaining over *work effort*, since the more workers per machine, the lower the effort required of each individual worker. According to this view, the bargain should then be modelled as occurring over wages and effort, with the level of employment remaining the managers' prerogative.[3] Unions may also affect employment indirectly through bargaining over the amount of redundancy pay, which affects the costs of labour turnover; therefore redundancy payments affect firms' hiring and firing decisions (Booth, 1993).

We will return to the issue of bargaining over employment in section 5.4 below, but for the moment suppose that the union and the firm bargain only over employee compensation, represented by wages. Since the two parties to the bargain are in a situation of bilateral monopoly, we need to impose additional structure on the model in order to generate a determinate solution. What is at issue is the division of the available surplus, or 'cake', between the two parties to the bargain. There are two broad approaches to modelling bargaining behaviour – the *axiomatic* approach, and the more recent *game-theoretic* approach. In section 5.2, we outline each of these solution concepts. Under certain conditions, these approaches generate identical predictions in spite of the fact that they proceed from very different assumptions. In section 5.3, we will use one of these solution concepts to examine the case where the union and the firm bargain over the wage rate w. Since management is assumed to retain the right to determine employment n unilaterally, this is referred to as the 'right-to-manage' model. A special case of this model, where the union has all the power, turns out to be the monopoly union model of the previous chapter.

However, the right-to-manage model turns out to be inefficient, in the sense that at least one party to the bargain could be made better off by adding employment to the bargaining agenda. Thus in section 5.4 we describe the efficient contract model, where the firm and the union simultaneously bargain over wages and employment. In section 5.5, the right-to-manage and the efficient bargaining models are compared, to try to determine which is the appropriate model of the unionised sector.

It has already been noted that an important element of the bargaining

---

[2] Table 4.1 shows that just over half of British manual and non-manual plants bargain over 'manning' issues or staffing levels.

[3] Models in this vein include Rosen (1989), Nickell *et al.*, (1992) and Moreton (1993).

process is the ability of one party to the bargain to impose costs on the other party, by withdrawing labour or locking out the workforce. Section 5.6 therefore examines approaches to modelling strike incidence and wage determination.

The analysis so far has examined wage and employment determination without considering how standard hours of work are determined. Yet unions do negotiate with firms and employers associations about standard hours of work; this issue is therefore examined in section 5.7. Conclusions are given in section 5.8.

5.2 Two approaches to modelling bargaining behaviour

This section considers two broad approaches to the problem of modelling bargaining behaviour – the axiomatic approach, and the game-theoretic approach. The *axiomatic approach* is static, and focuses on the outcome of the bargaining process. It supposes that the outcome must satisfy certain principles or axioms, which might be established by an objective arbitrator called in to resolve the dispute between the two parties. Essentially, this approach aims to find the weakest set of axioms under which a unique outcome can be found. Since the objective arbitrator is necessarily making interpersonal comparisons of the utility of each of the two parties, the axiomatic approach is regarded as normative. It can be shown that the satisfaction of four axioms that might be adopted by an independent arbitrator (invariance, Pareto efficiency, independence of irrelevant alternatives, and anonymity or symmetry) requires the maximisation of equation (1) (see appendix 5A). Let v_i be the utility payoff to bargainer i, and $\bar{v}_i$ be the utility payoff to bargainer i should no agreement be reached, sometimes known as the fall-back or status quo position. If the bargain is over wages, v_i is a function of the level of wages. Nash (1950, 1953) showed that $\mathbf{v}^*(v_1^*, v_2^*)$ satisfies these four axioms if $\mathbf{v}^*$ maximises the following:

$$\max_{v_1, v_2} \Phi = (v_1 - \bar{v}_1)(v_2 - \bar{v}_2) \qquad (1)$$

subject to $v_i \geq \bar{v}_i$, $i = 1, 2$. This is called the *Nash bargain*. If the axiom of anonymity is relaxed, satisfaction of the first three axioms requires the maximisation of the *generalised Nash bargain*:

$$\max_{v_1, v_2} \Phi = (v_1 - \bar{v}_1)^{\beta_1}(v_2 - \bar{v}_2)^{\beta_2} \qquad (2)$$

subject to $v_i \geq \bar{v}_i$, $i = 1, 2$, for some $\beta_1, \beta_2 \geq 0$. If the total size of the cake (or surplus) is unity, it is shown in appendix 5A that

$$v_i = \bar{v}_i + \frac{\beta_i}{(\beta_1 + \beta_2)} \cdot (1 - \bar{v}_1 - \bar{v}_2) \qquad (3)$$

The first term on the right-hand side of (3) is the disagreement payoff or status quo position, while the second term is a fraction $\beta_i/(\beta_1 + \beta_2)$ of the surplus $[1 - \bar{v}_1 - \bar{v}_2]$.[4] Finally, note that if $\beta_2 = (1 - \beta_1)$, and $0 \le \beta_1 \le 1$, then the fraction of the surplus going to the ith party is given by β_i.

Two problems with the axiomatic approach are as follows. First, there is no immediate economic interpretation of the parameter β. While researchers in this area often argue that β represents the relative bargaining strength of the union, this is rather an *ad hoc* interpretation. Secondly, the interpretation of the payoff in the event of disagreement, $\bar{v}_i$, is not straightforward. Suppose the union and the firm cannot agree on the bargaining outcome. Here it is reasonable to assume in the short term that the payoff for the union is what its members would receive while on strike, while the firm's payoff is any profits it may receive while production is shut down. This is termed the *inside option*. But if disagreement continues in the longer term, each of the two parties is likely to seek to replace its original bargaining partner and engage in some alternative economic activity. This is the *outside option*. Since the two options may be different, the problem arises as to how to incorporate this in the generalised Nash bargain.

One response to these problems is provided by a *game-theoretic approach* that involves modelling the bargaining *process* in order to determine the actual outcome (Rubinstein, 1982; Binmore, Rubinstein and Wolinsky, 1986; Sutton, 1986). It can be shown (see appendix 5A) that, in a simple alternating offers model with no uncertainty, the game-theoretic solution is the same as the generalised Nash bargaining solution. But the advantage of the game-theoretic method is that an economic interpretation can be given to β, namely that it represents the relative eagerness of the two parties to reach an agreement. The discount rate reflects the eagerness of a party to attain a settlement, and this can in principle be measured using economic information.

5.3 The right-to-manage model

In this model, the union and the firm are assumed to bargain over any surplus in order to determine w. The firm continues to choose the number of workers it wishes to employ once wages have been determined by the

---

[4] It is straightforward to show that the payoff of bargainer i, given by v_i, is increasing in β_i and $\bar{v}_i$, and decreasing in β_j and $\bar{v}_j$. To see this, partially differentiate (3) with respect to β_i, $\bar{v}_i$, β_j and $\bar{v}_j$. This yields

$$\partial v_i/\partial \bar{v}_i = 1 - [\beta_i/(\beta_1 + \beta_2)] > 0$$

$$\partial v_i/\partial \beta_i = (1 - \bar{v}_1 - \bar{v}_2)\beta_j/(\beta_1 + \beta_2)^2 > 0$$

$$\partial v_i/\partial \bar{v}_j = - [\beta_i/(\beta_1 + \beta_2)] < 0$$

$$\partial v_i/\partial \beta_j = - (1 - \bar{v}_1 - \bar{v}_2)\beta_i/(\beta_1 + \beta_2)^2 < 0$$

bargaining process. It turns out that the monopoly union model is simply a special case of the right-to-manage model, with the firm's bargaining power set to zero. The solution concept widely used in the literature is the generalised Nash bargaining solution, discussed above. According to this approach, wages are determined by maximisation of the product of each agent's gains from reaching a bargain, weighted by their respective bargaining strengths. Define a status quo or fall-back point for each party as its position if no bargain is reached. For the firm, the status quo position is zero. This is because, if it does not reach a bargain with the unionised workforce, it cannot obtain any other workers, since there are no nonunion workers in the sector. Therefore the firm's net gain is simply its profits function, $pq(n) - wn$. What is the net gain for the union? Its status quo position for a representative member is $u(b)$, since that is what a member will receive if no bargain is reached. But if there is a bargain, the expected utility of a member is given by:

$$\mathrm{EU} = \frac{n}{t} u(w) + (1-n)u(b) \qquad u'(w) > 0; \; u''(w) \leq 0 \tag{4}$$

The *net* gain to the union is thus (4) minus $u(b)$, which yields $[u(w) - u(b)]n/t$. We can now write the generalised Nash bargaining solution (the product of the weighted net gains to each party) as:[5]

$$\max_{w} B = \left\{ \frac{n}{t}[u(w) - u(b)] \right\}^{\beta} \{pq(n) - wn\}^{(1-\beta)} \tag{5}$$

where β measures the bargaining strength of the union, and $0 \leq \beta \leq 1$. Thus if $\beta = 1$, the outcome is the monopoly union model, since the last term in squiggly brackets in (5) becomes unity. The solution to this bargaining problem is contained in the following proposition.

Proposition 5.1.

Wages will be set by the union and the firm such that the proportional marginal benefit to both parties from a unit increase in wages is exactly equal to the proportional marginal cost to each party, weighted by each party's bargaining strength. This is given by the first-order condition for a maximum from (4):

$$\frac{\beta w u'(w)}{u(w) - u(b)} = \beta \epsilon + \frac{(1-\beta)wn}{pq(n) - wn} \tag{6}$$

where $\epsilon = -n'(w)w/n$, the wage elasticity of labour demand.

Proof. See appendix 5B.

---

[5] In the notation of equations (1) and (2), both v_1 and v_2 are functions of the endogenous variable, w. For the union, $\bar{v}_1 = u(b)$ and for the firm $\bar{v}_2 = 0$.

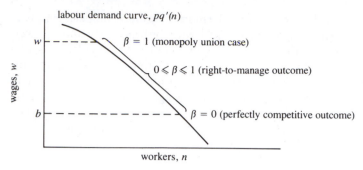

Figure 5.1. The right-to-manage outcome. Note that the monopoly union model is a special case of the right-to-manage bargaining model where $\beta = 1$, while the perfectly competitive model is a special case where $\beta = 0$.

The left-hand side of (6) represents the proportional marginal benefit to the bargain from the proportional increase in the wage. The benefit from a wage increase is felt only by the union, and thus it is weighted by the union's bargaining power β. The first term on the right-hand side is the union's proportional marginal cost (the percentage reduction in employment due to the proportional wage increase) weighted by the parameter representing union power, β. The second term on the right-hand side represents the firm's proportional marginal cost weighted by the firm's power $(1 - \beta)$.

    Note that the equation in proposition 5.1 (the right-to-manage model) differs from that in proposition 4.1 (the monopoly union model) in two respects. We rewrite the equation for the solution to the monopoly union model of proposition 4.1 as:

$$wu'(w)/[u(w) - u(b)] = \epsilon \qquad\qquad (7)$$

Now, comparing equations (6) and (7), note the following. First, the surplus is being shared between the union and the firm in accordance with their relative bargaining strengths, given by the parameter β. Thus if the firm has *all* the power, $\beta = 0$, and equation (6) becomes zero. The wage is then simply the alternative wage b. What happens if the union has all the power? Here $\beta = 1$, and the union is able to extract all the surplus; equation (6) collapses to equation (7), that is, the right-to-manage model collapses to the monopoly union model. For $0 < \beta < 1$, the employment and wage outcome will lie on the labour demand curve anywhere between the monopoly union extreme and the competitive outcome, as illustrated in figure 5.1.

    The second respect in which the right-to-manage outcome of (6) differs from the monopoly union outcome of (7) is in the inclusion of an extra term on the right-hand side of (6), representing the proportional marginal cost of a wage increase to the firm. The inclusion of this term in the optimal solution for the right-to-manage model reflects the fact that bargaining occurs between both parties over w, and therefore the impact of a wage rise on the firm's profits must also be taken into account.

What are the comparative static predictions of the right-to-manage model? The optimal wage is given by (6) in proposition 5.1. It has already been noted that an increase in union strength leads to a movement up the labour demand curve, and the bargained wage therefore increases with β, while employment is reduced. What impact might the business cycle have on the negotiated wage? It is clear from (6) that alternative opportunities b affect only union preferences. As b increases, we have seen from the monopoly union model that wages increase, and this result holds for the right-to-manage model too. As product demand increases, we have seen from the monopoly union model that if the labour demand curve shifts rightwards isoelastically, then wages are independent of demand fluctuations, which will affect only employment. This result also holds for the right-to-manage model. However, when considering the impact of the business cycle in the right-to-manage model, there is an extra effect working through the parameter β which needs to be considered. For if union bargaining strength is weakened during a recession, the negotiated wage will decline down the labour demand curve, and employment will increase. A decline in b will cause a similar movement down the labour demand curve, while an isoelastic fall in labour demand causes the demand curve to shift to the left. Wages will decline, but the employment impact will depend on the relative strengths of the positive impact through the fall in b and β, and the negative impact through the demand shift.

Finally, note that the empirically testable predictions of the right-to-manage model are the same as for the monopoly union model, with the addition of the prediction that variables proxying union strength will affect wages directly, but not employment.

Is the wage and employment outcome of the right-to-manage model Pareto-efficient? Or can at least one of the two parties to the bargain be made better off by shifting to some other (w,n) pair? Consider the monopoly union model in figure 5.2, which shows isoprofit curves representing different levels of profits for the firm, as well as union indifference curves. The isoprofit curves are labelled IP_0 and IP_1 (with the higher subscript denoting a higher level of profits) and the union indifference curves are denoted by IC, with expected utility increasing as the union moves northeast. Suppose that the equilibrium predicted by the model is $(\tilde{w},\tilde{n})$ at point A. Then it is clear that the union could be made better off while keeping the firm on the same isoprofit curve by shifting to point B. Alternatively, the firm could shift to a higher isoprofit curve, while keeping the union on the

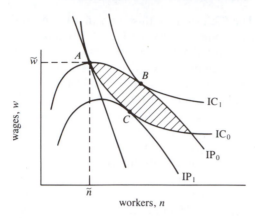

Figure 5.2. Inefficiency of the monopoly union model. Points *B* and *C* Pareto-dominate point *A*.

original indifference curve, through a move to point *C*. And *both* parties could be made better off by a shift from A on the labour demand curve to any point in the shaded area.

Recall that points on the labour demand curve represent the outcome of bargaining between the union and the firm over wages alone, leaving the firm with the right to determine employment. Yet positions on the labour demand curve are Pareto-*inefficient*. Either the union or the firm or both could be made better off by bargaining over *employment as well as wages*, that is, by a shift from a point such as *A* to *B* or *C* or anywhere in the shaded area. Note, that bargaining over employment as well as wages will not guarantee that the outcome of *any* bargaining process is efficient (although for the assumed Nash bargain the outcome does turn out to be efficient). Efficiency in the context of this model is where the marginal rates of substitution of employment for wages, for both the union and the firm, are equal. We will examine this more rigorously below.

5.4 The efficient bargaining model

In this model, the union and the firm simultaneously determine wages *and* employment. There is considerable evidence to suggest that unions and firms do *not* bargain simultaneously over wages and employment. Yet this approach has assumed importance in the literature because of its efficiency properties. We have seen that the right-to-manage model (and its special case, the monopoly union model) represent inefficient results, in the sense that at least one of the two parties involved can be made better off without making the other worse off. If both the union and the firm were to bargain simultaneously about wages and employment, the outcome would be efficient in that at least one could be made better off by shifting from the monopoly union case, without making the other worse off. The fact that this does not appear to happen in practice suggests that there may be something economists are missing in their modelling here, and we shall discuss this issue further at the end of the section. It must also be emphasised that the wage and employment outcome predicted by the efficient bargaining model is *not* efficient from the viewpoint of society as a whole.

In general, for efficiency we require only that one party's welfare be maximised, subject to any arbitrarily fixed level of welfare of the other. It is therefore possible to characterise an efficient outcome simply by considering union and managerial preferences, without imposing a particular bargaining structure. Although this does not yield a *unique* outcome, it serves to illustrate the necessary conditions for efficiency. In figure 5.2, point A is Pareto-dominated by points B and C, where the slopes of the isoprofit and union indifference curves are equal. We will prove this result formally below. It will also be seen that all possible points of tangency between isoprofit and union indifference curves trace out a locus of (w,n) pairs, known as the *contract curve*. Later we will use the generalised Nash bargain to produce a determinate outcome on the contract curve.

Since, for efficiency, we require only that one party's welfare be maximised, subject to any arbitrarily fixed level of welfare of the other, an efficient bargain over (w,n) solves:

$$\max_{w,n} pq(n) - wn \qquad n \geq 0; \; w \geq b$$

subject to (8)

$$\frac{n}{t}[u(w) - u(b)] + u(b) = \bar{U}$$

From the first-order conditions is obtained the following result.

Proposition 5.2.

An efficient (w,n) pair is given by equating the marginal rates of substitution of employment for wages for the union and the firm. Thus in equilibrium

$$pq'(n) - w = -\frac{[u(w) - u(b)]}{u'(w)} \tag{9}$$

Proof. See appendix 5B.

Equation (9) states that an efficient wage and employment outcome is one where the slopes of an isoprofit curve and an indifference curve are the same, as for example at point C in figure 5.2. The slope of the isoprofit curve is given by the left-hand side of (9) (equation (15) in chapter 4), while the right-hand side of (9) represents the slope of the union indifference curve (equation (10) in chapter 4). Note that in (8) we chose to maximise the firm's profits subject to the union achieving an arbitrarily given level of utility $\bar{U}$. We could also have chosen to maximise union expected utility subject to the firm achieving an arbitrarily given level of profits $\bar{\pi}$. The equilibrium condition is still given by (9). The contract curve is defined as the locus of all pairs (w,n) satisfying (9). We can rewrite (9) as

$$pq'(n) = w - [u(w) - u(b)]/u'(w) \tag{10}$$

From (10), note first that the value of the marginal product of labour is less than the wage rate, by an amount that is equal to the union marginal rate of substitution of employment for wages. Hence the contract curve must lie to the right of the labour demand curve for $w > b$. Secondly, if $w = b$, then (10) shows that $pq'(n) = w$, the perfectly competitive result. Thus the contract curve and the labour demand curve coincide where $w = b$.

The slope of the contract curve in (w,n) space is found by totally differentiating (10) with respect to w and n, which yields:

$$dw/dn = \frac{pq''(n)u'(w)^2}{[u''(w)][u(w) - u(b)]} \tag{11}$$

Proof. See proof of proposition 5.2 in appendix 5B.

What does (11) tell us about the slope of the contract curve? For the competitive firm to generate a surplus, its production function must be characterised by decreasing returns, as noted in chapter 3 ($q''(n) < 0$). Risk-averse members are characterised by a concave (indirect) utility of income function ($u''(w) < 0$). Thus from (11) the slope of the contract curve is positive. The intuitive explanation of this positive slope is as follows. As wages are increased above the competitive level, any members who are laid off have an increasing opportunity cost of being unemployed. The union therefore insures members against this risk by bargaining for increased employment (Ulph and Ulph, 1990a). Notice that if members were risk-neutral ($u''(w) = 0$), the contract curve would be vertical; members are not offered insurance against the risk of being unemployed. If members were risk-loving ($u''(w) > 0$), the contract curve would be negatively sloped. These possibilities are illustrated in figure 5.3.

Since for efficiency we require only that one party's welfare be maximised subject to any arbitrarily fixed level of welfare of the other, any point on the contract curve in the shaded area or 'core' in figure 5.2 represents an

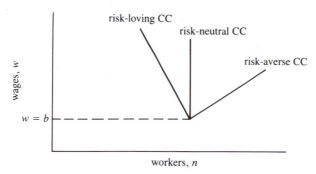

Figure 5.3. The contract curve under various assumptions about risk.

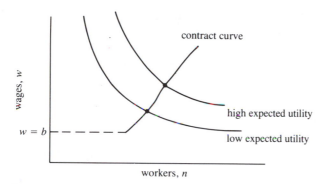

Figure 5.4. The contract curve.

efficient outcome for a particular arbitrarily fixed level of welfare of one
agent. Clearly, if the firm were maximising profits subject to a very high
level of expected utility for the union, the outcome would be to the far
north-east of the contract curve, as shown in figure 5.4. However, if the firm
were maximising profits subject to a low level of expected utility for the
union, the outcome would lie on the contract curve close to $w = b$.

So far, in order to determine where on the contract curve a unique (w,n)
outcome will lie, we have to rely on the arbitrarily fixed level of welfare of
one of the parties, and then examine the maximum welfare of the other
party subject to this constraint. This obviously cannot explain what unique
(w,n) pair might arise from union–firm bargaining behaviour. We therefore
now add to the model a means of determining a *particular* solution to the
bargaining process. We use the generalised Nash bargaining solution (used
also for the right-to-manage model), modified to allow for bargaining over
both w and n. Thus the generalised Nash bargaining solution $\tilde{B}$ is now
written as:

$$\max_{n,w} \tilde{B} = \left\{\frac{n}{t}[u(w) - u(b)]\right\}^{\beta} \{pq(n) - wn\}^{(1-\beta)} \tag{12}$$

The solution to this maximisation problem is as follows:

Proposition 5.3.

The union and the firm under the generalised Nash bargain will set w and n such that the wage is equal to the sum of the average and marginal revenue products of labour, weighted respectively by the union's bargaining strength β, and the firm's bargaining strength $(1-\beta)$. This will lie on the contract curve. The equilibrium is characterised by

$$w = \beta pq(n)/n + (1-\beta)pq'(n) \qquad \text{rent division curve} \tag{13}$$

and

$$w = pq'(n) + [u(w) - u(b)]/u'(w) \qquad \text{contract curve} \tag{14}$$

Proof. See appendix 5B.

Equations (13) and (14) represent the first-order conditions from maximisation of (12) with respect to w and n. Notice that $pq(n)/n$ represents the value of the average product of labour, while $pq'(n)$ is the value of the marginal product of labour. Equation (13) will be referred to as the *rent division curve*, while (14) is the by now familiar equation for the contract curve. The rent division curve is a weighted average of the average and marginal revenue product of labour curves, with the weights given by the relative bargaining strengths of each party (β and $(1-\beta)$). The rent division curve is negatively sloped in (w,n) space. This follows from the concavity of the production function $pq(n)$. Although both the average and marginal revenue product of labour curves are positive everywhere in the relevant domain of n, both are decreasing as employment increases. This is illustrated in figure 5.5. The equilibrium wage and employment levels w^* and n^* are given by the intersection of the rent division curve and the contract curve. If the union has no power ($\beta = 0$), then the rent division curve collapses to the labour demand curve (MRPL), and $w = pq'(n)$ – the perfectly competitive outcome. If the firm has no power ($\beta = 1$), the rent division curve becomes the average revenue product of labour curve (ARPL).

What are the predictions of the efficient bargaining model for wage and employment behaviour during the business cycle?[6] First, consider the

[6] The analysis here follows the approach of McDonald and Solow (1981). See Leontief (1946) for an early account of the efficient bargaining model.

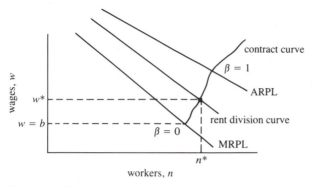

Figure 5.5. The generalised Nash bargaining outcome where bargaining occurs over wages and employment.

impact of union strength, β. It has already been noted that if β increases, we move north-east up the contract curve, and the rent division curve shifts right towards the ARPL curve. Thus negotiated wages and employment will rise with an increase in union strength. Secondly, it can be shown that an increase in alternative opportunities b leads to a leftwards shift of the contract curve, as illustrated in figure 5.6a. However, the rent division curve remains unaffected by changes in b (since b does not enter equation (12)). As figure 5.6a shows, the negotiated wage will increase, but by less than the full amount of the increase in b. Thus the opportunity cost of not being employed in the union sector has fallen, because the difference between the union wage and alternative remuneration has shrunk. The union can now offer its membership less insurance against the risk of not being employed in the union sector. Thus negotiated employment falls.

Finally, it can be shown that an improvement in the product market leading to an increase in labour demand will cause the contract curve to shift out and the rent division curve (RDC) also to shift rightwards.[7] This will have an ambiguous effect on wages, but will increase employment unambiguously, as illustrated in figure 5.6b. With isoelastic demand shifts, the wage rate will be rigid.

Note that, as we also found for the right-to-manage model, the employment effects of an improvement in alternative opportunities and in the product market work in opposite directions. It is likely that the product market effect will dominate, for when there is limited mobility between sectors, and union workers typically receive unemployment benefits when

---

[7] For a formal proof, see McDonald and Solow (1981). Suppose that there is a shift parameter θ in front of the ARPL and MRPL curves in (13) and (14). Then clearly an increase in θ will lead to an outward shift of the ARPL and MRPL curves. As shown in figure 5.6b, this causes both the contract curve and the rent division curve to shift rightwards.

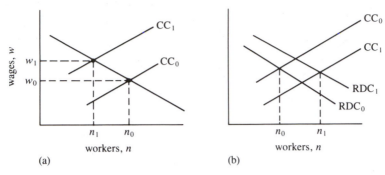

Figure 5.6. Some comparative statics: (a) An increase in b; (b) product demand rises.

not employed in the union sector, the impact of the business cycle on b is likely to be negligible. If we assume the product market effect dominates, then employment will move procyclically, and wages will be rigid over the business cycle. However, if β varies procyclically over the business cycle,[8] there will be limited wage flexibility; employment adjustment will be reduced, since the employment implications of changes in β and in demand are of opposite sign. Notice that the comparative static predictions of all of the models considered in this and the previous chapters have similar implications for wage stickiness and unemployment changes in the unionised sector. But employment levels in the efficient bargaining model are greater than in the right-to-manage model.

5.5 The right-to-manage model versus the efficient bargaining model

The decision as to which is the appropriate model of the unionised sector is an important issue because the models have different implications for unemployment and economic welfare, with the efficient bargaining model predicting overemployment and the other models predicting unemployment. In principle, we can adopt two approaches to making this decision. One approach is to appeal to the available evidence from collective bargains and surveys to see what issues are bargained over by unions and firms. The other is to test the various models against the data to try to discriminate between the models.

The orthodox models described above show that there are efficiency gains from extending bargaining from wages alone to both wages and employment. However, even if we were to observe that firms and unions bargain over both wages and employment, this would be a necessary but not sufficient condition for an efficient bargain (Farber, 1986: 1052). Any

[8] For example, since β proxies union power, then it might be expected to decline in a recession.

wage and employment outcome is feasible – both efficient and inefficient. Moreover, any particular (w,n) pair will depend on the form of the bargaining model.[9] In addition, as was noted in section 5.1, it is rare to find instances of union–firm bargaining over both wages and employment (see also table 4.1).

Why do we not observe bargaining over w and n, when economic theory suggests there are efficiency gains from doing so? One reason is that the efficiency gains may be an artifact following from one of the simplifying assumptions of the model. For example, suppose that we drop the assumption of certainty, and assume more plausibly that there is uncertainty about future product demand at the time the union and management bargain over wages and employment. This uncertainty may mean that a contract over both wages and employment is no longer incentive-compatible. Suppose union and management sign a contract about the level of wages and employment for the next period, based on expected demand. If it turns out that product demand is very low, management will want to renege on the agreement, and determine employment unilaterally. Hence the contract over wages and employment turns out not to be 'incentive-compatible', in that one party may have in the future an incentive to break the agreement. (See Bean (1984) for an application of this logic to implicit contract models.)

In Britain, collective agreements are not legally enforceable, and thus it is possible for either party to cheat on any agreement after the event, as described above. In the USA, collective agreements *are* legally enforceable, and industrial action is not allowed during the term of the contract. Since the term of the agreement is usually three years in the USA, then it would be surprising indeed to see management locking itself into wage and employment contracts allowing no *ex post* adjustment in bad states of the world. And, indeed, in US contracts, management typically retains the right to determine the level of employment.

Is the available empirical research able to discriminate between the right-to-manage model and the efficient bargaining model? The answer is no, but we briefly outline below a procedure that has been used in the literature, and then examine the problems and inadequacies of this procedure. According to the right-to-manage model (and its special case, the monopoly union), employment will be given from the labour demand curve, once the wage has been determined. The equilibrium (w,n) pair will lie on the labour demand curve. However, in the case of an efficient bargain over wages and employment, there will be 'overemployment' of labour; the equilibrium (w,n) pair will lie to the north-east of the labour demand curve, as shown in figure 5.2. Is it possible to test empirically which of these two types of model

---

[9] The literature simply *assumes* that the generalised Nash bargaining model (or, equivalently, a simple game-theoretic form as shown in appendix 5A) is the appropriate solution concept.

is not rejected by available data? There has been a small body of work which aims to do this, and which has relied on a simple (but flawed) test (see, for example, Brown and Ashenfelter (1986), Card (1986) and Bean and Turnbull (1988)).[10]

Consider the right-to-manage model. Employment in this model is determined by the firm's profit-maximising condition that wages should be equal to the value of the marginal product of labour, which we rewrite as equation (15):

$$\text{right-to-manage model: } pq'(n) = w \qquad (15)$$

Now consider the efficient bargaining model, and the equation for the contract curve (where the slope of the union indifference curve is equal to the slope of the firm's isoprofit curve) (equation (10)). We rewrite this equation here for ease of comparison with (15) above:

$$\text{efficient bargaining model: } pq'(n) = w - [u(w) - u(b)]/u'(w) \qquad (10)$$

Comparison of (15) and (10) reveals that there is an additional variable on the right-hand side of (10), namely the variable measuring alternative opportunities, b. This enters the model through its presence in the last term on the right-hand side of (10), the marginal rate of union substitution of employment for wages. Equations (10) and (15) therefore may appear initially to offer a promising means of establishing a test between the two models, but this is not the case. In the right-to-manage case, the equilibrium condition is that the value of marginal revenue product of labour $pq'(n)$ is exactly equal to the union wage, while in the efficient bargaining case the equilibrium condition is that $pq'(n)$ is equal to the union wage less an additional term which measures the substitutability at the margin of union employment for wages. Intuitively, since alternative opportunities enter this additional term, one might expect that the two models could be tested in an empirical estimation of a reduced-form employment equation in which alternative opportunities are included as a regressor (as well as other explanatory variables). If the coefficient to alternative opportunities is insignificantly different from zero, then this might suggest that the right-to-manage model is not supported by the available data.

There are a number of problems with this procedure, which will be addressed below, but beforehand it is worth considering formally how this testing procedure has been implemented. First, some simplifying assumptions must be made in order to derive an estimating equation. Suppose that

[10] Abowd (1989) tests not only for contract efficiency, but also for a vertical contract curve (see figure 5.3). A vertical contract curve is implied by risk-neutrality; here workers have utility functions that are linear in wages, and the union objective function is therefore rent maximisation. An increase in wages under these assumptions raises union utility by the same amount as it reduces the firm's profits. See Pencavel (1991: 112–14) for a critique.

union preferences can be represented by the following Stone–Geary function:

$$U(w,n) = (w - b)^{\phi} n^{1-\phi} \tag{16}$$

where $0 \leq \phi \leq 1$. Substitution of (16) into the constraint of (8) and simplification produces the following version of equation (10):[11]

$$pq'(n) = (1 - \psi)w + \psi b \tag{17}$$

where $\psi = (1 - \phi)/\phi$. (In the right-to-manage model, $\psi = 0$ and $pq'(n) = w$.) Now, in order to estimate equation (17), an assumption must be made about the labour demand curve. Following Andrews and Harrison (1991), we assume that the labour demand curve $pq'(n)$ can be represented by the following linear equation:

$$pq'(n) = a_0 + \mathbf{X}'a_1 + a_2 n \tag{18}$$

where $\mathbf{X}$ denotes a vector of exogenous variables affecting labour demand, a_0 is a constant, a_1 is a vector of coefficients, and n is employment and a_2 is its coefficient. Now substitute (18) into (17) and rearrange to obtain an employment equation which, with the addition of an error term, is ready for estimating against the available data:[12]

$$n = \beta_0 + \mathbf{X}'\beta_1 + \beta_2 w + \beta_3 b \tag{19}$$

where β_0 is a constant given by $(-a_0/a_1)$, $\beta_1 = -a_1/a_2$, $\beta_2 = (1 - \psi)/a_2$ and $\beta_3 = \psi/a_2$. In the right-to-manage model, $\psi = 0$, which is now a testable hypothesis. Note that β_1 is a vector.

There are, however, a number of problems with this approach. First, it can be shown (see, for example, Andrews and Harrison, 1991) that the specification of (17) is sensitive to the particular form assured for the union objective function. For example, suppose that union utility is weakly separable,[13] and given by

---

[11] The efficiency condition is that the slope of the isoprofit curve is equal to the slope of the union indifference curve in (w,n) space. We can totally differentiate (16) with respect to w and n to find the slope of the union indifference curve, and equate this to the slope of the isoprofit curve. This yields

$$[pq'(n) - w]/n = -(w - b)(1 - \phi)/\phi$$

[12] An alternative to imposing the restriction that labour demand follows this linear form is to assume a particular technology for the firm, for example, a Cobb–Douglas production function. Substitute the Cobb–Douglas production function into the firm's profit equation, and follow through with the maximisation process. The ensuing first-order condition can be solved explicitly for employment, yielding an employment equation similar to (19) in the text. For an example, see Bean and Turnbull (1988), who also use a constant elasticity of substitution (CES) production function in one of their models.

[13] Weak separability in the context of the union objective function is where the substitution effects between 'goods' are limited.

$$U(w,n) = (w/b)^\phi n^{1-\phi} \tag{20}$$

Then it can be shown that the efficiency condition becomes

$$pq'(n) = (1 - \psi)w \tag{21}$$

so that b has no impact on the efficient bargain either.[14] Secondly, it can be shown, under certain specific functional forms for union utility and the labour demand curve, that b can affect the right-to-manage outcome also (see, for example, Pencavel (1991: 110)). Thus if the estimated coefficient to b in (19) were found to be significant, this would be consistent with both the efficient bargaining *and* the right-to-manage hypotheses. These points make it clear that researchers need to investigate a variety of specific functional forms when using such a restriction on a coefficient to discriminate between competing hypotheses. It is vital to see if the restriction arises because of the theory or because of the assumed explicit functions employed to make the theory operational.

Thirdly, even if empirical studies were to reveal that ψ is significantly different from zero, this would not vindicate the efficient bargaining model. Other labour market theories, such as efficiency wage theory, may also be consistent with a non-zero ψ.[15] Moreover, the right-to-manage and the efficient bargaining models are not the only trade union theories; there is a broader framework even within the trade union literature.[16] It is also the case that a significant positive estimated coefficient to b is consistent with the textbook perfectly competitive spot market for labour. If the labour market operates in this fashion, alternative opportunities enter the structural supply equation. The reduced-form employment equation obtained from this textbook auction market also contains alternative opportunities as a right-hand-side variable. Thus a significant positive estimated

---

[14] To see this, totally differentiate the union objective function in (20) with respect to w and n, keeping union utility fixed. Rearrangement of this gives the slope of the union indifference curve;

$$\left. \frac{dw}{dn} \right|_{\bar{u}} = -(1-\phi)w/\phi n$$

where it can be seen that b does not appear at all.

[15] Under the efficiency wage hypothesis, the firm pays workers more than their alternative income even in the absence of trade unions. This yields greater profits to the firm than if it paid a wage equal to alternative income. This is because higher wages reduce shirking by workers who want to avoid being sacked; as a result, morale and co-operation are increased, resulting in higher profits.

[16] Manning (1987) suggests that wages and employment may be determined by a sequence of Nash bargains between the union and the firm: the first stage is a bargain over wages, while the second is one over employment, given the bargained wage level. The power of the union may differ at each stage. This approach nests as special cases both the right-to-manage and the efficient bargaining models. In the right-to-manage model the power of the union at the second stage is zero. In the efficient bargaining model, the power of the union at each stage is the same.

coefficient to b in a reduced-form employment equation is unable to discriminate between a number of hypotheses, including the perfectly competitive spot labour market.

MaCurdy and Pencavel (1986) adopt an alternative approach in testing to see whether or not employment satisfies equation (15), where the wage is equal to the marginal product of labour. Their approach takes as a null hypothesis that wages are equal to marginal productivity, in contrast to the studies outlined above that take the efficient bargaining model as the null hypothesis by estimating reduced-form employment equations. MaCurdy and Pencavel (1986) estimated production functions (using data on the number of typesetting machines of various types, the amount of advertising sales and the number of typographers) for the typographers labour market in thirteen US towns over the period 1945–73. They obtained estimates of the marginal product of labour from the first derivative of their estimated production functions with respect to labour. From the property that in equilibrium $w/\text{MPL} = r/\text{MPK}$, then $w = r.\text{MPL}/\text{MPK}$. Estimates of the marginal products of labour and capital were obtained from the respective first derivatives of their estimated production function. Observations on r are proportional to an annual user cost of capital, r^*, where the factor of proportionality is given by γ. The test is then to see if variations in wages w are proportional to variations in $r.\hat{\text{MPL}}/\hat{\text{MPK}}$ (where the hat over the marginal products indicates that these are estimates), with no other significant variables explaining the variation. Their estimates rejected the labour demand curve equilibrium model but, as they note, this is not proof of the efficient bargaining model, since employment might not lie on the contract curve even though it does not appear to be on the labour demand curve.

A fourth problem associated with the empirical tests aiming to discriminate between the right-to-manage and efficient bargaining models is that, in a dynamic framework, it can be shown that alternative wages affect employment. Lockwood and Manning (1989), in a model with quadratic employment adjustment costs, show that all variables affecting profits, union utility and union power influence the employment equation.

A fifth problem associated with the empirical tests aiming to discriminate between the right-to-manage and efficient bargaining models is that, under certain conditions, the contract curve may actually lie on the labour demand curve, as shown in several papers (see Carruth and Oswald, 1987; Oswald, 1993; and Booth, 1993). In Carruth and Oswald (1987), it is assumed that the union cares only about the welfare of employed members, or 'insiders', perhaps because workers who are laid off leave the trade union. While this does not characterise all union types (in particular, it is inappropriate for many craft unions whose unemployed workers retain union membership), it is arguably applicable to the general unions. The union objective function of (4) can therefore be written as

$$\text{EU} = \frac{n}{m} u(w) + \left[1 - \frac{n}{m}\right] u(b) \qquad n < m \qquad (22)$$

$$= mu(w) \qquad\qquad\qquad n \geq m$$

Since the union cares only about insiders, the union indifference curve is kinked at $n = m$, where m represents the inherited pool of incumbent workers at the firm. The slope of the union indifference curve for $n < m$ is $dw/dn = -[u(w) - u(b)]/nu'(w)$ as before, but for $n \geq m$ the slope is zero. Now suppose further that a fraction of workers retire each period. Assume that the firm has begun with an inherited pool of incumbent workers where $n \geq m$, and hence the kink of the union indifference curve lies to the right of the labour demand curve initially. Suppose that the union and the firm bargain over employment as well as wages, so that the outcome is efficient and also to the right of the labour demand curve. Over time with attrition through retirement, the kink in the union indifference curve will be moving leftwards, since m contracts in each period through attrition. Long-run equilibrium will be reached where the union indifference curve kink (where $dw/dn = 0$) is on the labour demand curve. The slope of any isoprofit curve is also zero at this point (because the locus of the turning-point of each isoprofit curve traces out the labour demand curve, as we saw in the previous chapter). At this point, the (w,n) outcome will not only be efficient (since the slopes of the isoprofit and indifference curves are the same), but it will also be on the labour demand curve.[17] Hence it may be impossible for any empirical test to distinguish between the right-to-manage and the efficient bargaining models, since the outcome of each is identical.

The same result – that the outcome of the efficient bargaining model coincides with the outcome of the right-to-manage model – can also be found if the scope of the bargain is extended to cover severance pay. In Booth (1993), the presence of redundancy payments on the bargaining agenda has the implication that the wage and employment predictions of both the right-to-manage and the efficient bargaining models coincide; both outcomes lie on the labour demand curve. Moreover, both outcomes have the additional property of efficiency from the viewpoint of society.[18]

What conclusions can be reached about the appropriateness of using the efficient bargaining model where employment is included on the bargaining agenda? Economists quite naturally like to believe that if an outcome is efficient, it should be followed by rational agents, since at least one party

[17] See also Layard et al. (1991: 112–16).

[18] This result is the same as the implicit contracts model with bargaining over wages, redundancy pay and employment, but is derived from different assumptions about whether or not the labour market is competitive.

would be made better off. However, there is little evidence from union contracts that unions and firms bargain over employment. Moreover, the empirical literature has not as yet been able to find an appropriate test to distinguish between the principal models. Furthermore, some theoretical studies have shown that the efficient outcome lies on the labour demand curve. It seems sensible in these circumstances to adopt a pragmatic approach. This might involve the use of the right-to-manage model where appropriate, and to undertake further research into examining bargaining over the issues that do appear in collective bargains, such as effort, 'manning' arrangements and the size of redundancy payments.[19]

5.6 Bargaining and strikes

The conditions under which a union can achieve a wage rate greater than the competitive level are that there must be some surplus to be shared, and that the union must have some bargaining power to induce the firm to share the surplus. The bargaining power arises wherever it is costly for the firm to replace its incumbent workforce. One source of bargaining power is the threat of complete labour withdrawal – the strike – a threat which is only credible if the firm cannot immediately replace its striking workforce. Hence the extent of unionisation and the degree of substitutability of union and nonunion workers is obviously important. Labour withdrawal allows the union to impose costs on the firm; the threat of these costs may induce the firm to accede to the union's demand for a higher wage. In this section we briefly examine a strike model that allows for the simultaneous determination of union wages and strike incidence. Although the model does not determine employment, it rests on a framework of bargaining between the union and the firm, and it is therefore appropriate to include the strike model in this chapter on union bargaining models.

A problem with early bargaining models attempting to explain the occurrence of strikes is that in such models the strike is not Pareto-optimal *ex ante*.[20] Although these models generate a unique post-strike wage level, the assumption of perfect information on which the models are based implies that both the union and the firm would know the outcome before embarking on the strike. If both parties are rational, they should therefore agree to the outcome *ex ante*, thereby avoiding the strike and its associated costs – the *Hicks' paradox*.[21] Following recognition of this paradox, the

---

[19] Recent papers have examined bargaining over wages and some of these issues. See *inter alia* Rosen (1989), Nickell *et al.*, (1992), Andrews and Simmons (1992), and Moreton (1993), for wages and effort; and Johnson (1990) and Clark (1990) for wages and the capital-to-labour ratio.

[20] For surveys of the strikes literature, see Kennan (1986) and Sapsford (1990).

[21] See Hicks (1963).

strikes literature has developed in three different directions. The first direction is to relax the assumption of rationality, the second involves a rejection of the theoretical approach in favour of *ad hoc* empiricism, while the third involves a relaxation of the assumption of perfect information. Since individual rationality is a fundamental behavioural paradigm of neo-classical economics, it is somewhat curious that some of the strikes literature should travel the first direction and assume irrationality. This irrationality is, however, only on the part of the rank-and-file union membership, and follows from Hicks' view that workers are concerned with fair wages, comparable worth and other 'more or less sentimental consider-ations of this sort' (Hicks, 1963: 153).

A pioneering study by Ashenfelter and Johnson (1969) developed a formal model in this vein, and tested its predictions for strike frequency against US data. In their model the firm maximises its present value, subject to an *ad hoc* union 'concession schedule' that indicates the minimum wage increases acceptable to union rank-and-file members after a strike of given length. The concession schedule assumes that union rank-and-file workers are overly optimistic about the wage increase they can extract from the employer, and require a strike to reduce their wage aspirations. Thus there is a negative relationship between wage increases and strike length. While the union concession schedule is arbitrary, the Ashenfelter and Johnson (1969) paper represents an important landmark in the modelling of strikes, for it can be interpreted as showing that strikes may occur because some information is private. In their model, the union rank-and-file are imper-fectly informed about the firm's profits, and need the strike in order to bring their wage demands into line. This approach has been followed in a number of other studies, and the model now appears in labour economics textbooks as a widely accepted model of strike behaviour. Below we consider a development of the Ashenfelter and Johnson approach provided by Farber (1978a) and Sapsford (1990).

The union's 'concession' or 'resistance' curve plots wage increases on the vertical axis and strike length on the horizontal axis, and the curve is negatively sloped to reflect the fact that union members require a strike to reduce their wage aspirations. The union concession curve is given by the following equation, where $\mu = \Delta w / \bar{w}$ and $\bar{w}$ is the pre-existing union wage:

$$\mu = \mu(s); \qquad \mu(0) = \mu_0; \qquad \mu(\infty) = \bar{\mu}; \qquad \mu'(s) < 0; \qquad (23)$$

The union concession curve is illustrated in figure 5.7. The vertical axis is the proportionate wage increase $\mu = \Delta w / \bar{w}$ (where $\Delta w = w - \bar{w}$), and the horizontal axis is strike length s. The union initially demands a wage increase given as μ_0, but as the strike proceeds the union modifies its wage demands, and hence the concession schedule is negatively sloped. The

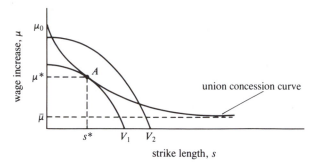

Figure 5.7. Wage increases and strike length.

concession schedule is asymptotic to some minimum wage increase given by $\bar{\mu}$, which is so low that the strike would continue indefinitely if this were the wage increase on offer.

The firm is assumed to maximise the present discounted value (PDV) of its future profit stream, given by

$$V = \int_0^\infty \pi e^{-rt} dt \qquad (24)$$

where π denotes profits which are decreasing in wages, r is the rate at which the firm discounts future earnings and t denotes time. It can be shown that the iso-PDV curves plotted in wage-increase μ and strike length s space are negatively sloped, as illustrated in figure 5.7.[22] The negative slope of the iso-PDV curves reflects the fact that the firm's profits decline with strike length because no production occurs during the strike. Iso-PDV curves that are closer to the origin represent higher present discounted value of profit

---

[22] Assume that the union concession curve is given by a particular functional form,

$$\mu = \bar{\mu} + (\mu_0 - \bar{\mu})e^{-as} \qquad (25)$$

where a denotes the rate of decay of the union's wage demands.

The firm's profits are given by

$$\pi = pq - wn \qquad (26)$$

From the definition of $\mu = \Delta w / \bar{w}$, we can write $\mu = (w - \bar{w})/\bar{w}$, and hence

$$w = \bar{w}(1 + \mu) \qquad (27)$$

Substitute (25), (26) and (27) into (24) in the text to obtain

$$V = \int_s^\infty \{pq - n\bar{w}[1 + \bar{\mu} + (\mu_0 - \bar{\mu})e^{-as}]\}e^{-rt} \, dt \qquad (28)$$

Integration of (28) yields

$$V = \{pq - n\bar{w}[1 + \bar{\mu} + (\mu_0 - \bar{\mu})e^{-as}]\}\frac{e^{-rs}}{r} \qquad (29)$$

which can be graphed in (μ, s) space as the firm's iso-PDV curves as shown in figure 5.7.

streams to the firm, since wage increases are lower and strike length is shorter. What is the final wage settlement and strike length? This is indicated as point A in figure 5.7, where the union concession schedule and the firm's iso-PDV schedule are tangential. This equilibrium point is achieved by the firm maximising its PDV subject to the union's concession curve.

The equilibrium in this model is not Pareto-optimal. The union has achieved the wage increase of μ^*, but only after a costly strike; had the firm paid μ^* immediately without the union going on strike, the firm would have been on an iso-PDV curve closer to the origin, which represents higher levels of profits. Moreover, the union would also have avoided the income loss associated with the strike. The fact that the strike occurred at all in the Ashenfelter and Johnson (1969) and Farber (1978a) models is because the union rank-and-file were assumed to be imperfectly informed about the wage increases that the firm could offer, and the length of strike was therefore a means of inducing the rank-and-file to lower their unrealistic expectations. But there is in these models no satisfactory explanation as to why the rank-and-file were misinformed. If the rank-and-file had had full information, then no strike should have occurred.

As noted by Kennan (1986: 1102), 'the empirical content of the Ashenfelter and Johnson model comes almost exclusively from intuitive guesses about the determinants of the workers' resistance curve, rather than from any analyses of rational economic behaviour'. Since the concession schedule is a vital part of this model, its *ad hoc* nature is of particular concern. In the model, the firm is assumed to have perfect knowledge of the union's concession schedule, which it then takes into account in its maximising strategy. The strike occurs because the union rank-and-file are either behaving irrationally, which was the original interpretation of the model, or have imperfect information about the firm's profitability, which is the more recent interpretation. But in the Ashenfelter–Johnson paper the means by which imperfect information might affect the outcome is not modelled.

By the mid-1980s, following developments in perfect equilibrium game theory by Rubinstein (1982) among others, the strikes literature developed in a third direction to allow for rationality and *private* information to generate a strike outcome that is Pareto optimal *ex ante*. Such game-theoretic models are found in Hayes (1984), Hart (1989), Tracy (1987), and Booth and Cressy (1990); in these studies, the firm possesses private information about its own profitability, while workers have imperfect information about the firm's profits – they know only the parameters of the distribution of profits across firms in the industry or sector. The process of bargaining reveals information to the union about the firm's profitability over time. The union makes an initial wage demand that will be accepted if the firm's profits are high, but which will be rejected if the firm has low profitability. The firm's refusal of a wage demand and its willingness to initiate a strike reveals to the union the information that profits are too low to support the initial wage demand. The union therefore lowers its wage demand.

Since rejection by the firm of the first wage demand results in a strike, which will occur only if the wage demand is too high, the union must weigh the advantage of a higher wage in the initial period if the demand is accepted against the advantage of more information (net of the 'costs of delay') if the demand is rejected.

These bargaining models generate testable predictions for the probability of a strike and its expected length. The theory is predicated on the assumption that the union does not know the precise profits of its employer, but only knows a distribution of profits. Therefore, empirical work needs to find proxies that will measure the union's uncertainty about the employer's profitability. For example, Tracy (1987) uses the volatility of the firm's market value as a measure of the union's uncertainty about profits in his estimates of strike incidence and duration in US manufacturing industries in the mid-1970s. He finds this measure has a positive impact on strike incidence and duration. But, as emphasised by Pencavel (1991: 139), empirical work attempting to test the predictions of asymmetric information models of strikes faces the problem that the results are not simply testing the asymmetric information hypothesis, but they are also relying on hypotheses about how to proxy union's uncertainty about firms' profits. It may not be possible to disentangle the effects of these hypotheses in empirical work.[23]

So far in the asymmetric information models of strikes, the union has been the party that has been imperfectly informed while the firm possesses private information about its profitability. Yet how plausible is this assumption? For many firms, it is relatively easy for outsiders to obtain access to company accounts. Moreover, workers in a given firm, or analysts in union research departments, are able to track sales, output, labour input and the like. What about future profitability? Here *both* parties are likely to have imperfect information, not just one. It is not immediately clear why each party would have a different distribution about future profitability. However, where there is bilateral asymmetry of information, it may be in each party's interest to behave strategically and reveal (or, perhaps, misrepresent) their true position. Examination of these issues may offer a promising area for future research.[24]

---

[23] See Card (1990) and McConnell (1989) for estimation of the relationship between union wage demands and strike duration using data for the US and Canada respectively. Card finds no contemporaneous correlation between real wages and strike incidence or duration, while McConnell finds a negative impact.

[24] See Black and Bulkley (1988) and references therein for analysis of strategic information transmission in a bargaining model with private information.

5.7 Bargaining over wages and standard hours

So far in this book, we have ignored the issue of union hours determination, and have focused predominantly on the influence of trade unions on wages and employment. This has been done to keep the modelling simple, for incorporation of hours into the bargaining framework rapidly complicates the analysis. However, hours are an important issue in the labour market. In Britain, there is a well-developed statutory structure covering the maximum length of the working week for women, and youths and children of both sexes. This legislative framework dates back to the nineteenth century, and arose out of public concern over the long hours worked, in particular in factories. However, hours of work for British men over the age of eighteen years have typically not been covered by legislation, largely because of the view that trade unions were able to safeguard the interests of men. Notable exceptions for male workers are found in industries where fatigue may cause negative externalities, for example public transport. (See Bienefeld (1972) and Bosworth and Dawkins (1981) for interesting accounts.) Thus for British men standard hours are typically negotiated by union–firm bargaining. Unions in the USA also bargain over the length of the standard working week. US collective bargains typically cover hours, overtime and holidays (Bureau of National Affairs, 1983). Therefore in this section we briefly consider the implications of the inclusion of hours into the union–firm bargaining framework. There is so far only a very small literature on union–firm determination of hours, and this topic would benefit from analysis by the next generation of researchers.

Hours worked over any year are affected not only by the length of the standard working week, but also by the number of weeks of paid holiday. Moreover, a given standard number of hours may be achieved by a working week of four, five or more days. In the economic approach, to date, attention has focused only on either a standard working week or a standard working day.

In what follows we present a simplified version of Booth and Ravallion (1993), and allow the union and firm to bargain over wages and hours. However, the firm retains the 'right to manage', that is, to determine *ex post* employment once hours and wages have been agreed.[25] Thus in this approach, hours and wages are determined efficiently, but employment is not. As in the model developed in section 5.4, we require only that one party's welfare be maximised, subject to any arbitrarily fixed level of

---

[25] For models of wages and hours determination in a monopoly union framework, see Calmfors (1985), Hoel (1986) and Booth and Schiantarelli (1987). The latter contains a dynamic formulation of the problem. See Oswald and Walker (1993) for a model of bargaining over wages, hours *and* employment.

welfare of the other. It is therefore possible to characterise an efficient outcome simply by considering union and managerial preferences, without imposing a particular bargaining structure.

Suppose also that the individual worker's utility function can be written as

$$u = u(y,h) \qquad u_y > 0; \ u_h < 0 \tag{30}$$

where y is weekly income, given by $y = wh$, and w is the hourly wage rate and h is the number of hours worked in a week. A worker's utility is increasing in weekly income, but decreasing in hours worked. Thus hours have both a negative effect on utility because workers prefer leisure to supplying labour, and a positive effect because income increases with hours worked at any given wage rate. To obtain a formal model of wages and hours determination, we now insert (30) into the usual union objective function, and suppose that the union chooses wages and hours to maximise this objective function, subject to the firm achieving at least some fixed level of profits π_0. (We could equivalently have allowed the firm to choose wages and hours, allowing the union to achieve a given level of utility.) If we assume the union has a utilitarian objective function, the union's problem is to choose wages and hours to maximise

$$nu(y,h) + (m - n)u(b)$$

subject to

$$\tag{31}$$

$$[q(hn) - whn] \geq \pi_0$$

Note that the firm's revenue function is now written as $q(hn)$ to allow for the fact that the number of hours worked by each individual affects the total product. Since w represents the hourly wage rate, the wage bill is given by the hourly wage rate for each worker times his or her hours worked, multiplied by the number of workers employed; thus the wage bill is whn.

Proposition 5.4.

Where the firm retains the right to choose employment but wages and hours are set efficiently, the union and the firm will set w and h such that the wage rate is equal to minus the marginal rate of substitution of wages for hours, given by $w = -u_h/u_y$. The efficient contract allows union workers to be on their individual labour supply curves.

The equilibrium is characterised by

$$-u_h = u_y w \tag{32}$$

Proof. See appendix 5B.

Notice that (32) states that the equilibrium is where the marginal cost of working an extra hour is exactly equal to the marginal benefit.

The model sketched out above represents the situation where wages and hours are set at the same level of collective bargaining, by negotiation between a union–firm pair. But in many situations, wages and hours are determined at different bargaining levels. For example, in Britain hours are frequently determined at the industry level, while wages may be determined at the level of the organisation or establishment. Moreover, wages may be bargained over annually, while hours may appear on the bargaining agenda less frequently. The model above is inapplicable for cases where legislation covers standard hours of work while unions and firms bargain over wages. It is therefore most important that the appropriate institutional framework is taken into account when economists model union wages and hours determination in a particular country or industry.

It is also apparent that there are a *number* of avenues through which hours may be affected in a unionised economy. For example, in the model sketched out above, union–firm bargaining determines the length of the standard working week. But union–firm bargaining may also affect the number of overtime hours.[26] Moreover, union bargaining occurs not only over the length of the standard working week, but also over issues affecting *annual* hours, such as the length of paid vacations, the number of public holidays and sick leave. Thus there is another avenue through which trade unions can affect the length of the working *year* in addition to the length of the working week.[27]

Unions may affect hours determination not only through the fact that hours and vacations appear explicitly on the bargaining agenda, but also indirectly through the fact that unions sometimes bargain over issues affecting employment adjustment costs. Examples of these are severance or redundancy payments and redeployment. Moreover unions (particularly in the USA) bargain over certain additional fringe benefits (such as health insurance, pensions, vacations, supplementary unemployment insurance and the like), the cost of which also varies with the number of workers and not the number of hours worked. Thus unionised firms face greater *fixed* employment costs relative to variable employment costs than do nonunion firms. The presence of these fixed employment costs can reduce the relative flexibility of the unionised firm in managing workforce reductions. To the extent that these adjustment costs differ systematically between the union

---

[26] For models incoporating overtime, see Hart (1984a), Fitzroy and Hart (1985), Booth and Schiantarelli (1987) and Calmfors and Hoel (1988, 1989), *inter alia*.

[27] In Booth and Ravallion (1993), the number of hours worked affects productivity or efficiency per hour. This 'efficiency hours hypothesis' is based on evidence from industrial psychologists.

and nonunion sectors, we would expect to see differences in employment and hours fluctuations in the union and nonunion sectors. Where there are substantial fixed costs associated with hiring or firing workers, we would expect to observe firms changing hours of work of a given number of employees (rather than changing the number of employees working a given number of hours) in response to small demand fluctuations.

The presence of fixed employment costs that differ between the union and nonunion sectors, and the appearance of hours of work on the union–firm bargaining agenda, suggest that a careful distinction should be made between hours and employment in estimation of union–nonunion effects. These issues will be further discussed in chapter 7.

All of the factors just outlined represent potentially interesting areas for future theoretical research. Moreover, as we shall see in chapter 7, there is very little empirical evidence about the joint determination of hours, employment and wages in unionised economies.

5.8 Conclusion

This chapter has covered a number of important models and issues in trade union theory. It began by considering how to model wage *bargaining* by the trade union and the firm. Several models were examined. First, we outlined the 'right-to-manage' model where employer and union bargained over wages, leaving management with the right to determine *ex post* employment. However, the right-to-manage model is inefficient, in the sense that at least one party to the bargain can be made better off by moving to a situation where both wages and employment are on the bargaining agenda. Thus the second model outlined in this chapter – the 'efficient bargaining' model – allows both employment and wages onto the bargaining agenda. But why do we typically not observe this form of contract in practice? Several reasons were advanced in the chapter; it was also pointed out that relaxation of one or more of the restrictive assumptions underlying this model can produce the prediction that the efficient bargaining outcome and the right-to-manage outcome coincide.

Throughout this book, we have argued that an important element of the bargaining process is the ability of one party to the bargain to impose costs on the other party – in the form of either a strike or a lockout. Thus in section 5.5 we also examined approaches to modelling strike incidence and wage determination. In the majority of union models in the literature, the issue of union influence over hours of work has been assumed away. And yet hours of work, in one form or another, appear frequently in collective agreements. Section 5.6 of this chapter therefore briefly examined hours and wages determination in a right-to-manage framework where the firm

determines *ex post* employment. This represents an under-researched area
of the economics of trade unions.

Appendix 5A. The non-cooperative bargaining problem

5A.1 The Nash solution to the bargaining problem

Denote by **V** the set of feasible payoffs, and let v_i be the payoff to the ith bargainer,
$i = 1,2$, and $\bar{v}_i$ be the status quo or fall-back point for the ith bargainer. The solution
to the bargaining problem is given by $\mathbf{v}^* = (v_1^*, v_2^*)$ which depends on the set of
feasible payoffs **V**, plus the status quo or disagreement points of $\bar{v}_1$ and $\bar{v}_2$. The four
axioms generating the solution are:

(1) *Invariance*. The solution is independent of the units in which utility is measured.
(2) *Efficiency*. The solution must be Pareto-efficient, in that neither party to the
   bargain can be made better off without making the other worse off. Formally, if
   $\hat{v}_i > v^*$, then $\hat{v}_i$ is not in **V**.
(3) *Independence of irrelevant alternatives*. Removal of part of the feasible set **V**,
   which does not contain the solution, will not affect the solution.
(4) *Anonymity*. Altering the labels on the bargainers does not change the solution.

Nash (1950, 1953) showed that $\mathbf{v}^*$ satisfies these four axioms if $\mathbf{v}^*$ maximises
$(v_1 - \bar{v}_1)(v_2 - \bar{v}_2)$ subject to $v_i \in \mathbf{V}$ and $v_i \geq \bar{v}_i$ for $i = 1,2$.
   Now consider the solution to the generalised Nash bargain, where the axiom of
anonymity is relaxed. This is given by (2) in the text, which we reproduce here:

$$\max_{v_1, v_2} \Phi = (v_1 - \bar{v}_1)^{\beta_1} (v_2 - \bar{v}_2)^{\beta_2} \tag{A1}$$

subject to $v_i \geq \bar{v}_i$, $i = 1, 2$, for some $\beta_1, \beta_2 \geq 0$. If the total size of the cake (or surplus) is
unity, then $1 \geq v_1 + v_2$. Assume that the cake is exactly exhausted and form the
Lagrangean $\mathscr{L}$, taking the natural logarithm of (A1), as

$$\mathscr{L} = \beta_1 ln(v_1 - \bar{v}_1) + \beta_2 ln(v_2 - \bar{v}_2) + \lambda(1 - v_1 - v_2) \tag{A2}$$

The first-order conditions are

$$\mathscr{L}_\lambda = 1 - v_1 - v_2 = 0 \tag{A3}$$
$$\mathscr{L}_{v_1} = \beta_1/(v_1 - \bar{v}_1) = \lambda \tag{A4}$$
$$\mathscr{L}_{v_2} = \beta_2/(v_2 - \bar{v}_2) = \lambda \tag{A5}$$

Equate (A4) to (A5), solve for v_i and substitute into (A3) to obtain

$$v_2 = (1 - \bar{v}_1)\frac{\beta_2}{\beta_1 + \beta_2} + \bar{v}_2 \frac{\beta_1}{\beta_1 + \beta_2} \tag{A6}$$

$$= (1 - \bar{v}_1)\frac{\beta_2}{\beta_1 + \beta_2} + \left[1 - \frac{\beta_2}{\beta_1 + \beta_2}\right]\bar{v}_2$$

$$= \bar{v}_2 + \frac{\beta_2}{(\beta_1 + \beta_2)}(1 - \bar{v}_1 - \bar{v}_2) \tag{A7}$$

which is (3) in the text. If neither party had any fall-back utility ($\bar{v}_i = 0$), then the division of the surplus would simply reflect relative bargaining strengths.

5A.2 The game-theoretic solution to the bargaining problem

This is the non-cooperative bargaining model of Rubinstein (1982), simplified by Tirole (1988). See Sutton (1986) and Binmore *et al.*, (1986) for extensive comparisons of the Nash and game-theoretic approaches to the bargaining problem.

Suppose there are two players, sharing a cake of size 1. The players make sequential alternating offers as to how the cake should be shared. Let x_t ($0 \leq x_t \leq 1$) be the share of the cake offered to player 1 at time t, and thus $(1 - x_t)$ is the share of player 2. To avoid confusion we label player 1 as Agnes and player 2 as Bob. What will the value of x be?

5A.2.1 The finite horizon case

We initially consider a model in which there is a finite horizon, and proceed by backward induction. Suppose that the discount factor for both players is $0 < \delta < 1$. Assume T time periods, and consider the last period. The player making the offer at the terminal date demands the entire cake, since the other player cannot make a further offer. Because the other player has nothing to gain by refusal (since the game is terminating), he or she accepts. If at time 0 Agnes is the first mover in the game, $x_T = 0$ if T is even, and $x_T = 1$ if T is odd. We will use this result to determine exactly what Agnes' equilibrium share will be.

Suppose that it is Agnes' turn to make the final offer at T (and thus T is odd). She will make Bob an offer of none of the cake, keeping all for herself. He will accept, since he gains nothing by refusing. At $T - 1$, it is Bob's turn to make an offer: Bob will offer Agnes a share making her just indifferent between accepting this offer, and having the entire cake (suitably discounted) in the following period. Thus Bob offers Agnes $\delta(1)$, keeping $(1 - \delta)$ for himself. At $T - 2$, it is Agnes' turn to offer, and she will offer Bob sufficient to make him just indifferent to accepting the offer, or waiting till the next period when he will get $(1 - \delta)$. Thus Agnes will offer Bob $\delta(1 - \delta)$, and keep $[1 - \delta(1 - \delta)]$ for herself. At $T - 3$ it is now Bob's turn to offer. To ensure Agnes is indifferent between acceptance and waiting till the next period, Bob offers $\delta[1 - \delta(1 - \delta)]$ for Agnes and retains $1 - \delta[1 - \delta(1 - \delta)]$ for himself.[28]

It should now be clear that, by induction on the number of time periods, in the limit as $T \to \infty$ we will find:

$$x_1 = 1 - \delta + \delta^2 - \delta^3 + \delta^4 - \ldots$$
$$= \frac{1 - \delta}{1 - \delta^2} = \frac{1}{1 + \delta} \tag{A8}$$

and therefore

$$1 - x_1 = \frac{\delta}{1 + \delta} \tag{A9}$$

[28] Obviously, at $T - 4$ Agnes offers Bob $\delta\{1 - \delta[1 - \delta(1 - \delta)]\}$.

These represent what are termed the subgame perfect equilibrium payoffs to the players. Note that, in equilibrium, the first offer will always be accepted, since it is chosen to ensure that the player receiving the offer is just indifferent between accepting and continuing into the next period.

Now suppose that the time between successive offers is given by Δ, and each party's discount factor can be written as $\delta = e^{-r\Delta}$. Then

$$\lim_{\Delta \to 0} x_1 = \lim_{\Delta \to 0} 1/(1 + e^{-r\Delta}) = 1/2 \qquad (A10)$$

Thus with each party characterised by the same discount factor, the surplus is split equally. This is analogous to the Nash bargaining outcome where each party has equal bargaining strength, and fall-back utilities are set to zero.

5A.2.2 The infinite horizon case

Here it is not possible to use backward induction, and instead we use valuation functions, following the simplified Rubinstein model of Tirole (1988: 430). In the infinite horizon case, if the game has not been terminated, it will appear the same at all even time periods, and the same at all odd time periods. We therefore know that the solution will be 'stationary', in the sense that offers and payoffs will be independent of the time period. Let V_i be player i's expected payoff when making an optimal offer (that is, an offer that will always be accepted, since it is chosen to ensure that the player receiving it is just indifferent between acceptance and continuation). Given stationarity, we need only consider two offers: where it is Agnes' turn to make the offer, and then where it is Bob's turn to make the offer. We now define x_A as Agnes' share of the cake when Agnes makes the offer, and x_B as Agnes' share when Bob makes the offer. When Agnes moves first, her valuation will be $V_A = x_A$. But when Bob moves first, his valuation will be $V_B = (1 - x_B)$.

Consider the situation where Agnes moves first. She makes an offer to Bob to make him just indifferent between accepting now and waiting until the next round, that is, his share now is equal to his next period's valuation V_B, discounted by δ, which is

$$(1 - x_A) = \delta V_B$$

Rearrangement yields

$$x_A = 1 - \delta V_B$$

which is Agnes' valuation, since $V_A = x_A$. Thus we can write

$$V_A = 1 - \delta V_B \qquad (A11)$$

Now suppose it is Bob's turn to move first. He makes an offer to Agnes to make her just indifferent between accepting now and waiting until the next round, that is, her share now is equal to her next period's valuation, discounted by δ. Thus $x_B = \delta V_A$. Therefore Bob's valuation is $V_B = 1 - x_B$, which we can write as

$$V_B = 1 - \delta V_A \qquad (A12)$$

The subgame perfect equilibrium is where the offer will always be accepted. To find this, solve (A11) and (A12) simultaneously, yielding:

$$V_A = V_B = \frac{1-\delta}{1-\delta^2} = \frac{1}{1+\delta} \tag{A13}$$

The person *not making the first move* will receive $[1 - 1/(1+\delta)] = \delta/(1+\delta)$. Thus this result is the same as in equations (A8) and (A9) above.

5A.2.3 The infinite horizon case with unequal discount rates

Now suppose that Agnes and Bob are characterised by different discount rates, δ_A and δ_B respectively. If Agnes moves first, she offers Bob

$$(1 - x_A) = \delta_B V_B$$

and since $V_A = x_A$, this becomes

$$V_A = 1 - \delta_B V_B \tag{A14}$$

Where Bob moves first, he offers Agnes

$$x_A = \delta_A V_A$$

and his own valuation $V_B = 1 - x_B$ is given by

$$V_B = 1 - \delta_A V_A \tag{A15}$$

Solve (A14) and (A15) simultaneously to obtain

$$V_A = \frac{1 - \delta_B}{1 - \delta_A \delta_B} \tag{A16}$$

and

$$V_B = \frac{1 - \delta_A}{1 - \delta_A \delta_B} \tag{A17}$$

Since $\delta_i = e^{-r_i \Delta}$, then we have

$$\lim_{\Delta \to 0} V_A = \lim_{\Delta \to 0} (1 - e^{-r_B \Delta})/[1 - e^{(r_A + r_B)\Delta}]$$

Using l'Hôpital's rule we find

$$\lim_{\Delta \to 0} V_A = \lim_{\Delta \to 0} [e^{(r_A + r_B - r_B)\Delta}].[r_B/(r_A + r_B)]$$

$$= r_B/(r_A + r_B) \tag{A18}$$

Dividing through each term on the right-hand side of (A18) by $r_A r_B$, we obtain:

$$V_A = (1/r_A)/(1/r_A + 1/r_B) \tag{A19}$$

Thus from (A19) it can be seen that, as $\Delta \to 0$ (the time between successive offers approaches zero), the solution for V is the same as for the generalised Nash solution in (A7), where $\beta_i = 1/r_i$, and $\bar{v}_i = 0$, $i = A, B$.

Appendix 5B

5B.1 Proof of proposition 5.1

Here the generalised Nash bargain B is over w alone; the firm determines n unilaterally. Thus

$$\max_{w} B = W^{\beta}F^{1-\beta} \tag{B1}$$

where

$$W = n(w)[u(w) - u(b)] \tag{B2}$$

$$W_w = n'(w)[u(w) - u(b)] + n(w)u'(w) \tag{B3}$$

and

$$F = pq[n(w)] - wn(w) \tag{B4}$$

$$F_w = n'(w)[pq'(n) - w] - n(w)$$
$$= -n(w) \tag{B5}$$

by the envelope theorem, since the firm will choose employment such that $pq'(n) = w$. The first-order condition of the Nash bargain is given by

$$B_w = \beta W^{\beta-1}F^{1-\beta}W_w + (1-\beta)W^{\beta}F^{-\beta}F_w = 0 \tag{B6}$$

thus

$$\beta W_w / W = -(1-\beta)F_w / F \tag{B7}$$

Insert (B2) to (B5) into (B7) and multiply through by w:

$$\frac{\beta wu'(w)}{u(w) - u(b)} = \beta\epsilon + \frac{(1-\beta)wn}{pq(n) - wn} \tag{B8}$$

This is equation (6) in the text. It states that the marginal benefit from a percentage increase in the wage rate is equal to the sum of the percentage marginal cost to the union (the first term on the right-hand side of (B8)) and the percentage marginal cost to the firm.

5B.2 Proof of proposition 5.2

Form the Lagrangean for the constrained maximisation problem of (8):

$$\max_{w,n} \Theta = pq(n) - wn + \lambda\{\bar{U} - [u(w) - u(b)]n/t - u(b)\} \tag{B9}$$

$$\Theta_w = -n - \lambda u'(w)n/t = 0 \tag{B10}$$

$$\Theta_n = pq'(n) - w - \lambda[u(w) - u(b)]/t = 0 \tag{B11}$$

$$\Theta_\lambda = \bar{U} - [u(w) - u(b)]n/t - u(b) = 0 \tag{B12}$$

Substitution of the value for λ obtained from (B10) into (B11) yields

$$pq'(n) - w = -[u(w) - u(b)]/u'(w) \tag{B13}$$

which is the equation for the contract curve, (9) in the text. To find the slope of the contract curve in (w,n) space, totally differentiate (B13) with respect to w and n:

$$dw\{[u(w) - u(b)]u''(w)/u'(w)^2\} = pq''(n)dn \tag{B14}$$

Rearrangement yields equation (11) in the main text.

5B.3 Proof of proposition 5.3

The generalised Nash bargain over w and n is given by

$$\max_{w,n} \tilde{\beta} = W^\beta F^{1-\beta} \tag{B15}$$

which yields, after some simplification of the first-order conditions, the following:

$$\tilde{B}_w = \beta W_w/W + (1-\beta)F_w/F = 0 \tag{B16}$$

$$\tilde{B}_n = \beta W_n/W + (1-\beta)F_n/F \tag{B17}$$

Recall that

$$W = [u(w) - u(b)]n/t \tag{B18}$$

Thus

$$W_w = u'(w)n/t \tag{B19}$$

$$W_n = [u(w) - u(b)]/t \tag{B20}$$

Recall also that

$$F = pq(n) - wn \tag{B21}$$

Thus

$$F_w = -n \tag{B22}$$

$$F_n = pq'(n) - w \tag{B23}$$

Substitution of (B18), (B19), (B21) and (B22) into (B16) yields:

$$\beta[pq(n) - wn] = (1-\beta)n[u(w) - u(b)]/u'(w) \tag{B24}$$

Substitution of (B18), (B20), (B21) and (B23) into (B17) yields:

$$\beta[pq(n) - wn] = -(1-\beta)n[pq'(n) - w] \tag{B25}$$

By equating (B24) with (B25), we find the equation for the contract curve

$$pq'(n) = w - [u(w) - u(b)]/u'(w) \tag{B26}$$

To find the first equation in proposition 5.3, the rent division curve, use (B25), which can be rearranged yielding

$$pq'(n) - w = [w - pq(n)/n]\beta/(1 - \beta) \tag{B27}$$

which on further rearrangement yields equation (13) in the main text.

Notice that, since the bargain is over both w and n, employment is not on the labour demand curve. The bargaining outcome thereby differs from that of the right-to-manage outcome of proposition 5.2, where $n^* = n(w^*)$.

5B.4 Proof of proposition 5.4

The union chooses wage w and hours h to maximise the Lagrangean:

$$\mathcal{L}(w,h,\lambda) = nu(y,h) + (m-n)u(b) + \lambda\{\pi_o - [q(hn) - whn]\} \tag{B28}$$

The first-order conditions are given by the following:

$$w: \quad u_y + \lambda = 0 \tag{B29}$$

$$h: \quad u_h + u_y w - \lambda[q'(nh) - w] = 0 \tag{B30}$$

$$\lambda: \pi_o - [q(hn) - whn] = 0 \tag{B31}$$

Eliminating λ using (B29) and (B30) and noting that $w = q'(nh)$, we obtain

$$u_h + u_y w = 0 \tag{B32}$$

which can be rewritten as (32) in the text.

It can be shown that union wages and hours are negatively related. To see this, totally differentiate (B32) with respect to w and h, and rearrange to find dw/dh. Use the result that the second-order condition for (B32) to represent a maximum requires $u_{yh} > 0$.

6   Empirical estimates of the union wage differential

6.1 Introduction

The union–nonunion wage differential has often been used as a measure of union power. Macroeconomic models, and models of the aggregate labour market, commonly use it for this purpose, since this differential is argued to be positively correlated with union power (see, for example, Layard, Metcalf and Nickell (1978), Nickell and Andrews (1983) and Layard and Nickell (1985, 1986)). In chapter 3 it was argued that, at the microeconomic level, although the existence of economic rents was a necessary condition for union differentials, higher union wages would be found only where the trade union had the necessary power to force the firm to give up some of its surplus. Therefore the union differential would be positively correlated with union power, as assumed in macroeconomic work.

Calculation of the union wage differential is sensitive to the method of estimation and to the degree of aggregation of the data. Estimates of the differential range from over 70% (Minford, 1983), to insignificantly different from zero, as we shall see in this chapter. Estimates obtained using aggregate data are typically far larger than those from individual cross-section data, and these in turn are larger than estimates from panel studies. Which estimates can we believe? What are the problems involved in the calculation of these estimates? To understand the issues involved it is vital that we understand the methods used to estimate union wage differentials and the econometric problems facing researchers in this field.

In this chapter we examine the impact of trade unions on worker remuneration, focusing in particular on wages. There is an enormous body of empirical research on trade union wage differentials. This literature is largely descriptive. It generally does not test economic theories of trade union behaviour, but instead is typically based on a definition of the union–nonunion wage differential. It can, however, be related to the theory developed in previous chapters, and this is shown in appendix 6A. The theory shows that the union wage differential over nonunion alternatives is increasing with union power, and decreasing with the elasticity of labour demand, with product market competitiveness and with labour intensity.

This chapter will not attempt to survey all the empirical descriptive research on the impact of trade unions on worker remuneration, since this would require an entire book. The interested reader who wishes to study in more detail the impact of US unions on key economic and industrial relations variables is referred to Freeman and Medoff (1984), Hirsch and Addison (1986) and Lewis (1986) and the extensive bibliographies therein. Here, we examine just a few typical empirical studies which attempt to quantify the impact of trade unions on wages. In the next chapter, we will look at the impact of trade unions on firms' profitability and investment behaviour, employment and hours, and labour productivity. Because it is necessary when evaluating estimates of the union wage differential to understand potential sources of bias, we will be carefully considering the econometric issues throughout. These will be presented non-technically, so that the intuitive reasoning can be understood by a reader who has followed a standard econometric course.

6.2 The union–nonunion wage differential: definition

In section 3.2, the union wage differential was defined as the difference between the union wage and the nonunion wage. This wage differential is the concept that is used in estimation of the union wage effect. Throughout this chapter, the terms union–nonunion wage 'gap', 'differential' and 'markup' are used interchangeably. These terms are quite distinct from the term 'wage gain' first defined in section 3.2.

The union–nonunion wage differential d can be written as

$$d_i = \frac{w_i^U - w_i^N}{w_i^N} \qquad i = 1,...,n \tag{1}$$

where w denotes the wage rate, the superscripts U and N represent union and nonunion respectively, and the subscript i denotes the ith individual. Calculation of the wage differential for an individual therefore requires wages information for the individual when unionised (w_i^U) and also when not unionised (w_i^N). However, only one of these is observed for any individual. Therefore the researcher's task is to *estimate* the wages that would be received by an individual were his or her union status altered, all other variables being held constant. This must be done in order to obtain an estimate of the wage differential d_i.

In chapter 3, it was argued that the ability of a union to achieve a wage rate higher than the nonunion level depends on the existence of economic rents or surplus in the product market, *and* on the power of the union to act as a monopolist in the supply of labour. Economic rents will typically be greatest where the degree of product market competition is low. Indeed, even if a trade union controls all the labour supplied to a particular sector, it will only be able to negotiate a large wage increase if there is low elasticity of labour demand in the sector. For given union power, Marshall's rules for the derived demand for labour indicate that wage increases will be largest where it is hard for firms to substitute in production, and consumers to substitute in consumption. Therefore, variations in the observed union wage differentials across sectors are likely to be related to differences in the surplus available to firms, and to the ability of trade unions to appropriate some of these rents. Variables proxying these factors are those that reflect the degree of product market competition, the elasticity of labour demand, trade union density and coverage, and other variables reflecting trade union power, such as the extent of closed-shop or union-shop practices. Empirical analysis is complicated by the fact that it is also necessary to control for wage variations due to compensating differentials. In the absence of unionisation, there will still be variations in wage rates, because, as a famous quotation from Adam Smith's *The Wealth of Nations* makes clear:

The five following are the principal circumstances which ... make up for small pecuniary gain in some employments, and counterbalance a great one in others; first, the agreeableness or disagreeableness of the employments themselves; secondly, the easiness and cheapness, or the difficulty and expense of learning them; thirdly, the constancy or inconstancy of employment in them; fourthly, the small or great trust which must be reposed in those who exercise them: and fifthly, the probability or improbability of success in them. (Adam Smith, 1977 [1776]: 202)

In estimating the union wage gap, it is necessary to separate out the impact of trade unionism from these other factors contributing to wage differentials in the absence of trade unionism. Not all empirical studies of the union wage gap have done so, in part because of data limitations.

6.3 Aggregate cross-section estimates of the union wage differential

Until the late 1960s in the USA and the 1970s in Britain, data on union membership or coverage was generally available only at an aggregate level, for example across groups of individuals in different industries, cities, states or occupations. Although there were large surveys of individuals, they typically did not ask if respondents were union members or covered by collective bargains negotiated by a trade union.[1] Separate wages data for

---

[1] The earliest survey of individuals in Britain that combined wages data, individual union membership information, and data on worker and industry attributes was the 1975 National Training Survey, used to estimate union wage differentials by Stewart (1983).

union and nonunion members were therefore not available; researchers had to use average wages information for *all* workers. Initially we will consider estimation of the union–nonunion wage differential in this context.

The mean log wage is a weighted average of the mean log wages for union and nonunion workers, where the weights are given by the proportion of workers unionised in a particular group of individuals:[2]

$$\ln w_i = D_i \overline{\ln w_i^{U}} + (1 - D_i) \overline{\ln w_i^{N}}$$

$$= D_i (\overline{\ln w_i^{U} - \ln w_i^{N}}) + \overline{\ln w_i^{N}} \qquad (2)$$

where D_i is the proportion of workers in group i covered by the union agreement.[3] From (1) we can write (dropping the bars denoting means, for ease of exposition):[4]

$$\ln(1 + d_i) = \ln w_i^{U} - \ln w_i^{N} \qquad (3)$$

Substitute (3) into (2) and suppose that d does not vary across individuals or groups. This yields:

$$\ln w_i = D_i \ln(1 + d_i) + \ln w_i^{N}$$
$$= \beta D_i + \ln w_i^{N} \qquad (4)$$

where $\beta = \ln(1 + d)$. In order to estimate (4), suppose that the log of nonunion wages is some function of a vector $\mathbf{X}_i'$ of observable industry and worker attributes, for example suppose $\ln w_i^{N} = \mathbf{X}_i' \gamma$, where γ is a vector of coefficients to be estimated. With the inclusion of an error term μ_i (whose expected value is zero), (4) becomes

$$\ln w_i = \beta D_i + \mathbf{X}_i' \gamma + \mu_i \qquad (5)$$

This equation has been used to estimate the union–nonunion wage differential (typically by ordinary least squares) in a number of aggregate

---

[2] An equivalent way of expressing this identity is that the log of the geometric mean wage is a weighted average of the logs of the geometric means of union and nonunion wages.

[3] Typically US studies have used for D_i the fraction of workers in the group who are members of a trade union. The difference between membership density and union coverage in the USA is typically small – between 2 and 3% (Hirsch and Macpherson, 1993). However, in Britain there is considerable divergence between membership density and coverage. The British studies based on aggregate statistics largely used the coverage data from the 1973 New Earnings Survey, which indicated 80% coverage for the full-time adult manual workforce, as compared to 55% union density. Recent estimates of the extent of free-riders in Britain indicate that it is between 13 and 17% (see chapter 1).

[4] Rearrangement of equation (1) gives

$$d_i w_i^{N} + w_i^{N} = w_i^{U}$$
$$(1 + d_i) w_i^{N} = w_i^{U}$$
$$(1 + d_i) = w_i^{U} / w_i^{N}$$

Take natural logarithms of both sides of this equation to obtain (3) in the text.

studies (see Lewis (1986: ch. 3) for an extensive survey of the US literature). An estimate of the average union–nonunion wage differential is obtained from the estimated coefficient $\hat{\beta}$; the average differential is given by $[\exp(\hat{\beta}) - 1]$ (where the hat over a variable indicates that it is an estimate).[5] A refinement of (5) is provided by postulating that the relative wage impact of unionism, β, is also a function of observable variables in $\mathbf{X}$, for example $\beta = \mathbf{X}_i'a$, where a is a vector of coefficients to be estimated. Thus (5) can be written as

$$\ln w_i = D_i \mathbf{X}_i' a + \mathbf{X}_i' \gamma + \mu_i \tag{6}$$

where the first term on the right-hand side of (6) is an interaction term between union membership status and the vector of explanatory variables. The advantage of estimating (6) is that it allows for union wage effects to differ across demographic or industrial groups. However, to its disadvantage, it uses up degrees of freedom, which may be a problem with the limited number of observations typical of aggregate work.

A large number of studies have estimated (5) using aggregate (or grouped) data,[6] and a smaller number have estimated variants of (6). The estimates of the union–nonunion wage differential obtained using this procedure are generally high; they also vary tremendously across different studies. For example, British estimates of aggregate or grouped cross-section union markups range from 18 to 47%. (Summaries are provided by Metcalf (1977) and Blanchflower (1984). US aggregate or grouped cross-section estimates range from 8 to 32% (Lewis, 1986: 45)). But there are a number of problems with this method of estimation of the union markup that raise questions about the reliability of the results, and which suggest that the estimates are upward biased.

The first problem relates to omitted variable bias. It can be shown that the omission of any variables influencing wage determination that are positively (negatively) correlated with the union coverage variable D_i will cause the estimated coefficient β to be upward (downward) biased. As an example, consider labour quality. It is often argued that firms that have become unionised respond to the higher union wage by carefully vetting prospective new hires in order to employ higher quality workers. Yet in the aggregate wage equations, it is generally impossible to control for labour quality. Therefore, $\hat{\beta}$ may actually be picking up the impact of the higher quality workforce in unionised establishments, *as well as* the monopoly

---

[5] The percentage wage differential is therefore $[\exp(\hat{\beta}) - 1].100$. Note that approximation of the log differential by the proportionate differential is valid only for small values of β, for example $\beta < 0.15$. See Halvorsen and Palmquist (1980).

[6] The reader is reminded that the term aggregate or grouped cross-section studies denotes studies estimating wages across *groups* of individuals, that is, individuals aggregated by industry, city, state or occupation.

union markup. A similar argument can be made for labour turnover. To the extent that the presence of trade unions reduces labour turnover, if labour turnover data are unavailable β will be picking up the impact of seniority on earnings *in addition to* the direct union wage impact.

The estimated union markup may also represent some form of compensating wage differential. If nonunion jobs are predominantly in small establishments with a less hierarchical system of human resource management, the lower pay associated with these jobs may be due to particular individuals being willing to work there for lower wages. Since firm size and other industrial relations features are typically not included in these aggregated cross-section models, because of lack of data, the union wage markup may be picking up the effect of wages in unionised plants compensating for other less salubrious features of the work environment. Therefore the estimates of the union wage gap are likely to be unreliable.

A further problem with estimation of the model of (5) or (6) is that $\hat{\beta}$ conflates the impact of several possible sources of trade union influence. The grouped data do not allow for estimation of the impact on wages of individual union status separate from the impact on wages of trade union density or coverage. An *individual's* wages are likely to be affected by the degree of unionisation in the negotiating group (union coverage) and by the individual's union status. For *establishment*-level data, the establishment's wages are likely to be affected by the degree of unionisation and whether or not there is a recognised union. Industrial relations scholars have long argued that there is a minimum critical size of membership necessary to achieve recognition, but that at higher levels of union density there may well be a saturation effect, where marginal changes in union density do not affect the union's bargaining strength conditional on recognition, and where at the margin 'each per cent of growth requires greater and greater effort on the part of the unions' (Rezler, 1961: 4). This view suggests that the degree of unionisation should be included as an explanatory variable in the wages regressions, as well as union status. But this generally cannot be done with aggregate level data.

Union density is typically used in aggregate or grouped studies as an explanatory variable to estimate the union–nonunion wage differential. But union density may be simultaneously determined with wages. The union markup represented by the coefficient β was obtained through manipulation of the identity of (2) and was not based on a theory of union wage and membership behaviour. Yet it is likely that the decision to unionise will be affected by union wage-setting policies, just as union wages will be affected by the level of membership.[7] Thus the estimates of the union wage markup

---

[7] Indeed, in the few theoretical models in which membership is allowed to vary, the models predict that wages and membership will be simultaneously determined. See, for example,

that do not control for this possible simultaneity may suffer from simultaneous equation bias.

Finally, many studies use weekly rather than hourly earnings as the dependent variable, since weekly earnings are generally all that is available. Weekly earnings frequently include earnings received for overtime, night shifts and the like. To the extent that overtime and shift work may be more prevalent in union rather than nonunion establishments, the use of weekly earnings may lead to an overestimate of the union markup.

With the availability since the late 1960s in the USA, and the 1970s in Britain, of large 'microdata' survey results containing information about union status in addition to wages, researchers have had access to wages data for both union and nonunion individuals. Thus it has no longer been necessary in many situations to estimate average wages equations of the form just described. Instead what is frequently done is to estimate separate wage equations for unionised and nonunionised workers, based on data for individuals or, less frequently, establishment-level data. We examine this approach in the next section.

6.4 Individual cross-section estimates of the union wage differential

6.4.1 Estimation methodology

In individual-level surveys with data on both union status and earnings, it is possible to estimate the earnings of union and nonunion workers separately, thereby overcoming a weakness of (5) that earnings determination was not allowed to vary between union and nonunion sectors.[8] Concomitant with the availability of these survey data since the late 1960s has been the development of human capital models of wage determination, stimulating the formulation of more sophisticated models of earnings determination. Individual cross-section estimates of the union wage markup now frequently rely on separate estimation of wage determination in the union and nonunion sectors; these estimates are then used to calculate an estimate of the union wage markup.

Suppose that wages in the union and nonunion sector are determined respectively by

$$\ln w_i^U = \mathbf{X}_i' \gamma^U + \mu_{1i} \tag{7}$$

$$\ln w_i^N = \mathbf{X}_i' \gamma^N + \mu_{2i} \tag{8}$$

Grossman (1983), Booth (1984), Booth and Chatterji (1993a, 1993b) and Naylor and Raaum (1993).

[8] Estimation of (6) with its interaction terms does allow for the wage determination process to vary between union and nonunion sectors.

where $\mathbf{X}_i$ is a vector of exogenous explanatory variables, γ^U and γ^N are vectors of coefficients to be estimated, and the error terms are given by μ_{1i} and μ_{2i}. From equations (3), and (7) and (8), the wage differential β_i is given by

$$\beta_i = \ln w_i^U - \ln w_i^N$$
$$= \mathbf{X}_i'(\gamma^U - \gamma^N) + e_i \tag{9}$$

where $e_i = (\mu_{1i} - \mu_{2i})$ is the error term. The estimated differential for the ith individual is given by

$$\hat{\beta}_i = \mathbf{X}_i'(\hat{\gamma}^U - \hat{\gamma}^N) \tag{10}$$

The estimate of the mean differential across union members is therefore given by

$$\hat{\bar{\beta}} = \bar{\mathbf{X}}'(\hat{\gamma}^U - \hat{\gamma}^N) \tag{11}$$

where $\bar{\mathbf{X}}$ is a vector of means of variables in the sample. Note that $\bar{\mathbf{X}}$ can represent union means, nonunion means, or means of the entire union and nonunion sample. For example, if we are interested in considering the predicted wage differential between employment in the union and non-union sectors for an individual *with average characteristics for the entire sample*, we use $\bar{\mathbf{X}}$ – the means of the entire sample. Equations (7) and (8) have been used to estimate the union wage gap (11) in a number of studies.

6.4.2 Estimates of union wage gaps

For the USA, there is a huge volume of cross-section, single equation studies estimating the mean union wage gap from a variety of data sources, for both broad and specific groups of US workers. Lewis (1986, 1990) provides comprehensive analyses of these. Lewis (1986) suggests that the mean wage-gap estimates for the USA vary between 12 and 20%. In contrast, there are relatively few studies of British wage gaps using cross-section micro data. These estimates range between -0.04 and 19%, and are summarised in table 6.1.

There is very little empirical work examining the impact of trade unions on women's wages, perhaps in part because of the fact that it is desirable to treat the female employment decision as endogenous, which complicates the estimation procedure.[9] However, Green (1988) using the General Household Survey (GHS) of 1983 finds that non-manual women have a union markup of 2.7% while manual women have a markup of 8.6%. Green's estimates are obtained from the coefficient of a sex dummy variable

---

[9] There are also few British attempts to control for simultaneity of union status (an exception is that of Murphy, Sloane and Blackaby (1992)).

Table 6.1. *British union wage-gap estimates*

Author	Year and survey	Earnings	Union measure	Mean union markup (%)
Stewart (1983)	1975 NTS individual	weekly	membership	7.7 full-time manual males
Blanchflower (1984)	1980 WIRS1 plants	weekly	recognition	10.2 semi-skilled manual −0.04 unskilled manual (insign.) 0.7 clerical (insign.) 4.0 middle manager
Shah (1984)	1969 Townsend individual	hourly	membership	10–13 manual males
Stewart (1987)	1980 WIRS1 private sector plants	weekly	recognition	8 semi-skilled manual 3 skilled manual (insign.)
Green (1988)	1983 GHS household	weekly hourly	membership	12 manual 4 non-manual 14 manual 4 non-manual
Stewart (1990)	1984 WIRS2 plants	weekly	recognition	0–10 semi-skilled manual
Symons and Walker (1990)	pooled 1979–84 FES individual, male	hourly	membership	13 manual males 5 non-manual males
Yaron (1990)	1983 GHS individual	hourly	membership	18 manual males 10 manual females
Blanchflower and Oswald (1990)	WIRS1 and 2 private sector plants	weekly	recognition	3 clerical, 1980 (insign.) 3 clerical, 1984 3 middle manager, 1980 1 foreman/supervisor, 1984 (insign.)
	pooled 1983–6 BSA individuals	annual	membership	10 non-manuals
Blanchflower (1991)	pooled 1983–6 and 1989 BSA individuals	annual	membership	10 non-manuals
Stewart (1991)	WIRS1 and 2 private sector plants	weekly	recognition	6.6 semi-skilled, 1980 8.4 semi-skilled, 1984 1.7 skilled, 1980 (insign.) 2.8 skilled, 1984 (insign.)

Table 6.1. (*cont.*)

Author	Year and survey	Earnings	Union measure	Mean union markup (%)
Main and Reilly (1992)	1986 SCELI individual, female	hourly	membership	14.6 full-time females 15.3 part-time females

Metcalf and Stewart (1992)	WIRS2 private sector plants	weekly	recognition and membership	semi-skilled manual:
				  7–10 density > 95 or post-entry closed shop
				  17–19 pre-entry closed shop

Murphy, Sloane and Blackaby (1992)	1986 SCELI individual, male	hourly	membership	13 manual males 10 non-manual males
Machin, Stewart and van Reenen (1993)	WIRS2 private sector plants	weekly	recognition; multi-union joint/separate bargaining	4 skilled 10 semi-skilled 6 unskilled Markup for multi-union separate bargaining vs. single bargaining: 8 skilled 5 semi-skilled 5 unskilled
Stewart (1994)	WIRS3 private sector plants	weekly	recognition	1 skilled (insign.) 7 semi-skilled 7 unskilled

Notes: The Townsend data refer to the Survey of Household Resources and Standards of Living in the UK, which contains both household and individual level data. These data were collected by Townsend (1979).

SCELI Social Change and Economic Life Initiative (a survey of six distinct local labour markets sponsored by the Economic and Social Research Council)
FES Family Expenditure Survey
GHS General Household Survey
BSA British Social Attitudes Survey
WIRS Workplace Industrial Relations Survey.

in a sample that has proportionally more men, and there are grounds for stratifying the sample on the basis of sex and estimating the entire model separately. Yaron (1990) also uses the 1983 GHS but divides the sample into manual men and manual women, finding a union markup of 10% for manual females and 18% for manual males. Main and Reilly (1992) use the Social Change and Economic Life Initiative Survey of six distinct local labour markets, and their unconditional estimates are of a union wage markup of 14.6% for full-time women and 15.3% for part-time women.

Thus it appears that women in Britain gain more from unionisation than men.

Stewart (1983) estimated the first individual-level union wage markups for Britain. Using data from the 1975 National Training Survey (NTS), he estimated an average union *membership* wage differential of 7.7% for full-time manual males in UK manufacturing industry, using weekly pay. There was considerable variation, however, in the membership wage differential, both with individual characteristics and across industries. As shown in table 6.1, Shah (1984) and Green (1988) estimated union membership markups of between 4 and 14%, using individual-level and household-level data respectively. Green used data for all workers from the 1983 General Household Survey. It is interesting to compare his estimates based on hourly earnings and weekly earnings, as shown in table 6.1. For manual workers, the union markup is larger when hourly earnings are used than when weekly earnings are used. Notice that the average differentials using micro data reported in table 6.1 are substantially smaller than the union coverage wage differential estimates based on British cross-section data aggregated at the industrial or occupational level.

The three surveys used by Stewart (1983), Shah (1984) and Green (1988) contained information about an individual's union status, but did not indicate union coverage for an individual worker.[10] Subsequent work by Blanchflower (1984), Stewart and others, using the Workplace Industrial Relations Surveys, estimates the union–nonunion differential where workers can be categorised according to whether their pay is determined by a recognised union or not – a union recognition wage differential. Their average estimates are shown in table 6.1. The distinction between a union membership and a union recognition wage differential is important for Britain, although less so for the USA where an individual covered by a collective agreement will typically be a union member.[11] In the USA, just 2–3% of the labour force are nonunion, but covered by a collective agreement. In Britain, individual wages are more frequently determined by a collective bargaining agreement, negotiated by a recognised union, regardless of individual union status, as we saw in chapter 2. This suggests that for

[10] However, the percentage of male manual workers in an individual's industrial Minimum List Heading, obtained from the 1973 New Earnings Survey, was included by Stewart (1983) as an explanatory variable in calculation of the union markup, and found to be insignificant. Both the proportion covered by a collective agreement, and the proportion who were union members had positive impacts on union wages only above the 8% significance level.

[11] Lewis (1986: 111–12) examines differences between the union membership wage differential and the union coverage wage differential for three studies using US data (Jones, 1982; Katz, 1983; Mincer, 1983). The estimates in Jones (1982) and Mincer (1983) are from the National Longitudinal Surveys (NLS), while Katz (1983) used the May 1979 Current Population Survey. Lewis finds that on average the membership differential exceeds the coverage differential but by only a small amount.

Britain, where coverage data are available, equation (7) should be estimated for individuals who are covered by a union agreement, rather than
just for individuals who are union members. If this is not possible, the
sample of nonunion members for which (8) is estimated may contain
individuals whose wages are determined by union agreements, and hence
the estimated differential may be an underestimate of the true impact of
trade unions.

We have argued earlier that the ability of a union to achieve a wage rate
higher than the nonunion level depends on the existence of economic rents
or surplus in the product market, *and* on the power of the union to act as a
monopolist in the supply of labour. Therefore, variations in the observed
union wage differentials across sectors are likely to be related to differences
in the surplus available to firms, and to the ability of the trade union to
appropriate some of these rents. US studies using the industry concentration ratio as a proxy for the firm's market power have largely found that
there is a negative relationship between the concentration ratio of the
industry in which a worker is employed, and the union wage differential.[12]
This negative relationship is rationalised by arguing that in concentrated
industries firms use their monopoly rents to withstand long strikes against
unions' wage demands. However, using US data, Mishel (1986) finds that in
unionised manufacturing establishments the union–nonunion wage differential is significantly greater for non-competitive industries than competitive ones, where the measure of competition used combines both the degree
of concentration and the presence of entry barriers. However, the *industry*
concentration ratio is not necessarily a good measure of the individual
firm's market power and profitability.

Stewart examines variation in union *recognition* wage differentials with
the type of collective bargaining arrangements at the establishment (Stewart, 1987, 1990), and with variations in the degree of competition in the
product market (Stewart, 1990). Using gross weekly pay for semi-skilled
manual workers in the private sector from the establishment-level data of
WIRS2, Stewart (1990) finds a mean union recognition pay differential of
8–10% where establishments have some degree of monopoly power. A zero
differential is found in competitive market conditions. The differentials are
over twice as large where there is a pre-entry closed shop in addition to
product market monopoly.[13] Firms with market power were found to pay

[12] See for example Bloch and Kuskin (1978), Freeman (1983), Mellow (1982), Kwoka (1983),
    Long and Link (1983). Evidence of a positive relationship is found in Freeman (1981) and
    Hirsch and Berger (1984).
[13] Estimates from WIRS1 also indicate the importance of the pre-entry closed shop. Stewart
    (1987) finds an average union recognition wage differential of 8% for semi-skilled workers,
    but only 3% (not significantly different from zero) for the skilled. The presence of a pre-
    entry closed shop roughly doubles the differential for the semi-skilled, while it increases it to
    9% for the skilled.

more than competitive firms even in the nonunion sector. This evidence of rent-sharing in the absence of recognised trade unions may reflect insider power, efficiency wages, or threat and spillover effects (Stewart, 1990: 1128).[14]

6.4.3 Summary of findings

The mean union wage-gap estimates for the USA vary between 12 and 20% (Lewis, 1986), whereas those for Britain vary between 3 and 19%. Average estimates of the mean union wage gap from cross-section models are around 15% for the USA and 8% for Britain.

However, there is considerable diversity in union wage-gap estimates across individuals, sectors and bargaining structures. A part of this diversity appears to reflect differences in economic rents in different product markets, and in the monopoly power of unions to extract a share of these rents. The studies by Stewart and others in Britain using the remarkably rich establishment-level data provided by the three Workplace Industrial Relations Surveys make a number of interesting points about variations in union–nonunion weekly earnings gaps. First, the evidence suggests that while on average there is a positive union–nonunion wage differential, when disaggregated calculations are made, unions are not always associated with positive wage gaps. (Thus, for example, Stewart (1990), using WIRS2 data for semi-skilled manual workers, showed that where product markets are competitive, there is a zero union weekly earnings gap.) Moreover, firms with market power pay more than competitive firms even in the absence of unionisation. Secondly, it is clear that, for Britain at least, the collective bargaining structure is an important determinant of the size of union wage gaps. In particular, multi-unionism combined with separate bargaining, and the presence of closed shops (notably, pre-entry closed shops), are associated with significantly larger than average union–nonunion wage gaps.[15]   Other British studies using differ-

---

[14] In order to incorporate a variety of collective bargaining arrangements that may explain variation in union wage differentials, Stewart (1987) added an extra set of variables into (7), which becomes

$$\ln w_i^U = \mathbf{X}_i' \boldsymbol{\gamma}^U + \mathbf{T}_i' \boldsymbol{\delta}^U + \mu_{1i} \tag{12}$$

where i refers to the establishment, $\mathbf{T}_i$ is a vector of bargaining characteristics, and $\boldsymbol{\delta}^U$ is a vector of coefficients to be estimated. The union recognition differential for an individual establishment becomes

$$\hat{\beta}_i = \mathbf{X}_i' (\hat{\boldsymbol{\gamma}}^U - \hat{\boldsymbol{\gamma}}^N) + \mathbf{T}_i' \boldsymbol{\delta}^U \tag{13}$$

In Stewart (1990), interactions were used as an alternative to estimating two separate wage equations, because of the relatively small number of observations.

[15] It is not yet possible to relate US union wage gaps to the collective bargaining structure, as there are no data available.

ent surveys for estimation of union wage gaps find that the wage differential for manual workers in Britain is greater than for non-manuals, and union wage gaps for women appear to be larger than for men.[16]

Lewis (1986: ch. 7) surveys and summarises US union wage differentials for particular workforce characteristics. His findings reveal, for example, that US wage gaps are greater for private sector than public sector workers, are roughly comparable for men and women, are greater for manual than non-manual workers, and are larger for non-manufacturing than manufacturing workers.

6.4.4 Potential problems with union wage-gap estimation

We now consider a number of caveats about estimation of union wage gaps using micro data-sets. These reservations arise because lack of appropriate data means that researchers are forced to use variables that are not perfectly measured from the econometrician's viewpoint. Moreover, some control variables that we might like to include are unobservable. The importance of these reservations must be emphasised, however, since an understanding of the potential problems may assist the reader in interpreting different estimates of union–nonunion wage differentials.

We have already mentioned the problems that may arise where the dependent variable is measured as weekly or annual earnings, rather than hourly earnings. This is an issue where trade unions affect the number of hours worked, so that, for example, the income reported by the union group may exceed that of the nonunion group because of extra hours worked in the union sector, and not through a union wage-rate markup.[17] If hourly wages cannot be used and it is impossible to control for shift work or overtime, which may be offered systematically more to union workers, union wage gaps may be overestimated. A problem with all of the published British estimates of the union wage differential using the WIRS data is that they are based on weekly earnings rather than an hourly wage rate. While this was necessary for studies using WIRS1 because the 1980 survey did not contain a question about hours worked, it was not necessary for the second and third WIRS. Yet not only is any theory about union influence on wages based on wage rates rather than total hours worked, but there are also differences in hours worked by union and nonunion workers (Millward, 1993). Union workers in Britain appear to work significantly longer total

---

[16] For a more detailed breakdown of variations in union wage gaps, the interested reader is referred to the original studies cited in table 6.1.
[17] Lewis (1986: 104–6) calculates, from sixteen US studies, 'hours gap' estimates which attempt to control for differences in hours worked. Hours gap estimates are discussed in the following chapter.

hours than do nonunion workers. We might therefore expect the estimates of the union wage gap based on WIRS data to be upward biased.

A related problem arising in the interpretation of estimates of union–nonunion wage gaps concerns the treatment of fringe benefits or perquisites that may be provided by the firm to workers in addition to wages. Since these are rarely included in the earnings measures used in empirical studies (often, but not always, because they are unavailable), union wage gaps may be incorrect. Lewis (1986: 95–104) calculates that inclusion of fringe benefits would raise average union wage-gap estimates for the US labour force by between 2 and 3 percentage points. Freeman and Medoff (1984) show that there is a union fringe benefit gap, analogous to the union wage gap. The US union sector is characterised by a higher proportion of labour cost attributable to voluntary fringe benefits such as health insurance and pensions, than in the nonunion sector. There are as yet no studies in Britain estimating the union–nonunion fringe benefit differential.

In considering union wage markups, careful thought must also be given to potential differences between estimates based on individual-level data and those based on establishment-level data. The use of individual-level data allows for the control of differences in *individual* attributes; this is usually not possible using establishment-level data. However, the use of establishment-level data allows control of *establishment* characteristics impossible with individual survey data.

Estimates based on individual survey data allow for each worker to have a different wage. But in practice wages are not exactly related to all observable characteristics of any one worker, especially not in the union sector where wages are typically 'determined by some procedure for a reference worker or a reference job' (Pencavel, 1991: 24). Thus wages are generally related to broad attributes of a type of worker, information about which is available through establishment data like WIRS. Moreover, plant data allow the firm's industrial relations and management policies to be controlled for, as in Stewart (1990). However, it is interesting that, in both the USA and Britain, estimates from individual and establishment data are generally similar, with the establishment-level estimates sometimes slightly lower.

As we have already noted, a problem associated with estimation of the union wage gap arises from the fact that some variables that are important from a theoretical perspective are not measured or are unobservable. A particular problem is labour productivity. Following unionisation, firms might be forced to pay higher wages but can typically hire whom they please. They can therefore choose higher quality workers, for the advent of higher wages encourages a queue of workers from which the firm can select the best. Therefore, we would expect to observe a positive correlation between union status and worker quality or productivity, after firms and workers have had time to adjust to the advent of unionisation. If worker productivity cannot be measured, then estimation of the union impact is likely to be picking up the impact not just of unionism but also of the worker's productivity, with which it is positively correlated. Hence the estimated coefficient to union status is upward biased. One way of dealing with this problem is to estimate a fixed effects model, where the worker is observed at two points in time.

The *fixed effects* model, using longitudinal or panel data, requires the same individual (or the same establishment, for plant-level data like WIRS) to be observed at two dates. Suppose each individual has some fixed effect such as ability or innate productivity; although this differs across individuals, it does not change over time, and it may be correlated with both wages and union status. The impact of this fixed effect can be removed by taking the difference between individual real earnings at two points in time, yielding an earnings growth equation in which the impact of individual ability has been netted out. To see this, consider the model of equation (14), where the first subscript i refers to the individual, and the second subscript refers to the time period t ($= 1, 2$). The individual's union status in a two-period wage growth model can take one of four possibilities – a union member in both periods, in neither period, in the first period but not the second (a quitter), and in the second period but not the first (a joiner). Denote a two-period member by D^{11}, a two-period non-member by D^{00}, a union quitter by D^{10} and a union joiner by D^{01}. The coefficients to be estimated are similarly superscripted. Since these are dummy variables, we let D^{00} be the omitted category. Assume that the error terms in each time period can be represented by $\mu_{it} = \phi_i + e_{it}$, where the ϕ_i represent individual-specific fixed effects, and it is assumed that only the ϕ_i are correlated with D_i, and the e_i are random. The wage growth model is

$$\ln w_{i2} - \ln w_{i1} = \mathbf{X}_i'(\gamma_2 - \gamma_1) + d^{11}D_i^{11} + d^{10}D_i^{10} + d^{01}D_i^{01}$$
$$+ (\phi_i - \phi_i) + (e_{i2} - e_{i1}) \tag{14}$$

Clearly the fixed effects vanish through this differencing procedure, and we are left with an estimating equation without omitted variable or selectivity bias. This equation can then be estimated using OLS. Notice that estimation of union–nonunion wage gaps from this equation relies on individuals who are changing union status over the estimation period – the joiners and the quitters. We will return to this in the following section.

Another potential problem affecting micro cross-section estimates (as well as aggregate estimates of union wage gaps) is the issue of simultaneity. In the context of wage equations, this means not only that wages are affected by union status, but also that the probability of being in a union is affected by the union wage gap. Failure to control for the endogeneity of union status may well lead to simultaneous equation bias in the estimates of β. Essentially the problem arises if selection into union status is non-random (Robinson, 1989). In the following section, we examine several approaches adopted in the literature to overcome this and related estimation problems.

It must be emphasised that these criticisms do not invalidate research aiming to quantify the impact of unions on wages. The reader should not regard empirical estimation of union wage gaps as of no value because of the possibility that estimates might suffer from the various problems outlined above. A good piece of empirical work not only carries out the modelling and estimation carefully, but also relates the analysis to the relevant environment, and is therefore able to provide considered justification for the possible direction of any biases.

6.5 Simultaneous equation and panel studies estimating the union wage differential using micro data

This section examines estimates of union wage differentials based on simultaneous equation estimation and on panel studies. First, consider the *simultaneous equation approach*. How can the possible endogeneity of union membership be allowed for in a model attempting to estimate the union wage gap? There are several popular methods in the literature. These include simultaneous equation estimation of both wages and membership, and the use of instrumental variables (IV) or control function methods such as the inverse Mills ratio (see Lewis (1986) and Robinson (1989) for further discussion). Since the simultaneous equation approach relies on estimation of a union membership equation in addition to wages, it is helpful initially to consider the theoretical background to membership determination.[18]

The simultaneity issue directs attention to the union status variable for individual data. Where individual data are being used, this amounts to estimating an equation explaining why individuals unionise. If an individual decides to join a union because there is a positive union–nonunion wage differential, then the unionisation equation should be estimated simultaneously with the wages equations, or at least an attempt should be made to control for simultaneity. Studies estimating a unionisation equation as well as wage equations in order to calculate union wage gaps have generally followed an *ad hoc* approach in specifying the unionisation equation. Indeed, the empirical literature on union wage gaps in a simultaneous equation framework, and the theoretical literature examining

---

[18] There is a very small theoretical literature on simultaneous wage and membership determination; see footnote 7 of this chapter.

unionisation decisions, have largely proceeded separately, with little inter-action between the two. For this reason, it is worth considering briefly the union membership decision, before we move on to discuss the estimates of the union wage gap derived from simultaneous equation models.

In chapter 3, the 'free-rider' problem was mentioned in the context of union membership. Here it was argued that, for the *individual*, the level of union wages is a collective good applying to all covered workers irrespective of their union status. Hence the individual, facing positive membership costs (union dues or subscription costs) might take a free ride on union membership. According to this view, workers will unionise only if they are committed to the union movement, or gain positive utility from the private services like grievance procedures offered by unions to their membership.[19] These factors will affect the individual demand for union membership. It is also necessary to consider the supply of union jobs, that is, jobs in which there is a recognised union or any union representation at all. Clearly factors like employer resistance, and union recognition or derecognition will also affect the union decision (Farber, 1983; Freeman, 1986; Disney *et al.*, 1993; Naylor and Raaum, 1993). Freeman (1986) suggests that the magnitude of the union wage differential will affect the intensity of managerial opposition to union recognition. While a wage gap may encourage workers to unionise, it will also encourage firms to resist unions. Hence the net effect on union status is ambiguous.[20] The upshot of this discussion is that the specifications of union status in the simultaneous equation estimates to be discussed below may suffer from misspecification and omitted variable bias, since many of the factors outlined above have not been included.[21]

The simultaneous equation approach to estimation of union wage gaps generally first estimates the probability of union membership, typically as a reduced-form equation (without the wage gap as a regressor).[22] Then

---

[19] For *empirical* models of union membership in this vein, see Bain and Elias (1985), Booth (1986), Blanchflower *et al.* (1990) and Booth and Chatterji (1993b).

[20] In the US institutional framework, managerial resistance takes the form of opposing union organisation in NLRB-supervised elections, as discussed in chapter 2. In Britain with its different institutional structure, the closest analogy is with recognition or derecognition of a union, or with the refusal of management to recognise a union on a greenfield site.

[21] Moreover, identification problems arise in estimation of simultaneous equation models of wage and membership that are not grounded in any theory, since there is no clear theoretical reason for any variables determining membership not also to determine the wage rate. The theoretical model in Booth and Chatterji (1993b) offers a potential means of identification, since the union incentive goods affect membership but not wages. See also Symons and Walker (1990), whose data offer a potential means of identification, as membership is signalled by payment of union dues, which do not affect the wage rate.

[22] Since at the individual level union status is effectively a dummy variable taking the value 1 if the person is a union member and 0 otherwise, the equation for unionisation has a dichotomous dependent variable. This equation is typically estimated using a logit or probit model.

predicted values, or transformations of predicted values, for union status
are used as a regressor in the earnings equation, either instead of or as well
as observed union status. Finally, the predicted mean log wage differential
is calculated; this should be an unbiased estimate (but more below). This
predicted wage differential may then be added as an explanatory variable
into final estimation of the union probability equation, which is now in
structural form. The full structural model is now equations (7) and (8)
augmented by the union membership equation, that is:

$$\left. \begin{aligned} D_i &= \mathbf{Z}_i'\alpha + \rho(\ln w_i^U - \ln w_i^N) + \mu_i \\ \ln w_i^U &= \mathbf{X}_i'\gamma^U + \mu_{1i} \\ \ln w_i^N &= \mathbf{X}_i'\gamma^N + \mu_{2i} \end{aligned} \right\} \tag{15}$$

where ρ is the coefficient to the union wage-gap estimates used in the
structural unionisation equation, $\mathbf{Z}_i$ is a vector of exogenous variables
explaining unionisation, and α is a vector of coefficients to be estimated.

What are the estimated union wage markups from the simultaneous
equation models? Lewis (1986) surveys those simultaneous equation estimates from US studies for which there are corresponding OLS estimates of
wages equation(s), and is rather pessimistic about the results. He finds that
the simultaneous equation estimates are neither systematically smaller nor
larger than the OLS estimates.[23] But they possess a disadvantage that does
not characterise the OLS estimates. This is their extreme sensitivity to the
method used for estimation, the inclusion of additional variables, assumptions about the error terms, and the data used. Because of this lack of
robustness, Lewis prefers the OLS estimates, although it must be borne in
mind that these are likely to be overestimates, owing to possible omitted
variable bias. It must be emphasised, however, that there is disagreement in
the literature about the simultaneous equation estimates.[24]

Now consider *panel estimates* of the union wage gap. How do the
estimates of the union–nonunion wage gap obtained from estimation of
(14) compare with those from OLS cross-section equations? So far there
have been no published studies estimating wage gaps from British longitudinal data, largely because of the relative paucity of panel data on both
union membership and wages. Our discussion will therefore be confined to
US estimates, but in view of the institutional differences between the two

---

[23] There appears to be just one published study using British data that addresses the
simultaneity issue (see Murphy *et al.*, 1992). However, while their sample selectivity
estimates suggested a downward bias to the estimated union wage gap for both non-manual
and manual men, the results were not significant.

[24] Robinson (1989) for example argues that, if the simultaneous equation estimates obtained
from large individual micro data sets are considered on their own (and estimates from
smaller less reliable data sets are ignored), the simultaneous equation estimates consistently
show a larger union wage differential than those obtained from OLS estimation.

countries, it should not be assumed that these estimates would necessarily apply to Britain. Lewis (1986: ch. 5) has carried out a painstaking analysis of seventeen panel studies using US data, and has compared these with cross-section estimates using the same data-sets.[25] His analysis shows that the panel estimates are generally smaller than corresponding cross-section wage-gap estimates by a factor of one-half. Recall from the previous section that the US cross-section estimates were in the order of 12 to 20%. However, Lewis argues that it is inappropriate to assume that the cross-section estimates are upward biased by a factor of two, first because the variance of the ratio of panel to cross-section estimates is large, and secondly because of measurement error associated with union status in panel studies. Mincer (1983), Freeman (1984) and Lewis (1986) *inter alia* investigate the extent of measurement error.[26]

Why should measurement error associated with union status be greater in longitudinal analyses than in cross-sectional ones? Suppose that only a small number of workers are misclassified by union status, and that misclassification is random. There will be a larger number of misclassified workers in the longitudinal data (two periods) than in the cross-section data (one period). Moreover, because the number of individuals changing union status in longitudinal studies is typically small[27] (even though the surveys on which they are based are large), there will be fewer correct observations. Consequently, there will be a larger proportion of incorrect observations in panel data, and therefore a larger measurement bias to the union wage-gap estimates (Freeman, 1984: 5).

A further problem with longitudinal studies also relates to the fact that they rely for estimation of the union–nonunion wage differential on individuals who have changed union status over the period. Some of these individuals have changed union status because of changing job from a union to a nonunion firm, or vice versa – the 'movers'. Job 'movers' may be very different from 'stayers', and therefore an estimation procedure that relies on the movers may be introducing further selectivity bias into the estimates of union wage gaps. For those individuals who move voluntarily, it might be assumed that the move follows from a higher wage offer. Consider a worker moving from a union job to a job with no recognised union. To the extent that s/he has accepted the job because of a potential wage increase, then it is likely that the nonunion firm is characterised by higher than average wages. Reliance on these workers to estimate the union

---

[25] These are principally the National Longitudinal Survey (NLS) and the Panel Study of Income Dynamics (PSID).

[26] Mincer (1983) using the NLS and the PSID finds that stayers typically outnumber movers among those individuals who changed their union status, and argues that this suggests measurement error in the job stayers through misreporting.

[27] See Freeman and Medoff (1984, table 3.2).

Table 6.2. *British manual union weekly earnings gaps 1980–90*

	% mean wage gap		
	skilled	semi-skilled	unskilled
1980	1.7*	6.6	—
1984	3.4*	10.0	10.2
1990	1.5*	6.3	7.2

Notes: * denotes insignificant.
The change in the differential across time periods for each skill group is insignificantly different from zero.
Source: Stewart (1991, 1994).

wage gap leads to an *underestimate* of the true effect. Now consider the alternative – a worker moving from a job with no recognised union to a union job. To the extent that the presence of union wage gaps leads to a queue for union jobs, and that higher quality workers can obtain these jobs, then an individual who is able to move from nonunion to union is likely to be of higher than average ability and therefore to have been paid more than average in the nonunion sector. This also will lead to an *underestimate* of the union wage gap in panel studies (Freeman and Medoff, 1984).

In summary, it is likely that while a cross-section microdata estimate is likely to be an overestimate of the union wage gap owing to selectivity or missing variable bias, panel data studies may yield underestimates, owing to the problems outlined above. Freeman (1984) suggests that the panel study estimates can be regarded as a lower bound, and the cross-section estimates as an upper bound, of the true union wage gap.[28]

6.6 Changes in the union wage differential over time

Estimates of the union wage differential over time can be obtained by gathering together all the cross-section estimates for different years, and also by estimating a model such as (6) using aggregated or grouped cross-section data for a number of years. A striking finding is that, for Britain, the manual union–nonunion weekly earnings gap has remained roughly constant over the periods 1980–4 and 1984–90. A comparison of cross-section estimates using the three Workplace Industrial Relations Surveys, summarised in table 6.2, reveals very little change in the average union wage

[28] See Robinson (1989) for further (technical) discussion of these issues.

Table 6.3. *US union wage gaps 1967–79*

	% mean wage gap
1967	12
1968	12
1969	12
1970	13
1971	16
1972	13
1973	16
1974	15
1975	17
1976	20
1977	19
1978	19
1979	14

Source: Lewis (1986, table 9.7).

differential for manual workers over the decade. This stability is remarkable, given the considerable changes in the external environment (Stewart, 1991, 1994).

There are as yet insufficient British microdata studies using similar data-sets at different time periods to allow us to comment reliably on wage gaps of types of workers other than manual ones. However, two studies using pooled British cross-section surveys over the first half of the 1980s do suggest that the average union wage gap for *all* workers has not altered significantly over this period (Symons and Walker, 1990; Blanchflower, 1991), in spite of the increase in unemployment and the anti-union legislation of the period.

For the USA, Lewis (1986) has gathered together the estimates from cross-section microdata studies using similar US data sources; these are summarised in table 6.3. He suggests these are upper bounds, since they are likely to suffer from selectivity bias, as we discussed earlier in this chapter. The mean over the period 1967–79 is 15%. The US union wage gap increased during the 1970s, but fell at the end of the decade. Studies by Edwards and Swaim (1986) and Linneman and Wachter (1986) indicate that the wage gap has been relatively stable since.[29]

---

[29] Using cross-section data from the Current Population Surveys, both studies estimated cross-section wage equations across industries, with Edwards and Swaim estimating the union coverage wage gap for the years 1979 and 1984, and Linneman and Wachter estimating the union status wage gap for the years 1973 to 1984. Their estimates cannot be

6.7 Unions and wage dispersion

The focus of this chapter is on the estimation of the union–nonunion wage gap, but it is also interesting to consider briefly the impact of unions on wage dispersion. The available empirical evidence suggests that on average there is a positive union–nonunion wage differential, although when disaggregated calculations are made, unions are not always associated with positive wage gaps. Thus for example, Stewart (1990), using WIRS2 data for semi-skilled manual British workers, showed that where product markets are competitive, there is a zero union wage gap. Moreover, firms with market power paid more than competitive firms even in the absence of unionisation.

The presence of positive union–nonunion wage differentials suggests that, on average, unionisation is associated with wage dispersion *across* an economy. However, the question also arises as to the impact of trade unions on wage dispersion *within* the union sector. Given that the stated goals of the trade union movement are to standardise rates of pay across firms, and to attach wage rates to jobs rather than to individuals, it might be expected that the dispersion of wage rates would be reduced within the union sector. There has been surprisingly little research into the impact of unions on wage dispersion and wage inequality. However, the available evidence for both the USA and Britain indicates that trade unions significantly reduce wage dispersion. Freeman (1980a, 1982) and Hirsch (1982) show that US unions reduce intra-industry wage dispersion, inter-firm and intra-firm wage dispersion, and wage dispersion across certain labour markets. Gosling and Machin (1993) show that trade unions in Britain also reduce wage dispersion within the union sector; they show that both the inter-establishment and intra-establishment wage distributions for manual workers are narrower in plants with recognised unions.[30]

directly compared with those in table 6.3, since, although they are based on cross-section regressions, the data are aggregated at the industry level. Both studies find that the average aggregate wage gap is stable over the period. Edwards and Swaim find, for their sample, that trade union membership declined from 27.8% in 1979 to 19.0% in 1984. It is an interesting question why trade union membership has declined, but the union wage gap has increased in the 1970s and remained relatively stable since. Freeman (1986) finds a positive correlation between the wage gap and a proxy for managerial resistance to union organisation – the number of unfair labour practices per worker in NLRB elections over the period 1950 to 1980. He argues that almost one-quarter of the decline in union membership over the period is due to the increasing wage premium of the 1970s causing an increase in managerial resistance.

[30] They also find that, over the period 1980 to 1990, pay dispersion for the semi-skilled increased in both union and nonunion establishments, but increased more in the *nonunion* establishments. An interesting issue is the extent to which the increase in earnings dispersion is due to declining union density. Both the USA and Britain have experienced increasing earnings dispersion. See Card (1991) and Freeman (1991) for discussion of unions and changes in US earnings dispersion.

6.8 Conclusion

This chapter has examined empirical estimates of union wage gaps and discussed problems associated with different methods of estimation. While the estimates from individual-level or establishment-level cross-section data may be upward-biased, they appear to be more robust than simultaneous equation models. Average estimates of the union wage gap from cross-section models are around 15% for the USA and 8% for Britain. Moreover, average union wage gaps in the USA and, in particular, in Britain appear to have been relatively stable over recent years.

However, there is considerable diversity in union wage gap estimates across individuals, sectors and bargaining structures. A part of this diversity appears to reflect differences in economic rents in different product markets, and in the monopoly power of unions to extract a share of these rents.

An enormous number of US studies have established that there is a positive average union–nonunion wage gap in the USA. A considerably smaller body of research in Britain has found that there is also a positive average union–nonunion wage gap in Britain. A very small literature has found that unions appear to have decreased wage dispersion within the union sector. But what impact do trade unions have on other economic variables? In the following chapter, we consider the available stylised facts about trade unions and economic performance, as measured by productivity and productivity growth, investment and employment.

Appendix 6A. Derivation of the union–nonunion wage differential from the right-to-manage model

The derivation of an expression for the union wage gap in this appendix follows the approach of Layard et al. (1991: 25–8, 100–3). Suppose that the union–firm pair bargain over wages, but the firm retains the right to determine ex post employment after the wage bargain has been struck. Assume further that union workers are risk-neutral, that is, that a worker's utility is linear in wages. This is a very restrictive assumption, but one which considerably simplifies the analysis.

Suppose the union associated with firm i has a utilitarian objective function, given by

$$U_i = n_i w_i + (1 - n_i) r \tag{A1}$$

where n_i is the number of workers employed by the ith firm next period, and r denotes alternative income from employment in the nonunion sector. The generalised Nash bargain becomes

$$\max_w \phi = \{n_i(w_i).[w_i - r]\}^\beta \Pi_i^{1-\beta} \tag{A2}$$

where Π denotes profits. Take natural logarithms of (A2) to obtain

$$\max_{w} \ ln \ \phi = \beta ln \ n_i(w_i) + \beta ln[w_i - r] + (1 - \beta)ln \ \Pi_i \tag{A3}$$

The first-order condition from maximisation of (A3) is

$$\frac{\beta}{w_i - r} + \frac{\beta n_i'(w_i)}{n_i} + \frac{(1 - \beta)\Pi_i'}{\Pi_i} = 0 \tag{A4}$$

where $\Pi_i' = -n_i$ by the envelope theorem.[31] Multiply (A4) by w_i and invert to obtain

$$\frac{w_i - r}{w_i} = \frac{1}{\epsilon} + \frac{\beta \Pi_i}{(1 - \beta)w_i n_i} \tag{A5}$$

Equation (A5) gives an expression for the union wage gap. It shows that the union wage gap is higher the smaller is the elasticity of labour demand ϵ. What is the impact on the wage differential of the second term on the right-hand side of (A5)? The term $\Pi_i/w_i n_i$ is related to the degree of competitiveness in the product market, and to labour intensity. To see this, we now impose more structure on the model, and assume that the firm faces a constant elasticity of substitution (CES) product demand equation, given by

$$q = p^{-\eta} \tag{A6}$$

where the subscripts have been dropped for expositional convenience. The elasticity of product demand is given, after differentiation of (A6) and rearrangement, as $\eta = -\frac{dq.p}{dp.q}$. Rearrange (A6) to obtain

$$p = q^{-1/\eta} \tag{A7}$$

and substitute into the firm's revenue function to obtain

$$\text{Revenue} = pq = q^{-1/\eta}q = q^{\kappa} \tag{A8}$$

where $\kappa = 1 - 1/\eta$. The more elastic is product demand η, the greater the degree of product market competitiveness given by κ. If $\eta \to \infty$, $\kappa \to 1$ and there is much competition. As $\eta \to 1$, $\kappa \to 0$ and there is little competition.

Now suppose that the firm's technology is Cobb–Douglas so that output is given by

$$q = n^a k^{1-a} \tag{A9}$$

and that only labour is variable in the short run. Short-run profits are given (from (A8) and (A9)) by choosing employment to satisfy

$$\max_{n} \ \Pi = (n^a k^{1-a})^{\kappa} - wn \tag{A10}$$

---

[31] The firm's profits Π are given by $\Pi = pq[n(w)] - wn(w)$. When profits are differentiated with respect to w, we obtain

$$\Pi_w = (pq' - w)n' - n = 0$$

But since the firm will always choose employment *ex post* so that $w = pq'$, that is, the wage rate is equal to the marginal product of labour, we can write $\Pi_w = -n$.

The first-order condition of (A10) is given by

$$\kappa q^{\kappa-1} a n^{a-1} k^{1-a} = w \tag{A11}$$

which can be rearranged to yield

$$\frac{n}{k} = \left(\frac{w}{a\kappa p}\right)^{-1/(1-a)} \tag{A12}$$

We now want to eliminate p from (A12). Substitute for p from (A7), and eliminate q from the result using (A9). Subsequent simplification ultimately yields

$$\frac{n^*}{k} = \left(\frac{w}{a\kappa} . k^{1/\eta}\right)^{-1/(1-a\kappa)} \tag{A13}$$

We want now to use (A13) to obtain an expression for Π/wn in (A5). Profits at the optimum are given by

$$\Pi^* = q^{\kappa^*} - wn^* \tag{A14}$$

where the asterisks denote optimum values. Notice that we can rearrange the first-order condition in (A11) to obtain an expression for q^κ, given by

$$q^\kappa = wn/a\kappa \tag{A15}$$

Substitute this expresssion for q^κ into (A14) to obtain

$$\Pi = wn[(1/a\kappa) - 1]$$

$$= wn[(1-a\kappa)/a\kappa] \tag{A16}$$

Thus we can now write that, at the optimum, $\Pi/wn = (1-a\kappa)/a\kappa$. Substitute this into the expression for the wage gap in (A5) to obtain

$$\frac{w_i - r}{w_i} = \frac{1}{\epsilon} + \frac{\beta(1-a\kappa)}{(1-\beta)a\kappa} \tag{A17}$$

Equation (A17) can now form the basis for estimating the markup of union wages over the outside alternative r. From (A17) it is clear that the wage markup is increasing in union power (β), and is declining in product market competitiveness (κ) and also in labour intensity (a).

7 The impact of trade unions on productivity, investment, profitability, employment and hours

7.1 Introduction

The orthodox view of monopoly trade unions is that they achieve a monopoly wage gain at the expense of one or more parties: nonunion workers who may receive lower wages; consumers if the cost increases can be passed on in the form of higher prices; or capitalists whose profits may be reduced. We saw in chapter 3 that a necessary condition for wage gains is the existence of economic rents in the product market. It was also argued that in order for a union to achieve wage gains, it must have the necessary power to force the firm to share the surplus. Alternatively, the firm must be willing to share any surplus with the union in exchange for higher productivity.

The latter view – that unions may be associated with productivity increases – is the focus of the first part of this chapter. While the monopoly 'face' of trade unions focuses on the negative aspects of unionism, an alternative view of unions is that in some circumstances they may be efficiency-enhancing, in the sense that the presence of a union may result in improvements in the organisation of the workplace and the productivity of the workforce. How does this improved productivity come about? There are two popular views in the literature, both of which can be placed under the broad heading of organisation theories, since unionisation may affect organisation of production and workers' incentives. The first organisation theory is the view that the advent of unionisation, with its associated higher labour costs, 'shocks' management into operating the firm more efficiently. This approach assumes that prior to unionisation the firm was not efficient. Following Leibenstein (1966), suppose that output in a firm depends not only on capital and labour inputs, but also on 'X-efficiency', which encompasses such factors as the firm's incentive structure to encourage effort, managerial organisation and supervision, and working conditions. If these inputs are not least-cost combinations, as might be the case if the firm is not fully competitive, then the advent of unionisation might 'shock' management into more efficient practices rather than face the alternative of going out of business.

The second organisation theory suggesting that trade unions may alter productivity encompasses the notion that the advent of unionisation is associated with changes in procedural arrangements and improvements in worker morale and co-operation (Slichter, 1941; Slichter, Healy and Livernash, 1960). This approach was extensively discussed in chapter 3, and therefore only the broad thrust of the argument will be repeated here. The theory assumes plausibly that the firm operates in a world of imperfect information or uncertainty, and that employment relationships are frequently long-term, perhaps because of specific human capital or other labour turnover costs. However, problems may arise, after a worker has begun employment with a firm, that were not perceived *ex ante*. In such an environment, the trade union may be viewed as an organisation acting on behalf of workers, expressing their views and looking after their interests. Some of the benefits provided by the union as agent are relevant to the firm's performance, for example communication of workers' preferences to management (Freeman and Medoff, 1979). Union provision of these benefits may be cheaper than individual provision, through economies of scale. It may also be the case that individual provision is not feasible. In addition, many aspects of labour contracts and workplace characteristics are collective in nature, for example grievance and promotion procedures and safety arrangements, and are therefore subject to the usual problems of preference revelation. Individuals may be unwilling to reveal their true preferences to management, because of fear of retaliation. So dissatisfied workers may leave the firm.[1] The union, however, is able to provide a collective voice, and can prevent managerial retaliation through the strike weapon. Even if the firm were able to devise institutional arrangements with individual workers, it could still cheat on legally non-enforceable arrangements if external conditions should change, as individual workers do not possess a credible means of punishment.

Firms may also desire trade union presence, since such presence may reduce labour turnover. The importance of this to the firm will be greater if employment continuity is in the interests of management. This is likely to be the case where there are substantial costs to labour turnover, for example with hiring and training costs. Where both parties desire employment

---

[1] A second problem associated with the collective nature of the workplace is the following. Suppose that a particular production technology is characterised by complementarities in production, for example, assembly line production (Duncan and Stafford, 1980). Output per period will be determined by the productivity or effort level of the slowest worker. If joint effort inputs can be jointly determined, then pressure may be brought to bear on the lowest-effort worker to increase productivity. The union may be an appropriate organisation to negotiate with the firm about joint effort levels.

continuity, but the firm has a degree of latitude over adjustment to exogenous shocks, both workers and management may prefer well-specified procedures for the resolution of disputes, the latter because such procedures reduce the cost of negotiation and the risk of incurring labour turnover costs.

But procedural arrangements may be achieved in the absence of trade unions.[2] What advantage is there to the arrangement of such procedures with a trade union rather than with individuals? At least two advantages have been suggested in the literature. First, negotiation costs may be lower when a union is involved, since the firm can deal with the unions' specialists instead of undertaking individual negotiations with each worker. Secondly, arrangements between individuals and managers may not be incentive-compatible. Trade unions may prevent management reneging on legally non-enforceable agreements (Malcomson, 1983). The union has a credible threat to prevent this – the withdrawal of *all* labour – a punishment strategy not possessed by individual workers. Through its collective nature, the trade union thus possesses two advantages over individual monitoring of the firm or individual negotiation – the union has a monopoly control of labour supply, and it also has the resources to investigate more thoroughly than the individual the firm's case.

In a nutshell, this view of the trade union implies that unions may be associated with increased labour productivity. Thus, although unions may cause wages to increase in the union sector, neither employment nor firms' profitability need necessarily be greatly affected, since the higher labour cost may be offset by improved labour productivity. However, an alternative view is that unionisation reduces morale and motivation, and obstructs the efficient organisation of capital and labour, since it constrains the choice set of management. Moreover, some unions enforce restrictive practices, for example overmanning rules, that are likely to reduce productivity. Unionisation is also at times associated with industrial action that may have an adverse effect on productivity, and unions may also adversely affect investment. Further, some unions follow an adversarial rather than a co-

[2] For example, a survey of the US Bureau of National Affairs Personnel Policies Forum in 1968 indicated that some 30% of nonunion firms are characterised by formal grievance procedures (Freeman, 1980b: 645). This may of course be an effect of the threat of unionisation. In Britain, procedural arrangements are found in both union and nonunion workplaces. Using WIRS3 data for 1990, Millward *et al.* (1992) found that in the nonunion private sector, 82% of workplaces had procedures for discipline and dismissals, 77% for individual grievances, 77% for health and safety procedures, and 46% for pay procedures. In the *unionised* private sector, the comparable figures were 96%, 93%, 93% and 84%. Where unions were present, the procedures were almost always jointly agreed. The increase in the spread of procedural arrangements since 1980 is attributed by Millward *et al.* (1992: 212) to the expansion of individual employment legislation, and to industrial tribunals increasingly examining employer practice after disagreements.

operative approach to industrial relations, engendering a low level of co-operation and morale, and thereby lower productivity. Therefore, the sign and the magnitude of organisational effects of unions on productivity and performance are ultimately empirical issues.[3] Given available data, it is not possible to estimate the individual impact of all the factors outlined above on productivity; instead, studies typically estimate the productivity impact of all of these influences taken together.

There are a number of testable hypotheses arising from the organisational view of the trade union as enhancing (or altering) productivity. First, union presence should be associated with a lower turnover rate, since it is argued that trade unions are a mechanism allowing workers to voice complaints to management, rather than being forced to find another job if they are dissatisfied with their present employer. Secondly, union workers should have higher job satisfaction. Thirdly, worker productivity and effort should be higher in unionised firms than nonunion firms, *ceteris paribus*. Fourthly, conditional on union workers being characterised by higher labour productivity than nonunion workers, the impact of union wage gains on employment and profits might be small, depending on the price-setting behaviour of firms.[4] Note that this latter hypothesis assumes that firms are on their labour demand curves, an assumption which is itself a research hypothesis, as we saw in chapter 5 when examining the contract curve model of union wage determination.[5] The impact of trade unions on productivity is likely to differ across unions and plants; any reading of the industrial relations literature for the USA and for Britain indicates that different trade unions are characterised by often widely diverging attitudes to enhancing industrial co-operation.

This fourth hypothesis – that conditional on unions raising productivity, employment may be unaffected – is illustrated in figure 7.1. Suppose that the union determines a wage rate of w^U, and the nonunion wage rate is given by w^N. If the value of the marginal product of labour (denoted in the figure by VMPL) increases as a result of unionisation, then even though the union causes *wages* to increase, the net impact on employment for the competitive

---

[3] Both views, about the improvement or worsening of industrial relations after unionisation, suggest that both the intercept and the slope of the VMPL curve may be affected by unionisation. Empirical work should therefore treat this as a research hypothesis.

[4] For example, suppose that firms have a degree of product market power, and choose employment in order to achieve a markup of price over marginal cost that is equal to market power, as is shown in appendix 3A. If unions raise productivity *ceteris paribus*, marginal cost to firms falls and therefore prices fall. If there is a simple cost structure, such that marginal cost equals average cost, then the firms' profits will be the same.

[5] The last two hypotheses may be consistent with several theories about unionisation. For example, it is not possible to distinguish clearly between the 'shock' theory (where management is shocked by unionisation into adopting more efficient managerial practices), and the 'collective voice' theory (whereby unionisation improves workers' morale by giving them a voice at the workplace, thereby increasing their willingness to supply effort).

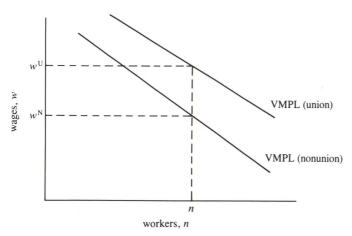

Figure 7.1. Illustrating the possibility that employment may be unchanged by unionism if productivity improvements are sufficiently large.

firm may be small, or there may even be no employment impact, as illustrated. Initially, it might be tempting to think that there is resource misallocation in this case, because unionisation has resulted in differences in marginal products between the union and nonunion sectors. Suppose that prior to unionisation, there were just two sectors of the economy, and that wages and marginal products were equated across sectors, in other words there was allocative efficiency (see figure 3.3). After unionisation in one sector, union wages increase but union productivity also increases sufficiently to maintain employment in each sector at the pre-union levels. Then it is straightforward to see that the VMPL will be higher in the union sector than the nonunion sector. This is *not* to say, however, that there is resource misallocation. For according to the institutional view of trade unions as efficiency-enhancing, the productivity increase was not feasible in the absence of trade unions.

Sections 7.2 to 7.5 examine the various approaches that have been adopted in the literature to *test empirically* the hypothesis that unions increase productivity. Section 7.6 looks at the impact of unions on investment, profitability, employment and hours. As in the rest of this book, our approach is not to survey all the empirical studies in this area. Instead, the purpose is to provide the reader with an understanding of the methodological framework adopted to test the hypothesis that unions increase productivity, and to make clear the econometric problems – many unresolved but being investigated by econometricians and applied economists – in so doing. The principal stylised facts or empirical regularities emerging from the literature will be briefly summarised.

7.2 Modelling union effects on productivity

A typical version of the production function approach to estimating the union–nonunion productivity differential is developed below. Suppose that an industry, sector or economy has a production function that can be written generally as

$$q = q(n,k) \tag{1}$$

where q denotes output, n is the number of workers and k represents capital. Suppose there are two types of labour, union workers, denoted by n^U, and nonunion workers, denoted by n^N. To proceed further, assume that the product market is competitive and the production technology is Cobb–Douglas. Equation (1) can therefore be rewritten as the following explicit function of labour and capital:

$$q = Ak^a(n^N + \gamma n^U)^{1-a} \tag{2}$$

where A is a technical efficiency parameter representing the influence of variables explaining output differences between firms or industries, and $0 < a < 1$. The superscripts U and N denote union and nonunion labour respectively. The production function in (2) assumes constant returns to scale, since the exponents sum to unity.[6] Notice that the exponents a and $(1 - a)$ indicate the relative share of that input in the total product,[7] and can also be interpreted as the partial elasticity of output with respect to the respective input (Chiang, 1984). If $\gamma > 1$, unionised workers are more productive than nonunionised workers; if $\gamma = 1$, there is no difference between the productivity of union and nonunion workers; if $\gamma < 1$, union workers are less productive than nonunion workers.

   Equation (2) assumes that the production functions characterising the union and nonunion sectors are the same. This follows from the fact that, in (2), the *only* way in which the union and nonunion sectors differ is through

---

[6] See Chiang (1984) for a discussion of the properties of the Cobb–Douglas production function.

[7] Suppose that profits Π are given by

$$\Pi = pq - wn - rk = pn^a k^{1-a} - wn - rk$$

where p is product price, and the firm is a price taker. The two first-order conditions are given by

$$\partial\Pi/\partial n = apn^{a-1}k^a - w = 0$$

$$\partial\Pi/\partial k = (1 - a)pn^a k^{-a} - r = 0$$

Rearrangement of the first-order conditions yields

$$a = wn/pq = \text{share of wage bill in total output}$$

$$(1 - a) = rk/pq = \text{share of capital in total output}$$

the coefficient γ. Equation (2) allows for trade unions to affect productivity through labour-augmenting (capital-saving) technical change. This is a strong assumption, particularly when it is remembered that a facet of the theoretical justification for a positive union–nonunion productivity differential was that technology in union establishments differed from that in nonunion ones, that is, $a^U \neq a^N$. Moreover, the theory also suggested that union presence is more likely to be found in particular technologies, for example where there are complementarities in production, skill specificities or a non-competitive market structure providing a surplus that can be bargained over. This may well imply that $A^U \neq A^N$.

Another strong assumption underlying the use of the Cobb–Douglas production function of equation (2) is that the elasticity of substitution is constrained to be unity (Wallis, 1979: 43). Some researchers, concerned with the restrictive nature of the Cobb–Douglas specification, have used a translog production function, which nests the Cobb–Douglas as a special case.[8] However, an advantage of the Cobb–Douglas production function is its tractability. From (2), an estimating equation for labour productivity can easily be derived. Manipulation of (2) yields

$$q = Ak^{\alpha}n^{1-\alpha}[1 + (\gamma - 1)D]^{1-\alpha} \tag{3}$$

where D is the proportion of the total workforce unionised, n^U/n.[9] Since (3) measures total output and what we are after is a measure of labour productivity, divide both sides of (3) by n, and take the natural logarithm to linearise the equation. This yields[10]

$$\ln(q/n) = \ln A + \alpha\ln(k/n) + (1 - \alpha)\ln[1 + (\gamma - 1)D] \tag{4}$$

where the second term on the right-hand side controls for capital substitution following union wage increases. It can be shown, by the use of a first-order Taylor series expansion, that $\ln(1 + x)$ is approximately equal to x for *small* values of x, where $x = (\gamma - 1)D$ in this case. Hence (4) can be written as

$$\ln(q/n) \cong \ln A + \alpha\ln(k/n) + (1 - \alpha)(\gamma - 1)D \tag{5}$$

If the assumption of constant returns to scale is relaxed, (5) is augmented by the variable $\ln n$, which can be interpreted as establishment size if

---

[8] Pencavel (1977) uses a constant elasticity of substitution (CES) production function to estimate total output. Bemmels (1987) uses a translog production function and his data reject the restrictions that the production function is Cobb–Douglas.

[9] The intermediate steps in the derivation of (3) from (2) are as follows:

$$q = Ak^{\alpha}(n^N + \gamma n^U)^{1-\alpha}$$
$$= Ak^{\alpha}(n^N + \gamma n^U - n^U + n^U)^{1-\alpha}$$
$$= Ak^{\alpha}[n + (\gamma - 1)n^U]^{1-\alpha}$$

[10] The term $(1 - \alpha)\ln(n/n)$ drops out, since $\ln 1$ is zero.

estimation is carried out using establishment-level data.[11] To estimate (5), assume that $\ln(q/n)$ is also a function of a vector of observable firm or industry attributes $\mathbf{X}'\delta$, where δ is a vector of coefficients to be estimated. If it is believed that management is likely to respond to unionisation and its associated higher labour costs by substituting higher quality workers, then $\mathbf{X}$ might also include human capital variables measuring worker quality. With the inclusion of an error term μ, (5) becomes

$$\ln(q_t/n_t) = \ln A_t + \alpha\ln(k_t/n_t) + (1-\alpha)(\gamma-1)D_t + \mathbf{X}'_t\delta + \mu_t \qquad (6)$$

where the subscript t denotes the time period.[12] Equation (6) forms the basis for an estimating equation in many production function studies attempting to measure the union–nonunion productivity differential. Notice that in (6) both capital per worker and labour quality have been controlled for, and hence the estimated coefficient $(1-\alpha)(\gamma-1)$ represents the logarithmic union–nonunion productivity differential. The union–nonunion productivity differential in percentage terms is given by $\{\exp[(1-\alpha)(\gamma-1)].100\}$.

Equation (6) can also be interpreted in terms of total factor productivity (TFP). Subtract $\alpha\ln(k/n)$ from both sides of (5), to obtain the following equation measuring the impact of unionisation on TFP:

$$\ln q_t - \alpha\ln k_t - (1-\alpha)\ln n_t = \text{TFP} = \\ \ln A_t + (1-\alpha)(\gamma-1)D_t + \mathbf{X}'_t\delta + \mu_t \qquad (7)$$

If $\gamma > 1$, then unions are interpreted as increasing both labour productivity through (6) and TFP through (7). Notice that α is the share of capital in total output, and $(1-\alpha)$ is the share of labour; this derives from profit maximisation under perfect competition. Equation (7) can be interpreted as TFP *growth* through taking first differences; TFP growth by definition is the rate of growth of output less the weighted sum of the growth rates of the inputs, where the weights are given by the shares of each input.

7.3 Some problems with this approach

There are a number of problems associated with this approach to measurement of the union–nonunion productivity differential. Some of these

[11] Replace $(1-\alpha)$ in (2) and (3) by θ (where the special case of constant returns to scale is given by $\theta + \alpha = 1$). It can easily be verified that (5) becomes

$$\ln(q/n) \cong \ln A + \alpha\ln(k/n) + (\theta+\alpha-1)\ln n + \theta(\gamma-1)D \qquad (5a)$$

A significantly positive (negative) estimated coefficient to $\ln n$ would suggest that the production function is characterised by increasing (decreasing) returns to scale, while an estimated coefficient not significantly different from zero would suggest constant returns to scale.

[12] Of course, the model might also be estimated using cross-section data, in which case the convention is to subscript by i, where i represents the ith firm or industry.

problems pertain to the production function methodology in general, while others are econometric problems arising in the estimation of (6) or (7). We have already noted that the Cobb–Douglas production function is restrictive, but has the advantage of tractability.[13] We also noted that it assumes both the union and nonunion sectors are characterised by similar technology: production functions in the union and nonunion sectors are assumed to be identical in equation (6). This assumption is unlikely to hold, because the conditions characterising union emergence and power are different from the conditions characterising perfectly competitive labour markets with no unions. A conclusion of chapter 3 was that a necessary condition for union emergence and power was the existence of a surplus; for the union to gain a share of this surplus, it requires monopoly power over labour supply. Indeed, a stylised fact emerging from chapter 6 was that the union wage markup is higher the less competitive the product market. This would also suggest that sectors of the economy with a strong trade union presence are likely to be associated with a different technology or market structure than sectors with no trade unions or with only a weak union presence. It may be the case, therefore, that in equation (6) union density D is endogenous, and that unions may organise in less competitive or productive industries. Furthermore, the advent of unionisation will arguably alter work rules and the industrial relations framework; any studies ought therefore at the minimum, to test the hypothesis that production functions differ between union and nonunion establishments.[14]

It is sometimes argued that a union–nonunion productivity differential simply follows from a union–nonunion *wage* differential (Reynolds, 1986). Consider the labour demand curve in figure 7.1. Suppose that unionisation does *not* result in an outward shift of the value of the marginal product of labour curve, VMPL. Instead, when faced with the higher union wage w^U, the firm shifts from the competitive situation where VMPL $= w^N$ up the labour demand curve to the position where VMPL $= w^U$, laying off workers in the process. Since the firm is now at a higher point on the VMPL curve, marginal productivity is obviously higher. Therefore, studies estimating

[13] The constant elasticity of substitution (CES) production function is more general, and nests the Cobb–Douglas production function as a special case. But it is more difficult to use empirically. Because the CES production function is not readily linearised, in contrast to the Cobb–Douglas, its estimation requires either estimation of its first-order conditions, or direct estimation by *non-linear* methods, or linearisation through making further restrictive assumptions. See Wallis (1979) for discussion of its properties and estimation, and also for the translog production function.

[14] This problem – that (6) assumes both union and nonunion firms are characterised by similar technology – can be met to some extent by interacting the variable measuring the proportion unionised, D, with the other explanatory variables in the equation estimating labour productivity.

equation (5) that find a positive union–nonunion productivity differential are simply picking up this fact.[15]

What are the *econometric* problems associated with estimation of a production function as represented by (6)? First, there is the potential problem of sample selection bias. Suppose that we are estimating (6) using a sample of union and nonunion firms. Are the union firms in the sample representative of all firms that may have become unionised? Or are they simply those unionised firms that managed to survive unionisation by becoming more productive? If the answer to the last question is yes, then the estimates of (6) from our sample of nonunion and *surviving* union firms may suffer from *sample selection bias*. In this case, OLS estimation of (6) will produce biased and inconsistent estimated coefficients. The measured union–nonunion productivity differential will be an overestimate, since it has been estimated on a sample in which there is overrepresentation of efficient surviving unionised firms.

A second problem associated with the empirical implementation of (6) concerns the measure of output q used in the dependent variable, $\ln(q/n)$. Ideally, output should be measured in physical units. But most studies are forced to use value added as an output measure, because output in physical units may not be available. However, value added is measured in terms of prices. To the extent that union wage increases result in higher product prices (if firms are able to pass on cost increases to the consumer), then

---

[15] We can see this formally as follows. Partial differentiation of (2) with respect to union and nonunion labour respectively yields the following:

$$\partial q / \partial n^U \equiv \text{VMPL}^U = \gamma(1-a)q/(n^N + \gamma n^U) \tag{8}$$

and

$$\partial q / \partial n^N \equiv \text{VMPL}^N = (1-a)q/(n^N + \gamma n^U) \tag{9}$$

Using the first-order condition from profit maximisation that the ratio of marginal products is equal to the ratio of wage rates, we find

$$\frac{\text{VMPL}^U}{\text{VMPL}^N} = \frac{w^U}{w^N} = \gamma \tag{10}$$

where w^U is the union wage and w^N is the nonunion wage. Thus the ratio of union–nonunion productivity is equal to the ratio of union to nonunion wages, in turn given by γ. The measured productivity differential simply tracks the union–nonunion wage differential. Reynolds' criticism assumes that firms are on their labour demand curves. We saw in chapter 5 on theory, that if unions and firms bargain over employment *as well as* wages, it is not necessarily optimal for the firm to be on its labour demand curve. According to this theory, union and firm both gain from moving from a position on the labour demand curve to a point where $w^U > \text{VMPL}^U$. Hence the union–nonunion productivity differential will be less than the union–nonunion wage differential. If this is the case, the labour demand curve cannot be used to infer the impact of unions on productivity. If it turns out that firms are not always on their labour demand curves but are instead at a position where $w^U > \text{VMPL}$, as suggested by this theory, the union–nonunion productivity differential will be less than the union–nonunion wage differential (Addison and Hirsch, 1989).

value added in the union sector will be higher than in the nonunion sector simply because union product prices are higher. It follows, therefore, that part of any observed productivity differential may be due to higher prices; thus the estimates of (6) using value added or sales as an output measure will be overestimates of the true union–nonunion productivity differential.

A third problem arising in the empirical implementation of (6) relates to the possibility of omitted variable bias. This is, of course, a potential problem with any empirical estimation. Omitted variable bias might arise in estimation of a union–nonunion productivity differential in the following fashion. Suppose that there are factors such as the quality of management or industrial relations, and that these factors are correlated with unionisation. Suppose that the impact of these variables on the dependent variable cannot be modelled directly, because there is no information on managerial quality or industrial relations in available data. However, if these unobservables are correlated with unionisation, then it can be shown that the estimated coefficient to the unionisation variable D will pick up some of the impact of the unobservable variables, and will therefore not reflect the 'true' impact of unionisation on productivity. If the quality of managerial inputs or industrial relations is systematically higher (lower) in unionised establishments, then the estimated union–nonunion productivity differential will be upward (downward) biased. In this context the direction of the bias might be interpreted as going either way, depending on the *a priori* beliefs of the investigator, unless there is some supplementary evidence from another data source indicating whether unionisation and the variables mentioned in our example – managerial quality and industrial relations – are positively or negatively correlated with unionisation.

Simultaneity bias might also occur in estimation of the union–nonunion productivity differential. Consider equation (6). The inputs on the right-hand side are unlikely to be exogenous, since a positive union–nonunion wage differential will induce firms to alter inputs, as noted in chapter 3. It might therefore be argued that (6) should properly be considered as just one equation in a structural simultaneous equation system in which there are additional equations specifying the determinants of the quantity of the various inputs into the production system. An alternative way of controlling for the fact that the production inputs are simultaneously determined is to replace these inputs on the right-hand side of (6) by 'instrumental' variables, that is, variables that are correlated with the input quantities but not with the left-hand side variable. Another approach is to estimate, in place of a production function, cost and profit functions.[16]

[16] Allen (1987) overcomes the problem of endogeneity of input quantities in the production function approach by the use of translog cost and profit functions to estimate the union–nonunion efficiency differential.

Perhaps the major problem with production function studies in general, aside from the problem of measuring union effects, is the following. Suppose that all firms in a particular sector face the same technology and the same input prices. This is likely to be the case with a cross-section of firms in a particular industry. In such a situation, it might be expected that all firms would have the same inputs and outputs, and therefore the same levels of productivity. But this is never observed. In cross-sections of firms facing the same technology and input prices, there is heterogeneity in firms' choices of inputs and outputs. Even without trade unionisation, there is considerable diversity in firms' choices of inputs, outputs and productivity. Firms appear to be characterised by *individual fixed effects*. This heterogeneity makes it hard to distinguish between individual idiosyncracies affecting a particular firms' choices, and union-induced differences in choices. Possible ways for the applied economist to overcome these problems when attempting to estimate productivity equations are to use panel data, and to estimate productivity growth equations, where differencing eliminates the fixed effects as we noted in the previous chapter.

It was observed in the previous chapter that there is a positive average union–nonunion wage differential. Given that employers are free to adjust inputs in response to wage differentials, we would expect outputs to differ between union and nonunion firms.[17] The impact of input price differences between union and nonunion sectors should be picked up by measures of the differing factor mixes, which are endogenous in productivity equations. Much of the union–nonunion productivity literature has not yet been able to establish whether observed output differences are due to productivity differences or arise instead out of input price differences. This raises questions about relying on many of the currently available empirical estimates as a basis for economic policy.

7.4 Empirical evidence for the USA

7.4.1 The impact of unions on US productivity

Is unionisation associated with higher productivity in the USA? Empirical evidence suggests that unions do not *on average* significantly increase productivity. However, some industries are characterised by a significant positive union–nonunion productivity differential, while others are characterised by a significant negative differential. Indeed, this is what one would expect, given the variety of different forms of unionisation, as a reading of industrial relations case studies makes clear. For surveys of the many

[17] Consider the substitution and scale effects illustrated in figure 3.5.

production function studies, see Freeman and Medoff (1984), Hirsch and
Addison (1986) and Addison and Hirsch (1989). Brown and Medoff (1978)
pioneered the use of the production function methodology to examine
union effects on productivity. Their estimates of a large positive union–
nonunion productivity differential generated a wave of studies, and it is
worth examining their work in detail. They estimated, using 1972 aggregate
data for twenty-nine states for twenty two-digit standard industrial classification manufacturing industries, the following model:

$$\ln(q/n)_{ij} = \mathbf{Z}_i' b_1 + \mathbf{X}_j' b_2 + b_3 \ln(k/n)_{ij} + b_4 D_{ij} + b_5 [\ln(k/n).D_{ij}] + \mu_{ij} \quad (11)$$

where $\mathbf{Z}$ and $\mathbf{X}$ are vectors of industry and regional dummy variables
respectively, the b are coefficients to be estimated, and output q is proxied
by value added. The subscript i represents industries, while j denotes
regions. The total number of usable observations was 341. Labour and the
unionisation variable are adjusted by an index of labour quality, to allow
for the possibility that unionisation may cause firms to substitute higher
quality labour. The coefficient b_3 indicates the share of value added
accruing to capital. Based on their estimates for b_4, they conclude that the
union-nonunion productivity differential is of the order of 22%. This is a
remarkably high figure, and implausibly so. The theoretical and econometric problems outlined earlier are relevant to this study, as Brown and
Medoff recognise: the dependent variable uses value added rather than a
measure of physical output (thereby potentially conflating union effects on
output price with union effects on productivity), the hypothesis that
production function parameters differ between the union and nonunion
sectors is not tested, input quantities are not instrumented, and there is
likely to be omitted variable bias. Further, the dependent variable and the
hourly wage are highly positively correlated, and the estimated union
productivity differential may be tracking the union wage gap: Brown and
Medoff experimented with replacing the dependent variable by the natural
logarithm of hourly wages, and found that both the magnitude and
significance of their estimate of b_4 remained much the same. As Addison
and Hirsch (1989: 77–8) point out, some of these problems are unavoidable
and are recognised by the authors. However, 'any generalization of their
results must meet the dual criteria of plausibility and consistency with
subsequent studies. By either standard, their estimate of the union productivity effect is too high.'

Other US studies of all manufacturing, or economy-wide analysis, do not
support the findings of Brown and Medoff. For example, Clark (1984),
Bemmels (1987), Lovell, Sickles and Warren (1988) and Hirsch (1990)
conclude that, in general, unionisation lowers productivity, although in

some industries unionisation is associated with a positive productivity differential.[18]

These studies have used aggregate data. But what are the union productivity estimates from studies using disaggregated data? There are compelling reasons for using less aggregated data, even though it is not easy to generalise from the results. In particular, the use of firm-level data from one particular industry lends some credibility to the assumption underlying (6) of a common technology. Moreover, if data are available on union status at the level of the establishment, then all the coefficients in the production function represented by (2) can be allowed to differ between union and nonunion establishments.[19] Furthermore, it is easier to obtain output data in *physical* units than in value added for firms in a particular industry; this avoids the problem that union output price effects are conflated with union productivity effects. Finally, if panel data are available, where the same plants are surveyed at different points in time, it is possible to control for unobservable fixed effects associated with any particular establishment. If the impact of these fixed effects can be eliminated, for example through differencing, then the resulting equation is less likely to suffer from omitted variable bias. However, as was also the case when we considered panel estimates of the union wage gap in chapter 6, estimation of the union–nonunion differential requires the panel sample to contain some establishments that changed union status during the sample period. Thus productivity differentials calculated this way will suffer from some of the problems discussed in section 6.4.

A particularly interesting and careful study is that by Clark (1980a), who uses panel data from the US cement industry to estimate a Cobb–Douglas production function for the period 1953 to 1976; his sample comprises six cement plants that changed from nonunion to union status at various dates over the period. This gives 104 observations when the data from the six plants are pooled over the time period. The strengths of this study are that output is measured in physical units (tons of cement); that the production function coefficients are allowed to differ between the union and nonunion plants; that fixed firm effects are controlled for; and that person-hours of supervisory workers are included as an explanatory variable, providing a measure of control for supervisory workers. The dependent variable is the natural logarithm of tons of finished cement per production worker per person-hour. The estimated union–nonunion productivity differential is

---

[18] For example, Clark (1984) finds positive union productivity differentials in just three two-digit industries – textiles, furniture and petroleum.

[19] This can be done by interacting union status with all the appropriate right-hand-side variables in (6). This allows one to test the hypothesis that union status might affect the dependent variable through either neutral technical change, labour-augmenting technical change, or capital-augmenting technical change.

between 6 and 8%. A further strength of Clark's approach is that he not only meets many of the criticisms of production function studies outlined earlier, but he also carefully relates his analysis to the relevant environment. For example, he examined the collective agreements with the union held by each plant. He also interviewed both union and management personnel to elicit their views on any organisational changes accompanying unionisation which may have affected labour productivity, and came to the conclusion that unionisation significantly alters the process of management.

Rather than survey the findings of a number of other studies of the union productivity differential, we summarise the main 'stylised facts' or empirical regularities to emerge from these studies. First, unions in the USA do not appear to increase productivity *on average*. Secondly, it seems that significant positive union productivity differentials are typically found in the private sector, in particular where there is a degree of product market competition.[20] It appears that product market competition encourages efficiency improvements in unionised labour markets. Thirdly, there is a positive correlation between union productivity differentials and union wage gaps: industries with large union wage gaps are also likely to have large union productivity differentials. This should not be asserted too strongly as a stylised fact, since it may occur because the productivity differential simply tracks the wage gap; as unions increase wages, the firm moves up the VMPL curve until the new wage is equal to a higher level of VMPL, as we discussed in the previous section. Alternatively, the finding may be a result of management organising itself more efficiently when faced by substantial union wage differentials. Moreover, the finding that there is a positive correlation between union wage gaps and union productivity differentials is at odds with the finding that union productivity differentials are positively correlated with product market competition, for unions are less likely to obtain higher wages in competitive product markets. Clearly, further work is required to investigate these relationships.

7.4.2 The impact of unions on US productivity growth

All the studies mentioned so far estimate the union impact on *levels* of labour productivity. It was noted in the previous section that a problem with estimation of the production function represented by equations (6), (7) or (11) is the possibility of omitted variables biasing the estimated coefficient to the union variable D. Intuitively, this problem arises if the available data do not include a full set of variables likely to affect worker producti-

---

[20] See, for example, Clark (1980b, 1984), Ehrenberg, Sherman and Schwarz (1983), Noam (1983), Allen (1986, 1987) and Eberts and Stone (1987).

vity. If these unobservable variables are also correlated with the unionism variable, then the estimated coefficient will be picking up not only the impact of unionisation on productivity, but also the impact of the unobservables. Thus the estimated coefficient to D will be biased – upwards if the correlation between unobservables and unionisation is positive, and downwards if the correlation is negative. This problem can be reduced if, instead of estimating productivity *levels*, the investigator estimates productivity *growth*. Consider the following simple equation in levels, and suppose this is to be estimated using firm-level data:

$$\ln(q_{it}/n_{it}) = \ln A_{it} + a\ln(k_{it}/n_{it}) + (1-\alpha)(\gamma-1)D_{it} + \mu_{it} \qquad (12)$$

where the subscripts i denote the ith firm. Suppose that data on these firms are available at two points in time, so that $t = 1,2$. Suppose that there are unobservables, such as firm-specific factors affecting productivity, encapsulated in the error term, which can be written as

$$\mu_{ij} = \phi_i + v_{ij} \qquad (13)$$

where ϕ_i represents firm-specific effects which are fixed across time periods, for example managerial quality, and v_{ij} is an error term with zero expected value. Substitution of (13) into (12), followed by the taking of first differences, yields the following:

$$\Delta\ln(q_{it}/n_{it}) = \Delta\ln A_{it} + a\Delta\ln(k_{it}/n_{it})] + (1-\alpha)(\gamma-1)\Delta D_{it} + \Delta v_{it} \quad (14)$$

where it will be noted that the fixed effect ϕ_i has vanished, reducing the danger that the estimates of the model will suffer from omitted variable bias. Now the model estimates the impact of changing density or union status on productivity *growth*.[21]

It is interesting that the few productivity growth studies for the USA appear to suggest either a negative or insignificant correlation between unionisation and productivity growth,[22] while the productivity level studies suggest that the union productivity effect may be positive, negative or

---

[21] Any consideration of productivity growth over time raises the issue of the relationship between research and development, and innovation, on the one hand, and the firm's performance on the other hand. Studies specifically examining the impact of R&D on productivity which also include a union density or status explanatory variable find that unionism has a negative (and sometimes insignificant) impact on TFP growth (Addison and Hirsch, 1989: 98).

[22] Hirsch and Link (1984) estimate a version of productivity growth as represented by (14), using two-digit US manufacturing industry data for the period 1957 to 1973. They find that increases in union density significantly reduce productivity growth. Freeman and Medoff (1984: 169) estimate the effect of union density on manufacturing productivity growth from three data-sets, and conclude that 'current empirical evidence offers little support for the assertion that unionization is associated with lower (or higher) productivity advance'. Their conclusion appears to be as valid now for the USA as it was in 1984.

insignificant, depending on the particular industry. However, it is rather premature to conclude that there is a conflict between the results of the productivity level and growth studies. Only when careful comparisons have been made of productivity level and growth estimates from identical datasets can such a conclusion be reached.

7.4.3 The impact of unions on quits and job tenure

It will be recalled from the introduction to this chapter that the organisation (or collective voice) theory of trade unions has several testable implications in addition to the hypothesis that unions increase productivity. First, union presence should be associated with a lower turnover rate, since it is argued that trade unions are a mechanism allowing workers to voice complaints to management, rather than being forced to find another job if they are dissatisfied with their present employer. Secondly, union workers should have higher job satisfaction. There have been relatively few empirical studies on the impact of unionisation on labour turnover and worker satisfaction, perhaps owing to poor data availability, and these studies relate principally to the US environment. For example, Freeman (1980b) finds that US workers covered by collective agreements are less satisfied than comparable nonunion workers; however, covered workers are less likely to state they wish to change jobs, and also have lower quit rates. These findings might be construed as suggesting that union workers are more vocal about expressing dissatisfaction, and less likely to use the exit option. Freeman and Medoff (1984) find that unionisation significantly reduces quits and increases job tenure with a firm, and argue that reduced turnover is equivalent to a 1–2% increase in productivity, an effect clearly not large enough to outweigh the negative union wage effect. The finding that unions reduce quits and increase tenure has also been established for Australia (Miller and Mulvey, 1993). Freeman (1980b), Blau and Kahn (1983) and Mincer (1983) also find that labour turnover in the USA is significantly lower among union workers. But does reduced union turnover contribute to productivity in unionised establishments? There has been little analysis of this issue, although work by Clark (1980a) suggests that it may for his sample of firms in the cement industry.

Katz, Kochan and Gobeille (1983) and Ichniowski (1986) find the number of grievances filed in union workplaces in the USA has a negative impact on productivity. Allen (1984) estimates that absenteeism in the USA is significantly higher among union workers than nonunion, and that this contributes a very small amount to productivity decrease. There are obvious problems in this literature in determining what absenteeism would have been in the absence of unions.

It is interesting to note that simple cross-tabulations from the 1990 Workplace Industrial Relations Survey indicate that private sector non-union establishments have higher quit rates and lower rates of absenteeism than do unionised establishments in the private sector (Millward *et al.*, 1992: 342). No doubt in the future there will be multiple regression analyses of these data from new questions in the 1990 Workplace Industrial Relations Survey.

7.5 Evidence on productivity for Britain

US evidence suggests that unions do not *on average* significantly increase productivity and that unions decrease productivity growth. The British evidence as to the impact of unions on productivity is mixed. Unions appear in general to have had a negative impact on the *level* of productivity, although there are so far only a small number of British studies estimating the union–nonunion productivity differential. It is therefore too early to state categorically that in Britain unions decrease productivity. However, in the first half of the 1980s, unionisation had a significant positive impact on productivity *growth*.[23]

Two principal questions have been addressed in the British literature: first, do trade unions on average reduce productivity and, secondly, was the dramatic productivity improvement in British manufacturing in the 1980s a result of weakening trade union power and anti-union legislation? We will first consider the available evidence as to the impact of unions on productivity levels in general, given in table 7.1. From this, it is evident that there is a negative correlation between unions in Britain and productivity levels. However, we can conclude very little about the average impact of British trade unions on productivity until a larger number of studies using a number of different data-sets have produced consistent results. Until then we can only tentatively conclude that the available evidence is consistent with unions in some circumstances having a negative effect on productivity levels, and in other circumstances having an insignificant effect.

How does unionisation affect productivity *growth* in Britain? This question has been a major focus of recent research on the effects of trade unions. A stimulus to this research was the increase in productivity growth in British manufacturing in the 1980s, at the time of the anti-union legislation of the Thatcher government and declining union density. Table 7.2 shows productivity growth in the business sector of several OECD countries, including the United Kingdom. The figures for levels have been calculated using purchasing power parity exchange rates, since compari-

---

[23] For comprehensive surveys of the British evidence on the impact of unions on productivity levels and growth, see Metcalf (1989a, 1990a, 1990b).

Table 7.1. *Estimates of the impact of unions on productivity levels*

Study	Data-set	Time period	Union measure	Productivity effect
Firm-level studies				
Pencavel (1977)	4 coalfields	1900–13	union density	negative
Edwards (1987)	650 manufacturing plants	1977–8	union density	negative
Wilson and Cable (1991)	52 engineering firms	1978–82	union density	negative
Machin (1991)	"	"	union density	none
Industry-level studies				
Ball and Skeoch (1981)	15 manufacturing industries	1973	union coverage	negative
Davies and Caves (1987)	86 3-digit manufacturing industries	1967–8 1977	union density, strikes	negative (density); negligible (strikes)
Knight (1989)	52 3-digit manufacturing industries	1968	strike frequency	positive
Moreton (1993)	1-digit (aggregate data)	1950–87	union density, strikes	negative (density); insign. (strikes)

Note: The productivity measure for all studies is value added per employee, with the exception of Pencavel (1977) where it is annual output in tons of coal.

sons at prevailing exchange rates are often misleading. Notice that in the 1960s and 1970s, both the UK and the USA are near the bottom in terms of productivity growth.[24] However, since the 1960s all countries have been characterised by a fall in productivity growth, and this has been over a sufficiently long period to suggest a trend rather than short-run demand factors. Finally, observe that relative productivity growth of both the UK and the USA improved in the 1980s (Crafts, 1991: 83).

Investigators, eager to examine the impact of trade union legislation on Britain's improvement in productivity growth in the 1980s, have also considered the impact of trade unions on productivity growth in general through the productivity effects hypothesised at the beginning of this

[24] See Crafts (1991) for an analysis of Britain's poor productivity performance for the three decades following the Second World War. See also Metcalf (1989a).

Table 7.2. *Productivity growth in the business sector (% per year)*

Country	Labour productivity			Total factor productivity		
	1960–73	1973–9	1979–88	1960–73	1973–9	1979–88
Australia	3.2	2.0	1.1	2.9	1.2	1.0
Austria	5.8	3.3	1.8	3.4	1.4	0.7
Canada	2.8	1.5	1.5	2.0	0.7	0.3
France	5.4	3.0	2.4	3.9	1.7	1.5
Germany	4.6	3.4	1.9	2.7	2.0	0.7
Italy	6.3	3.0	1.6	4.6	2.2	1.0
Japan	9.4	3.2	3.1	6.4	1.8	1.8
UK	3.5	1.5	2.6	2.2	0.5	1.9
USA	2.8	0.6	1.6	1.8	0.1	0.7

Source: Crafts (1991).

chapter. Productivity growth may be influenced by unionisation in a number of different ways. In general, if there is any weakening of previously productivity-reducing organisational arrangements that characterise only the union sector, then after this change there will be observed a relative improvement in productivity growth in the union sector. For example, productivity growth may be enhanced if restrictive practices in the union sector are weakened, and the estimated union impact on productivity growth will be positive through the elimination of these practices. Or if industrial relations become more co-operative or managerial input more effective, unions will be observed to be associated with a higher growth rate. To the extent that the anti-union legislation of the Thatcher government (outlined in chapter 2) has weakened union restrictive practices and returned the right-to-manage to management, then the legislation can be said to have contributed to the increase in British productivity growth in the 1980s.

Of course, other factors apart from the anti-union legislation may have influenced the rise of labour productivity growth in the 1980s (Muellbauer, 1986; Metcalf, 1988, 1989a, 1990a, 1990b). Cross-country comparisons of long-run growth have focused on the 'catch-up hypothesis'. According to this view, at a particular point in time one country might be at the technological frontier, but over time there will be convergence of the growth rates of all countries at a similar stage of development and with similar levels of human capital. These countries will 'catch up' the lead country through technology transfer, international competition and emulation of the institutions and practices of the lead country (Baumol, 1986; Abramovitz, 1986; Dowrick and Nguyen, 1989; Chatterji, 1992). Both

Britain and the USA were more developed than European countries and Japan in the 1950s, but by the 1980s had fallen so far behind that they then had scope for catching up.

Another reason advanced for the surge in productivity growth is what is often termed a 'shock' effect, where the shock in this context is the adverse demand shock of the recession of 1979–81 (Metcalf, 1988; Layard and Nickell, 1989). Britain suffered badly from this negative demand shock, with the largest one-year fall in manufacturing output ever recorded in the UK. Exchange rates and interest rates increased, fiscal and monetary policies were tight, subsidies were withdrawn for companies in difficulties, and Britain suffered a fall in international competitiveness. The recession with its enormous employment losses gave both workers and management the choice of either increasing their productivity or losing their jobs. The Thatcher goverment removed industrial subsidies and instructed nationalised industries to break even prior to privatisation. Managers, faced with the fear of both bankruptcy of their firm and job loss, were forced to become more competitive and eliminate restrictive practices. Restrictive practices, long held to be a cause of Britain's poor economic performance, began to disappear during the 1980s (see, for example, Morris and Wood (1988), Marsden and Thompson (1988), Machin and Wadhwani (1989), Purcell (1991) and Millward *et al.* (1992)).[25] Moreover, increasing capital market integration has made firms more vulnerable to takeover than before (Bean and Symons, 1989).

While the shock hypothesis might be valid for both union *and* nonunion firms, it is generally held that restrictive practices have been found in workplaces with a strong union presence (Oulton, 1990). Where the shock effect works through the elimination of union-initiated restrictive practices, it might be expected that productivity increases would be greater in unionised plants or industries. Thus changes in industrial practices might have resulted from two ways in which trade union power was weakened – the anti-union legislation, and the shock effect – and in practice it is

---

[25] The 1980 Workplace Industrial Relations Survey shows that in 1980 some 76% of union plants bargained over manning levels. However, this had declined to 55% by the time of the second Workplace Industrial Relations Survey in 1984 (Millward and Stevens, 1986). The 1990 Workplace Industrial Relations Survey indicates that managers in over a third of workplaces reported changes in working practices (reducing job demarcation or increasing the flexibility of working) over the three years prior to the survey (Millward *et al.*, 1992: 334). Some 72% of establishments changing working practices reported improvements in labour productivity, as compared with 56% of plants where work practices were unchanged.

Machin and Wadhwani (1989) use the 1984 WIRS to examine the extent to which British plants experienced changes in work practices or work organisation (not involving new plant, machinery or equipment) in the three years prior to the survey. They find that changes in work practices were more likely to occur in plants where unions were recognised, with the presumption that union plants were more restrictive to begin with.

extremely hard to distinguish between these two hypotheses. Notice that if indeed trade unions are now less able to resist the introduction of new technology and work practices, we would expect to see a permanently higher rate of productivity growth in Britain. However, if union power is weakened predominantly through the shock effect, the higher rate of productivity growth may not be a permanent phenomenon.

Another hypothesis explaining improvements in British productivity growth in the 1980s is the 'batting average' effect (Muellbauer, 1986). To the extent that the recession of 1979–81 resulted in the closure of inefficient firms with inferior quality workers, the average productivity of the remaining higher quality workers would have increased simply because less efficient workers were no longer present. However, Oulton (1987) shows that large plants were characterised by higher labour productivity than small plants, and that large plants were disproportionately affected by the recession. To carry through the batting analogy, since it was the openers who vanished rather than the tail-enders, labour productivity should have been reduced (Metcalf, 1989a: 12).

An alternative explanation of the rise in British labour productivity is that it was brought about in part by the end of labour hoarding that was associated with the recession; the 1970s had been characterised by hoarding of workers rather than layoffs, but the 1979–81 recession was so bad that it generated a labour shakeout, bringing about a once-and-for-all increase in productivity (Darby and Wren-Lewis, 1992). To the extent that unionised firms may be more prone to hoarding labour than nonunionised ones, then once the labour hoarding ends in a severe recession, union firms may be observed to be associated with relatively faster productivity growth.[26]

It is also sometimes suggested that the 1980s were characterised by a surge of innovations associated with the microchip, which led to Britain's productivity growth. Yet this would suggest increasing productivity internationally, which, as table 7.2 shows, has not been the case (Muellbauer, 1990). Finally, it has been argued that labour market changes in the 1980s were but one influence on productivity growth, and that changes in the product market (in particular, a decline in concentration) were also an important part of the productivity growth story (Haskel, 1991).

A potential problem with British productivity figures is that they may be affected by the degree of labour utilisation. Mendis and Muellbauer (1984) and Muellbauer (1986, 1991) devise a measure of labour utilisation based on weekly hours of overtime as a fraction of the normal working week.[27]

---

[26] Union firms may be more likely to hoard labour because of high costs of redundancy, either through union-negotiated non-statutory redundancy pay agreements or through strike action by threatened workers.

[27] They also emphasise the need for researchers to consider carefully the biases inherent in particular output measures. In particular, there are problems associated with measuring deflators of value added (see also Muellbauer, 1986).

Table 7.3. *Residual annualised rates of TFP growth in British manufacturing*

Period	Annual TFP growth (%)
1956 Q1 to 1959 Q3	1.8
1959 Q4 to 1972 Q4	2.9
1973 Q1 to 1979 Q2	0.7
1979 Q3 to 1980 Q2	− 1.6
1980 Q3 to 1990 Q4	3.3

Source: Muellbauer (1991: 105).

Using a production function approach similar to that discussed in section 7.2, they augment the labour input variable to control for variations in utilisation reflecting short-run cyclical effects. Their results indicate a substantial upturn in British manufacturing total factor productivity (TFP) growth in the 1980s, where TFP growth is defined as 'changes in output that cannot be explained by other variables, chiefly weeks worked, number of workers, effective weekly hours of work, the measured capital stock, and the output bias terms' (Muellbauer, 1991: 105). The implication is then that the residual TFP growth must be due to the various hypotheses put forward above, between which it is not possible to distinguish using their data. Table 7.3 shows the Muellbauer estimates of annualised rates of TFP growth not accounted for by the factors outlined above.

We now consider the results of some studies attempting to distinguish between these explanations of British productivity growth in the 1980s, in order to see to what extent the decline in trade union power has caused the 'productivity miracle'. Unfortunately, while the evidence clearly indicates that unionised firms had relatively greater productivity growth than low-density or nonunion firms in the first half of the 1980s, it is not possible to distinguish clearly between the various explanations of this stylised fact, and the impact of the anti-union legislation remains debatable.

The British studies addressing these issues typically use an extension to the production function approach, in order to take into account bargaining between the union and the firm. This extension involves estimation of a production function of the following form:

$$q = A(en^a)k^{1-a} \qquad (15)$$

The novelty of this approach lies in the inclusion in the production function of observed effort, denoted by e. The rationale for inclusion of e is through union bargaining theory (developed for models without effort in chapter 5). It is assumed that the union and the firm bargain over the level of observed effort, as well as over the level of wages.[28] The justification for the inclusion of observed effort e is that it either measures restrictive practices such as job demarcation, manning ratios, or length of smoke breaks, which might increase total employment, or, alternatively, it measures the intensity of individual effort. Workers might be willing to accept lower wages in return for a more comfortable workpace or because total employment might increase. Once the union and firm have determined wages and effort, the firm then determines the number of workers to employ for the bargained level of wages and effort.

How do the union and the firm determine e and the union wage? Rosen (1989), Nickell *et al.*, (1989) and Moreton (1993) give details, but the basic idea is the following. A union worker's utility is assumed to be increasing in wages as usual, but decreasing in effort; thus $u = u(w,e)$. The firm's profits are increasing in worker effort, through the production function of (15). Substitute the worker's utility function into the union objective function, and substitute (15) into the profits equation; then maximise the generalised Nash bargain with respect to both wages w and effort e. The bargain provides a solution for observed effort and union wages as a function of a number of exogenous variables, such as the product market structure within which the firm operates, proxies for factors affecting union power, the level of unemployment (reflecting alternative opportunities), and industry control variables where appropriate. It is therefore possible now to substitute out e in (15) by the appropriate exogenous variables. Equation (8) can then be linearised by taking logarithms, and estimated by OLS techniques.

The studies in table 7.4 use (15) in differenced form to estimate the determinants of productivity growth. As noted earlier, differencing has the advantage of eliminating unobservable fixed effects. We will focus briefly 'on the results from the two company-level studies reported in table 7.4. Nickell *et al.* (1992), using data for large companies from an (unbalanced) panel, find that productivity growth was higher in union firms over the period when union firms were becoming weaker (1979–84), but was in some specifications lower over the period when unions were in a strong bargaining position (1975–8). They attribute these results to a reduction in restrictive practices in the 1980s. It is not possible to tell whether the anti-union legislation or the shock of the 1979–81 recession was the major impetus for changes in working practices from the early 1980s. However, a proxy for the impact of the recession on productivity growth from 1981 is

---

[28] This approach appears first in the literature in Rosen (1989) and Nickell, Wadhwani and Wall (1989). See Layard *et al.* (1991) and Moreton (1993) for formal models of bargaining over wages and effort, and a comparison of equilibrium wages and effort arising from this model with those from a model in which effort is not subject to bargaining.

Table 7.4. *British estimates of productivity growth and the union effect*

Study	Data-set	Time period	Union measure	Productivity measure	Union productivity effect
Firm-level studies					
Nickell, Wadhwani and Wall (1992)	100–18 firms Exstat and Datastream panel (manfg.)	1972–84	proportion of manual employees covered by union collective agreement	real sales	1975–8: lower; 1979–: higher
Gregg, Machin and Metcalf (1993)	328 firms Exstat panel (production, construction, retail, transport)	1984–9	recognition	real sales	1984–7: none; 1988–9: positive
Industry-level studies					
Denny and Muellbauer (1988)[29]	75 3-digit mnfg. industries	1980–4	density	value added	negative
Oulton (1990)	94 3-digit mnfg. industries	1971–86	coverage	value added	1971–82: negative; 1983–: positive
Haskel (1991)	81 3-digit mnfg. industries	1980–6	density	output volume per head	insignificantly negative

given by the proportional fall in employment experienced by each company from 1979 to 1981, which is held to be responsible for a 0.9% per annum increase in productivity growth for the period 1982–4 (but with no significant effect thereafter). Firms with higher debt–equity ratios also

---

[29] There are problems with generalising from any of the studies using Census of Production three-digit industrial-level data, with which the WIRS density data have been merged in order to calculate the union effect. This is because, at the three-digit level of industrial classification, there are very few observations in each category in the WIRS data. (An equivalent way of stating this is that the cell size is very small.) Therefore the values of the unionisation variables deriving from this procedure may not be representative of the true population values for the particular industrial group.

experienced higher productivity growth, reflecting the view, the authors argue, that debt acts to discipline managers to improve productivity.[30]

The study by Gregg, Machin and Metcalf (1993), also using panel data at the company level,[31] is particularly interesting because it is the first company-level British study to estimate the impact of changes in union arrangements over the period (for example, partial or full derecognition, and repudiation of closed-shop arrangements). Their data show that between 1984 and 1989 more than a quarter of those companies recognising trade unions at the start of the period (who account for two-thirds of the full sample) had partially or completely derecognised trade unions and partly or completely repudiated the closed shop. Their estimates of the determinants of productivity growth show that there were no differences in productivity growth between union and nonunion companies over the period 1984–7. However, over the period 1988–9, productivity growth was highest on average in companies experiencing a change in union arrangements, such as repudiation of a closed shop or derecognition. Productivity growth was second highest in companies recognising trade unions and with no change in union arrangements, and lowest in nonunion companies. Their results taken in conjunction with those of Nickell *et al.* suggest that during the late 1970s productivity growth in union firms was lower than in nonunion firms, but by the 1980s union companies either narrowed or reversed the productivity differential due to two separate 'bursts of differential productivity growth 1980–3 and 1988–9', only the first of which was a period of high and rising unemployment (Gregg *et al.*, 1993: 906).

It is also interesting to consider the impact of changes in the product market on British productivity growth. Haskel (1991), using a panel of 81 3-digit manufacturing industries over the period 1980–6, finds that industries in which concentration fell the most had the highest productivity growth. However, changes in union density had a negative but insignificant impact.

The primary conclusion of the majority of studies listed in table 7.4 is that the weakening of trade unions in the 1980s has been an important factor explaining productivity growth over the same period. We now turn to consideration of the impact of trade unions on investment, profitability, employment and hours.

---

[30] Another significant factor affecting productivity growth is market share. Increases in market share were associated with lower *levels* of productivity, while firms with a higher market share in general have higher productivity *growth* rates.

[31] Their companies are preponderantly large and are not representative of the population of all British companies; the panel is not balanced since a number of firms either were not operating or did not have company accounts reported for the whole period. Their estimating sub-sample comprises only those companies with at least six continuous data observations between the years 1982 and 1989.

7.6 The impact of unions on investment, profitability, employment and hours

7.6.1 Unions and investment

Chapter 3 noted a number of potential effects of unionisation on firms' investment in capital. Theoretical studies by Baldwin (1983), Grout (1984) and van der Ploeg (1987) show that the presence of a union may lead to underinvestment. This may arise because, once a firm has invested in a new project, the union has an incentive to demand higher wages in order to capture a share of the quasi-rents. Firms, knowing this *ex ante*, have a reduced incentive to invest. Thus unionisation may be associated with lower investment *ceteris paribus*. According to this rent-seeking view, union wages will be an increasing function of the firm's capital stock. However, this underinvestment result may carry through to situations where there is no union. For example, *any* incumbent workers with some bargaining power have an incentive (in the absence of binding contracts) to demand higher wages after the firm has made an investment, in order to gain a share of the surplus. Another instance of underinvestment in situations with no unions is the following. Suppose that the firm pays efficiency wages to deter shirking, where the cost to the firm of shirking may depend on capital intensity. Here *nonunion* wages will also be an increasing function of the firm's capital stock (Machin and Wadhwani, 1991). Hence both union *and* nonunion firms may underinvest.

In contrast, the traditional view is that the firm is free to determine employment and capital, after the determination of input prices either competitively or, in the case of wages, through a bargaining model of wage determination. If a powerful trade union or group of incumbent workers extracts higher wages, the relative price of capital declines; the profit-maximising firm then adjusts its employment and capital inputs, and output. Depending on the relative strengths of the scale effect and the substitution effect, firms may want to increase their capital input, and investment may increase. According to this approach, unionisation may increase or decrease investment activity. Finally, if trade unions oppose investment in new technology and associated changes in work practices, the effective cost of capital will also be increased through higher installation costs, through the provision of redundancy payments or other methods of buying workers' acquiescence in the face of change.

There is scanty empirical evidence on the impact of unionisation on investment in both the USA and Britain. In the USA, empirical evidence suggests that unionisation is associated with significantly less investment in physical capital (Bronars and Deere, 1986; Hirsch, 1990); significantly less innovation (Acs and Audretsch, 1987; Hirsch and Link, 1987); significantly less investment in R&D (Connolly, Hirsch and Hirschey, 1986); but significantly more investment in employer-related training (Tan *et al.*, 1992). The British evidence as to the impact of unions on investment is given in table 7.5.

The first two studies, using the WIRS data, show insignificant and positive union impacts, respectively, on the particular measure of investment. But, as the authors acknowledge, it is inappropriate to generalise on the basis of one cross-section, especially since unions were weak over the period 1981–4. The third study, by Denny and Nickell (1992), uses industry-level data, for manufacturing, from the Census of Production, merged with data from the 1980 and 1984 Workplace Industrial Relations Surveys on union recognition, density conditional on recognition, and the pre-entry closed shop. They thus have two data points for each industry – 1980 and 1984 – and take first differences to eliminate industry-specific fixed effects. Their estimates of investment growth indicate that the rate of investment is about 16% lower in competitive firms with a recognised union and the average level of union density, than in competitive firms in which a union is not recognised. The reduction in the rate of investment is about 3% for non-competitive firms.[32]

What impact do unions have on investment in human capital at the workplace? Booth (1992) and Greenhalgh and Mavrotas (1992), using data from the British Social Attitudes 1987 Survey and the General Household Survey respectively, find that unionism is associated with a significantly higher probability of receiving formal training. Tan *et al.* (1992) in a comprehensive study examining company-provided training in the USA, Britain and Australia, find that union membership or union coverage are associated with a greater probability of formal company-provided training. However, Claydon and Green (1992) find that unionisation is associated with a significantly greater level of training only for non-manual employees in small workplaces.

The British evidence as to the impact of unions on investment is not only sparse but has mixed results, as table 7.5 indicates. There is so far conflicting evidence from the handful of British studies on the impact of unionisation on physical investment activity. The study by Denny and Nickell (1992) is arguably the most representative, since it covers a broader time period than the cross-section studies, and estimates investment growth

---

[32] Denny and Nickell (1992) estimate a gross reduction in investment of 28%. Since unions also affect wages, product prices and productivity, it is necessary to allow for the indirect impact of unionisation on investment through these variables. After using estimates of union wage effects from Stewart (1990) and productivity effects from Metcalf (1988), Denny and Nickell calculate the net union impact on the rate of investment.

Table 7.5. *British estimates of union–nonunion physical investment effects*

Study	Data-set	Time period	Union measure	Investment measure	Union investment effect
Machin and Wadhwani (1991)	WIRS2 630 private mnfg. and service sector plants	1984	recognition	new equipment/ new micro-electronic equipment introduced three years prior to survey	positive but insignificant
Latreille (1992)	WIRS2	1984	recognition	micro-electronic equipment ever introduced	positive
Denny and Nickell (1992)[33]	Census of Production 72 3-digit mnfg. industries	1980–4	merged WIRS recognition, density and closed shop, 1980 and 1984	real expenditure on plant and machinery	negative
	54 3-digit industries	1973–85	coverage		negative

controlling for fixed effects across manufacturing industries. However, it is clear that substantially more empirical studies need to be carried out before the findings discussed in this subsection, of the impact of trade unions on investment activity, acquire the status of stylised facts.

7.6.2 Unions and profitability

Trade unions are often held to reduce the profitability of firms through their rent-seeking activities, which reduce the surplus available to capitalists. The availability of any surplus in the first instance is likely to depend on the structure of the product market in which the firm operates. Economic theory suggests that supernormal profitability will be a function of market

---

[33] Denny and Nickell (1991) use the first data-set reported in their 1992 study to reach broadly similar conclusions. They additionally find that the presence of joint consultative committees had a positive impact on investment growth over the period 1980–4.

structure; the extent to which the owners of capital are able to appropriate this surplus will be determined by their bargaining power relative to that of the union. Thus, where there are supernormal profits arising from market structure, any lowered profits associated with unionisation raise distributional issues about the relative shares of the surplus going to capital and labour. In contrast, the relationship between market structure and profitability raises efficiency issues.

Market power may in part be a function of innovations carried out by the firm. Innovation provides economic rents that may be regarded as a 'normal' return on R&D investment, but to the extent that this investment represents sunk costs the union or group of workers may be able to appropriate a share of the rents to innovation. Van Reenen (1993) estimates the extent to which union workers share in the rents to innovation in the form of higher wages. He uses a panel of 154 listed UK manufacturing firms with a recognised union in at least some part of the company, over the period 1976–83.[34] His estimates suggest that firm-level innovations are associated with higher wages for up to seven years, and van Reenen interprets these findings as evidence that the surplus from innovation is shared in the form of higher wages in these unionised companies.[35]

The availability of any surplus which may be appropriated by unions in the form of higher wages depends on market structure, the degree of innovation as outlined above and the extent to which unions are able to increase rents accruing to the firm through improved co-operation and morale (the 'organisational' view of unions with which this chapter began). The relationship between market structure and profitability has been the focus of a considerable empirical literature in the industrial organisation field. In general, these studies have found that profitability is significantly affected by variables proxying market structure (for surveys, see Geroski (1989) and Schmalensee (1989)). Some of the studies have also controlled for the degree of unionisation or union status, and have therefore as a by-product estimated the impact of unionisation on profitability. More recently, labour economists have begun to estimate specifically the effect of unions on profitability. It is a theoretical possibility that unions might *increase* the surplus available to the firm through any union productivity-enhancing effects. For example, if unions increase productivity, and if this effect more than offsets the higher wages paid to union workers, then unions might have a positive effect on profitability. However, as Clark (1984)

---

[34] These company accounts data are from Datastream and Exstat. The innovations measures are total innovations *produced* in the two-digit SIC and total innovations *used* in the two-digit SIC. These measures are obtained from the Science Policy Research Unit.

[35] It is interesting that interactions of firm-level union density with innovations have a negative impact on wages, although of course density may be endogenous in such a model.

points out, it is not possible to infer profitability from information on union wage and productivity effects alone, although these may provide useful indicators. For the union impact on the performance of the firm will depend on the particular collective bargaining structure, the product market structure and the production technology. This is because the ability of the trade union to extract a share of profits depends on both union bargaining power and the extent of any surplus, and both these factors are related in turn to the collective bargaining structure, market structure and technology. It is therefore clear that empirical profitability studies need to consider the interaction between these variables in estimating union profit effects. Recent US studies examining this interaction find conflicting evidence about the degree to which union profit effects are more prevalent in firms or industries with high market power. However, the general consensus of the US studies is that unions lower profitability (see, for example, Freeman (1983), Clark (1984), Karier (1985), Domowitz, Hubbard and Peterson (1986) and Hirsch and Connolly (1987)).[36]

There are so far few British studies estimating the union impact on profitability (table 7.6). The first three studies reported in the table use industry-level data, while the remainder use firm-level data.[37] With the exception of Machin (1990), all the British *firm-level* studies reported in table 7.6 are based on a subjective measure of financial performance – managers' responses to a question about their own establishment's financial performance relative to establishments in the rest of the industry. As Blanchflower and Oswald (1988a: 724) note, 'managers reported that, on the whole, establishments in the sample performed better than average'. So it would appear that managers tended to have a rosy picture of their own performance relative to that of the industry. Nonetheless, even though this measure is a subjective and probably biased measure of the establishment's financial performance, it is interesting that the studies using this approach consistently reveal that unions have a negative impact on this measure of financial performance.

With the exception of the industry-level studies of Cowling and Waterson (1976) and Haskel and Martin (1992) (who find that unionism has an

---

[36] For a survey, see Addison and Hirsch (1989).
[37] Studies at the industry level focus principally on estimating the price–cost margin, defined as total revenue less variable costs, divided by total revenue. In practice, this might be measured by value added less payroll and advertising costs, as a proportion of total shipments (Addison and Hirsch, 1989). Firm-level studies attempting to measure profitability might use accounting measures of either the rate of return on capital (earnings as a proportion of assets), or the rate of return on sales (earnings as a proportion of sales). An alternative measure for firms whose shares are publicly traded is Tobin's q (market value as a proportion of the replacement cost of assets), a forward-looking measure of *expected* earnings. Each of these measures has problems (see Addison and Hirsch (1989) and Machin and Stewart (1990) for a discussion).

Table 7.6. *British estimates of union–nonunion profitability effects*

Study	Data-set	Time period	Union measure	Profitability measure	Union profitability effect
Industry-level studies					
Cowling and Waterson (1976)	industry	1963–8	density	gross output less wages and salaries less raw materials divided by sales revenue	none
Conyon and Machin (1991)	90 3-digit mnfg. industries	1983–6	coverage in 1985	value added less wages, divided by value added	negative
Haskel and Martin (1992)	81 3-digit mnfg. industries	1980–6	density	value added less wages less employer taxes, divided by value added	none
Firm/plant-level studies					
Blanchflower and Oswald (1988a)	WIRS2 1209 private sector plants	1984	recognition closed shop	managerial ranking of financial performance above average (subjective)[38]	negative (recognition and closed shop)
Machin and Stewart (1990)	private mnfg. plants WIRS1: 623 WIRS2: 511	1980 and 1984	recognition pre-entry closed shop	financial performance ranking (subjective)	negative (recognition and closed shop)
Machin (1991b)	pooled mnfg. firm-level data	1984 and 1985	recognition	profits to sales ratio	negative
Machin, Stewart and van Reenen (1993)	WIRS2 566 private mnfg. union plants	1984	particular features of unionism	financial performance ranking (subjective)	negative (multiple unions and separate bargaining)

insignificant effect on changes in profitability and profitability respectively), the general consensus arising from the other five British studies is that unions have a *significant negative* impact on profitability in British manufacturing.

The negative union–nonunion profitability differential found by the majority of the British studies is what we would expect, if unions are unable to increase productivity enough to offset the positive average union–nonunion wage differential, discussed in chapter 4. Moreover, we also observed in the previous chapter that high union density and the closed shop are associated with larger wage differentials, and therefore lower profits *ceteris paribus*. It is also evident from Stewart (1990) that union wage differentials are greater where the firm has some market power. Therefore the negative impact of unions on profits may simply reflect the fact that the union is extracting a share of supernormal profits. It is interesting that Machin and Stewart (1990), Machin (1991b) and Conyon and Machin (1991) all find that the union profitability effect is most pronounced when the firm has product market power.[39]

It is early days yet to give the finding of a negative union–nonunion profitability differential the status of a stylised fact, particularly in the light of the fact that half of the British studies use a subjective measure of financial performance. Moreover, the studies do not indicate whether or not any impact of unions on profitability has changed over the period from the 1970s to 1980s. Although it is not appropriate as yet to regard as a stylised fact the negative association between unions and profitability observed in a few studies, it is worth asking the question: if unions do reduce profitability, what are the likely effects through this channel on the British economy? If the impact of unions has been to reduce supernormal profits at the expense of owners of capital, while still allowing a sufficient margin to attract capital investment, then we may not want to worry about the negative union impact on profits. But we may want to worry about the market structure from which are generated supernormal profits. Metcalf (1989b) notes that a negative union impact on profits matters 'if, as a consequence, unionised firms invest less in physical and human capital and in research and development. Such an adverse union impact would lower the underlying growth rate of the economy. Unfortunately there is very little evidence of this important issue.' (Metcalf, 1989b: 28)

---

[38] This ranking by managers was based on a question about whether the plant's financial performance relative to other establishments in the same industry was better, the same or worse.

[39] Machin and Stewart (1990) point out that, owing to data availability, studies are not able to gauge how profitability alters in response to the emergence of a union, and can only address the issue of how the distribution of profits between capital and labour alters in response to union bargaining power.

7.6.3 Unions and employment

According to the simple textbook model of labour demand, if a trade union increases the wage rate above the competitive level, the firm will respond by moving up its labour demand schedule, reducing employment until the new union wage is equal to the (higher) value of the marginal product of labour (VMPL). Therefore the prediction of this model is that unions reduce employment, and that the extent of employment reduction can be calculated as the product of the wage elasticity of labour demand and the union wage differential. However, there are several problems with this prediction. First, the advent of unionisation may lead to a change in both the intercept and slope of the VMPL curve. Unionisation may be associated, not just with higher wages, but also with changes in work organisation and procedures, which may improve (or worsen) worker morale and co-operation. As a result, there may be a negligible or zero union impact on employment, as illustrated in figure 7.1. Secondly, this prediction derives from the particular 'right-to-manage' model, and this may not be the appropriate model, as noted in chapter 5.

A third problem is that higher union wages may not affect employment where labour or product markets are not competitive. For example, suppose that there is a monopsonistic buyer of labour (as is arguably the case in 'company towns' – see Boal (1993)). In such a situation, unions can increase the wage rate above that set by the firm and engender an associated *increase* in employment.[40] Moreover, if the firm is imperfectly competitive prior to unionisation, then the advent of a union and an associated higher wage will simply have the effect of redistributing some of the supernormal profits from the firm to workers, without necessarily affecting employment.[41]

It is instructive to consider a simple model of labour demand, in order to highlight the potential dangers associated with inferring the union–nonunion employment effect directly from estimates of the union–nonunion wage differential and the wage elasticity of product demand. Following (Pencavel, 1991: 33), consider a simple constant elasticity labour demand curve, given by

[40] See appendix 3A.
[41] Some researchers (see, for example, Long (1993)) suggest that the finding of a negative union–nonunion profitability differential implies that ultimately unionised firms will vanish, as shareholders switch from union to nonunion firms to achieve a greater share of profits. However, if unions emerge and extract wage differentials in imperfectly competitive sectors where there are supernormal profits, it may still be more profitable to retain shares and receive a reduced share of supernormal profits in these firms than to switch to the nonunion sector.

$$n = w^a x^b \qquad (16)$$

where n represents labour demanded, w is the wage rate, x denotes exogenous factors affecting labour demand, and a and b are constants. Taking natural logarithms of (16) we obtain

$$\ln n = a\ln w + b\ln x \qquad (17)$$

Now suppose that we are considering a union and a nonunion sector, whose labour demand n^U and n^N respectively are given by

$$\ln n^U = a^U\ln w^U + b^U\ln x^U \qquad (18)$$

and

$$\ln n^N = a^N\ln w^N + b^N\ln x^N \qquad (19)$$

Recall that the elasticity of labour demand is given in the union sector by $\frac{d\ln n^U}{d\ln w^U} = a^U$ and in the nonunion sector by $\frac{d\ln n^N}{d\ln w^N} = a^N$.[42] Now the union–nonunion employment differential is given by $(\ln n^U - \ln n^N) \equiv d$. To obtain this, subtract (19) from (18), yielding

$$d = a^U(\ln w^U - \ln w^N) + (a^U - a^N)\ln w^N + b^U\ln x^U - b^N\ln x^N \qquad (20)$$

where the union–nonunion wage differential, β, is given by $(\ln w^U - \ln w^N)$, as we saw in the previous chapter.[43] The first term on the right-hand side of (20) represents the product of the wage elasticity of labour demand in the union sector (a^U), and the union–nonunion wage differential (β). Clearly the union–nonunion *employment* differential d is only equal to the product of the wage elasticity of labour demand and β if all the other terms on the right-hand side of (20) are zero. In any work attempting to obtain the union–nonunion employment differential, the hypothesis that these other terms are zero must be tested. It seems unlikely *a priori* that $a^U = a^N$ or that $x^U = x^N$. In particular, trade unions reduce the flexibility of firms in managing workforce reductions through, for example, bargaining over

---

[42] Thus the elasticity is constant in each sector. This is why a function such as that in (16)–(19) is known as constant elasticity.

[43] The intermediate steps to obtain (20) are as follows. First, subtraction of (19) from (18) yields

$$d \equiv (\ln n^U - \ln n^N) = a^U\ln w^U + b^U\ln x^U - a^N\ln w^N - b^N\ln x^N \qquad (21)$$

Now add and subtract $a^U\ln w^N$ from the right-hand-side of (21) to obtain

$$(\ln n^U - \ln n^N) = a^U\ln w^U - a^U\ln w^N + a^U\ln w^N - a^N\ln w^N + b^U\ln x^U - b^N\ln x^N \qquad (22)$$

Rearrangement of (22) yields (20) in the text.

severance payment schemes and redeployment.[44] Therefore union firms are more likely to hoard labour, and to vary hours rather than bodies, than are their nonunion counterparts. (This possibility has not been explored in the empirical studies.) Therefore x is likely to differ between the union and nonunion sectors, as are the estimated coefficients.

Unfortunately, the available empirical evidence about the union–nonunion *employment* differential is sparse, both for the USA and for Britain. This is surprising given the enormous literature estimating union wage effects, but may in part be a result of the (erroneous) view that employment effects can be calculated simply as the product of the elasticity of labour demand and the union wage differential.

Leonard (1992) and Long (1993) find negative union–nonunion employment growth differentials for California and Canada respectively. Leonard (1992) examines approximately 1800 manufacturing plants over the period 1974–80, and finds that employment growth in union plants is 4 percentage points less than in nonunion plants. Long (1993) finds, for a sample of 510 establishments over the period 1980 to 1985, that in both the manufacturing and non-manufacturing sectors, union plants grew just under 4 percentage points more slowly than nonunion plants. Both these studies estimate reduced-form models of employment growth, and do not allow for union interactions nor do they examine issues such as whether or not the union sector is subject to more hours variation. Moreover, if these estimates are correct, we would expect to observe, after a number of years, employment in the unionised sector approaching zero. The Leonard and Long specifications are therefore unlikely to be measuring the long-run impact of trade unions on employment, although each may represent a disequilibrium position.

Boal and Pencavel (1994) estimate a full model of wages, employment and operating days for union and nonunion annual coal-mining data at the level of up to thirty-five counties in West Virginia over the period 1897–1938. The model is meticulously related to the institutional environment, is built on a full structural model of separate wages determination in the union and nonunion sectors, and explicitly takes into account the relationship between wage and employment determination outlined earlier in this subsection. Their estimates (controlling for fixed effects) reveal a positive

---

[44] The 1990 WIRS indicates that 42% of plants report bargaining at any level with a manual union over the size of redundancy pay, 57% report bargaining over redeployment, 78% over reorganisation of working hours, 50% over staffing levels, 76% over physical working conditions, and 32% over recruitment. The comparable figures for non-manuals are 51% (size of redundancy pay), 62% (redeployment), 46% (reorganisation of working hours), 56% (staffing levels), 78% (physical working conditions), and 40% (recruitment). See table 4.1 and Millward *et al.* (1992: 251–2). Many of these issues are likely to reduce the firm's flexibility in managing employment change.

union–nonunion *wage* differential, a negligible union-nonunion *employment* differential, and a significant union–nonunion *operating days* differential. From their estimates, the employment demand function for the union sector is steeper than for the nonunion sector, and suggests differences in the underlying union and nonunion production functions.

There are so far only two studies examining the impact of unionisation on employment with British data. These studies use the same data-sets – WIRS1 and WIRS2 – to produce conflicting evidence as to the employment effects of trade unions. The first study, by Blanchflower, Millward and Oswald (1991: 815), finds that employment in the typical British establishment grows approximately three percentage points more slowly than in a typical nonunion establishment.[45] Machin and Wadhwani (1991), using the same data source, produce estimates suggesting that the Blanchflower, Millward and Oswald (hereafter BMO) result is not robust.

The BMO result was found from estimation by OLS of an employment equation for private sector establishments in which the logarithm of employment in 1984 was regressed on a number of variables, including the logarithm of employment lagged one year and four years. The union impact was measured through the inclusion of a union density variable, and through dummy variables for nonunion, open-shop union, and closed-shop union. The authors interpret their specification as an employment growth equation, because the coefficient to the first lagged employment variable is close to one, while the coefficient to the logarithm of employment lagged four years is close to zero.[46] If these estimates are correct, we would expect to observe, after a number of years, employment in the unionised sector approaching zero – the same problem that arises with the studies by Leonard (1992) and Long (1993).[47] Pencavel (1991: 44) suggests that the lagged employment variables in the BMO model may be picking up the impact of (unobserved) technological, price and demand factors. If this is the case, the coefficient to the union recognition variable 'measures, in part, the impact of unions on the *level* (and not the change) of employment,

---

[45] This result, as reported in an earlier discussion paper by Blanchflower, Millward and Oswald (1989), was used in the British government's White Paper on *Employment in the 1990s* to justify a further attack on trade unions, and hence it is important to know how robust it is.

[46] In the BMO preferred specification equation (6) is as follows:

$$\ln N = 0.141 + 1.008\ln N_{t-1} - 0.030\ln N_{t-4} - 0.037\,D + X'\beta$$
$$(3.66) \quad (48.83) \qquad (1.49) \qquad (2.34)$$

where D is a union recognition dummy variable, N is employment, X' is a vector of exogenous variables including regional and industry dummy variables, and t-statistics are given in parentheses.

[47] The BMO specification therefore cannot be regarded as representing the long-run impact of unions on employment in the British economy, although it may represent a disequilibrium position in the early 1980s.

lagged employment doing little more than controlling for the string of unobserved determinants of current employment'.

Machin and Wadhwani (1991) have an alternative explanation for the BMO result. Their premise is that, over the period 1980–4, unionised firms were more likely to experience an erosion of restrictive practices, some of which related to overmanning arrangements and demarcation. The erosion of restrictive practices over the period meant that union firms were more likely to lay off workers, thereby generating a possibly one-off employment reduction. Hence estimation of the employment effects of unions over the sample period 1980–4, without controlling for these factors, would show a negative correlation between union measures and employment growth. To test this hypothesis, Machin and Wadhwani estimated the determinants of organisational change over the period 1980–4, and found that plants in which a union was recognised were significantly more likely to experience organisational change.[48] They then incorporated into a BMO-style employment equation interactions between union recognition and organisational change, to test the hypothesis that it was the combination of unionisation and elimination of restrictive practices (as proxied by their organisational change variable) that was associated with employment reduction over the period 1980–4. Their results indicate that for plants in which there was no organisational change, there is no significant correlation between union recognition and employment growth. Only for plants experiencing organisational change is a negative association found. These results 'are suggestive of the view that the disproportionate decline in employment in union plants during 1980–4 might have resulted from the fact that unionised plants were more likely to remove restrictive practices.' (Machin and Wadhwani, 1991: 852)

Even if the BMO results are robust to alternative specifications, there are compelling reasons for not using the results from one study alone to make inferences about the long-run union impact on employment in the British economy, not least because the WIRS data used refer to just two cross-sections, in 1980 and 1984, which may not be representative of other periods. In particular, at that time Britain was facing a major recession and the trade union movement was in a state of flux.

Machin and Wadhwani (1991) also examine company data from Exstat and Datastream (representing an unbalanced panel for the period 1975–86). Their estimates of the union–nonunion employment differential over

---

[48] They also estimated the determinants of what they term 'limits to managerial freedom', a zero–one variable based on data about whether or not management felt constrained in their organisation of work. They found that large unionised establishments were significantly more likely to report 'restrictions on managerial discretion *vis-à-vis* work practices' (Machin and Wadhwani, 1991: 852).

the period 1979–84 are negative: employment in firms with 100% union density grew 1.8 percentage points more slowly than did employment in equivalent nonunion firms. However, over the period 1977–8, employment in union firms grew more quickly – by 2.2 percentage points per annum. Thus it would appear that in some periods at least there has been a negative union–nonunion employment differential. However, there is as yet insufficient evidence to give this finding the status of a stylised fact regarding a union–nonunion employment differential for Britain.

7.6.4 Unions and hours of work

The previous subsection raised the hypothesis that employment and hours in the union sector may be determined differently to those in the nonunion sector. There are several avenues through which unions may affect hours determination. First, the advent of unionisation is sometimes associated with a switch to bargaining over issues affecting employment adjustment costs, such as severance or redundancy payments and redeployment.[49] Moreover, evidence from the USA suggests there are positive union–nonunion differentials for fringe benefits such as health insurance, pensions, vacations, supplementary unemployment insurance and the like.[50] These are costs that vary with the number of workers and not the number of hours worked, and are therefore fixed employment costs. Thus unionised firms face greater *fixed* employment costs relative to variable employment costs than do nonunion firms. The presence of these fixed employment costs can reduce the relative flexibility of the unionised firm in managing workforce reductions. To the extent that these adjustment costs vary systematically between the union and nonunion sectors, we would expect to see differences in employment and hours fluctuations between the union and nonunion sectors. Where there are substantial fixed costs associated with hiring or firing workers, we would expect to observe firms changing hours of work of a given number of employees (rather than changing the number of employees working a given number of hours) in response to small demand fluctuations.

The second way in which unions affect hours is that in unionised firms there is often bargaining between management and union over working hours. Union bargaining occurs not only over the length of the standard working week, but also over issues affecting annual hours, such as the

---

[49] In the USA, 39.2% of workers covered by major collective agreements covering at least 1,000 workers are also covered by severance payment agreements, with 53.6% coverage in manufacturing and 27.0% in non-manufacturing (Pencavel, 1991: 64). See also footnote 44.

[50] See Freeman (1981) and Lewis (1986). There is no comparable work as yet for Britain. See Hart (1984b) for non-wage labour costs across a number of OECD countries, including the USA and the UK.

length of paid holidays, the number of public holidays, and sick leave. We would therefore expect to observe differences in the hours worked in the union and nonunion sectors, for reasons in addition to the adjustment cost factors outlined above.

The presence of fixed employment costs that differ between the union and nonunion sectors, and the appearance of hours of work on the union–firm bargaining agenda, suggest that a careful distinction should be made between hours and employment in the estimation of union–nonunion effects. In some circumstances, however, workplaces may be characterised by bargaining between workers and management even in the absence of trade unions. For example, where both parties have some bargaining power, bargaining may be between individuals and management, or between a union and management. While bargaining may be more effective with a union, there may still be some scope for individual bargaining with management in some production processes, owing to the presence of labour turnover costs giving workers some monopoly power. In these circumstances, it may well be that individual bargaining also occurs over issues such as hours, holidays, severance pay, redeployment, and the like, and that, as a result, management responds to demand perturbations by varying hours rather than the number of workers. Such arguments suggest that researchers wishing to estimate hours and employment effects need to control carefully for the degree of fixity of non-wage labour costs.[51] What are the available estimates of union–nonunion *hours* differentials? Evidence from the USA suggests that there are considerable variations in union–nonunion hours differentials across worker type, occupation, and industry (Lewis, 1986; Earle and Pencavel, 1990). Earle and Pencavel (1990) found, using 1978 data, that white women have an average weekly hours differential of 9.9 per cent, an annual weeks differential of 9.3 per cent, and an annual hours differential of 20.2 per cent. For white men, the average union–nonunion weekly hours differential is −1.1 per cent, while the annual weeks differential is 3.0 per cent, and the annual hours differential is 1.8 per cent. Of course, a part of these estimated differentials may arise because individuals who wish to work more self-select themselves into the union sector.

As yet, there are no estimates of union–nonunion hours differentials for Britain. However, evidence from WIRS3 indicates that the mean number of hours worked in the union sector is 6% higher than in the nonunion sector (Millward, 1993).

---

[51] The hours issue also affects union–nonunion wage differentials, as we noted in the previous chapter. If the union and nonunion sectors differ systematically with respect to the number of hours worked, then studies using weekly or annual earnings to estimate the union wage gap may produce biased estimates.

7.7 Conclusion

Sections 7.2 to 7.5 examined the various approaches that have been adopted in the literature to *test empirically* the hypothesis that unions increase productivity. The remaining section looked at the impact of unions on investment, profitability, employment and hours. The principal stylised facts or empirical regularities emerging from the literature are as follows. First, unionisation in both Britain and the USA appears, on average, to have a negative impact on productivity and productivity growth; however, in Britain unionisation is associated with greater productivity growth in the 1980s. Secondly, while there is scanty US and British empirical evidence as to the impact of unions on investment, the US evidence is of a negative effect, while the British evidence is ambiguous. Thirdly, unionisation appears to have a negative impact on profitability, as is expected *a priori* given a positive union–nonunion wage gap *ceteris paribus*. Since it seems likely that unions induce firms to share their surplus and thereby reduce profits in the absence of an accompanying productivity increase, the issue of whether profits are supernormal or otherwise is of obvious relevance, and requires further investigation. Fourthly, there is some evidence that unions are associated with a negative impact on employment growth, in both North America and Britain. However, these studies have typically not allowed for the fact that unionisation is associated with bargaining over issues that are likely to encourage union firms to vary hours rather than workers, and this casts some doubt on the results. Finally, the few studies looking at union hours gaps reveal significant differences between union and nonunion hours.

It is clear that much more research is required in order to measure the impact of unions on economic outcomes (apart from the union impact on wages, the focus of most of the empirical union research). It is also clear that there are dangers in focusing narrowly on one aspect of unionisation, without also taking into account secondary union effects. Moreover, even where we may be confident about the measured union effect on one particular variable, it may be the case that because of the different structure of unions in different countries and in different sectors of a single economy, this effect is not found elsewhere. It is therefore necessary to have evidence on the union effects from a number of different studies before drawing any firm conclusions. Global or national generalisations on the basis of a handful of studies should be avoided. It is clear that the measurement of union effects remains an under-researched but exciting area for future researchers.

8 Unions and the macroeconomy

8.1 Introduction

Over the 1980s, macroeconomic modelling increasingly shifted from the Walrasian market-clearing approach to one in which account was taken of the fact that firms, trade unions and governments may be able to act strategically (Dixon and Rankin, 1994). The 'New Keynesian' approach to macroeconomics emerged in the 1980s as a response to the inability of the received macroeconomics to explain the phenomena of the period. By this decade, there were changes in the economic performance of all the major advanced economies compared with the 1960s and 1970s. Growth almost halved, unemployment increased dramatically through both the seventies and eighties, and inflation accelerated in the seventies, falling back in the eighties to a level higher than in the fifties and sixties. While most major industrialised countries had a poorer economic performance in the seventies and eighties, there were nonetheless considerable cross-country differences with respect to growth, unemployment and inflation. These changes contributed to a re-evaluation of macroeconomic modelling, of which the 'New Keynesianism' emerging in the 1980s was one approach. This new approach produces models with Keynesian features, through modelling the *imperfectly competitive* behaviour of firms and workers, thereby providing microeconomic foundations for the behaviour of macroeconomic aggregates such as equilibrium unemployment and inflation. In this chapter, we examine the contribution of the recent microeconomic trade union literature to the New Keynesian approach to macroeconomics, and focus in particular on the implications of union behaviour for nominal and real wage rigidity, and for aggregate unemployment.

Two points about the analysis of this chapter must be emphasised at this juncture. First, the aggregate bargained wage-setting curve obtained from models of the trade union (which replaces the aggregate labour supply curve of Walrasian analysis) is also predicted by several other wage-setting

224

theories in which there are no labour unions. For example, efficiency wage theory and insider–outsider models each have broadly similar predictions in the absence of unions.[1] Thus the macroeconomic policy implications that emerge from union models with nominal inertia are not necessarily absent in nonunionised economies.[2] Secondly, although we briefly outline some of the theories of imperfectly competitive firms' price-setting behaviour, we incorporate into our aggregate labour market model only the very simplest case of the price-setting behaviour that may characterise imperfectly competitive product markets – normal cost pricing. The reader interested in studying more complex pricing models is referred to Carlton (1989) and Layard *et al.* (1991), and references therein.

Section 8.2 examines the implications of trade unions for wage determination at the aggregate level, where we draw principally on a simple development of the monopoly union model of chapter 4. The model developed in section 8.2 starts from the partial equilibrium monopoly union model, and then aggregates across the economy by assuming that all firms are identical. Thus, in equilibrium, each firm's price and wage will equal the economy-wide levels of prices and wages. An aggregate *wage-setting* equation can be derived from this model of union behaviour, for parametrically given prices. In addition, an aggregate *price-setting* equation can be derived from the product market, for given wages; a *real* wage is implied by this price-setting equation. *Equilibrium* aggregate employment (and hence unemployment) and real wages are then obtained by the simultaneous interaction of the aggregate price-setting and the aggregate wage-setting equations.

Equilibrium unemployment may also be affected by the collective bargaining structure. In section 8.3, we therefore examine the implications of the collective bargaining structure – in particular, the degree of centralisation of wage bargaining – for aggregate models of union behaviour and wages, prices and unemployment. The experience of many European Community countries in the 1980s has been novel in the sense that, while unemployment has risen, the level of inflation has remained roughly constant. This suggests that the 'non-accelerating-inflation rate of unemployment', or NAIRU, must have risen. But, using the analysis of the determinants of NAIRU developed in section 8.2, it is not clear why this should have happened. Indeed, factors such as the fall in OPEC prices and declining union power suggest that equilibrium unemployment should

---

[1] See Salop (1979), Shapiro and Stiglitz (1984), and Akerlof and Yellen (1986) among others for efficiency wages, and Lindbeck and Snower (1985, 1988), Solow (1985) and Gregory (1986) for insider–outsider theory.

[2] Nominal inertia refers to delays or inertia in the adjustment of nominal wages and prices to exogenous shocks to the system.

have fallen. In section 8.4, we therefore look at new explanations for this phenomenon of 'hysteresis' or unemployment persistence. The final section of the chapter considers the validity of the models developed in this chapter for economies which are only partially unionised.

Now for a word about the notation used in this chapter: throughout this chapter, we will follow the general convention of principally using upper-case letters to denote variables at the macroeconomic or aggregate level.

8.2 The monopoly union model and macroeconomics

8.2.1 Background

Chapters 4 and 5 examined popular partial equilibrium models in which there is imperfect competition in the labour market but perfect competition in the product market. We assumed perfect competition in the product market in chapters 4 and 5 in order to concentrate on the modelling of the imperfectly competitive elements of the labour market, in particular, on the conflicting preferences of trade unions and management, and on methods of characterisation and reconciliation of these conflicting objectives. The general conclusion of these two chapters was that it seemed appropriate to assume that trade unions and firms typically bargain over wages, leaving the firm with the 'right to manage', that is, to determine employment once the wage package is settled.

In the present chapter, we consider how the partial equilibrium approach to modelling a unionised sector might be incorporated into a general or economy-wide model. For simplicity, we use the monopoly union model in order to predict the behaviour of nominal wages, employment and output. While it was clear from chapters 4 and 5 that the monopoly union model is an extreme case of the more plausible right-to-manage model, it makes our task considerably easier to use this special case. This approach can be extended to the right-to-manage model, as in Layard *et al.* (1991).

Because a focus of macroeconomics is the impact of exogenous shocks on macroeconomic aggregates, it is useful to return to the monopoly union model of chapter 4 to see its predictions for real wages and employment in response to exogenous aggregate demand shocks. Initially we consider the partial equilibrium real-wage-setting response of a union–firm pair to demand shocks given by θ. Suppose that the real wage set by the ith pair is given by $\omega_i = W_i/P$, where W_i is the nominal wage and P is the cost-of-living index. Assume that the firm can only hire union workers, and the total number of union workers available is given by M. Suppose θ is a random variable, distributed on $[\underline{\theta}, \bar{\theta}]$. If θ is high, the labour demand (or VMPL) curve shifts out as illustrated in figure 8.1; for low θ, the labour demand (VMPL) curve shifts in. Labour demand varies between a maximum level

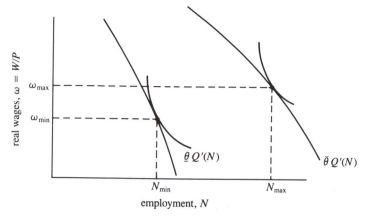

Figure 8.1. The monopoly union with exogenous aggregate demand shifts.

denoted by $\bar{\theta} Q'(N)$ in figure 8.1, and a minimum level of $\underline{\theta} Q'(N)$, depending on the realisation of θ, and we assume that $\theta = \bar{\theta}$ at $N_{max} < M$.[3] With union indifference curves as illustrated, union wages are relatively sticky in response to the exogenous shock, and the brunt of the adjustment falls on employment. In the case of an isoelastic increase in labour demand, union wages are rigid and all of the adjustment falls on union employment, as was proved in proposition 4.2(ii).

The monopoly union model with unemployment of union members ($N \leq M$) predicts that real wages will be rigid in response to *isoelastic* demand shocks; higher demand is translated into higher employment of union workers. But are there any conditions under which a demand shock might fall entirely on wages? If the exogenous demand shock θ is so large that $N > M$, then all union workers are employed. Under these conditions, the union is no longer concerned with trading off wage increases for higher levels of employment, and as a result, union wages increase. To see this formally, define $\hat{\theta}$ as that value of θ at which all union workers in the sector are employed, that is, where $N = M$. Now consider the objective function of the union. Suppose the union maximises the expected utility of a representative worker, and assume the following form of union objective function, used extensively in previous chapters:

$$\max_{\omega} EU = (N/M)\, u(\omega) + (1 - N/M)\, u(R) \qquad \text{for } N \leq M \qquad (1a)$$

$$= u(\omega) \qquad \text{for } N > M \qquad (1b)$$

Here R denotes the reservation wages or alternative opportunities of the

---

[3] Recall that the production function is denoted by $Q(N)$, where N is the number of workers the firm employs, and $Q(0) = 0$; $Q'(N) > 0$; $Q''(N) < 0$.

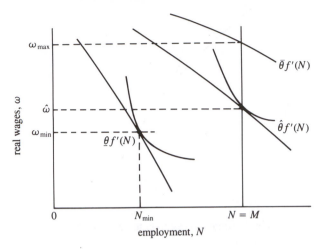

Figure 8.2. Aggregate demand shifts and monopoly union real wages.

representative union worker.[4] The union is assumed to take into account the employment implications of its wage-setting behaviour only if it expects labour demand to be such that some members are unemployed, as in (1a). If the union expects all members to be employed, it does not need to worry about employment, and hence its maximand is given by (1b).[5] The intuitive explanation for this is that, once all union workers in the sector are employed, the union no longer wishes to trade off lower union wages for higher levels of employment. Therefore, once labour demand is so buoyant that all workers are employed, which occurs at $\hat{\theta}$, the union will set higher wages and the level of employment will remain at $N = M$, as illustrated in figure 8.2. Thus for $\theta > \hat{\theta}$, ω will respond to aggregate demand shocks with N remaining fixed at $N = M$, while for $\theta < \hat{\theta}$, ω will be relatively sticky, while N fluctuates as shown, between $N_{\min}$ and $N = M$.

Now we move from the partial equilibrium model of the behaviour of a union–firm pair in response to aggregate demand shocks described above, to a model of the whole economy. How can the simple monopoly union model be expanded to provide a plausible model of a unionised economy? A popular method in the literature is to start from the partial equilibrium union model and to aggregate across the economy by assuming that all

---

[4] Note that in chapters 4 and 5 alternative opportunities were denoted by b. In this chapter, we will be allowing for alternative opportunities to be a weighted average of unemployment benefits and alternative wages, where the weights are given by the fractions unemployed and in employment respectively. We therefore denote alternative opportunities in this chapter by R.

[5] The union indifference curves are horizontal for $N > M$.

firms are identical, and that the entire economy is unionised or covered by union collective agreements. Thus, in equilibrium, the prices and wages of each union–firm pair will equal the economy-wide levels of prices and wages.[6] An aggregate *wage-setting* equation can then be derived, for given prices, from the wage-setting behaviour of labour unions and firms.

The aggregate wage-setting equation gives a union real wage curve. We also need to add to the model of the aggregate labour market an equation for the 'feasible' real wage, obtained from firms' price-setting behaviour. To obtain the feasible real wage, we derive an aggregate *price-setting* equation from the product market, for given nominal wages; the precise form of this depends on assumptions made about the way in which firms set prices, for given wage levels. Typically in macroeconomic models, it is assumed that firms' product markets are characterised by some form of imperfect competition. Prices in imperfectly competitive product markets are generally some markup of parametrically given wage costs and other variables. We will assume the simplest case of 'normal cost pricing' for the firm and give only passing reference to more sophisticated imperfectly competitive price determination models, in order to focus attention on the union impact on aggregate employment. The aggregate price-setting equation is derived from the price-setting behaviour of the firm, which is then aggregated, as for the wage-setting equation. A real wage is implied from the aggregate price-setting equation.

Equilibrium employment (and hence unemployment) and real wages are obtained by the simultaneous interaction of the aggregate price-setting and aggregate wage-setting equations. Both equations can be illustrated in (ω, N) space, since the aggregate price-setting equation can be inverted. For illustrative purposes, in the remainder of this section we will adopt the approach of Carlin and Soskice (1990) to the derivation of aggregate price- and wage-setting equations, and hence equilibrium unemployment in the economy.[7]

8.2.2 Derivation of the aggregate wage-setting equation

Suppose that there are v union–firm pairs in the economy, and denote the real wages set by the ith union–firm pair as $\omega_i = W_i/P$, where W_i is the nominal or money wage, P is the cost of living index and $i = 1,...,v$. Thus ω_i is the real consumption wage. The union objective function used in earlier

---

[6] Alternatively, if all unions are combined for bargaining purposes into a confederation of unions, and all firms into a confederation of employers, then the partial equilibrium model is effectively a model of the entire economy. The implications of the particular bargaining structure of an economy are discussed in section 8.3.

[7] This is a simpler exposition of the Layard *et al.* (1991) model.

chapters was typically the expected utility formulation, for the principal reason that this is used most widely in microeconomic work. In macroeconomic work, it is generally assumed for simplicity that the union is risk-neutral, that is, the utility function of union workers is linear in wages.[8] In the notation of this chapter, the union utilitarian objective function can now be written as

$$\max_{\omega} EU_i = N(\omega_i).\omega_i + [1 - N_i(\omega_i)]R$$

$$= N(\omega_i)(\omega_i - R) + R \tag{2}$$

Suppose that the alternative or reservation wage available to unemployed union workers is given by

$$R = (1 - U)\tilde{\omega} + Ub \tag{3}$$

where $\tilde{\omega}$ is the real wage available elsewhere in the economy, b is the real unemployment benefit, and U is the proportion of the population unemployed (thus $U = 1 - N/LF$, where N is aggregate employment and LF is the total labour force). A worker in the ith union–firm pair who does not get employment following the union wage-setting round seeks employment elsewhere; if successful, the worker receives $\tilde{\omega}$, but if unsuccessful, she receives the unemployment benefit b. Her probability of getting a job elsewhere is given by $(1 - U)$.

The first-order condition from maximisation of (2) with respect to ω_i can be written as equation (4) where we have divided through by N_i' ($N_i' \equiv \partial N_i/\partial \omega_i$):

$$N_i/N_i' + \omega_i = (1 - U)\tilde{\omega} + Ub \tag{4}$$

Now we want to convert (4) into an aggregate relationship. Assume that all firms behave in the same way, so that $\omega_i = \tilde{\omega} = \omega$. (This is sometimes known in the literature as the symmetry assumption.) Thus the alternative real wage for a worker laid off from the ith firm is the same as the union real wage. Equation (4) can now be written as

$$\frac{N\omega}{N'\omega} + \omega = (1 - U)\omega + Ub \tag{5}$$

and since the aggregate wage elasticity of labour demand can be written as

$$\epsilon = -(N'\omega/N) \equiv \frac{-\partial N}{\partial \omega}\cdot\frac{\omega}{N} \tag{6}$$

we can now rearrange (5) as

---

[8] See, for example, Blanchard and Fischer (1989), Layard *et al.* (1991), Dixon and Rankin (1994), and references therein. In addition, it is also frequently assumed that the union maximises rents, as given by equation (3) in chapter 4.

$$\omega[1 - 1/\epsilon - (1 - U)] = Ub \qquad (7)$$

Equation (7) can now be solved for the *aggregate union wage-setting curve*:

$$\omega = b[U/(U - 1/\epsilon)] \qquad (8)$$

In the monopoly union model in chapter 4, the condition was imposed that wages must be greater than unemployment benefits, in order to induce workers to supply labour.[9] In the aggregate wage-setting equation of (8), we also impose the restriction that $\omega > b$.[10] The aggregate real wage is decreasing in U, and increasing in b.[11] Moreover, the more elastic is labour demand, the lower is the markup of the union wage over b, and hence the lower the aggregate union wage-setting curve[12]. This can be illustrated in (ω, N) space (and thus (ω, U) space), as shown in figure 8.3. Note that employment is shown on the horizontal axis increasing from left to right, and unemployment is therefore increasing from right to left. Because the aggregate bargained wage is decreasing in U, it is increasing in N. Thus the curve is upward-sloping as illustrated.

How does the curve shift in response to changes in parameters b and ϵ? First, consider the impact of an increase in b on the bargained wage, *ceteris paribus*. Since we know from (8) that the bargained wage is increasing in b for a given level of unemployment, then, in figure 8.3a, an increase in b can be shown as an upward shift in the bargained wage curve, from b to b'. As unemployment benefits increase, the union becomes more aggressive in its wage demands, secure in the knowledge that any workers who are laid off as a result will have a higher level of unemployment income. Secondly, consider the impact on the bargained wage of an exogenous increase in ϵ, for given U and b. From (8), it can be seen that as $\epsilon \to \infty$, $\omega \to b$. Thus the wage-setting curve with elastic ϵ is lower than the wage-setting curve with inelastic ϵ. The union knows that by setting $\omega > b$, some unemployment will result. If labour demand is very elastic, a small wage increase results in a larger unemployment increase than where labour demand is very inelastic. This constrains the union facing elastic labour demand from demanding

[9] The model assumed that there is some disutility associated with work.

[10] This condition then imposes a restriction on ϵ.

[11] Differentiation of (8) with respect to U yields $\partial\omega/\partial U = -(b/\epsilon)/(U - 1/\epsilon)^2 < 0$. This is negative regardless of the sign of $(U - 1/\epsilon)$, since this term is squared in the expression for $\partial\omega/\partial U$. (The negative slope of the aggregate wage-setting curve can also be seen by examining the term $[U/(U-1/\epsilon)]$. A unit reduction in U reduces the denominator by a larger proportion than it reduces the numerator.) Notice that the fact that $\partial\omega/\partial U < 0$ provides a theoretical basis for the empirical finding of the 'wage curve' of Blanchflower and Oswald (1994).

To see the impact of a small increase in b on ω, we find $\partial\omega/\partial b = [U/(U - 1/\epsilon)]$. This is positive, provided we restrict attention to situations where $(U - 1/\epsilon) > 0$.

The set of restrictions required on the parameters of this version of the union wage-setting curve are quite stringent. For a less restrictive and more plausible model (albeit more difficult), see Layard *et al.* (1991: ch. 2).

[12] From equation (8), as ϵ approaches infinity, ω approaches b.

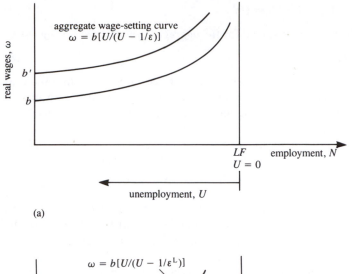

(a)

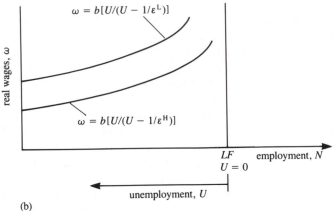

(b)

Figure 8.3. (a) Aggregate wage-setting curve shifts up as b increases; (b) aggregate wage-setting curve shifts up as ϵ becomes less elastic (where ϵ^L and ϵ^H denote low and high elasticity respectively).

wage increases as large as those demanded by a union facing inelastic product demand. In figure 8.3b, aggregate wage-setting curves are drawn for high (ϵ^H) and low (ϵ^L) elasticities of labour demand ϵ. In general, factors that increase the bargaining power of trade unions will lead to an upward shift of the bargained wage-setting curve.

8.2.3 *Derivation of the aggregate price-setting equation*

The aggregate wage-setting equation developed in the previous subsection replaces the aggregate labour supply equation in a macroeconomic model with imperfect competition in the labour market. We now turn to the derivation of an aggregate price-setting curve, for parametrically given wages, in order to be able to close the model of the aggregate labour market. It is an empirical regularity that firms react to demand shifts predominantly by varying quantities, rather than prices, for given wage rates (see, for example, Coutts, Godley and Nordhaus (1978), Encaoua and Geroski (1986), and Brack (1987)). In this subsection we examine how the assumption of imperfect competition in the product market can provide a theoretical basis for this stylised fact. Initially, however, we will examine the price-setting behaviour of a monopoly. This allows us not only to compare the outcome with that of the competitive firm, but, more importantly, to have a basis for subsequent discussion of the behaviour of imperfectly competitive firms, characterised by setting prices as a markup over marginal cost, a markup that is inversely related to the elasticity of product demand. Labour demand for the monopolistic firm depends crucially on the elasticity of product demand. However, since there is some evidence that the elasticity of product demand varies procyclically with output and employment, we will find that under these conditions the aggregate price-setting curve may be rather flat in (ω, N) space.

The behaviour of firms in setting prices with regard to costs has obvious implications for the real wage. This is because firms' derivation of prices as a function of parametrically given nominal wages results in an implied real wage. In the case of *perfect competition*, each firm's profit-maximising behaviour results in the condition that the price-determined real wage equals the marginal product of labour (MPL). To see this, recall from earlier chapters that the firm chooses employment to maximise profits Π, given by

$$\max_{N} \Pi = PQ(\mathrm{N}) - WN \tag{9}$$

where the firm's production function is $Q(N)$, N is the number of workers the firm employs, and $Q(0) = 0$; $Q'(N) > 0$; $Q''(N) < 0$. The first-order condition yields

$$PdQ/dN = W \tag{10}$$

and since dQ/dN is the marginal product of labour, we know that the real wage W/P is equal to MPL. Since the MPL declines as employment is increased (due to diminishing returns to labour), the real wage also declines.

We now consider the familiar textbook case of *monopoly*. Here the firm faces a downward-sloping demand curve for its product, and is aware of the fact that product price decreases with the quantity of output sold. An extra unit of output produced generates a consequent decline in product price for all units of output. Suppose the monopolist's price is given by $P(Q)$, where P is product price as a function of output Q, and $P'(Q) < 0$. Thus revenue R is given by

$$R(Q) = P(Q)Q \tag{11}$$

and the firm's short-run production function is given by $Q = Q(N)$. The firm chooses N to maximise profits, given by

$$\max_{N} \Pi = P[Q(N)].Q - WN \tag{12}$$

Manipulation of the first-order condition yields the equilibrium condition[13]

$$(1 - 1/\eta).dQ/dN = W/P \tag{13}$$

where dQ/dN is the marginal product of labour and $\eta = -\dfrac{dQ}{dP}.\dfrac{P}{Q}$, the elasticity of product demand. As $\eta \to \infty$, the real wage given by (13) approaches the perfectly competitive real wage given by (10). Equation (13) can be rewritten, using the fact that marginal cost (MC) is given by $W/$ MPL, as

$$(P - \mathrm{MC})/P = 1/\eta \tag{14}$$

which shows that the markup of price over marginal cost is inversely related to the elasticity of product demand η.[14]

Equation (13) provides a comparison of the real wages implied by price-setting behaviour in the perfectly competitive and monopolistic models; this is illustrated in figure 8.4. Notice that the slopes of both curves are negative, and that for η that is constant across levels of output and

[13] The first-order condition is

$$\frac{dP}{dQ}.\frac{dQ}{dN}.Q + P(.).\frac{dQ}{dN} - W = 0$$

where dP/dQ is marginal revenue and dQ/dN is the marginal product of labour. With the first term on the left-hand side of this equation multiplied by P/P, and with $\eta = -(dQ/Q)/(dP/P)$ (the elasticity of product demand), the equation can be written as

$$P(1 - 1/\eta) = W/\mathrm{MPL}$$

The real wage is then given from this price-setting equation as

$$W/P = (1 - 1/\eta).\mathrm{MPL}$$

[14] To see this, rewrite (13) as $\mathrm{MC} = P[1 - 1/\eta]$. Rearrangement yields (14).

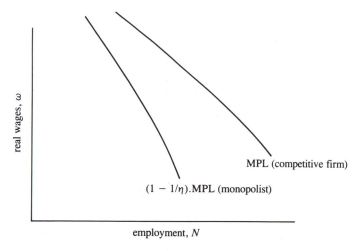

Figure 8.4. Labour demand under monopoly and under perfect competition.

employment, the monopolist's curve deviates from that of the perfectly competitive firm by a constant fraction.

However, it is often argued that the price-setting behaviour of imperfectly competitive firms generates a *flatter* curve than that shown for the monopolist in figure 8.4. The empirical regularity that prices do not respond much to demand fluctuations is more pronounced in imperfectly competitive markets. But, there is little consensus as to why firms' pricing behaviour might be unresponsive to demand fluctuations, although a number of different hypotheses have been advanced.[15] From (14) we can see that there are two avenues through which demand fluctuations may potentially affect prices: first, through the markup on marginal cost, given by $1/\eta$, and, secondly, through marginal cost itself.

Suppose that the elasticity of product demand η is not constant as employment and output increase in response to an increase in aggregate demand. Some empirical studies have suggested that η moves procyclically (and therefore the markup of price over marginal cost moves counter-cyclically) with employment and output (Bils, 1987, 1989; Haskel and Martin, 1992). If this is the case, then the price-setting curve will be flatter than where η is constant for all output levels. Hypotheses supporting the view that the markup of price over marginal cost moves counter-cyclically are varied. For example, suppose that there are 'customer markets' for firms' products. Customers become attached to particular firms; during

[15] See Layard *et al.* (1991: ch. 7) and Carlton (1989) for detailed discussion of these issues.

booms, firms reduce their prices in order to attract new customers who then become attached to the firm and remain with it during subsequent reductions in aggregate demand (Bils, 1989; Ball and Romer, 1990; McDonald, 1990). Another hypothesis suggesting that the markup moves counter-cyclically relies on collusion between firms. The degree of collusion between oligopolistic firms in a particular industry may vary across the business cycle, quite independently of η (Rotemberg and Saloner, 1986; Bils, 1987; Carlton, 1989; Rotemberg and Woodford, 1992). The incentives for oligopolistic firms to undercut their rivals are greatest during a boom, since this is when, by cheating on the cartel, an individual firm's gains are greatest. Hence it may be difficult to enforce collusion when demand is high, and the markup will therefore be lower during a boom.

We now consider the second argument for a flat price-setting curve under imperfect competition – that the slope of the marginal cost curve is flat for the relevant range (Fudenberg and Tirole, 1983; Hall, 1988). Firms may invest in excess capacity as a means of deterring entry into the industry by potential competitors because output can then be expanded at negligible marginal cost. Thus, from (14), for a given η, the markup of price over (constant) marginal cost will be constant for most output levels. Yet another hypothesis for a flat price-determined real wage curve is that firms may have implicit contracts with purchasers of their products, where delivery time rather than price may vary in response to demand pertur-bations, or, alternatively, product price may be sticky, reflecting an element of insurance across states of nature (Carlton, 1986, 1989). According to this implicit contracts view, firms do not vary prices in response to demand fluctuations; however, the theory of adjustment through delivery times implies that firms may not have flat marginal cost curves, otherwise they would simply increase output in response to demand increases (Layard *et al.*, 1991).

These various hypotheses about why the markup should vary counter-cyclically represent an interesting area of research, but as yet there is no consensus about the relative importance of each approach. For simplicity, therefore, we follow Carlin and Soskice (1990) in confining our attention to the simplest model of firms' price-setting behaviour, which assumes that imperfectly competitive firms set prices as a fixed markup over normal unit labour costs – what is termed *normal cost pricing*.

Define normal unit labour costs as WN/Q, the wage bill divided by total output. Denote labour productivity by Q/N. Let $\rho = Q/N$ at normal capacity utilisation, and write normal unit labour costs as W/ρ. Suppose the ith firm sets prices as a markup over normal labour costs. Then

$$P_i = (1 + \mu)W_i/\rho \tag{15}$$

where μ denotes the markup. Both μ and ρ are assumed to be invariant with changes in output or employment. Carlin and Soskice (1990: 142) further decompose (15) in order to show how output per head is broken up into real profits per head and real wages per head. Let $m = \mu/(1 + \mu)$. Now (15) can be rewritten as

$$P = W/[(1 - m)\rho] \tag{16}$$

Equation (16) indicates that prices are decreasing in labour productivity ρ. After further rearrangement, (16) yields

$$\rho = m\rho + W/P \tag{17}$$

which gives output per head ρ broken down into real profits per head and real wages per head on the right-hand side. This has the advantage of emphasising the competing claims of capitalists and workers to output per head.

Now return to equation (15) and suppose that all firms in the economy are identical, so that $P_i = P$ and $W_i = W$. Thus the *aggregate price-setting curve* is given from (15) by

$$P = (1 + \mu)W/\rho \tag{18}$$

From (18), we can write the aggregate price-determined real wage as

$$W/P = \rho/(1 + \mu) \tag{19}$$

which is horizontal in (ω, N) space, as illustrated in figure 8.5. Imperfectly competitive firms use their market power to maximise profits by setting prices in relation to production costs. Aggregated over all the economy, output per head is thus divided into the real wage and real profit per worker, as (17) indicated.

Finally, we would emphasise that the horizontal aggregate price-setting curve developed in this subsection has been introduced for pedagogic reasons, and that under other hypotheses about firms' price-setting behaviour this curve might be expected to have a negative slope. We are now in a position to consider equilibrium real wages and unemployment in our simple closed-economy macro-model.

8.2.4 General equilibrium unemployment

We now combine the aggregate wage-setting and price-setting curves, to allow for the simultaneous determination of equilibrium aggregate real wages and unemployment in the economy. This is shown in figure 8.6. The equilibrium level of unemployment is given by U^*, at the intersection of the aggregate wage-setting and price-setting curves. At U^* the real wage

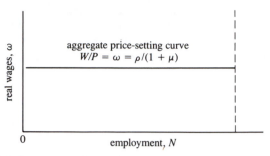

Figure 8.5. Aggregate price-setting curve.

determined by firms' price-setting behaviour is equal to the real wage determined by unions' bargaining behaviour, that is, feasible and targeted real wages are the same. This equilibrium level of unemployment is often termed in the literature the 'non-accelerating-inflation rate of unemployment', or NAIRU for short. This term provides a reminder that at U^* price and wage expectations of workers and firms are exactly realised, and therefore the inflation rate is constant.[16] Equilibrium unemployment is where unions achieve their bargained real wage and firms achieve their desired share of profits, and the wages and price levels are exactly as anticipated. This is at U^* in figure 8.6, where the price-setting and wage-setting curves intersect. Here real wage and profit claims are consistent: there is no conflict of interest between firms and unions over the division of output per head.[17]

What is the process of adjustment that will lead the economy to U^*? First, consider the situation where $U < U^*$. At low levels of unemployment (high employment), unions feel they are in a strong bargaining position and demand a higher level of nominal wages for given prices than that consistent with U^*. With normal cost pricing, all firms in the economy will pass this on in the form of higher prices. Thus workers' real wages will not rise. However, if the monetary authorities do not accommodate the general price increase by increasing the nominal money supply, the real money supply will contract, and so too will aggregate demand. As a result, aggregate unemployment will increase. Only when $U = U^*$ will the conflict-

[16] The intuitive reasoning behind this is as follows. Suppose that there is some stable level of inflation pertaining in the economy, say 5%. At the next wage round, the union will want a 5% money wage increase in order to keep workers' real wages constant. For a given money wage increase of 5%, firms will need to increase their prices by 5% in order to maintain their share of profits. Therefore, the actual price level will increase by 5%; thus the price-determined real wage will remain constant.

[17] The model has some analogies with Marxian analysis since it emphasises the importance of unemployment in reducing workers' power – the notion of the 'reserve army of labour'. See, for example, Bowles (1985).

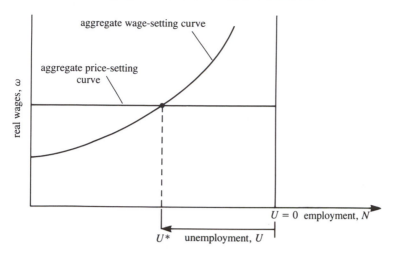

Figure 8.6. Equilibrium real wages and unemployment.

ing claims of firms and unions to output per head be reconciled. Now consider the opposite situation, where $U > U^*$. Here the high level of unemployment has dampened down union bargaining power, and union leaders therefore ask for lower nominal wages. Firms pass this cost saving on in the form of lower prices. As a result, the real money supply expands, and so too does aggregate demand; aggregate employment therefore increases. Unemployment falls to U^*.

Is U^* in figure 8.6 voluntary or involuntary unemployment? To answer this question, we superimpose in figure 8.7 a labour supply curve on the usual wage- and price-setting diagram. The labour supply curve shows the real wage necessary to induce individual workers to accept a job offer. This lies below the bargained real wage-setting curve, which shows the real wage negotiated by trade unions for each level of employment. The price-determined real wage curve or price-setting equation set by imperfectly competitive firms lies below the aggregate labour demand curve at U^* (where the real wage determined by firms' price setting behaviour is equal to the real wage determined by unions' bargaining behaviour). There is thus involuntary unemployment, represented by the horizontal distance AB on the price-setting curve between the bargained wage curve and the labour supply curve. At this particular level of the real wage, there are individuals who would like to work more at the prevailing wage. Moreover, there are firms who would like to produce additional output, but are constrained by the fact that, for additional demand above U^*, the bargained real wage lies above the price-setting curve.

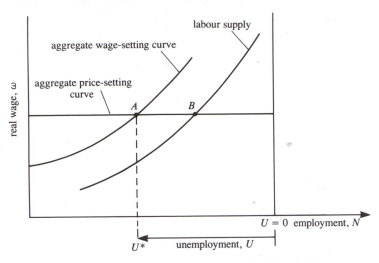

Figure 8.7. Equilibrium real wages and involuntary unemployment.

At the equilibrium level of unemployment U^*, or NAIRU, unions achieve their bargained real wage, and firms achieve their desired share of profits, and the wage and price levels are exactly as anticipated. The plans of all agents are consistent at U^*, and inflation is stable.[18] But will the economy *always* operate at this point of intersection between the aggregate wage-setting and price-setting curves? Or are there nominal rigidities that slow down the adjustment process? To obtain answers to these questions, we need to reconsider the process of adjustment that leads the economy to U^* after a disequilibrating shock.

First, suppose there is an exogenous increase in aggregate demand. This causes employment to increase, and as unemployment falls, unions feel in a stronger position to demand higher nominal wages. Therefore nominal wages increase for a given price in the wage-setting equation. Since firms

[18] To see what happens to inflation *out of equilibrium*, consider the following scenario. Suppose that at U^* the non-accelerating inflation rate is, say, 5%. Now assume that, for some reason, unemployment is below U^*, so that the union bargained wage is above the real wage implied by firms' price-setting behaviour. Away from U^*, inflation is no longer constant. For $U < U^*$, unions are pushing for a nominal wage increase greater than the expected inflation rate of 5%, because of their stronger bargaining position. But firms want to maintain their desired profit margins, and in the face of wage demands greater than 5% set price increases greater than 5%. The outcome is that both nominal wages and profits increase by more than 5%. Thus $U < U^*$ is associated with an accelerating inflation rate.

But what happens if $U > U^*$? Here the unions have lower bargaining power, and they demand a nominal wage increase of less than the expected inflation rate of 5%. Firms can therefore maintain their desired profit margins by increasing prices by less than 5%. As a result, actual price and wage inflation is less than expected. Only at $U = U^*$ is inflation constant.

follow normal cost pricing and set prices as a markup on nominal wages, prices also increase, leaving real wages in the pricing equation unaltered. If the price rise is not accommodated by an expansion of the nominal money supply, the real money supply will contract, as we noted earlier, and so too will aggregate demand, until once more $U = U^*$.

Secondly, suppose that there is a negative supply shock.[19] This causes the aggregate bargained wage-setting curve to shift upwards for all levels of employment. If this shift is permanent, real aggregate demand must fall in order to stabilise inflation. As a result, the labour market will be left with a higher U^*. This analysis serves to emphasise the importance of supply-side shocks to an understanding of the NAIRU.[20]

It is clear that the answer to our question about whether or not the economy will always operate at U^* will depend on the speed of adjustment of the process sketched out above. With instantaneous wage and price adjustment, the economy will immediately move to U^* after exogenous demand shocks, and therefore there will be no employment and output fluctuations (as in the classical macroeconomic model). However, if there are nominal rigidities, then aggregate shocks may be associated with output and employment fluctuations, or persistence of unemployment after exogenous demand shocks. The imperfectly competitive model alone is not associated with non-neutrality of monetary policy unless it is combined with nominal rigidities or inertia. If there are no nominal rigidities, prices and wages adjust instantly to any demand shocks.

What factors might cause nominal inertia? A number of theories as to potential sources of nominal inertia have emerged in the macroeconomic literature over the 1980s.[21] First, the periodic nature of wage bargaining means that wage adjustment is not instantaneous (see Taylor, 1983). For example, in the UK union sector, wages are negotiated annually, while in the USA negotiations are typically every three years. With periodic bargaining, the negotiators need to form expectations about inflation over the relevant period, and thus the aggregate wage-setting curve becomes W/P^e instead of W/P, where P^e denotes expected prices. Expectations may be wrong if they are formed adaptively; at $U < U^*$, inflation accelerates, and wage bargainers are always one step behind the play. With rational

---

[19] Examples of such shocks (causing the aggregate wage-setting curve to shift upwards in (ω, N) space) are the introduction of legislation giving unions greater strength, the introduction of employment protection legislation, or an increase in the income tax rate. See also the discussion about variables proxying wages pressure in section 8.5.

[20] What is also evident from our discussion of equilibrium in the aggregate labour market is that the real wage predicted by our simple model will, in equilibrium, always be the same, regardless of the configuration of the aggregate wage-setting curve. This of course follows from our simplifying assumption of imperfectly competitive firms following normal cost pricing.

[21] See Dixon and Rankin (1994) for a detailed survey.

expectations, or *without* periodic bargaining, the acceleration in inflation would be infinite.

A second potential source of nominal rigidity is adjustment or 'menu' costs; these are small lump-sum costs associated with adjusting wages or prices. These might represent the costs of producing new price lists or menus, hence the term (see, for example, Akerlof and Yellen (1985), Mankiw (1985), Blanchard and Kiyotaki (1987), Benassy (1987), Ball and Romer (1989, 1990), and Frank (1990)). These costs imply that the economy is not always on the aggregate price-setting curve.

A third group of explanations for nominal inertia relaxes the assumption of unit-elastic expectations of future prices with respect to current ones (see, for example, Hart (1982), Dehez (1985), D'Aspremont, Dos Santos Ferreira and Gerard-Valet (1989), Silvestre (1990), Jacobsen and Schultz (1989), and Rankin (1992)). Finally, there are theories that combine imperfect competition with a small nominal rigidity in some sector of the economy (Dixon, 1990, 1991; Fender and Yip, 1990; Moutos, 1991).

All theories have in common the combination of imperfect competition with some other distortion resulting in the non-neutrality of aggregate demand policy.[22] If there is nominal inertia for whatever reason, a change in aggregate demand will not be associated with an immediate change in prices or wages. This has the clear implication that demand policies can be used to raise output and employment in imperfectly competitive economies with some nominal inertia. (See Dixon and Rankin (1994) for discussion of the differences between fiscal and monetary policy in imperfectly competitive economies with and without nominal rigidities.) Of course, as in the classical macroeconomic model, supply-side policies can also be used to alter the equilibrium unemployment rate. In the imperfectly competitive framework of this chapter, such policies would be those that shift the aggregate wage-setting or price-setting curves or both.[23]

What is the importance of this flat aggregate price-setting curve for macroeconomic modelling? The answer is that, with a flatter aggregate price-setting curve, demand shocks in combination with nominal inertia are associated with larger employment and output fluctuations than in the case of perfect competition. A flat price-setting curve means that output and

---

[22] This suggests an example of the theory of second best, for while monetary policy is incapable of causing Pareto improvements with either imperfect competition or the other distortion on its own, it is Pareto-improving where both are present (Dixon and Rankin, 1994).

[23] For example, an increase in government expenditure on training lowers the equilibrium unemployment rate through two mechanisms. First, a better trained workforce is more productive, hence the price-determined real wage will shift up. Secondly, more training may lower the bargained wage curve through an expansion in the supply of skilled workers, thereby reducing the monopoly power of skilled union workers. See Carlin and Soskice (1990: ch. 7) for extensive discussion of supply-side policies.

employment are demand-determined: firms supply the level of output that is demanded. However, this does not mean that the government can use demand management policy to achieve any level of output and employment, since attempts to lower U below the NAIRU, or U^*, will be associated with accelerating inflation.

The model of the aggregate labour market developed in this subsection specifically takes into account how real wages are set when the economy is unionised, or when all workers have some bargaining power. We do not embed this model of the aggregate labour market into a full macroeconomic open-economy model, since that is beyond the scope of this book. The interested reader is referred to Carlin and Soskice (1990) and Layard *et al.* (1991) for models of the aggregate labour market that are embedded in a broader model of the macroeconomy.

It is also possible that, instead of having a unique U^*, the aggregate labour market may be characterised by multiple (stable) equilibria or by a range of equilibria.[24] In more complex (and realistic) models of wage- and price-setting behaviour, the curves may not be linear, or may not be monotonic, or may be of a 'perverse' slope. Discussion in this chapter has focused on a horizontal price-setting equation, whilst noting that more generally the price-setting curve might be negatively sloped in (ω, N) space (although relatively flat to reflect the stylised fact that firms appear to adjust quantities rather than prices). But if the economy is characterised by an increasing-returns aggregate production function, at least over some levels of output, then the price-setting curve will be positively sloped in (ω, N) space. This may generate multiple equilibria for real wages and aggregate unemployment (Manning, 1990).[25]

8.3 Aggregate unemployment and the wage bargaining structure

Over the 1980s it was increasingly argued that the institutional structure of wage bargaining may have an important impact on macroeconomic performance. Initial research by economists tried to incorporate the institutional structure by following the notion of 'corporatism' developed in political science. Corporatism has been loosely and variously defined, ranging from the extent of government involvement in wage bargaining, through trade union involvement in policy in return for wage restraint, to

---

[24] See Dixon (1988) and McDonald (1990) for macroeconomic models, with imperfectly competitive labour and product markets, that generate a natural *range* of unemployment rather than a single rate.

[25] See also Chatterjee and Cooper (1989), and Frank (1993) for stories of multiple equilibria that do not rely on increasing returns. The model of Frank (1993) is characterised by perfect competition and decreasing returns, showing that multiple equilibria are not a characteristic of increasing-returns imperfectly competitive models alone.

the degree of consensus in the goals of unions and firms. In the 1980s, a number of the empirical studies estimating aggregate wage and/or price equations included as an explanatory variable an 'index of corporatism' (McCallum, 1983; Bruno and Sachs, 1985; Bean, Layard and Nickell 1986; Newell and Symons, 1987). These studies show a significant positive correlation between the degree of corporatism and real wage moderation. More corporatist economies are those characterised by some combination of greater centralisation of wage bargaining, employer co-ordination, union power and works councils. However, estimated results for the impact of the 'corporatism index' are subject to a variety of interpretations, and the index itself is subjective. Moreover, the inclusion of the index in these studies lacks any theoretical underpinning. It has been suggested by Calmfors and Driffill (1988) *inter alia* that it is the degree of centralisation of pay bargaining that may be of particular importance, and Calmfors and Driffill (1988) attempt to provide a coherent justification as to why, as we shall see.[26]

In OECD countries, there are three broad categories of pay bargaining structure. At one end of the spectrum, wage bargaining and price setting may be *decentralised* to the level of the individual firm. Countries character- ised by decentralised pay bargaining include the USA, Canada, Japan and Switzerland. (However, since Japan is characterised by a high degree of wage-setting co-ordination between large firms, its wage determination cannot really be regarded as decentralised.) At the other end of the spectrum, bargaining may be *centralised* to the economy level. Here confederations of trade unions and employers' federations negotiate the level of wages; countries in this category include Austria, Denmark, Finland, Norway and Sweden. In between these extremes, there may be *intermediate* bargaining at the industry level, as occurs for example in the UK, France, Italy, Germany, the Netherlands, Australia and Belgium (Calmfors and Driffill, 1988: table 2).

By the late 1980s, an empirical regularity appeared to have been discovered: a hump-shaped relationship between the degree of centralisa- tion of wage bargaining and the maintenance of low unemployment in the face of aggregate supply shocks. Countries with either a very high or a very low degree of centralisation of wage bargaining appeared to suffer lower unemployment perturbations following major supply shocks. Although

---

[26] The level of wage bargaining also has ramifications for the relationship between unions and government; for example, government policy may be endogenous for a centralised monopoly union (Calmfors and Horn, 1985, 1986). See also Hoel (1991) for analysis of the relationship between wage determination and the degree of centralisation of wage bargaining.

this 'stylised fact' is based on less than twenty observations, it is nonetheless an interesting hypothesis.[27]

What is the theory for the impact of bargaining structure on economic performance? We follow the Calmfors and Driffill (1988) approach here, which relies on the elasticity of product substitution (see also Carlin and Soskice, 1990). Suppose that union utility is defined over both the real consumption wage, $\omega_i = W_i/P$, and employment (and therefore unemployment), as we have been assuming throughout this book. Unions are aware of the fact the higher wages mean lower employment in the centralised and decentralised situations. This trade-off effectively limits the power of the union, albeit for different reasons in the centralised and decentralised situations. First, consider the case of *decentralised* bargaining. If the decentralised union sets a high money wage, the firm will want to pass this on in the form of higher prices for its product. Since the firm is one of many in the industry, the firm's product will be a close substitute for that of other firms. Therefore, if the firm passes on higher nominal wage costs in the form of higher prices, demand for its output will drop, and so too will employment.[28] Thus any real wage gain obtained by the union will be at the cost of higher unemployment. Since the union executive is aware of this, it will not push for too high money wage increases. Because the overall economy comprises many firms, there will therefore be low equilibrium aggregate unemployment.

There are of course other reasons for any moderation associated with decentralised pay bargaining. To the extent that firms impose sanctions on any firm in the industry granting too large a wage increase, it may be co-ordination between employers rather than a high elasticity of product demand that restrains wage increases.

How are wage increases restrained in the case of *centralised* bargaining? Suppose the union confederation were to increase nominal wages. All firms in the economy, it is argued, will pass this on in the form of higher product prices. Thus workers' real wages will not rise. If the monetary authorities adopt a non-accommodation policy, the real money supply will contract, reducing aggregate demand and resulting in an increase in aggregate

---

[27] More empirical evidence is required before the hypothesis of a hump-shaped relationship can be treated as an empirical regularity or a stylised fact. Honkapohja (1988) suggests the use of panel data. The hypothesis might also be tested for a country like Britain which has some industries characterised by industry-level bargaining, and others by establishment-level bargaining.

[28] This follows from Marshall's rules of the derived demand for labour, where the wage elasticity of labour demand ϵ is greater the more elastic is demand for the firm's product, η. Intuitively, if an increase in the price of a product causes a large drop in the quantity of that product demanded, then firms will consequently produce less output and reduce their demand for their factor inputs including labour.

unemployment. The confederation of unions knows that a cost of raising nominal wages is a higher level of unemployment. Therefore it will set wages such that there is a low equilibrium aggregate unemployment. The centralised trade union (or confederation of trade unions) takes into account the impact of increased union money wages on the general price level and unemployment, and therefore its wage increases are constrained by this.[29]

Although centrally agreed wage settlements are supposedly applicable to all sectors of the economy, such centralised arrangements are frequently accompanied by wage drift. Wage drift refers to the tendency for certain sectors in strong bargaining positions to negotiate for themselves local wage increases substantially above the central wage agreement. Therefore the success of centralised bargaining in constraining wage increases and maintaining a low U^* depends crucially on the ability of the central confederation to co-ordinate its constituent unions, and in particular to keep them in line in order to minimise wage drift.[30]

A second potential problem with centralised wage bargaining is that it is associated with fixed wage relativities across sectors, which thereby make it difficult for fluctuations in relative wages to be used to attract labour to sectors experiencing shortages. Thus fixed relativities emerging from centralised wage negotiation may be associated with allocative inefficiencies. However, the available evidence on this question, although extremely sparse, does suggest tentatively that fixed relativities may not be very costly (Bell and Freeman, 1985).

How are aggregate wages and unemployment affected by *intermediate-level* bargaining structures? Here the nominal wage W_i is set at the level of the ith industry, in an economy with many industries. Given a low degree of substitutability between products of different industries (cricket bats are not good substitutes for dishwashing machines), then the industry union knows that high W_i can be passed on in the form of higher prices for the output of the ith industry, P_i. Since industry demand is argued to be relatively inelastic, then industry output will not contract too much. Because there are many industries in the economy, the union believes the price increase in the ith industry will not affect the consumer price index P. Thus real wages $\omega_i = W_i/P$ increase, but unemployment is not much affected. Obviously, if *all* industrial unions behave in the same fashion, P

[29] Blanchard in the discussion to Calmfors and Driffill (1988) suggests that the interests of the unemployed are more likely to be represented in centralised than in decentralised bargaining, and that bargaining structure might therefore have implications for unemployment persistence and hysteresis. We believe this is particularly likely to be the case if, at the aggregate level, union leaders are concerned with long-term union survival and membership dynamics.

[30] See Soskice (1990) and Rowthorn (1992).

will increase also, and therefore real wages will be unaffected. However, the level of nominal wages and prices will have increased. With a fixed nominal money supply, the real money supply will contract, reducing aggregate demand and increasing aggregate unemployment. But the union at the industry level will not take this into account in its wage setting. (Here there is a problem of co-ordination, a need to internalise a negative externality, that may be overcome by industrial-level unions combining.)

How can the bargaining structure be incorporated into the aggregate wage- and price-setting framework? We follow the approach of Carlin and Soskice (1990: 411) developed in the previous section, and illustrated in figure 8.8 for decentralised and intermediate levels of wage bargaining. The principal difference between the decentralised and intermediate levels in the preceding discussion related to the product demand elasticity. It was argued that, owing to substitution possibilities, the decentralised individual union-firm pair would be faced by a relatively more elastic product demand than would unions and firms bargaining at the industry level. From figure 8.3b and equation (8) (the wage-setting curve, $\omega = b[U/(U - 1/\epsilon)]$), we know that the markup of aggregate real wages above the level of unemployment benefits declines with labour demand elasticity ϵ. We also know from Marshall's rules of derived demand that the greater is product demand elasticity η (where $\eta = -\dfrac{dQ}{dN} \cdot \dfrac{N}{Q}$), the greater is labour demand elasticity ϵ.

Hence with very elastic *product demand*, we know that *labour demand* is also elastic, and therefore the wage-setting curve is lower in (ω, N) space than if product demand is inelastic. Therefore the wage curve for the decentralised wage bargaining structure will be lower than the curve for the intermediate-level bargaining structure, as shown in figure 8.8. Aggregate unemployment (U^d) will therefore be lower (and aggregate employment higher) for decentralised bargaining than for intermediate-level bargaining (U^i).

Notice that the impact of centralised wage bargaining on aggregate employment depends on the precise interpretation of the intuitive argument outlined earlier in this section. With the flat aggregate price-setting curve, the centralised union federation knows exactly what the real wage must be. It might therefore be expected that the utility-maximising position of the central union would be to eliminate all involuntary unemployment, and therefore that the aggregate wage-setting curve would be congruent with the labour supply curve shown in figure 8.7. This does not appear a plausible position, although there is no doubt that Austria and the Scandinavian countries, which are characterised by centralised wage bargaining, have experienced relatively low levels of aggregate unemployment.[31]

---

[31] The position for Sweden has altered recently. See Calmfors (1993).

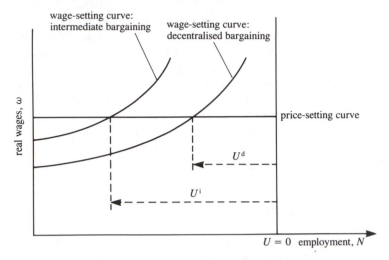

Figure 8.8. Equilibrium unemployment and bargaining structure.

The analysis in the literature of the impact of the wage bargaining structure on aggregate unemployment and wages, interesting though it is, leaves open avenues for further research. In particular, the bargaining structure is assumed exogenous. Yet, as was asked in chapter 3, why do countries adopt a particular bargaining structure? Is it historical accident alone? Or is there an economic rationale for the choice of a particular bargaining structure, which affects the power of the relevant parties to achieve their own goals?[32] Do firms choose decentralised structures where unions are weak, to allow variations in relative wages to enhance resource allocation? What is the role of management in the choice? We have mentioned the degree of centralisation or co-ordination of unions and its importance for the wage outcome, and have tacitly assumed that employers are also co-ordinated in such circumstances. But what has been somewhat neglected is the rationale for firms to centralise (but see Soskice (1990)). These are interesting questions for future research.

8.4 Unemployment persistence and hysteresis

The experience of many OECD countries in the 1980s was novel in the sense that, while unemployment rose dramatically, the level of inflation remained roughly constant. This suggests that the NAIRU (non-accelerating-inflation rate of unemployment) or U^* must have risen. But, using the conventional analysis of the determinants of NAIRU that we have examined in this chapter, it is not clear why this should be the case.

[32] These goals may range more widely than the level of wages alone.

According to this analysis, unanticipated changes in demand and supply cause deviations of actual unemployment from equilibrium, where equilibrium unemployment is determined by the particular institutional structure of the economy. When actual unemployment deviates from equilibrium, changes in the behaviour of workers and firms alter the inflation rate, and this in turn ultimately leads to unemployment returning to its equilibrium.

This approach has not been borne out by recent experience in many OECD countries. Both actual and equilibrium unemployment (as estimated from Phillips curves) have risen together. But increases in unemployment have not been accompanied by declining inflation.[33] Indeed, inflation has been roughly constant. Moreover, there has been a decline in OPEC prices, and in many countries a reduction in union power, suggesting that NAIRU should have fallen.

The failure to account for the phenomena of apparently increasing equilibrium unemployment and roughly constant inflation has led to a search for alternative theories of aggregate unemployment. Of particular interest in some of the recent macroeconomic literature is the notion of *hysteresis*, whereby equilibrium unemployment is held to be path-dependent: it depends on the history of actual unemployment. Any changes to actual unemployment can affect equilibrium for a long time; there is unemployment persistence. There are a number of interesting theoretical developments aiming to explain hysteresis. We consider two of these – *duration* theories, based on the view that only the short-term unemployed affect wage determination, and *insider–outsider* theories, where wages are determined by insiders only.[34]

First, we consider *unemployment duration* theory. There are various theories as to why unemployed workers may affect unemployment persistence; the duration theory is just one, and it rests on the belief that the job-seeking behaviour of the long-term unemployed differs significantly from that of the short-term unemployed (Layard and Nickell, 1986, 1987; McCormick, 1990).[35] According to this approach, union bargaining power

[33] In Britain, for example, high levels of unemployment for long periods have been found to have little effect on wage inflation (Gregory, Lobban and Thomson, 1986, 1987).

[34] Not all of the theories of unemployment persistence relate to trade union theory in even an indirect fashion. For example, two potential sources of persistence operate through the labour demand side; these are firing costs and capital shortages. See Bean (1993) for an outline.

[35] Outsiders may affect persistence in a number of ways (see Bean (1994) for a survey). If skill deterioration of unemployed workers is such that the wage they could command drops below their reservation wage, then these workers effectively drop out of the labour force, although they remain as registered unemployed. An extension of this view is that skill deterioration is less dramatic but that firms, faced with a queue of applicants all demanding the same wage, prefer to hire the short-term unemployed (Blanchard and Diamond, 1990). Lockwood (1991) assumes that firms have imperfect information about applicants' ability; duration dependence may emerge to the extent that ability is partially correlated with unemployment history.

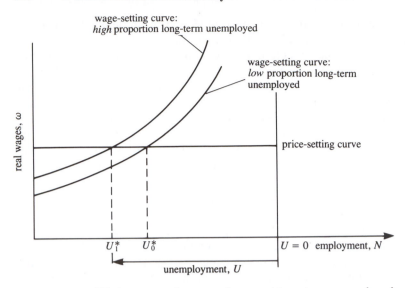

Figure 8.9. Equilibrium unemployment: short- and long-term unemployed.

is greater the larger the proportion of long-term unemployed in the pool of unemployed workers. Firms are unwilling to hire the long-term unemployed, because they have lost their skills and work confidence, and perhaps because of suspicions that they are the rejects from other firms. Moreover, the long-term unemployed may be so discouraged and lacking in confidence that they have effectively given up job search. For a variety of reasons, therefore, the long-term unemployed may have effectively withdrawn from the labour force. Thus, from the viewpoint of the union, the unemployed workers relevant to the bargained wage are the short-term unemployed: only these unemployed workers affect union bargaining power. For a given unemployment level, the greater the proportion of long-term unemployed, the higher the union-negotiated wage *ceteris paribus* (and thus the higher the wage-setting curve in (ω, N) space). Thus U^* alters with changes in the long-term unemployed, from U^*_0 to U^*_1 as shown in figure 8.9.

Secondly, we consider *insider–outsider* theories as an explanation for unemployment persistence. Suppose each firm has N_i^* incumbents or employed members. The trade union is assumed to represent *only the interests of the employed members*, who are employed by the firm first owing to workers' market power to enforce this employment rule. Unemployed workers are not in a position to undercut the employed insiders. Only when all N_i^* insiders are employed can outsiders (new entrants to the firm) be hired. Of course, a distinction between insiders and outsiders can still be made in the absence of trade unions, as emphasised by Lindbeck and Snower (1988). All that is required is that there should be labour turnover costs giving the insiders some market power.[36] This can give insiders, whether unionised or not, sufficient power to capture some of the firm's available surplus when making wage demands. The notion that insider–outsider models may be applicable to the labour market even in the absence of a trade union is important to the following section also, where we look at the modelling of economies with both union and nonunion sectors.

What are the implications for aggregate unemployment and hysteresis of labour unions in the context of insider–outsider models? The work by Blanchard and Summers (1986, 1987) suggests that any level of unemployment may be self-perpetuating, to the extent that insiders determine wages in order to ensure that all insiders are employed, but without regard to the employment consequences for outsiders. Suppose that there is some exogenous demand shock that temporarily lowers employment, resulting in some of the insiders losing their jobs and their insider status. The remaining pool of insiders then sets the next period's wage taking into account the employment implications for the smaller pool of insiders that remains. The new insiders thus set wages to maintain permanently the lower level of employment. As a result, employment will not be restored to its original level when demand recovers; instead, wages will increase but employment will remain the same. Thus unemployment will be characterised by hysteresis.

What are the predictions of this model for unemployment persistence in terms of the diagrammatic framework developed in section 8.2? An unexpected temporary adverse shock to labour demand leads to a fall in employment, which causes the number of insiders to contract. When labour demand recovers, because the insiders care only about employed members, wages increase instead of employment. The wage-setting curve therefore shifts upwards. Employment will only return to its original level if there are temporary incomes policies or other factors shifting the wage-setting curve downwards, or instead if there is an off-setting unexpected labour demand shock leading firms to take on new workers.

This insider hysteresis approach has a number of theoretical problems. In Blanchard and Summers (1986), wage-setting behaviour depends only on changes in unemployment, and not on the level. The steady-state implications of this are rather odd. If two economies have each experienced a stable long-run inflation rate, but one has a high unemployment level while the other has a low level, each should be characterised by similar wage

---

[36] These labour turnover costs might be, for example, hiring, training or firing costs, costs associated with harassment of new entrants by incumbents, and/or costs of reduced effort or lack of co-operation by incumbents if turnover is high (Lindbeck and Snower, 1988).

demands according to this model. A second point of criticism relates to the fact that the labour market typically has a number of people changing jobs each year. So the question arises as to why employment has not declined due to labour turnover, if unions only take into account in their wage setting the surviving incumbents (Layard *et al.*, 1991). Finally, the insider view of hysteresis is not a coherent story of union membership, since a series of negative shocks should see union membership dwindling in the face of massively high wages, which is not what we observe.

Does this model explain the *empirical* pattern of unemployment persistence in the European Community? The Blanchard and Summers (1986) estimates for the period 1953–84 suggest that there is a hysteresis effect for European countries, to the extent that changes in employment matter for wage growth. However, the importance of changes in unemployment (as well as levels) in wage-equation and Phillips curves is well recognised. As noted by Alogoskoufis and Manning (1988a) and Bean (1994), it is difficult to distinguish between competing hypotheses explaining such persistence. For example, are persistence mechanisms insider-generated, outsider-generated, or wage aspiration-generated? Alogoskoufis and Manning (1988a, 1988b) estimate a generalised version of the Blanchard and Summers model for 16 OECD countries over the period 1952–85. They argue that it is persistence in real-wage aspirations that matters rather than insider membership dynamics. Although this study is carefully executed it is worth noting this conclusion by Calmfors (1988: 460):

It is a disturbing fact that different cross-country studies tend to come up with different explanations of inter-country employment differences . . . So what have we learnt from the increasing number of cross-country studies on the causes of unemployment? My answer is: not much! The main reason is that there are simply not enough cross-section observations to be able to draw any safe empirical conclusions from country comparisons.

It is also interesting to consider the results of microeconometric studies estimating wage equations, which may shed some light on the hysteresis question. These studies typically distinguish between the impact of firm-specific or 'insider' factors on wage determination, and the impact of 'insider hysteresis' effects. The latter are generally proxied by a variable measuring employment changes (see, for example, Nickell and Wadhwani (1990)). Outsider variables are also incorporated. These studies suggest that firm-specific factors or 'insider' variables are relatively unimportant in the Scandinavian countries, are very important in the USA and Japan, and are somewhere in between in Britain and Germany (see Nickell and Kong (1988), Brunello and Wadhwani (1989), Nickell and Wadhwani (1990), and Holmlund and Zetterberg (1991)). The finding that insider variables are relatively unimportant in Scandinavian countries is what we would expect, given the centralised nature of wage-setting institutions in these countries. Nickell and Wadhwani (1990) use individual firm-level panel data for 219 manufacturing companies over the period 1972–82. While they find in their principal specification that the 'insider-based hysteresis effect' (for employment change) has a positive effect on wages, this finding is not robust to alternative specifications.[37] In conclusion, we might note that evidence as to the existence of insider hysteresis effects is sparse. It is also generally not supportive of the insider persistence impact, although there are as yet too few studies to draw firm conclusions.

8.5 Empirical estimation of the wage- and price-setting curves

We now turn to a more detailed empirical examination of the aggregate labour market model developed in the previous sections. It is common practice in the literature to estimate a structural model of the aggregate labour market in a form similar to the following two log-linear equations, which are obtained from the influential work of Nickell (1987) and Layard and Nickell (1987):

$$\text{price-setting: } p - w = a_0 - a_1(p - p^e) - a_2 u - a_3(k - l) \tag{20}$$

$$\text{wage-setting: } w - p^e = \beta_0 + \beta_1(p - p^e) - \beta_2 u + \beta_3(k - l) + z \tag{21}$$

where the variables are written in lower case to denote that they are the natural logarithms of the upper-case variables used earlier in this chapter, p^e represents expected prices, and z denotes variables proxying wage pressure.[38] It is assumed that z is exogenous.[39] Where $p = p^e$, prices are correctly forecast and there are no price 'surprises'. Clearly, in the short run, there is scope for price surprises. In the *price-setting* equation (20), the left-hand-side variable is the markup of prices over hourly wage costs, and the level of unemployment u is included on the right-hand side as an indicator of labour market activity. The last term on the right-hand side of (20) measures the impact of the growth of the capital stock; since this causes productivity to

[37] Blanchflower, Oswald and Garrett (1989) report an employment growth variable as having a negative impact on wages, where they use data from the 1984 Workplace Industrial Relations Survey.

[38] Variables proxying wage pressure might be the degree of mismatch, employment protection, the ratio of unemployment benefits to earnings, and proxies for union power, incomes policies or payroll taxes. See, for example, Bean *et al.* (1986), Layard and Nickell (1987: 137), and Layard *et al.* (1991:404).

[39] This will not be true in an open economy, because wage pressure arises in part through the real price of imports entering the wedge between consumption and production wages (see Layard and Nickell (1986) and Alogoskoufis (1990)).

increase, it is expected that $(k-l)$ will have a negative impact on firms' markup of prices over labour costs.[40] Finally, notice that if $a_2 = 0$, (20) represents the normal cost pricing model, where the markup is unaffected by demand fluctuations in the short run.

In the *wage-setting* equation (21), we expect a positive price surprise $(p > p^e)$ to be associated with a negative effect on the wage markup, as the real wage will be lower than bargained for. As in the model of section 8.2, we expect unemployment to have a negative impact on the wage markup. Finally, increasing $(k-l)$ should be associated with productivity improvements, encouraging unions to bargain for higher wages. The wage pressure variable z reflects the institutional environment affecting wage bargaining.

The structural model represented by the price- and wage-setting equations of (20) and (21) respectively is typically derived from theoretical models of imperfectly competitive firms' price-setting behaviour and of wage bargaining between unions and firms. Since the theoretical model is generally static (for reasons of tractability), the specification of (20) and (21) is then augmented by the inclusion of lagged and/or differenced variables (see Nickell (1987) and Layard *et al.* (1991: ch. 8)). For example, Nickell (1987) assumes that price surprises associated with changes in the inflation rate Δp are represented by $\Delta^2 p$, and the dynamic structure of the unemployment term in the wages equation is assumed to be as indicated in equation (23), which captures hysteresis effects. Estimates of the preferred dynamic specification of (20) and (21), as reported in Layard and Nickell (1987), are given below; estimation is based on annual aggregate data for Britain over the period 1956–83.[41]

price-setting:
$$p - w = a_0 - 0.61\Delta^2 w - 0.51\Delta^2 w_{-1}$$
$$- 0.253u + 0.075\Delta u - 0.338\Delta^2 u - 1.07(k - l) \tag{22}$$

wage-setting:
$$w - p = \beta_0 + 0.36\Delta^2 p - 0.104\ln u$$
$$+ 0.532u - 1.174\Delta u - 0.356\Delta^2 u + 1.07(k - l) + z \tag{23}$$

where the subscript -1 represents the variable lagged one period.

How can the long-run or steady-state NAIRU be calculated from

---

[40] From (16), it can be seen that prices are decreasing in labour productivity. If the capital-to-labour ratio increases, labour productivity increases; as a result, more output is produced for a given labour input and wage rate. Firms can therefore reduce their product price, while maintaining a fixed level of profits.

[41] A restriction is imposed that $a_3 = \beta_3$. If $\beta_3 - a_3 > 0$, firms and workers would take more than 100% of increases in trend productivity. Note that t-statistics are not reported in Layard and Nickell (1987).

equations (22) and (23)? Expand the wage equation around an unemploy-ment level of $\bar{u}$, and set the differenced terms to zero (see Nickell (1987) for full details). Thus we obtain steady-state prices and wages as

$$\text{prices: } p - w = a_0 - 0.253u - 1.07(k - l) \tag{24}$$

$$\text{wages: } w - p = \beta'_0 - \left(\frac{0.104}{\bar{u}} - 0.532\right)u + 1.07(k - l) + z \tag{25}$$

Now add (24) and (25) to obtain

$$u = \left(0.253 + \frac{0.104}{\bar{u}} - 0.532\right)^{-1}(z + a_0 + \beta'_0) \tag{26}$$

Thus, in the long run, the particular value of the NAIRU will depend on z – the wages pressure variable, reflecting a number of institutional features of the economy.

To conclude this section, we note that a major problem with the *estimation* of a simultaneous equation model of the form of (20) and (21) is that of *identification* of the wage equation (Layard *et al.*, 1991: 405).[42] As Manning (1993: 99) notes: 'In practice, identification is achieved by arbitrary exclusion restrictions (i.e. omitting one of the productivity variables from the wages equation) and/or *ad hoc* dynamics. There is a certain act of faith in assuming that one gets sensible results from such practices.' As a means of checking if their simultaneous equation estimates are sensible, Layard *et al.* (1991) compare these with reduced-form estimates, and argue that their story of unemployment is unaffected by the changed estimation procedure.[43]

[42] An intuitive explanation of the identification problem is as follows. Suppose that we have observed at yearly intervals three data points in (ω, N) space, as shown in graph (a). Suppose we believe these points to each represent the equilibrium from a labour market model of aggregate price- and wage-setting behaviour. It is clear, however, that there are a number of possible structural models consistent with these observed data, as illustrated in graphs (b) and (c). For (b) to represent the appropriate structural model, we would need to know that wage-setting behaviour had been constant over the period, while price-setting behaviour had been altering. As a crude rule-of-thumb, we require for *identification* of the correct structural model a variable in the wage equation that is not in the price equation, and vice versa. See Greene (1993) for an advanced exposition, and any basic econometrics text for a simpler approach.

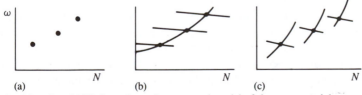

(a) (b) (c)

[43] See Manning (1993) for a dynamic structural model of the aggregate labour market that overcomes the identification problems inherent in the estimation of (20) and (21).

8.6 Conclusion

It is clear that many countries are characterised by having both unionised and nonunionised sectors, yet partially unionised economies are not encapsulated in the macroeconomic model outlined in the previous sections. In the USA, for example, some sectors of the economy are not unionised.[44] Even in Britain, which, as we noted in an earlier chapter, has a far higher aggregate trade union density than the USA, there are some sectors of the economy with very low levels of unionisation (see Beatson and Butcher, 1993).

What are the implications of partial unionisation for modelling of the macroeconomy? If an economy is partially unionised but wages for all workers are effectively determined by confederations of trade unions and employers, the model of section 8.2 may be a reasonable approximation to reality. An example of such an economy is Germany, which is also characterised by a very stable wage-setting system. If an economy is partially unionised but wages are determined locally, the macroeconomic model of this chapter may still be a reasonable approximation, provided that the *coverage* of collective agreements is high and the model is modified to allow for the degree of decentralisation. Thus both the bargaining structure and the bargaining coverage are institutional features of an economy that need to be considered before constructing an aggregate model of the labour market. Since these features typically vary across countries, it is clear that a model developed for one particular economy may not be appropriate for another. We have already noted in this chapter the importance of the level of bargaining. In earlier chapters we also noted that in some countries union coverage differs considerably from union membership. According to Layard *et al.* (1991: 52) all European countries with the exception of Switzerland have over three-quarters of workers covered by union collective bargains, as does Australia. Japan, New Zealand and Canada have union coverage of between 25 and 75%, while only in the USA are less than one-quarter of workers covered by union collective agreements[45]. In the European Community, there are generally single-industry agreements, whch are usually binding on firms regardless of whether or not they are unionised.

However, for partially unionised countries without centralisation of wage fixing and with low levels of union coverage, while the macro-model of section 8.2 may be able to chart aggregate wages across time, the interpretation of the results will be debatable. For example, in the USA wages are typically determined at the firm level, and union membership *and*

---

[44] See Hirsch and Macpherson (1993).
[45] The union density figures for a number of OECD countries are given in chapter 1.

coverage are very low. If the nonunionised sector were competitive, the macroeconomic modelling problem would be relatively straightforward, to the extent that it could be modelled as for the two-sector general equilibrium model referred to in chapter 3.[46] But there is no general consensus as to how wages are determined in the nonunion sector. Is the nonunion sector competitive? Or is it characterised by efficiency wage determination? Alternatively, can the nonunion sector be represented by a model analogous to the union models outlined in this book, because nonunion workers also possess some bargaining power due to labour turnover costs? Or is the nonunion sector characterised by elements of all of these theories of wage determination? If wages in the nonunion sector are determined by efficiency wage considerations or because insiders have some market power due to labour turnover costs, then the wage-setting curve for the nonunion sector will be similar to the union wage curve derived in this chapter. However, the fact that the microeconomic behaviour underpinning the models is different will have implications for policy.

The reader interested in the problems of providing a realistic microfoundation for the US labour market is directed to Pencavel (1991: ch. 6), who discusses and models interactions among markets in an economy such as that of the USA with only very partial unionisation and coverage. For European countries, the imperfect competition model outlined in this chapter appears a reasonable first approximation to wage setting in unionised economies. It would be fair to state, however, that modelling at the aggregate level the imperfectly competitive wage- and price-setting behaviour of unions and firms is a relatively novel research area. No doubt, developments in this area will improve our understanding of the aggregate labour market.

[46] For macroeconomic models in this vein, see Chatterji and Price (1988) *inter alia*.

9   Conclusion

In the introduction to this book, it was argued that the textbook perfectly competitive model of the labour market, where labour is treated essentially as a commodity in an auction, is not a good characterisation when workers have some bargaining power. It is well known that labour is characterised by certain features that distinguish it from other inputs. These features may in some circumstances give workers or management a degree of bargaining power. Some examples of these characteristics were provided in chapter 1. In general, in circumstances where it is costly for the *firm* to replace existing workers by outsiders, incumbent workers have some market power. And where it is costly for the *worker* to be laid off for whatever reason (be it loss of firm-specific human capital or because there are no alternative jobs), management will have some bargaining power. In such a situation of bilateral monopoly, emerging as a result of labour turnover costs, wages may be determined through a bargaining process rather than through an auction process. In principle, such bargaining may be either between individuals and management, or between an agent of the workers and management, where the agent could be a trade union. While bargaining may be more effective between a trade union and management, there may still be scope for individual bargaining with management in some production processes.

In this book it is argued that, while the union models refer to labour contracts between a trade union and management, they are also relevant to a much wider class of situations than those in which a trade union explicitly represents workers. Indeed, union contracts may be viewed simply as an explicit formulation of a wider variety of labour contracts that are found in labour markets wherever incumbent workers have some bargaining power.

A major theme of the book is that, for a trade union to be able to increase workers' remuneration, it must have the necessary power to induce the firm to share any surplus. Bargaining power on the part of the union arises wherever the group of workers can impose costs on the firm by labour withdrawal. Workers can threaten costly labour withdrawal through strikes, or work-to-rule, or refusals to train or instruct new workers, or threats to find other jobs. Of course, labour turnover or withdrawal costs to the firm may arise quite naturally in the absence of trade unions, for example where there is skill specificity. But labour withdrawal costs may also arise when a trade union is able to control the supply of labour to a firm or sector, through for example closed-shop agreements. It is argued that union or worker control over labour supply is likely to be found in rather particular conditions. Examples are provided by craft unions where the union can control the supply of trained labour, and by technological processes in which skilled labour is vital for production and it is costly to the firm to obtain new workers. Indeed, an interesting research hypothesis is that bargaining situations are more likely to be determined by the characteristics of particular methods of work organisation or productive processes (in which trade unions may also be more likely to emerge) than by the mere presence of trade unions.

A second theme of the book is that, for a union to be able to increase workers' remuneration, there must exist some economic rent or surplus that is available for sharing. Economic rents arise wherever there is imperfect competition in the product market. We would therefore expect to observe greater union gains for workers in situations where there is a degree of market power arising from imperfect competition in the product market. Where there are supernormal profits arising from market structure, any lowered profits consequent on unionisation raise distributional issues about the relative shares of the surplus going to capital and labour. But such lowered profits do not raise allocative issues about unionisation, since the allocative inefficiency existed in the absence of unionisation, through the firm's market power. Thus, while society may gain from eliminating product market imperfections that confer market power on a firm, policies to weaken trade union power will not eliminate the allocative inefficiencies. Of course, market power may arise as a quasi-rent following innovation; if unions gain a share of such quasi-rents and in so doing reduce the incentive to innovate, then unionisation will be associated with allocative inefficiencies. But economists know very little as yet about the relationship between unions and innovation.

If it is the case that unions make wage gains only where there is a degree of market power, the implications for allocative efficiency are very different from the orthodox textbook view of the impact of unions on resource allocation. Where product markets are perfectly competitive, the impact of unionisation has a negative impact on allocative efficiency, as we saw in chapter 3. It is clear that different models of unionisation have very different predictions as to allocative inefficiencies. This remains a relatively unexplored area in the economic analysis of trade unions.

An alternative source of economic rents that might be shared between workers and the firm is any organisational change associated with the advent of unionisation. For example, improved co-operation and worker morale arising from unionisation may be a source of rents that can be shared between all parties. The evidence from the industrial relations literature is that forms of organisational structure and behaviour associated with trade unions vary considerably across unions, firms, industries and countries. Some unions are characterised by a very confrontational approach which may result in a reduced surplus to the firm, for example. An interesting and as yet unanswered question arises as to the extent to which bargaining power and hence rent sharing depend on the source of economic rents. If the rents arise in the product market, are firms better able to appropriate the surplus than if they arise from the labour market?

The book suggests that there are a number of questions, both theoretical and empirical, that have not yet been answered by the trade union literature. A lot of theoretical attention has focused on how to model union and, to a lesser extent, managerial objectives, and how to model the resolution of the conflicting preferences of unions and firms for wage and employment outcomes. The issue of whether the bargaining agenda includes only wages, or instead wages *and* employment, has also been an important research subject. But there are a number of other interesting questions that remain largely unanswered. These include the topic of what else may appear on the bargaining agenda; for example, unions and firms frequently negotiate hours of work, manning arrangements, effort, capital-to-labour ratios and redundancy payments. It is also clear that endogenous membership, union insiders and outsiders, and the relationship between seniority and wages represent important and under-researched theoretical issues. In addition, it would be fair to say that very few economic theories of the trade union have yet been adequately tested against the data, nor has it yet appeared possible to discriminate between the various competing hypotheses about wage and employment determination under bargaining.

Much of the theoretical modelling referred to in the book is broadly appropriate to the unionised economies of Europe, Australia and New Zealand, and to the unionised sectors of the USA. None the less, a theme of the book is that there are important institutional differences across countries, differences that may need to be incorporated into the modelling framework. The book pays particular attention to differences in collective bargaining structures between Britain and the USA. But even within each country, there is diversity in collective bargaining institutions across sectors. This diversity has emerged in response to variations in product market conditions and structure, political organisation and historical accident. It is important that students and researchers are aware of this heterogeneity, in order to avoid the pitfall of inappropriate applications of theoretical models characterising the behaviour of unions in one particular country or sector to another country or sector with a dissimilar institutional structure.

It was noted in chapter 1 that, coincident with the recent blossoming of research on trade unions, there has been a decline in trade union density in most major industrialised economies. Although union density appears to be declining, and in some countries only a minority of the workforce is unionised, an argument of this book is that we still need to be concerned with providing appropriate models of union behaviour. There are several reasons for this. Industrial relations and labour researchers in the USA, where union density has been declining since the mid-1950s, have long argued that union influence extends well beyond the unionised sector. In particular, the threat of union organisation of a nonunion sector may provoke management to provide wages and working conditions that mimic those negotiated in union firms. Nonunion workers will therefore be less likely to unionise, since there is little difference between their welfare in a union firm and a nonunion firm providing matching benefits. Another instance of union influence on the nonunion sector arises where the threat of union organisation provokes management into directing resources into anti-union activities, in order to prevent a union emerging. It is also clear that, even if aggregate union density is low, modelling the behaviour of unions is important for sectoral analysis of the parts of the economy that *are* heavily unionised, or where a powerful sector is unionised and there are knock-on effects for the rest of the economy.

For European countries and Australia and New Zealand, the influence of trade unions at the macroeconomic level is better indicated by the extent of coverage of the workforce by union collective agreements, rather than by the proportion of the workforce that are union members. Of the major industrial countries, only in the USA is less than one-quarter of workers covered by union collective agreements. Most European countries have coverage exceeding three-quarters. This suggests that an understanding of the economics of the trade union is vital for analysis of the workings of the macroeconomy for most industrialised countries, and that at the microeconomic level it is also important for the USA.

The theoretical analysis of trade unions has, to a large extent, proceeded separately from empirical measurement, and there is a much larger literature devoted to the latter. Indeed, there is an enormous body of empirical research on trade unions, a literature that documents the observed differences between union and nonunion sectors, jobs and outcomes. Much of the literature measuring the impact of trade unions on various outcomes has been largely descriptive with no theoretical foundation. It is predicated, often implicitly, on the orthodox view of trade unions as operating in perfectly competitive product markets; this is particularly the case in the US empirical literature. At best, the results of this empirical literature can be given the status of 'stylised facts', providing valuable information about empirical regularities associated with unionised labour markets. But our knowledge as to why there are differences between union and nonunion labour markets is still incomplete. In essence, while descriptive empirical research is instructive in summarising data sets and suggesting stylised facts that require explanation, the book has emphasised that care should be taken in using it to make inferences about the impact of trade unions.

What can we conclude about empirical regularities or stylised facts associated with trade unionism? Sadly, rather little. But we do know that the impact of unions on wages is nowhere near as large as was thought in the late 1960s and 1970s, when economists relied on aggregate data to estimate union–nonunion wage differentials. A combination of advances in computing facilities, econometric software and econometric modelling techniques has allowed the analysis of newly available large micro-level survey data, and the estimated average union wage gap is now believed to be only 7–8% for Britain,[1] and 15% for the USA. Moreover, British evidence indicates that in sectors of the economy with a competitive product market, the union–nonunion wage differential is far smaller than these average figures. This finding suggests that there may be other factors apart from wages sustaining union membership and recognition.

What about the impact of unions on other measures of economic activity? The principal stylised facts or empirical regularities emerging from the literature are as follows. First, unionisation in both Britain and the USA appears, on average, to have a negative impact on productivity and productivity growth in the 1980s. Secondly, while there is scanty empirical evidence as to the impact of unions on investment, the US evidence is of a negative effect, while the British evidence is ambiguous. Thirdly, unionisation appears to have a negative impact on profitability, as is expected *a priori* given a positive average union–nonunion wage gap *ceteris paribus*. It seems likely that unions typically induce firms to share their surplus and, in the absence of an accompanying productivity increase, thereby reduce profits. Therefore, the issue of whether profits are supernormal or otherwise is of obvious relevance, and requires further investigation. If the impact of unions has been to reduce supernormal profits at the expense of owners of capital, while still allowing a sufficient margin to attract capital investment, then we may not want to worry about the negative union impact on profits.

---

[1] The estimated British union–nonunion wage gap has remained stable over the decade 1980–90.

But we may wish to concern ourselves with the market structure from which are generated supernormal profits. It is therefore most important that applied researchers examine whether or not unions' negative impact on profits leads to lower investment in physical and human capital, and in innovation and research and development. These will obviously affect the growth rate of the economy.

A fourth measure of economic activity on which unions may have an effect is employment. There is some evidence that unions are associated with negative employment growth, in both North America and Britain. However, studies estimating union effects on employment growth have typically not allowed for the fact that unionisation is associated with bargaining over issues that are likely to encourage union firms to vary hours rather than workers, and this casts some doubt on the results. Finally, the few studies looking at union hours gaps reveal significant differences between union and nonunion hours.

It is clear that much more research is required in order to measure the impact of unions on economic outcomes (apart from the union impact on wages, the focus of most of the empirical union research). It is also clear that there are dangers in concentrating narrowly on one aspect of unionisation, without also taking into account secondary union effects. Moreover, even where we may be confident about the measured union effect on one particular variable, it may be the case that because of the different structures of unions in different countries and sectors of the one economy, this effect is not found elsewhere. It is therefore necessary to have evidence on the union effects from a number of different studies before drawing any firm conclusions. Global or national generalisations on the basis of a handful of studies should be avoided. It is clear that the measurement of union effects remains an under-researched area, but an exciting one for future researchers.

There are many interesting questions about trade unions that remain unanswered and generally unaddressed in the huge body of empirical literature measuring union effects, and yet the answers to which might inform the empirical work. For example, how do trade unions gain the power to obtain wage increases? Under what conditions is the union able to raise wages above the nonunion wage rate? Why do unions exist? In what circumstances might management acquiesce in the formation of a union or agree to recognise a union? How do unions affect hours of work?

Another area where further research is required is the role of trade unions in the macroeconomy. It is clear that many countries are characterised by both unionised and nonunionised sectors, yet partially unionised economies are not represented in the popular macroeconomic model outlined in chapter 8. Even for Britain, which has a far higher overall trade union density than the USA, there are some sectors of the economy with very low levels of unionisation. What are the implications of partial unionisation for modelling of the macroeconomy? If an economy is partially unionised but wages for all workers are effectively determined by confederations of trade unions and employers, the labour market model of chapter 8 may be a reasonable approximation to reality. If an economy is partially unionised but wages are determined locally, the macroeconomic model of chapter 8 may still be a reasonable approximation, provided that the *coverage* of collective agreements is high and the model is modified to allow for the degree of decentralisation. Thus both the bargaining structure and the bargaining coverage are institutional features of an economy that need to be considered before constructing an aggregate model of the labour market. Since these features typically vary across countries, it is clear that a model developed for one particular economy may not be appropriate for another.

However, for partially unionised countries without centralisation of wage fixing and with low levels of union coverage, while the macro-model of chapter 8 may be able to chart aggregate wages across time, the interpretation of the results will be debatable. For example, in the USA wages are typically determined at the firm level, and union membership *and* coverage are very low. If the nonunionised sector were competitive, the macroeconomic modelling problem would be relatively straightforward. But there is no general consensus as to how wages are determined in the nonunion sectors. Is the nonunion sector competitive? Or is it characterised by efficiency wage determination? Alternatively, can the nonunion sector be represented by a model analogous to the union models outlined in this book, because nonunion workers also possess some bargaining power due to labour turnover costs? Or is the nonunion sector characterised by elements of all of these theories of wage determination?

For European countries, the imperfect competition model of the labour market of chapter 8 appears a reasonable first approximation to wage setting in unionised economies. It would be fair to state, however, that aggregate-level modelling of the imperfectly competitive wage- and price-setting behaviour of unions and firms is a relatively novel research area. No doubt future developments in this area will improve our understanding of the aggregate labour market.

In conclusion, it is clear that the economics of the trade union remains an exciting research area, and one in which there is scope for the next generation of researchers to make important contributions to our understanding of unionised economies. While there has been a remarkable number of developments in the theoretical and empirical work on trade unions over the past two decades, there remain many unanswered questions. The answers to these questions will not only be of theoretical interest but also have important implications for economic policy, in particular if issues of resource allocation are explicitly addressed in a framework of imperfectly competitive product markets. Moreover, while trade union power and membership density declined over the 1980s during the so-called 'conservative revolution', it is extremely unlikely that trade unions will vanish from European labour markets. Indeed, we are likely to see an expansion of labour unions in the newly democratic countries of Eastern Europe. Even in the USA where union density stands at only 16% of the workforce, union bargaining models of wage determination are applicable wherever incumbent workers have some bargaining power arising from labour turnover costs. It is clear that much important work remains to be done in the economic analysis of the trade union.

References

Aaron, B., J.R. Grodin and J.L. Stern (1979), *Public-Sector Bargaining*, Washington D.C.: Bureau of National Affairs.

Abowd, J.M. (1989), 'The Effect of Wage Bargains on the Stock Market Value of the Firm', *American Economic Review*, 79(4): 774–809.

Abowd, J.M. and H.S. Farber (1990), 'Product Market Competition, Union Organising Activity and Employer Resistance', NBER Working paper no. 3353, Cambridge, Mass.

Abraham, K.G. and J.L. Medoff (1983), 'Length of Service, Terminations and the Nature of the Employment Relation', NBER Working paper no. 1086, Cambridge, Mass.

Abramovitz, M. (1986), 'Catching Up, Forging Ahead and Falling Behind', *Journal of Economic History*, 86: 385–406.

Acs, Z.J. and D.B. Audretsch (1987), 'Innovation in Large and Small Firms', *Economics Letters*, 23: 109–12.

Addison, J.T. and B.T. Hirsch (1989), 'Union Effects on Productivity, Profits and Growth: Has the Long Run Arrived?', *Journal of Labor Economics*, 7(1): 72–105.

Akerlof, G.A. and J.L. Yellen (1985), 'A Near-rational Model of the Business Cycle, with Wage and Price Inertia', *Quarterly Journal of Economics*, 100 (supplement): 823–38.

(1986) (eds.), *Efficiency Wage Models of the Labour Market*, Cambridge University Press.

Alesina, A. (1989), 'Politics and Business Cycles in Industrial Democracies', *Economic Policy*, 8 (April): 55–87.

Allen, S.G. (1984), 'Trade Unions, Absenteeism and Exit-Voice', *Industrial and Labor Relations Review*, 37(3): 331–45.

(1986), 'The Effect of Unionism on Productivity in Privately and Publicly Owned Hospitals and Nursing Homes', *Journal of Labor Research*, 7: 59–68.

(1987), 'Can Union Labor Ever Cost Less?', *Quarterly Journal of Economics*, 102: 347–73.

Alogoskoufis, G. (1990), 'The Labour Market in the Open Economy', in D. Sapsford and Z. Tzannatos (eds.), *Current Issues in Labour Economics*, London: Macmillan.

266

Alogoskoufis, G. and A. Manning (1988a), 'On the Persistence of Unemployment', *Economic Policy*, 7: 428–69.

(1988b), 'Wage Setting and Unemployment Persistence in Europe, Japan and the USA', *European Economic Review*, 32: 698–706.

Andrews, M.J. and A.H. Harrison (1991), 'Testing for Efficient Contracts in Unionised Labour Markets', University of Manchester, mimeo.

Andrews, M.J. and R. Simmons (1992), 'Effort Bargaining', University of Manchester, mimeo.

Ashenfelter, O. and G.E. Johnson (1969), 'Bargaining Theory, Trade Unions and Industrial Strike Activity'. *American Economic Review*. 59(1): 35–49.

Atherton, W.N. (1973), *Theory of Union Bargaining Goals*, Princeton University Press.

Atkinson, A.B. and J.E. Stiglitz (1980), *Lectures on Public Economics*. London: McGraw-Hill.

Bain, G.S., R. Bacon and J. Pimlott (1972), 'The Labour Force', in A.H. Halsey (ed.) *Trends in British Society since 1900*, London: Macmillan.

Bain, G.S. and P. Elias (1985), 'Trade Union Membership in Great Britain: An Individual-Level Analysis', *British Journal of Industrial Relations*, 23: 71–92.

Bain, G.S. and F. Elsheikh (1976), *Union Growth and the Business Cycle*, Oxford: Basil Blackwell.

Bain, G.S. and R.J. Price (1980), *Profiles of Union Growth: A Comparative Statistical Portrait of Eight Countries*, Oxford: Basil Blackwell.

Bain, T. (1987), 'Unions and Industrial Relations in Great Britain in the Past Ten Years', *Bulletin of Comparative Labour Relations*, 16: 27–57.

Baldwin, C. (1983), 'Productivity and Labor Unions: An Application of the Theory of Self-Enforcing Contracts', *Journal of Business*, 56: 155–85.

Ball, L. and D. Romer (1989), 'The Equilibrium and Optimal Timing of Price Changes', *Review of Economic Studies*, 56(2): 179–98.

(1990), 'Real Rigidities and the Non-neutrality of Money', *Review of Economic Studies*, 57(2): 183–203.

Ball, J.M. and N.K. Skeoch (1981), 'Inter-plant Comparisons of Productivity and Earnings', UK Government Economic Service, Working Paper no. 38, Department of Employment, London.

Bamber, G. and E. Snape (1987), 'British Industrial Relations', in G. Bamber and R. Lansbury (eds.), *International and Comparative Industrial Relations*, London: Unwin and Hyman.

Baumol, W.J. (1986), 'Productivity Growth, Convergence and Welfare: What the Long-run Data Show', *American Economic Review*, 76: 1072–85.

Bean, C. (1984), 'Optimal Wage Bargains', *Economica*, 51: 141–9.

(1994), 'European Unemployment: A Survey', *Journal of Economic Literature*, 32(2): 573–619.

Bean, C.R., R. Layard and S.J. Nickell (1986), 'The Rise in Unemployment: A Multi-country Study', *Economica*, supplement 53(S): S89–S120.

Bean, C. and J. Symons (1989), 'Ten Years of Mrs T', *NBER Macroeconomics Annual*, 4: 13–60.

Bean, C. and P. Turnbull (1988), 'Employment in the British Coal Industry: A Test of the Labour Demand Model', *Economic Journal*, 98: 1092–104.

Beatson, M. and S. Butcher (1993), 'Union Density across the Employed Workforce', *Employment Gazette* (January): 673–89.

Becker, G.S. (1962), 'Investment in Human Capital: Effects on Earnings', *Journal of Political Economy*, 70: 9–49.

Bell, L.A. and R.B. Freeman (1985), 'Does a Flexible Industry Wage Structure Increase Employment? The US Experience', NBER Working Paper no. 1604, Cambridge, Mass.

Bemmels, B. (1987), 'How Unions Affect Productivity in Manufacturing Plants', *Industrial and Labor Relations Review*, 40: 241–53.

Benassy, J.-P. (1987), 'Imperfect Competition, Unemployment and Policy', *European Economic Review*, 31: 417–26.

Berkowitz, M. (1954), 'The Economics of Trade Union Organization and Administration', *Industrial and Labour Relations Review*, 7(4): 537–49.

Bienefeld, M.A. (1972), *Working Hours in British Industry*, London: Weidenfeld & Nicolson.

Bils, M. (1987), 'The Cyclical Behavior of Marginal Cost and Price', *American Economic Review*, 77(5): 838–55.

(1989), 'Pricing in a Customer Market', *Quarterly Journal of Economics*, 104(4): 699–718.

Binmore, K., A. Rubinstein and A. Wolinsky (1986), 'The Nash Bargaining Solution in Economic Modelling', *RAND Journal of Economics*, 17(2): 176–88.

Bird, D., M. Beatson and S. Butcher (1993), 'Membership of Trade Unions', *Employment Gazette* (May): 189–96.

Black, J. and G. Bulkley (1988), 'The Role of Strategic Information Transmission in a Bargaining Model', *Economic Journal Conference Papers*, 98: 50–7.

Blackaby, D., P. Murphy, P. Sloane (1991), 'Union Membership, Collective Bargaining Coverage and the Trade Union Mark-up for Britain', *Economics Letters*, 36: 203–8.

Blair, D.H. and D.L. Crawford (1984), 'Labour Union Objectives and Collective Bargaining', *Quarterly Journal of Economics*, 99(3): 547–66.

Blanchard, O.J. and P.A. Diamond (1990), 'Ranking, Unemployment Duration and Wages', MIT Department of Economics, Working Paper 546.

Blanchard, O.J. and S. Fischer (1989), *Lectures on Macroeconomics*, Cambridge Mass.: MIT Press.

Blanchard, O.J. and N. Kiyotaki (1987), 'Monopolistic Competition and the Effects of Aggregate Demand', *American Economic Review*, 77(4): 647–66.

Blanchard, O.J. and L.H. Summers (1986), 'Hysteresis and the European Unemployment Problem', in S. Fischer (ed.), *NBER Macroeconomics Annual*, Cambridge Mass.: MIT Press.

(1987), 'Fiscal Increasing Returns, Hysteresis, Real Wages and Unemployment', *European Economic Review*, 31(3): 543–60.

Blanchflower, D.G. (1984), 'Union Relative Wage Effects: A Cross-section Analysis Using Establishment Data', *British Journal of Industrial Relations*, 22: 311–32.

(1991), 'Fear, Unemployment and Pay Flexibility', *Economic Journal*, 101: 483–96.

Blanchflower, D.G., R. Crouchley, S. Estrin and A.J. Oswald (1990), 'Unemployment and the Demand for Unions', NBER Working Paper no. 3251, Cambridge, Mass.

Blanchflower, D.G., N. Millward and A.J. Oswald (1989), 'Unionism and Employment Behaviour', NBER Working Paper no. 3180, Cambridge, Mass.

(1991), 'Unionism and Employment Behaviour', *Economic Journal*, 101: 815–34.

Blanchflower, D.G. and A.J. Oswald (1988a), 'Profit-related Pay: Prose Discovered?', *Economic Journal*, 98: 720–30.

(1988b), 'The Economic Effects of Trade Unions', *Economic Report* (Employment Institute), 3(10).

(1990), 'Working Internationally', London School of Economics, CLE, Discussion Paper 371.

(1994), *The Wage Curve*, Cambridge, Mass.: MIT Press.

Blanchflower, D.G., A.J. Oswald and M.D. Garrett (1989), 'Insider Power in Wage Determination', *Economica*, 57: 143–70.

Blau, F.D. and L.M. Kahn (1983), 'Unionism, Seniority and Turnover'. *Industrial Relations*, 22(3): 362–73.

Blaug, M. (1990), *Economic Theories, True or False? Essays in the History and Methodology of Economics*, Aldershot: Elgar.

Bloch, F. and M.S. Kuskin (1978), 'Wage Determination in the Union and Nonunion Sectors', *Industrial and Labour Relations Review*, 31(2): 183–92.

Boal, W.M. (1993), 'Estimates of Unionism in West Virginia 1900–1935', *Labor History*, in press.

Boal, W.M. and J.H. Pencavel (1994), 'The Effects of Labor Unions on Employment, Wages and Days of Operation: Coal Mining in West Virginia', *Quarterly Journal of Economics*, 109 (February): 267–98.

Booth, A.L. (1983), 'A Reconsideration of Trade Union Growth in the United Kingdom', *British Journal of Industrial Relations*, 21(3): 377–91.

(1984), 'A Public Choice Model of Trade Union Behaviour', *Economic Journal*, 94: 883–98.

(1985), 'The Free Rider Problem and a Social Custom Theory of Trade Union Membership', *Quarterly Journal of Economics*, 100 (February): 253–61.

(1986), 'Estimating the Probability of Trade Union Membership: A Study of Men and Women in Britain', *Economica*, 53(1): 41–61.

(1987), 'Extra-Statutory Redundancy Payments in Britain', *British Journal of Industrial Relations*, 25(3): 401–18.

(1989), 'The Bargaining Structure of British Establishments' *British Journal of Industrial Relations*, 27(2): 225–34.

(1991), 'Job-related Formal Training: Who Receives it and What is it Worth?', *Oxford Bulletin of Economics and Statistics*, 53(3): 281–94.

(1993), 'Layoffs with Payoffs: A Bargaining Model of Union Wage and Severance Pay Determination', CEPR Discussion Paper no. 843, forthcoming *Economica*.

Booth, A.L. and M. Chatterji (1989), 'Redundancy Payments and Firm-Specific Training', *Economica*, 56: 505–21.

(1993a) 'Reputation, Membership and Wages in an Open Shop Trade Union', *Oxford Economic Papers*, 45: 23–41.

(1993b), 'Union Membership and Wage Bargaining when Membership is not Compulsory', Birkbeck College, London, Department of Economics, Discussion paper no. 493.

Booth, A.L. and R. Cressy (1990), 'Strikes with Asymmetric Information: Theory and Evidence', *Oxford Bulletin of Economics and Statistics*, 52(3): 269–88.

Booth, A.L. and M. Ravallion (1993), 'Employment and Length of the Working Week in a Unionised Economy in which Hours of Work Influence Productivity', *Economic Record*, 69: 428–36.

Booth, A.L. and F. Schiantarelli (1987), 'The Employment Effects of a Shorter Working Week', *Economica*, 54: 237–48.

Booth, A.L. and D.T. Ulph (1990), 'Union Wages and Employment with Endogenous Membership', University College London, Department of Economics, mimeo.

Bosworth, D.L. and P.J. Dawkins (1981), *Work Patterns: An Economic Analysis*, Aldershot: Gower.

Bowles, S. (1985), 'The Production Process in a Competitive Economy: Walrasian, Neo-Hobbesian, and Marxian Models', *American Economic Review*, 75(1): 16–36.

Boyer, G.R. (1988), 'What Did Unions Do in Nineteenth Century Britain?', *Journal of Economic History*, 48(2): 319–32.

Boyer, G.R., T.J. Hatton and R. Bailey (1994), 'The Union Wage Effect in Late Nineteenth Century Britain', *Economica*, in press.

Brack, J. (1987), 'Price Adjustment within a Framework of Symmetric Oligopoly: An Analysis of Pricing in 380 US Manufacturing Industries, 1958–71', *International; Journal of Industrial Organization*, 5(3): 289–302.

Bronars, S.G. and Deere, D.R. (1986), 'The Real and Financial Decisions of Unionized Firms in a Dynamic Setting', University of California at Santa Barbara, mimeo.

Brown, C. and J. Medoff (1978), 'Trade Unions in the Production Process', *Journal of Political Economy*, 86: 355–78.

Brown, J.N. and O. Ashenfelter (1986), 'Testing the Efficiency of Employment Contracts', *Journal of Political Economy*, 94 (supplement): S40–S87.

Brown, W. (1981), (ed.), *The Changing Contours of British Industrial Relations*, Basil Blackwell: Oxford.

Brown, W. and S. Wadhwani (1990), 'The Economic Effects of Industrial Relations Legislation Since 1979', *National Institute Economic Review*, no. 131 (February): 57–70.

Brunello, G. and S. Wadhwani (1989), 'The Determinants of Wage Flexibility in Japan: A Comparison with the UK Using Micro Data', London School of Economics, CLE, Discussion Paper no. 362.

Bruno, M. and J. Sachs (1985), *Economics of Worldwide Stagflation*, Oxford: Basil Blackwell.

Bureau of National Affairs (1986), *Basic Patterns of Union Contracts* (11th edn), Washington, D.C.

(1989), 'Two-Tier Wage Plans 1988', *What's New in Collective Bargaining Negotiations and Contracts*, part 2 (23 February).

Burgess, K. (1975), *The Origins of British Industrial Relations*, London: Croom Helm.

Calmfors, L. (1985), 'Worksharing, Employment and Wages', *European Economic Review*, 27: 293–309.

(1993), 'Lessons from the Macroeconomic Experience of Sweden', *European Journal of Political Economy*, 9(1): 25–72.

Calmfors, L. and J. Driffill (1988), 'Bargaining Structure, Corporatism and Macroeconomic Performance', *Economic Policy*, 6: 13–62.

Calmfors, L. and M. Hoel (1988), 'Work Sharing and Overtime', *Scandinavian Journal of Economics*, 90(1): 45–62.

(1989), 'Work Sharing, Employment and Shiftwork', *Oxford Economic Papers*, 41: 758–73.

Calmfors, L. and H. Horn (1985), 'Classical Unemployment, Accommodation Policies and the Adjustment of Real Wages', *Scandinavian Journal of Economics*, 87(2): 234–61.

(1986), 'Employment Policies and Centralised Wage-Setting', *Economica*, 53: 281–302.

Calvo, G.A. (1978), 'Urban Unemployment and Wage Determination in LDCs: Trade Unions in the Harris–Todaro Model', *International Economic Review*, 19(1): 65–81.

Card, D. (1986), 'Efficient Contracts with Costly Adjustment: Short-run Employment Determination for Airline Mechanics', *American Economic Review*, 76: 1045–71.

(1990), 'Strikes and Wages: A Test of an Asymmetric Information Model', *Quarterly Journal of Economics*, 105: 625–60.

(1991), 'The Effect of Unions on the Distribution of Wages: Redistribution or Relabeling?', Princeton University, Industrial Relations Discussion Paper no. 287.

Carlin, W. and D. Soskice (1990), *Macroeconomics and the Wage Bargain: A Modern Approach to Employment, Inflation, and the Exchange Rate*, Oxford University Press.

Carlton, D.W. (1986), 'The Rigidity of Prices', *American Economic Review*, 76(4): 637–58.

(1989), 'The Theory and the Facts of How Markets Clear: Is Industrial Organisation Valuable for Understanding Macroeconomics?', in R. Schmalensee and R.D. Willig (eds.), *Handbook of Industrial Organisation*, Amsterdam: North-Holland.

Carmichael, L. (1983), 'Firm-specific Human Capital and Promotion Ladders', *Bell Journal of Economics*, 14(1): 251–8.

Carruth, A. and R. Disney (1988), 'Where have Two Million Trade Union Members Gone?', *Economica*, 55: 1–20.

Carruth, A. and A.J. Oswald (1985), 'Miners' Wages in Post-war Britain: An Application of a Model of Trade Union Behaviour', *Economic Journal*, 95: 1003–120.

(1987), 'On Union Preferences and Labour Market Models: Insiders and Outsiders', *Economic Journal*, 97: 431–45.

Carter, A.M. (1959), *Theory of Wages and Employment*, Homewood Ill.: Irwin.

Chatterjee, S. and R. Cooper (1989), 'Multiplicity of Equilibria and Competitive Economics', *American Economic Review*, 79(2): 353–7.

Chatterji, M. (1992), 'Convergence Clubs and Endogenous Growth', *Oxford Review of Economic Policy*, 8(4): 57–69.

Chatterji, M. and S. Price (1988), 'Unions, Dutch Disease and Unemployment', *Oxford Economic Papers*, 40: 302–21.

Chiang, A.C. (1984), *Fundamental Methods of Mathematical Economics*, (3rd edn), Tokyo: McGraw-Hill.

Clark, A. (1990), 'Efficient Bargains and the McDonald-Solow Conjecture', *Journal of Labor Economics*, 8(4): 502–28.

Clark, A. and A.J. Oswald (1993), 'Trade Union Utility Functions: A Survey of Union Leaders' Views', *Industrial Relations*, 32(3): 391–411.

Clark, K. B. (1980a) 'The Impact of Unionization on Productivity: A Case Study', *Industrial and Labor Relations Review*, 33: 451–69.

(1980b) 'Unionization and Productivity: Microeconometric Evidence', *Quarterly Journal of Economics*, 95: 613–39.

(1984), 'Unionization and Firm Performance: The Impact on Profits, Growth and Productivity', *American Economic Review*, 74: 893–919.

Claydon, T. (1989), 'Union Derecognition in Britain in the 1980s', *British Journal of Industrial Relations*, 27(2): 214–24.

Claydon, T. and F. Green (1992), 'The Effect of Unions on Training Provision', Leicester University, Department of Economics, Discussion Paper no. 92–3.

Clegg, H.A. (1980), *The Changing System of Industrial Relations in Great Britain*, Oxford: Basil Blackwell.

(1985), *A History of British Trade Unions since 1889*, vol. II: Oxford: Clarendon.

Clegg, H.A., A. Fox and A.F. Thompson (1964), *A History of British Trade Unions Since 1889*, vol. I: 1889–1911, Oxford: Clarendon.

Connolly, R.A., B.T. Hirsch and M. Hirschey (1986), 'Union Rent Seeking, Tangible Capital, and Market Value of the Firm', *Review of Economics and Statistics*, 68: 567–77.

Conyon, M. and S. Machin (1991), 'The Determination of Profit Margins in UK Manufacturing', *Journal of Industrial Economics*, 39: 369–82.

Cornes, R. and T. Sandler (1984), 'Easy Riders, Joint Production and Public Goods', *Economic Journal*, 94: 580–98.

Coutts, K., W. Godley and W. Nordhaus (1978), *Industrial Pricing in the United Kingdom*, Cambridge University Press.

Cowling, K. and M. Waterson (1976), 'Price-Cost Margins and Market Structure', *Economica*, 43: 267–74.

Crafts, N. (1991), 'Reversing Relative Economic Decline? The 1980s in Historical Perspective', *Oxford Review of Economic Policy*, 7(3): 81–97.

Darby, J. and S. Wren-Lewis (1992), 'Changing Trends in International Manufacturing Productivity', *Scandinavian Journal of Economics*, 94(3): 457–77.

D'Aspremont, C., R. Dos Santos Ferreira and L.-A. Gerard-Valet (1989), 'Unemployment in an Extended Cournot Oligopoly Model', *Oxford Economic Papers*, 41; 490–505.

Davies, S. and R. Caves (1987), *Britain's Productivity Gap*, Cambridge University Press for NIESR.

Deaton, D. and P. Beaumont (1980), 'The Determinants of Bargaining Structure: Some Large Scale Evidence for Britain', *British Journal of Industrial Relations*, 17: 202–16.

de Fina, R.H. (1983), 'Unions, Relative Wages and Economic Efficiency', *Journal of Labor Economics*, 1(4): 408–29.

Dehez, P. (1985), 'Monopolistic Equilibrium and Involuntary Unemployment', *Journal of Economic Theory*, 36: 160–65.

de Menil, G. (1971), *Bargaining: Monopoly Power versus Union Power*, Cambridge Mass.: MIT Press.

Denny, K. and J. Muellbauer (1988), 'Economic and Industrial Relations Explanations of Productivity Change: Some Evidence for the British Manufacturing Sector 1980–1984', Nuffield College, Oxford, mimeo.

Denny, K. and S.J. Nickell (1991), 'Unions and Investment in British Industry', *British Journal of Industrial Relations*, 29: 113–22.

  (1992), 'Unions and Investment in British Industry', *The Economic Journal*, 102: 874–87.

Dertouzos, J.N. and J. Pencavel (1981), 'Wage and Employment Determination under Trade Unionism: the International Typographical Union', *Journal of Political Economy*, 89(6): 1162–81.

Devereux, M.B. and B. Lockwood (1991), 'Trade Unions, Non-Binding Wage Agreements and Capital Accumulation', *European Economic Review*, 35: 1411–26.

Dickens, W.T. (1983), 'The Effect of Company Campaigns on Certification Elections: Law and Reality Once Again', *Industrial and Labor Relations Review*, 36(4): 560–75.

Dickens, W.T. and J.S. Leonard (1985), 'Accounting for the Decline in Union Membership 1950–1980', *Industrial and Labor Relations Review*, 38(3): 323–34.

Disney, R. (1990), 'Explanations of the Decline in Trade Union Density in Britain: An Appraisal', *British Journal of Industrial Relations*, 28(2): 165–77.

Disney, R., A. Gosling and S. Machin (1993), 'What has Happened to Union Recognition in Britain?', London School of Economics, CEP, Discussion Paper no. 130.

Disney, R. and H. Gospel (1989), 'The Seniority Model of Trade Union Behaviour: A (Partial) Defence', *British Journal of Industrial Relations*, 27(2): 179–95.

Dixon, H. (1988), 'Unions, Oligopoly and the Natural Range of Employment', *Economic Journal*, 98: 1127–47.

  (1990), 'Macroeconomic Policy with a Floating Exchange Rate and a Unionised Non-traded Sector', *Economic Journal*, 100 (supplement): 78–90.

  (1991), 'Macroeconomic Equilibrium and Policy in a Large Unionised Economy', *European Economic Review*, 35: 1427–48.

Dixon, H. and N. Rankin (1994), 'Imperfect Competition and Macroeconomics: A Survey', *Oxford Economic Papers*, 46(2): 171–99.

Doeringer, P.B. and M.J. Piore (1971), *Internal Labor Markets and Manpower Analysis*, Lexington, Mass.: D.C. Heath.

Domowitz, I., R.G. Hubbard and B.C. Peterson (1986), 'Business Cycles and the Relationship between the Concentration and Price-cost Margins', *RAND Journal of Economics*, 17(1): 1–17.

Dowrick, S. (1989), 'Union-Oligopoly Bargaining', *Economic Journal*, 99: 1123–42.

(1992), 'Enterprise Bargaining, Union Structure and Wages', Australian National University, Research School of Social Sciences, mimeo.

Dowrick, S. and T. Nguyen (1989), 'OECD Comparative Economic Growth 1950–85: Catch-up and Convergence', *American Economic Review*, 79: 1010–30.

Duncan, G.J. and F.P. Stafford (1980), 'Do Union Members Receive Compensating Wage Differentials?', *American Economic Review*, 70: 355–71.

Dunlop, J.T. (1944), *Wage Determination under Trade Unions*, London: Macmillan.

Eberts, R.W. and J.A. Stone (1986), 'On the Contract Curve: A Test of Alternative Models of Collective Bargaining', *Journal of Labor Economics*, 4: 66–81.

(1987), 'The Effect of Teacher Unions on Student Achievement', *Industrial and Labor Relations Review*, 40: 354–63.

Edwards, P.K. (1987), *Managing the Factory*, Oxford: Basil Blackwell.

Edwards, P.K. and G.S. Bain (1988), 'Why Are Trade Unions Becoming More Popular? Unions and Public Opinion in Britain', *British Journal of Industrial Relations*, 26(3): 311–26.

Edwards, R. and P. Swain (1986), 'Union–Nonunion Earnings Differentials and the Decline of Private Sector Unionism', *American Economic Review*, Papers and Proceedings, 76: 97–102.

Ehrenberg, R.G. and J.L. Schwartz (1983), 'Public Sector Labor Markets', NBER Working Paper no. 1179, Cambridge, Mass.

Ehrenberg, R.G., S.R. Sherman and J.C. Schwarz (1983), 'Unions and Productivity in the Public Sector: A Study of Municipal Libraries', *Industrial and Labor Relations Review*, 36: 199–213.

Encaoua, D. and P. Geroski (1986), 'Price Dynamics and Competition in Five OECD Countries', *OECD Economic Studies*, 6: 47–74.

Englander, A.S. and A. Mittelstadt (1988), 'Total Factor Productivity: Macroeconomic and Structural Aspects of the Slowdown', *OECD Economic Studies*, 10.

Evans, S. (1987), 'The Use of Injunction in Industrial Disputes', *British Journal of Industrial Relations*, 25(3): 419–36.

Faith, R.L. and J.D. Reid (1987), 'An Agency Theory of Unionism', *Journal of Economic Behavior and Organisation*, 8: 39–60.

Farber, H.S. (1978a), 'Bargaining Theory, Wage Outcomes, and the Occurrence of Strikes: An Econometric Analysis', *American Economic Review*, 68(3): 262–71.

(1978b), 'Individual Preferences and Union Wage Determination: The Case of the United Mine Workers', *Journal of Political Economy*, 86(5): 932–42.

(1978c), 'The United Mine Workers and the Demand for Coal: An Econometric Analysis of Union Behavior', *Research in Labor Economics*, 2: 1–74.

(1983), 'The Determination of the Union Status of Workers', *Econometrica*, 51(5): 1417–38.

(1986), 'The Analysis of Union Behavior', in O. Ashenfelter and R. Layard (eds.), *Handbook of Labor Economics*, vol. II, Amsterdam: North-Holland.

(1987), 'The Recent Decline of Unionism in the United States', *Science*, 238: 915–920.

(1990), 'The Decline of Unionisation in the United States: What Can be Learned from Recent Experience?', *Journal of Labor Economics*, 8(1), Part 2: S75–S105.

Fender, J. and C.Y. Yip (1990), 'Aggregate Demand Management Policies in an Intertemporal Macroeconomic Model with Imperfect Competition', Pennsylvania State University, Department of Economics, mimeo.

Fellner, W. (1947), 'Prices and Wages under Bilateral Monopoly', *Quarterly Journal of Economics*, 61(4): 503–32.

Fine, B. (1990), 'Gender Discrimination and Bargaining Structures in the Coal Industry', Birkbeck College, London, Department of Economics, mimeo.

Fitzroy, F.R. and R.A. Hart (1985), 'Hours, Layoffs and Unemployment Insurance Funding: Theory and Practice in an International Perspective', *Economic Journal*, 95: 700–13.

Flanagan, R.J. (1989), 'Compliance and Enforcement Decisions Under the National Labor Relations Act', *Journal of Labor Economics*, 7: 257–80.

(1990a), 'The Economics of Unions and Collective Bargaining', *Industrial Relations*, 29(2): 300–15.

(1990b), 'Union Labor Adjusted to a Change in the Climate', Stanford University, Graduate School of Business, mimeo.

Flanders, A. and H.A. Clegg (eds.) (1964), *The System of Industrial Relations in Great Britain*, Oxford: Basil Blackwell.

Frank, J. (1985), 'Trade Union Efficiency and Overemployment with Seniority Wage Scales', *Economic Journal*, 95: 1021–34.

(1990), 'Monopolistic Competition, Risk-aversion and Equilibrium Recessions', *Quarterly Journal of Economics*, 105 (November): 921–38.

(1993), 'Competitive Equilibrium Recessions', Essex University, Department of Economics, mimeo.

Frank, J. and J. Malcomson (1994), 'Insiders, Outsiders and Seniority Employment Rules', *European Economic Review*, in press.

Freeman, R.B. (1972), *Labor Economics*, Englewood Cliffs, N.J.: Prentice-Hall.

(1980a), 'Unionism and the Dispersion of Wages', *Industrial and Labor Relations Review*, 34(1): 3–23.

(1980b), 'The Exit–Voice Tradeoff in the Labor Market: Unionism, Job Tenure, Quits and Separations', *Quarterly Journal of Economics*, 94(4): 643–74.

(1981), 'The Effect of Unionism on Fringe Benefits', *Industrial and Labor Relations Review*, 34(4): 489–509.

(1982), 'Union Wage Practices and Wage Dispersion within Establishments', *Industrial and Labor Relations Review*, 36(1): 3–21.

(1983), 'Unionism, Price–Cost Margins, and the Return to Capital', NBER Working Paper no. 1164.

(1984), 'Longitudinal Analyses of the Effects of Trade Unions', *Journal of Labor Economics*, 2(1): 1–26.

(1986), 'The Effect of the Union Wage Differential on Management Opposition and Union Organization Success', *American Economic Review Papers and Proceedings*, 76: 92–6.

(1988), 'On the Divergence in Unionism Among Developed Countries', Harvard University, Department of Economics, mimeo.

(1991), 'How Much has Deunionization Contributed to the Rise in Male

Earnings Inequality?', NBER Discussion Paper no. 3826, Cambridge, Mass.

Freeman, R.B. and J.L. Medoff (1979), 'The Two Faces of Unionism', *Public Interest*, no. 57: 69–93.

(1984), *What Do Unions Do?*, New York: Basic Books.

Freeman, R. and J. Pelletier (1990), 'The Impact of Industrial Relations Legislation on British Union Density', *British Journal of Industrial Relations*, 28(2): 141–64.

Fudenberg, D. and J. Tirole (1983), 'Capital as a Commitment: Strategic Investment to Deter Mobility', *Journal of Economic Theory*, 31: 227–50.

Gennard, J., S. Dunn and M. Wright (1980), 'The Extent of Closed Shop Arrangements in British Industry', *Employment Gazette* 88: 16–22.

Geroski, P. (1989), 'Entry, Innovation and Productivity Growth', *Review of Economics and Statistics*, 71(4): 572–8.

Gosling, A. and S. Machin (1993), 'Trade Unions and the Dispersion of Earnings in UK Establishments, 1980–1990', London School of Economics, CEP, Discussion Paper no. 140.

Gospel, H.F. (1983), 'Trade Unions and the Legal Obligation to Bargain: An American, Swedish and British Comparison', *British Journal of Industrial Relations*, 21(3): 343–59.

Gravelle, H. and R. Rees (1983), *Microeconomics*, London: Longman.

Green, F. (1988), 'The Trade Union Wage Gap in Britain: Some Recent Estimates', *Economics Letters*, 27: 183–7.

Green, W.H. (1993), *Econometric Analysis* (2nd edn), New York: Maxwell Macmillan.

Greenhalgh, C. and G. Mavrotas (1992), 'The Role of Career Aspirations and Financial Constraints in Individual Access to Vocational Training', University of Oxford, Applied Economics Discussion Paper no. 136.

Gregg, P.A. and S.J. Machin (1988), 'Unions and the Incidence of Performance-Linked Pay Schemes in Britain', *International Journal of Industrial Organisation*, 6: 91–107.

(1992), 'Unions, the Demise of the Closed Shop and Wage Growth in the 1980s', *Oxford Bulletin of Economics and Statistics*, 54(1): 53–72.

Gregg, P., S. Machin and D. Metcalf (1993), 'Signals and Cycles: Productivity Growth and Changes in Union Status in British Companies, 1984–1989', *Economic Journal*, 103: 894–907.

Gregg, P., S. Machin and S. Szymanski (1993), 'The Disappearing Relationship between Directors' Pay and Corporate Performance', *British Journal of Industrial Relations*, 31(1): 1–10.

Gregory, M., P. Lobban and A. Thomson (1986), 'Bargaining Structure, Pay Settlements and Perceived Pressures in Manufacturing: Further Analysis from the CBI Databank', *British Journal of Industrial Relations*, 24: 215–32.

(1987), 'Pay Settlements in Manufacturing Industry, 1979–84: A Micro-data Study of the Impact of Product and Labour Market Pressures', *Oxford Bulletin of Economics and Statistics*, 49: 129–50.

Gregory, R.G. (1986), 'Wages Policy and Unemployment in Australia', *Economica*, supplement, 53(5): S53–S72.

Grossman, G.M. (1983), 'Union Wages, Temporary Layoffs, and Seniority', *American Economic Review*, 73(3): 277–90.

Grout, P.A. (1984), 'Investment and Wages in the Absence of Binding Contracts', *Econometrica*, 52(2): 449–60.

Hall, R.E. (1988), 'The Relationship Between Price and Marginal Cost in US Industry', *Journal of Political Economy*, 96(5): 921–47.

Halvorsen, R. and R. Palmquist (1980), 'The Interpretation of Dummy Variables in Semilogarithmic Equations', *American Economic Review*, 70(3): 474–5.

Hamermesh, D.S. (1975), *Labor in the Public and Non-profit Sectors*, Princeton University Press.

(1993), *Labor Demand*, Princeton University Press.

Hanson, C., S. Jackson and D. Miller (1982), *The Closed Shop*, Aldershot: Gower.

Harberger, A.C. (1954), 'Monopoly and Resource Allocation', *American Economic Review Papers and Proceedings*, 44(2): 77–87.

Hart, O.D. (1982), 'A Model of Imperfect Competition with Keynesian Features', *Quarterly Journal of Economics*, 97(1): 109–38.

(1989), 'Bargaining and Strikes', *Quarterly Journal of Economics*, 104(1): 25–44.

Hart, R.A. (1984a), 'Worksharing and Factor Prices', *European Economic Review*, 24: 165–88.

(1984b), *The Economics of Non-wage Labour Costs*, London: Allen & Unwin.

Hashimoto, M. (1981), 'Firm-specific Human Capital as a Shared Investment', *American Economic Review*, 71: 475–82.

Haskel, J. (1991), 'Imperfect Competition, Work Practices and Productivity Growth', *Oxford Bulletin of Economics and Statistics*, 53(3): 265–80.

Haskel, J.E. and J.A. Kay (1991), 'Mrs Thatcher's Industrial Performance: Lessons from the UK', in F.H. Gruen (ed.), *Australian Economic Policy*, Canberra: Australian National University.

Haskel, J. and C. Martin (1992), 'Margins, Concentration, Unions and the Business Cycle: Theory and Evidence for Britain', Queen Mary and Westfield College, London, mimeo.

Hayes, B. (1984), 'Unions and Strikes with Asymmetric Information', *Journal of Labor Economics*, 2(1): 57–83.

Hicks, J.R. (1963), *The Theory of Wages* (2nd edn), London: Macmillan.

Hieser, R.O. (1970), 'Wage Determination with Bilateral Monopoly in the Labour Market: A Theoretical Treatment', *Economic Record*, 46(1): 55–72.

Hirsch, B.T. (1982), 'The Interindustry Structure of Unionism, Earnings and Earnings Dispersion', *Industrial and Labor Relations Review*, 36(1): 22–39.

(1990), 'Innovative Activity, Productivity Growth and Firm Performance: Are Labor Unions a Spur or a Deterrent?', in A.N. Link and V.K. Smith (eds.), *Advances in Applied Microeconomics*, Vol. V, Greenwich, Conn: JAI Press.

Hirsch, B.T. and J.T. Addison (1986), *The Economic Analysis of Unions: New Approaches and Evidence*, Boston: Allen & Unwin.

Hirsch, B.T. and M.C. Berger (1984), 'Union Membership Determination and Industry Characteristics', *Southern Economic Journal*, 50(3): 665–79.

Hirsch, B.T. and R.A. Connolly (1987), 'Do Unions Capture Monopoly Profits?', *Industrial and Labor Relations Review*, 41: 118–36.

Hirsch, B.T. and A.N. Link (1984), 'Unions, Productivity and Productivity Growth', *Journal of Labor Research*, 5(1): 29–37.

Hirsch, B.T. and D.A. Macpherson (1993), 'Union Membership and Coverage Files from the Current Population Surveys: Note', *Industrial and Labor Relations Review*, 46(3): 574–8.

Hirschman, A.O. (1970), *Exit, Voice and Loyalty*, Cambridge, Mass.: Harvard University Press.

Hoel, M. (1986), 'Employment and Allocation Effects of Reducing the Length of the Workday', *Economica*, 53: 75–85.

(1990), 'Local versus Central Wage Bargaining with Endogenous Investments', *Scandinavian Journal of Economics*, 92: 453–69.

(1991), 'Union Wage Policy: The Importance of Labour Mobility and the Degree of Centralisation', *Economica*, 58: 139–53.

Holmlund B. and J. Zetterberg (1991), 'Insider Effects in Wage Determination: Evidence from Five Countries', *European Economic Review*, 35: 1009–34.

Honkapohja, S. (1988), 'Discussion', *Economic Policy*, 6: 48–51.

Horn, H. and A. Wolinsky (1988), 'Worker Substitutability and Patterns of Unionisation', *Economic Journal*, 98: 484–97.

Huizinga, F. and F. Schiantarelli (1992), 'Dynamics and Asymmetric Adjustment in Insider–Outsider Models', *Economic Journal*, 102: 1451–66.

Ichniowski, C. (1986), 'The Effects of Grievance Activity on Productivity', *Industrial and Labor Relations Review*, 40: 75–89.

Ingram, P., D. Metcalf and J. Wadsworth (1993), 'Strike Incidence in British Manufacturing Industry in the 1980s', *Industrial and Labor Relations Review*, 46(4): 704–17.

Jacobsen, H.J. and C. Schultz (1989), 'Wage Bargaining and Unemployment in a General Equilibrium Model', University of Copenhagen, Institute of Economics, Discussion Paper no. 89–01.

Johnson, G.E. (1984), 'Changes over Time in the Union–Nonunion Wage Differential in the United States', in J.-J. Rosa (ed.), *The Economics of Trade Unions: New Directions*, Boston: Kluwer-Nijhoff.

(1990), 'Work Rules, Featherbedding and Pareto-optimal Union–Management Bargaining', *Journal of Labor Economics*, 8: S237–59.

Jones, E.B. (1982), 'Union/Nonunion Wage Differentials: Membership or Coverage?', *Journal of Human Resources*, 17(2): 276–85.

Jones, S.R.G. (1987), 'Union Membership and Employment Dynamics', *Economics Letters*, 25: 197–200.

Jones, S.R.G. and C. McKenna (1989), 'The Role of Outsiders in Union Contracts', *European Economic Review*, 33: 1567–73.

(1994), 'A Dynamic Model of Union Membership and Employment', *Economica*, 61 (May): 179–89.

Kahn-Freund, O. (1977), *Labour and the Law* (2nd edn), London: Stevens.

Karier, T. (1985), 'Unions and Monopoly Profits', *Review of Economics and Statistics*, 67: 34–42.

Kassalow, E.M. (1969), *Trade Unions and Industrial Relations: An International Comparison*, New York: Random House.

Katz, H.C. (1983), 'Union Status, Union Wages, and the Free Rider Problems: The Issue of Membership vs. Coverage', Massachusetts Institute of Technology, Department of Economics, mimeo.

Katz, H.C., T.A. Kochan and K.R. Gobeille (1983), 'Industrial Relations Performance, Economic Performance, and QWL Performance: An Interplant Analysis', *Industrial and Labor Relations Review*, 37: 3–17.

Kennan, J. (1986), 'The Economics of Strikes' in O. Ashenfelter and R. Layard (eds.), *Handbook of Labor Economics*, vol. II, Amsterdam: North-Holland.

Kiander, J. (1993), 'Endogenous Unemployment Insurance in a Monopoly Union Model when Job Search Matters', *Journal of Public Economics*, 52: 101–15.

Kidd, D.P. and A.J. Oswald (1987), 'A Dynamic Model of Trade Union Behaviour', *Economica*, 54: 355–65.

Kmenta, J. (1971), *Elements of Econometrics*, New York: Macmillan.

Knight, K.G. (1989), 'Labour Productivity and Strike Activity in British Manufacturing Industries: Some Quantitative Evidence', *British Journal of Industrial Relations*, 27(3): 365–74.

Kochan, T.A., H.C. Katz and R.B. McKersie (1986), *The Transformation of American Industrial Relations*, New York: Basic Books.

Kwoka, J.E., Jr (1983), 'Monopoly, Plant and Union Effect on Worker Wages', *Industrial and Labor Relations Review*, 36(2): 251–7.

Latreille, P. (1992), 'Unions and the Inter-establishment Adoption of new Microelectronic Technologies in the British Private Manufacturing Sector', *Oxford Bulletin of Economics and Statistics*, 54(1): 31–51.

Layard, R., D. Metcalf and S. Nickell (1978), 'The Effect of Collective Bargaining on Relative and Absolute Wages', *British Journal of Industrial Relations*, 16(3), 287–302.

Layard, R. and S.J. Nickell (1985), 'The Causes of British Unemployment', *National Institute Economic Review*, 111: 62–85.

(1986), 'Unemployment in the UK', *Economica*, Supplement 53(5): S121–S166.

(1987), 'The Labour Market', in R. Dornbusch and R. Layard (eds.), *The Performance of the British Economy*, Oxford University Press.

(1989), 'The Thatcher Miracle?', *American Economic Review Papers and Proceedings*, 79(2): 215–19.

(1990), 'Is Unemployment Lower if Unions Bargain over Employment?', *Quarterly Journal of Economics*, 105(3): 773–87.

Layard, R., S.J. Nickell and R. Jackman (1991), *Unemployment: Macroeconomic Performance and the Labour Market*, Oxford University Press.

Layard, R. and A. Walters (1978), *Microeconomic Theory*, Maidenhead: McGraw-Hill.

Lazear, E.P. (1979), 'Why is There Mandatory Retirement?', *Journal of Political Economy*, 87(6): 1261–84.

Lebergott, S. (1984), *The Americans: An Economic Record*, New York: W.W. Norton.

Leibenstein, H. (1966), 'Allocative Efficiency vs. "X-Efficiency"', *American Economic Review*, 56(3): 392–415.

Leonard, J.S. (1992), 'Unions and Employment Growth', *Industrial Relations*, 31(1): 80–94.

Leontief, W. (1946), 'The Pure Theory of the Guaranteed Annual Wage Contract', *Journal of Political Economy*, 54(1): 76–9.

Lewis, H.G. (1986), *Union Relative Wage Effects: A Survey*, University of Chicago Press.

(1990), 'Union/Nonunion Wage Gaps in the Public Sector', *Journal of Labour Economics*, 8(1, part 2): S260–S328.

Lewis, R. (1991), 'Reforming Industrial Relations: Law, Politics and Power', *Oxford Review of Economic Policy*, 7(1): 60–75.

Lindbeck, A. and D. Snower (1985), 'Explanations of Unemployment', *Oxford Review of Economic Policy*, 1(2): 34–69.

(1987), 'Strike and Lock-out Threats and Fiscal Policy', *Oxford Economic Papers*, 39: 760–84.

(1988), *The Insider–Outsider Theory of Employment and Unemployment*, Cambridge, Mass.: The MIT Press.

Linneman, P. and M.L. Wachter (1986), 'Rising Union Premiums and the Declining Boundaries among Noncompeting Groups', *American Economic Review Papers and Proceedings*, 76: 103–8.

Lockwood, B. (1991), 'Information Externalities in the Labour Market and the Duration of Unemployment', *Review of Economic Studies*, 58: 733–53.

Lockwood, B. and A. Manning (1989), 'Dynamic Wage-Employment Bargaining with Employment Adjustment', *Economic Journal*, 99: 1143–58.

Long, J.E. and A.N. Link (1983), 'The Impact of Market Structure on Wages, Fringe Benefits, and Turnover', *Industrial and Labor Relations Review*, 36(2): 239–50.

Long, R.J. (1993), 'The Effect of Unionisation on Employment Growth of Canadian Companies', *Industrial and Labor Relations Review*, 46(4): 81–93.

Lovell, C.A.K., R.C. Sickles and R.S. Warren, Jr (1988), 'The Effect of Unionization on Labor Productivity: Some Additional Evidence', *Journal of Labor Research*, 9: 55–63.

Lovell, J. and B.C. Roberts (1968), *A Short History of the TUC*. London: Macmillan.

McCallum, J. (1983), 'Inflation and Social Consensus in the Seventies', *Economic Journal*, 93: 784–805.

McCarthy, W.E.J. (1964), *The Closed Shop in Britain*, Oxford: Basil Blackwell.

McConnell, S. (1989), 'Strikes, Wages and Private Information', *American Economic Review*, 79(4): 801–15.

McCormick, B. (1990), 'A Theory of Signalling During Job Search, Employment Efficiency and "Stigmatised" Jobs', *Review of Economic Studies*, 57(2): 299–313

MaCurdy, T.E. and J.H. Pencavel (1986), 'Testing Between Competing Models of Wage and Employment Determination in Unionized Markets', *Journal of Political Economy*, 94 (supplement): S3–S39.

McDonald, I.M. (1987), 'Customer Markets, Trade Unions and Stagflation', *Economica*, 54: 139–53.

(1990), *Inflation and Unemployment*, Oxford: Basil Blackwell.

McDonald, I.M. and R.M. Solow (1981), 'Wage Bargaining and Employment', *American Economic Review*, 71: 896–908.

Machin, S. (1991a), 'The Productivity Effects of Unionisation and Firm Size in British Engineering Firms', *Economica*, 58: 479–90.

(1991b), 'Unions and the Capture of Economic Rents: An Investigation Using British Firm-Level Data', *International Journal of Industrial Organisation*, 5: 327–50.

Machin, S. and M. Stewart (1990), 'Unions and the Financial Performance of British Private Sector Establishments', *Journal of Applied Econometrics*, 5: 327–50.

Machin, S., M. Stewart and J. Van Reenen (1993), 'The Economic Effects of Multiple Unionism', *Scandinavian Journal of Economics*, 95(3): 275–92.

Machin, S. and S. Wadhwani (1989), 'The Effects of Unions on Organisational Change, Investment and Employment: Evidence from WIRS', London School of Economics, CLE, Working Paper no. 1147.

(1991), 'The Effects of Unions on Organisational Change and Employment', *The Economic Journal*, 101: 835–54.

MacInnes, J. (1987), *Thatcherism at Work*, Milton Keynes: Open University Press.

Main, B. and B. Reilly (1992), 'Women and the Union Wage Gap', *The Economic Journal*, 102: 49–66.

Malcomson, J.M. (1983), 'Trade Unions and Economic Efficiency', *Economic Journal* (Conference Papers Supplement), 93: 50–65.

Mankiw, N.G. (1985), 'Small Menu Costs and Large Business Cycles: A Macroeconomic Model of Monopoly', *Quarterly Journal of Economics*, 100(2): 529–37.

Manning, A. (1987), 'An Integration of Trade Union Models in a Sequential Bargaining Framework', *Economic Journal*, 97: 121–39.

(1990), 'Imperfect Competition, Multiple Equilibria and Unemployment Policy', *Economic Journal*, 100 (supplement): 151–62.

(1992), 'Multiple Equilibria in the British Labour Market: Some Empirical Evidence', *European Economic Review*, 36: 1333–65.

(1993), 'Wage Bargaining and the Phillips Curve: The Identification and Specification of Aggregate Wage Equations', *Economic Journal*, 103: 98–118.

Marsden, D. and M. Thompson (1988), 'Flexibility Agreements in Britain and Their Significance in the Increase in Productivity in British Manufacturing since 1980', London School of Economics, Industrial Relations Department, mimeo.

Marshall, A. (1948), *Principles of Economics* (8th edn.), London: Macmillan.

Marshall, F.R., A.G. King and V.M. Briggs Jr (1980), *Labor Economics: Wages, Employment and Trade*, Homewood, Ill.: R.D. Irwin.

Medoff, J.L. (1979), 'Layoffs and Alternatives under Trade Unions in US Manufacturing', *American Economic Review*, 69(3): 380–95.

Mellow, W. (1983), 'Employer Size, Unionism and Wages', in J.D. Reid, Jr (ed.), *New Approaches to Labour Unions*, Greenwich, Conn.: JAI Press.

Mendis, L. and J. Muellbauer (1984), 'British Manufacturing Productivity 1955–83: Measurement Problems, Oil Shocks and Thatcher Effects', CEPR Discussion Paper no. 32.

Metcalf, D. (1988), 'Trade Unions and Economic Performance: The British Evidence', London School of Economics, CLE, Discussion Paper no. 320.

(1989a), 'Water Notes Dry Up: The Impact of the Donovan Reform Proposals and Thatcherism at Work on Labour Productivity in British Manufacturing Industry', *British Journal of Industrial Relations*, 27(1): 1–31.

(1989b), 'Trade Unions and Economic Performance: The British Evidence', *LSE Quarterly*, 3(1): 21–42.

(1990a), 'Labour Legislation 1980–1990: Philosophy and Impact', London School of Economics, Industrial Relations Department, mimeo.

(1990b) 'Union Presence and Labour Productivity in British Manufacturing Industry: A Reply to Nolan and Marginson', *British Journal of Industrial Relations*, 28(2): 249–66.

(1991), 'British Unions: Dissolution or Resurgence?', *Oxford Review of Economic Policy*, 7(1): 18–32.

(1993), 'Industrial Relations and Economic Performance', *British Journal of Industrial Relations*, 31(2): 255–83.

Metcalf, D. and M. Stewart (1992), 'Closed Shops and Relative Pay: Institutional Arrangements or High Density?', *Oxford Bulletin of Economics and Statistics*, 54(4): 503–16.

Miller, P. and C. Mulvey (1993), 'What Do Australian Trade Unions Do?' *Economic Record*, 69: 315–42.

Millward, N. (1993), 'Uses of the Workplace Industrial Relations Surveys by British Labour Economists', London School of Economics, CEP, Discussion Paper, no. 145.

Millward, N. and M. Stevens (1986), *British Workplace Industrial Relations 1980–84*, Aldershot: Gower.

Millward, N., M. Stevens, D. Smart and W. Hawes (1992), *Workplace Industrial Relations in Transition*, Dartmouth: Aldershot.

Milner, S. (1992), 'Unions and Profits', London School of Economics, CEP, mimeo.

Mincer, J. (1983), 'Union Effects: Wages, Turnover and Job Training' in J.D. Reid, Jr (ed.), *New Approaches to Labor Unions* (supplement no. 2 to R.G. Ehrenberg (ed.), *Research in Labor Economics*), Greenwich, Conn.: JAI Press.

Minford, P. (1983), 'Labour Market Equilibrium in an Open Economy', *Oxford Economic Papers* (November, Supplement): 207–44.

Mishel, L. (1986), 'The Structural Determinants of Union Bargaining Power', *Industrial and Labor Relations Review*, 40(1): 90–104.

Moene, K.O. (1988), 'Unions' Threats and Wage Determination', *Economic Journal*, 98: 471–83.

Molana, H. and T. Moutos (1992), 'A Note on Taxation, Imperfect Competition and the Balanced Budget Multiplier', *Oxford Economic Papers*, 43: 68–74.

Moreton, D. (1993), 'Trade Union Effects on Labour Productivity in UK Manufacturing, 1950–1987', University of Greenwich, London, mimeo.

Morris, T. and S. Wood (1988), 'Change and Continuity in British Industrial Relations', London School of Economics, Industrial Relations Department, mimeo.

Moutos, T. (1991), 'Turnover Costs, Unemployment and Macroeconomic Policies',

European Journal of Political Economy, 7: 1–16.

Muellbauer, J. (1986), 'The Assessment: Productivity and Competitiveness in British Manufacturing', *Oxford Review of Economic Policy*, 2(3): 1–25.

—— (1991), 'Productivity and Competitiveness', *Oxford Review of Economic Policy*, 7(3): 99–117.

Mulvey, C. (1978), *The Economic Analysis of Trade Unions* (Glasgow Social and Economic Research Studies 5), Oxford: Martin Robertson.

—— (1986), 'Wage Levels: Do Unions Make a Difference?', in J. Niland (ed.), *Wage Fixation in Australia*, Sydney: Allen & Unwin.

Murphy, P., P. Sloane and D. Blackaby (1992), 'The Effects of Trade Unions on the Distribution of Earnings: A Sample Selectivity Approach', *Oxford Bulletin of Economics and Statistics*, 54(4): 517–42.

Musson, A.E. (1972), *British Trade Unions, 1800–1875*, London: Macmillan.

Nash, J.F. (1950), 'The Bargaining Problem'. *Econometrica*. 18(2): 155–62.

—— (1953), 'Two Person Cooperative Games', *Econometrica*, 21(1): 128–40.

Naylor, R. (1989), 'Strikes, Free Riders and Social Customs', *Quarterly Journal of Economics*, 104(4): 771–86.

—— (1990), 'A Social Custom Model of Collective Action', *European Journal of Political Economy*, 6: 201–16.

Naylor, R. and O. Raaum (1993), 'The Open Shop Union, Wages and Management Opposition', *Oxford Economic Papers*, 45(4): 589–604.

Neumann, G. and E. Rissman (1984), 'Where Have All the Union Members Gone?', *Journal of Labor Economics*, 2(2): 175–92.

Newell, A.T. and J. Symons (1987), 'Corporatism, Laissez-faire and the Rise in Unemployment', *European Economic Review*, 31(2): 567–601.

—— (1988), 'Mid-1980s Unemployment', London School of Economics, CLE, mimeo.

Nickell, S.J. (1979), 'Fixed Costs, Employment and Labour Demand over the Cycle', *Economica*, 46: 329–45.

—— (1987), 'Why is Wage Inflation in Britain so High?', *Oxford Bulletin of Economics and Statistics*, 49: 103–28.

Nickell, S.J. and M. Andrews (1983), 'Unions, Real Wages and Employment in Britain, 1951–79', *Oxford Economic Papers* (November, Supplement): 183–206.

Nickell, S.J. and P. Kong (1988), 'An Investigation into the Power of Insiders in Wage Determination', University of Oxford, Institute of Economics and Statistics, Applied Economics Discussion Paper no. 49.

Nickell, S.J. and S. Wadhwani (1990), 'Insider Forces and Wage Determination', *Economic Journal*, 100: 496–509.

Nickell, S.J., S. Wadhwani and M. Wall (1989), 'Unions and Productivity Growth in Britain, 1974–86: Evidence from Company Accounts Data', London School of Economics, CLE, Working Paper no. 1149.

—— (1992), 'Productivity Growth in UK Companies, 1975–1986', *European Economic Review*, 36: 1055–91.

Noam, E.M. (1983), 'The Effect of Unionization and Civil Service on the Salaries and Productivity of Regulators', in J.D. Reid, Jr (ed.), *New Approaches to*

Labor Unions (supplement no. 2 to R.G. Ehrenberg (ed.), *Research in Labor Economics*), Greenwich, Conn.: JAI Press.

Nolan, P. and P. Marginson (1990), 'Skating on Thin Ice? David Metcalf on Trade Unions and Productivity', *British Journal of Industrial Relations*, 28(2): 227–47.

Oi, W.Y. (1962), 'Labor as a Quasi-Fixed Factor', *Journal of Political Economy*, 70: 538–55.

Olson, M., Jr (1965), *The Logic of Collective Action*, Cambridge, Mass.: Harvard University Press.

Osborne, M.J. (1984), 'Capitalist-Worker Conflict and Involuntary Unemployment', *Review of Economic Studies*, 51: 111–27.

Oswald, A.J. (1979), 'Wage Determination in an Economy with Many Trade Unions', *Oxford Economic Papers*, 31(3): 369–85.

  (1982), 'Trade Unions, Wages and Unemployment: What Can Simple Models Tell Us?', *Oxford Economic Papers*, 34(3): 526–45.

  (1985), 'The Economic Theory of Trade Unions: An Introductory Survey', *Scandinavian Journal of Economics*, 87(2): 160–93.

  (1986), 'Unemployment Insurance and Labour Contracts under Asymmetric Information: Theory and Facts', *American Economic Review*, 76: 365–77.

  (1993), 'Efficient Contracts are on the Labour Demand Curve: Theory and Facts', *Labour Economics*, 1(1): 85–113.

Oswald, A.J. and P.J. Turnbull (1985), 'Pay and Employment Determination in Britain: What are Labour Contracts Really Like?', *Oxford Review of Economic Policy*, 1: 80–97.

Oswald, A.J. and I. Walker (1993), 'Labour Supply, Contract Theory and Unions', London School of Economics, CEP, mimeo.

Oulton, N. (1987), 'Plant Closures and the Productivity "Miracle" in British Manufacturing', *National Institute Economic Review*, no. 121 (August): 53–9.

  (1990), 'Labour Productivity in UK Manufacturing in the 1970s and in the 1980s', *National Institute Economic Review*, no. 132 (May): 71–102.

Pelling, H. (1987), *A History of British Trade Unionism* (4th edn), London: Macmillan.

Pemberton, J. (1988), 'A Managerial Model of the Trade Union', *Economic Journal*, 98: 755–71.

Pencavel, J.H. (1977), 'The Distributional and Efficiency Effects of Trade Unions in Britain', *British Journal of Industrial Relations*, 15(2): 137–56.

  (1984), 'The Tradeoff between Wages and Employment in Trade Union Objectives', *Quarterly Journal of Economics*, 99(2): 215–31.

  (1985), 'Wages and Employment under Trade Unionism: Microeconomic Models and Macroeconomic Applications', *Scandinavian Journal of Economics*, 87(2): 197–225.

  (1991), *Labor Markets under Trade Unionism*, Oxford: Basil Blackwell.

Phelps Brown, H. (1959), *The Growth of British Industrial Relations*, London: Macmillan.

  (1986), *The Origins of Trade Union Power*, Oxford University Press.

Piore, M.J. (1986), 'Perspectives on Labor Market Flexibility', *Industrial Relations*, 25: 146–66.

Polachek, S.W. and W.S. Siebert (1993), *The Economics of Earnings*, Cambridge University Press.

Price, R. (1989), 'Trade Union Membership', in R. Bean (ed.) *International Labour Statistics*, London: Routledge.

Purcell, J. (1991), 'The Rediscovery of the Management Prerogative: The Management of Labour Relations in the 1980s', *Oxford Review of Economic Policy*, 7: 33–43.

Purcell, J. and K. Sisson (1983), 'Strategies and Practice in the Management of Industrial Relations', in G.S. Bain (ed.), *Industrial Relations in Britain*, Oxford: Basil Blackwell.

Rankin, N. (1992), 'Imperfect Competition, Expectations and the Multiple Effects of Monetary Growth', *Economic Journal*, 102: 743–53.

Rees, A. (1962), *The Economics of Trade Unions*, Cambridge University Press in association with the University of Chicago Press.

(1963), 'The Effects of Unions on Resource Allocation', *Journal of Law and Economics*, 6: 69–78.

Rezler, J. (1961), *Union Growth Reconsidered: A Critical Analysis of Recent Growth Theories*, New York: Kossuth Foundation.

Reynolds, L.G. (1978), *Labor Economics and Labor Relations* (7th edition), Englewood Cliffs, N.J.: Prentice Hall.

Reynolds, M.O. (1986), 'Trade Unions in the Production Process Reconsidered', *Journal of Political Economy*, 94(2): 443–7.

Richardson, R. (1976), 'Trade Union Growth', *British Journal of Industrial Relations*, 15(2): 280–1.

Richardson, R. and S. Wood (1989), 'Productivity Change in the Coal Industry and the New Industrial Relations', *British Journal of Industrial Relations*, 27(1): 33–55.

Riley, D. (1992), 'UK Trade Union Membership: 1892 to 1990', Birkbeck College, London, Department of Economics, mimeo.

Roberts, B.C. (1985), 'Great Britain', in B.C. Roberts (ed.) *Industrial Relations in Europe*. London: Croom Helm.

Roberts, B.C. and S. Rothwell (1973), 'Recent Trends in Collective Bargaining in the United Kingdom' in *Collective Bargaining in Industrialised Market Economies*, Geneva: International Labour Office.

Robinson, C. (1989), 'The Joint Determination of Union Status and Union Wage Effects: Some Tests of Alternative Models', *Journal of Political Economy*, 97(3): 639–67.

Rogers, J. (1989), 'Don't Worry, Be Happy: Institutional Dynamics of the Postwar Decline of Private Sector US Unionism', University of Wisconsin-Madison, School of Law, mimeo.

Rosen, A. (1989), 'Bargaining over Effort', London School of Economics, CEP, Discussion Paper no. 351.

Rosen, S. (1969), 'Trade Union Power, Threat Effects and the Extent of Organisation', *Review of Economic Studies*, 36(3): 185–96.

Ross, A.M. (1948), *Trade Union Wage Policy*, Berkeley: University of California Press.

Rotemberg, J.J. and G. Saloner (1986), 'A Supergame-Theoretic Model of Price

Wars During Booms', *American Economic Review*, 76(3): 390–407.

Rotemberg, J.J. and M. Woodford (1992), 'Oligopolistic Pricing and the Effects of Aggregate Demand on Economic Activity', *Journal of Political Economy*, 100(6): 1153–1207.

Rowthorn, R.E. (1992), 'Centralisation, Employment and Wage Dispersion', *Economic Journal*, 102: 506–23.

Rubinstein, A. (1982), 'Perfect Equilibrium in a Bargaining Model', *Econometrica*, 50(1): 97–109.

Salop, S.C. (1979), 'A Model of Natural Rate of Unemployment', *American Economic Review*, 69(1): 117–25.

Sampson, A.A. (1988), 'Unionized Contracts with Fixed Wage Rates and State-contingent Employment Levels' *Economica*, 55: 95–105.

Sapsford, D. (1990), 'Strikes: Models and Evidence', in D. Sapsford and Z. Tzannatos (eds.), *Current Issues in Labour Economics*, London: Macmillan.

Schmalensee, R. (1989), 'Interindustry Studies of Structure and Performance', in R. Schmalensee and R.D. Willig (eds.), *Handbook of Industrial Organisation*, Amsterdam: North-Holland.

Shah, A. (1984), 'Job Attributes and the Size of the Union/Non-union Wage Differential', *Economica*, 51: 437–46.

Shapiro, C. and J.E. Stiglitz (1984), 'Equilibrium Unemployment as a Worker Discipline Device', *American Economic Review*, 74(3): 433–44.

Silvestre, J. (1990), 'There may be Unemployment when the Labour Market is Competitive and the Output Market is Not', *Economic Journal*, 100: 899–913.

Simons, H.C. (1944), 'Some Reflections on Syndicalism', *Journal of Political Economy*, 52(1): 1–25.

Sisson, K. and W. Brown (1983), 'Industrial Relations in the Private Sector: Donovan Revisited', in G.S. Bain (ed.), *Industrial Relations in Britain*, Oxford: Basil Blackwell.

Slichter, S.H. (1941), *Union Policies and Industrial Management*, Washington, D.C.: Brookings Institute.

Slichter, S.H., J.J. Healy and E.R. Livernash (1960), *The Impact of Collective Bargaining on Management*, Washington, D.C.: Brookings Institute.

Smith, A. (1977), *The Wealth of Nations* [1776], Harmondsworth: Penguin.

Solow, R.M. (1985), 'Insiders and Outsiders in Wage Determination', *Scandinavian Journal of Economics*, 87: 411–28.

Soskice, D. (1990), 'Wage Determination: The Changing Role of Institutions in Advanced Industrialized Countries', *Oxford Review of Economic Policy*, 6(4): 36–61.

Stewart, M.B. (1983), 'Relative Earnings and Individual Union Membership in the UK', *Economica*, 50: 111–25.

(1987), 'Collective Bargaining Arrangements, Closed Shops and Relative Pay', *Economic Journal*, 97: 140–56.

(1990), 'Union Wage Differentials, Product Market Influences and the Division of Rents', *Economic Journal*, 100: 1122–37.

(1991), 'Union Wage Differentials in the Face of Changes in the Economic and Legal Environment', *Economica*, 58: 155–72.

(1993), 'Do Changes in Collective Bargaining Arrangements Imply Declining Union Wage Differentials into the 1990s?', University of Warwick, Department of Economics, mimeo.

(1994), 'Union Wage Differentials in an Era of Declining Unionisation', University of Warwick, Department of Economics, mimeo.

Stigler, G.J. (1974), 'Free Riders and Collective Action: An Appendix to Theories of Economic Regulation', *Bell Journal of Economics*, 5(2): 359–65.

Sutton, J. (1986), 'Non-cooperative Bargaining Theory: An Introduction', *Review of Economic Studies*, 53(5): 709–24.

Symons, E. and I. Walker (1990), 'Union/Non-union Wage Differentials 1979–1984: Evidence from the UK Family Expenditure Surveys', University of Keele, mimeo.

Szymanski, S. (1988), 'Wage Profiles, Commitment and Unions', Birkbeck College, London, Discussion Paper no. 88/5.

Tan, H., B. Chapman, C. Peterson and A. Booth (1992), 'Youth Training in the United States, Britain and Australia', *Research in Labour Economics*, 13: 63–99.

Taylor, B.J. and F. Witney (1971), *Labor Relations Law*, Englewood Cliffs, N.J.: Prentice-Hall.

Taylor, J.B. (1980), 'Aggregate Dynamics and Staggered Contracts', *Journal of Political Economy*, 88(1): 1–23.

(1983), 'Union Wage Settlements During a Disinflation', *American Economic Review*, 73(5): 981–93.

Tirole, J. (1988), *Theory of Industrial Organisation*, Cambridge, Mass.: MIT Press.

Towers, B. (1989), 'Running the Gauntlet: British Trade Unions under Thatcher, 1979–1988', *Industrial and Labor Relations Review*, 42(2): 163–88.

Tracy, J.S. (1987), 'An Empirical Test of an Asymmetric Information Model of Strikes', *Journal of Labor Economics*, 5(2): 149–73.

Troy, L. and N. Sheflin (1985), *Union Sourcebook: Membership, Structure, Finance, Directory*, West Orange, N.J.: Industrial Relations Data and Information Services.

Turnbull, P.J. (1988a), 'The Economic Theory of Trade Union Behaviour: A Critique', *British Journal of Industrial Relations*, 26(1): 99–118.

(1988b), 'Industrial Relations and the Seniority Model of Union Behaviour', *Oxford Bulletin of Economics and Statistics*, 50(1): 53–70.

Turner, H.A. (1962), *Trade Union Growth, Structure and Policy*, London: Allen & Unwin.

Ulph, A. and D. Ulph (1988), 'Bargaining Structures and Delay in Innovations', *Scandinavian Journal of Economics*, 80: 475–91.

(1990a), 'Union Bargaining: A Survey of Recent Work', in D. Sapsford and Z. Tzannatos (eds.), *Current Issues in Labour Economics*, London, Macmillan.

(1990b), 'Labour Markets and Innovation', *Journal of the Japanese and International Economies*, 3: 403–23.

(1994), 'Labour Markets and Innovation: Ex-Post Bargaining', *European Economic Review*.

van der Ploeg, F. (1987), 'Trade Unions, Investment, and Employment', *European Economic Review*, 31:1465–92.

van Reenen, J. (1993), 'The Creation and Capture of Rents: Wages, Market Structure and Innovation in UK Manufacturing Firms', University College London, Department of Economics, mimeo.

Waddington, J. (1992), 'Trade Union Membership in Britain, 1980–1987: Unemployment and Restructuring', *British Journal of Industrial Relations*, 30(2): 287–324.

Wadhwani, S. (1990), 'The Effect of Unions on Productivity Growth, Investment and Employment: A Report on Some Recent Work', *British Journal of Industrial Relations*, 28(3): 371–85.

Wallis, K.F. (1979), *Topics in Applied Econometrics*, (2nd edn), Oxford: Basil Blackwell.

Webb, B. and S. (1897), *Industrial Democracy*, London: Longmans and Green.

Weekes, B., M. Mellish, L. Dickens and J. Lloyd (1975), *Industrial Relations and the Limits of the Law*, Oxford: Basil Blackwell.

Weiler, P. (1983), 'Promises to Keep: Securing Workers' Rights to Self-Organisation Under the NLRA', *Harvard Law Review*, 98: 1769–827.

Weiss, A. (1991), *Efficiency Wages: Models of Unemployment, Layoffs and Wage Dispersion*, Oxford: Clarendon Press.

Wheeler, H. (1987), 'Management–Labour Relations in the USA', in G.J. Bamber and R.D. Lansbury (eds.), *International and Comparative Industrial Relations*, London: Unwin Hyman.

White, P.J. (1983), 'The Management of Redundancy', *Industrial Relations Journal*, 14: 32–40.

Williamson, O.E. (1985), *The Economic Institutions of Capitalism*, New York: Free Press.

Williamson, O.E., M.L. Wachter and J.E. Harris (1975), 'Understanding the Employment Relation: The Analysis of Idiosyncratic Exchange', *Bell Journal of Economics*, 6(1): 250–78.

Willman, P. (1989), 'The Logic of "Market-share" Trade Unionism: Is Membership Decline Inevitable?', *Industrial Relations Journal*, 20: 260–70.

(1990), 'The Financial Status and Performance of British Trade Unions, 1950–1988', *British Journal of Industrial Relations*, 28(3): 313–27.

Wilson, N. and J.R. Cable (1991), 'Union, Wages and Productivity: Some Evidence from UK Engineering Firms', *Applied Economics*, 23(1B): 219–27.

Wolman, L. (1924), *The Growth of American Trade Unions, 1880–1923*, New York: NBER.

Wragg, R. and J. Robertson (1978), *Post-war Trends in Employment, Productivity, Output, Labour Costs and Prices by Industry in the United Kingdom*, United Kingdom Department of Employment Research Paper no. 3.

Yaron, G. (1990), 'Trade Unions and Women's Relative Pay: A Theoretical and Empirical Analysis Using UK Data', Oxford University, Institute of Economics and Statistics, Applied Economics Discussion Paper no. 95.

Index